THE COMMUNITY OF JESUS

Fieldstead
and Company

ARTSEMPOWERINGLIFE
The Human Spirit Emboldened for Change

OPERA DI
SANTA MARIA
DEL FIORE
DAL 1296

Proceedings of the conferences

Paris, Institut Catholique
12–13 May 2017

Strasbourg, Faculté de Théologie Protestante,
Université de Strasbourg
19–20 May 2017

Florence, Facoltà Teologica dell'Italia Centrale
and Opera di Santa Maria del Fiore
25–7 May 2017

New Haven, Connecticut,
Institute of Sacred Music, Yale Divinity School
20–1 October 2017

Orleans, Massachusetts, Community of Jesus
27–9 October 2017

Art and Theology
in Ecumenical Perspective

edited by
TIMOTHY VERDON

mount
tabor
BOOKS

PARACLETE PRESS

Mandragora

ACKNOWLEDGMENTS

This volume has been published thanks to a generous grant from Fieldstead and Company, California (USA), and with a contribution from the Opera di Santa Maria del Fiore, Florence (Italy). The international conference which the book presents was sponsored by the Community of Jesus, Orleans, Massachusetts; by the Institut Supérieur de Théologie des Arts of the Theologicum of the Institut Catholique de Paris; by the Équipe d'accueil 4378 of the Faculté de Théologie Protestante of the Université de Strasbourg; by the Opera di Santa Maria del Fiore, Florence; and by the Institute of Sacred Music of Yale University, New Haven, Connecticut; co-sponsors of the conference were the Facoltà Teologica dell'Italia Centrale, Florence; the Mount Tabor Ecumenical Centre for Art and Spirituality, Barga, Italy; and the foundation Arts Empowering Life, Orleans, Massachusetts. Thanks also to Denis Hétier and Jérôme Cottin for arranging permission to publish in English translation conference papers already published in French in the *Acta* of the Paris and Strasbourg symposia (*La théologie au risque de la création artistique*, edited by Denis Hétier and Jérôme Cottin, Paris, 2018), and to Stefano Tarocchi and the Consiglio Direttivo of the review *Vivens homo* of the Facoltà Teologica dell'Italia Centrale, for permission to publish in English translation four papers of the Florence symposium already published in Italian (*Vivens homo, rivista di teologia e scienze religiose*, 28/2 [2017]). Our gratitude finally goes to the authors whose texts appear here, and to Giovanni Serafini, who efficiently and tirelessly served as editorial assistant for this project.

T.V.

ABBREVIATIONS

The books of the Bible in alphabetical order of abbreviations:

Ac . . . . Acts of the Apostles
Am . . . . Amos
Ba . . . . . . Baruch
1 Ch. . . . . . 1 Chronicles
2 Ch. . . . . . 2 Chronicles
1 Co. . . . . . 1 Corinthians
2 Co. . . . . . 2 Corinthians
Col. . . . . . . Colossians
Dn . . . . Daniel
Dt . . . . Deuteronomy
Ep . . . . Ephesians
Est . . . . Esther
Ex . . . . Exodus
Ezk. . . . . . . Ezechiel
Ezr . . . . Ezra
Ga . . . . Galatians
Gn . . . . Genesis
Hab . . . . . Habakkuk
Heb . . . . . Hebrews
Hg . . . . . . Haggai
Ho . . . . . . Hosea
Is . . . . Isaiah
Jb . . . . Job
Jdt . . . . . . Judith
Jg . . . . Judges
Jl . . . . Joel
Jm . . . . . . James
Jn . . . . John
1 Jn . . . . . . 1 John
2 Jn . . . . . . 2 John
3 Jn . . . . . . 3 John
Jon . . . . . . Jonah
Jos . . . . . . Joshua
Jr . . . . Jeremiah
Jude . . . . . Jude
1 K . . . . 1 Kings

2 K . . . . . . 2 Kings
Lk . . . . Luke
Lm . . . . . . Lamentations
Lv . . . . . . Leviticus
1 M . . . . . 1 Maccabees
2 M . . . . . 2 Maccabees
Mi . . . . Micah
Mk . . . . . . Mark
Ml . . . . Malachi
Na . . . . Nahum
Nb . . . . . . Numbers
Ne . . . . . . Nehemiah
Ob . . . . Obadiah
1 P . . . . 1 Peter
2 P . . . . 2 Peter
Ph . . . . . . Philippians
Phm . . . . . Philemon
Pr . . . . Proverbs
Ps . . . . Psalms
Qo . . . . . . Ecclesiastes (Qoheleth)
Rm . . . . . . Romans
Rt . . . . Ruth
Rv . . . . . . Revelation (Apocalypse)
1 S . . . . 1 Samuel
2 S . . . . 2 Samuel
Sg . . . . Song of Songs
Si . . . . Ecclesiasticus (Sirach)
Tb . . . . . . Tobit
1 Th . . . . . 1 Thessalonians
2 Th . . . . . 2 Thessalonians
1 Tm . . . . 1 Timothy
2 Tm . . . . 2 Timothy
Tt . . . . Titus
Ws . . . . . . Wisdom
Zc . . . . . . Zechariah
Zp . . . . . . Zephaniah

TABLE OF CONTENTS

Introduction.
An Ambitious Idea, a Complex Event, a Ground-breaking Book

TIMOTHY VERDON

This collection of essays has its origin in an exhibition by one of the contributors to the present volume, the artist Filippo Rossi, at the Abbey of Novacella near the Italian border with Austria in late April of 2015. To inaugurate the exhibition, the monastic community there sponsored a symposium on sacred art, and among the speakers, in addition to myself, was Jérôme Cottin, a university professor both at Strasbourg and in Paris whom I have known since the 1990s. In view of the up-coming celebrations for the fifth centennial of Martin Luther's publication of the 95 theses that launched the Protestant Reformation (1517–2017), I proposed to Cottin, a Calvinist, that together we organize a multi-sectioned international meeting on the arts in Christian history, involving our respective institutions: on my side the Catholic Archdiocese of Florence, in which I am a priest; the Cathedral Foundation (Opera di Santa Maria del Fiore), of whose museum I am Director; and the Community of Jesus, a U.S.-based monastic family in the Benedictine tradition with a branch in Barga, Tuscany: the Mount Tabor Ecumenical Centre for Art and Spirituality, of which I am Academic Director. On his side, Jérôme Cottin is Professor of Practical Theology at the Faculty of Protestant Theology of the University of Strasbourg, and also teaches in the program of the Institut Supérieur de Théologie des Arts at the Catholic Institute of Paris. Filippo Rossi, who was part of that opening conversation, offered to produce an exhibit to accompany the moveable feast Jérôme Cottin and I dreamed of creating.

The International Conference

After obtaining preliminary approval from these several institutions, and the commitment of the Community of Jesus to finance those parts of the multipartite event for which other funding would not be available, in December of 2015 I called a first planning meeting in Florence, attended by Jérôme Cottin and Denis Villepellet, then Director of the Catholic Institute's Theology of the Arts program, and by Denis Hétier, who would replace Villepellet in that role the following year. On that occasion it was decided to construct the conference not around the historical Luther event but around the broader theme of ecumenism and the arts, since, as Cottin pointed out, one of the unexpected developments of the present time is a renewed interest in the visual arts in Protestant denominations which in the 16th century rejected them. The specific focus of our conference was suggested by Denis Villepellet, who stressed the problem that both Catholic and Protestant theological communities experience whenever efforts are made to discuss art as more than 'illustration' or 'decoration'. Villepellet suggested the second part of what became the title of the overall conference: *Ecumenism and the Arts. What Theology Risks in Artistic Creation*. Our ambitious objective, that is, was not only to commemorate the Reformation but to challenge – from both the Protestant and the Catholic perspective – an ingrained prejudice of all academic theology, which hesitates to accept that the arts are themselves *loci* – venues – of original theological reflection, not mere illustrations of verbal formulas.

A further development was the decision of the Florence theology school – the Facoltà Teologica dell'Italia Centrale – to participate, together with the Opera di Santa Maria del Fiore, in the Florentine part of the conference. At that point, however, our inchoative program appeared not only entirely European but also predominantly Roman Catholic, and I asked Cottin and Villepellet if they would authorize me to approach to an American institution, Yale University, about the possibility of adding a transatlantic 'section' to the event. They agreed and, thanks to the collaboration of Martin Jean, Director of the Yale Institute of Sacred Music, a New Haven session was added to those in Paris, Strasbourg and Florence. It was also decided to conclude the now intercontinental meeting with three days at the monastery of the Community of Jesus on Cape Cod, in the township of Orleans, two hours north of New Haven. Since its foundation in the late 1950s, this ecumenical monastic community has devoted itself to the arts in the context of worship, and there seemed no more fitting place to tie together the many threads of thought and experience that our conference would treat than in a similarly creative setting.

The enthusiasm for the project on both sides of the Atlantic suggested a very high level of academic and ecclesial interest, and it was agreed that efforts should be made to publish the proceedings of the entire event in a single

work in today's international language, English. Thus, at my suggestion, the Community of Jesus asked the Fieldstead Company Foundation of California for a publication grant, which was duly given; the present collection of essays is the fruit of the Fieldstead Company's generosity and of the sympathetic interest of Roberta Ahmanson and her husband Howard, who lead the family foundation.

In late April 2016 a second planning meeting was convened by Denis Villepellet at the Institut Catholique in Paris, attended by myself and Filippo Rossi, Father Gianni Cioli of the Florence Theology School, Christopher Kanaga of the Community of Jesus, Jérôme Cottin of Strasbourg and Paris, and Denis Hétier, Villepellet's designated successor. The overall plan of the five-part conference began to emerge, and, with it, the principal themes of discussion and names of possible speakers; the program finally defined is found in Part 7 of the present work. It was agreed that the Paris session would lay the theological foundation of the entire event; Strasbourg would focus on the Reformation moment, Florence would recuperate earlier Eastern and Western experiences in the field of church art; Yale would look at the sacred arts in North America; and the final session at the Community of Jesus monastery, a Protestant setting which privileges painting, theater, music and sculpture, would ponder 'the Word in color, action, music and form'. To ensure *fils conducteurs* in what otherwise risked being disconnected symposia, it was agreed that a few of the organizers would give papers in several of the venues, and that a joint-exhibition of works by Filippo Rossi and Susan Kanaga, an artist of the Community of Jesus, would accompany each stage of the meeting; for logistical reasons, this exhibition, 'Creator Spirit' (see Part 6), was physically mounted only in Florence and at Orleans, while in Paris, Strasbourg and at Yale a short film recounting its genesis was projected, available with the present publication in link.

Organization of the book

The structure of the present volume differs substantially from that of the 2017 conference, which sought to distribute among the five separate venues common themes that, in a unified publication, it has seemed better to organize in more coherent groupings. The order of development of the themes, which in 2017 was determined by the participating institutions' scheduling needs, has now assumed a simpler form, roughly following the chronology of ideas and artworks discussed. For various reasons not all the papers given in 2017 are present here: the poet Florent Dumontier's moving presentation in Paris was ultimately impossible to translate in a meaningful way, as was Monsignor André Dupleix's demonstration of 'Spirit-inspired' music, given with a series of recorded examples. Other papers, including most of those in Yale symposium, had been previously committed and the authors preferred not to publish the same text twice. Lost too are the contextual debate and framing events of the 2017 meetings: in Paris, a 'soirée artistique' organized by Institut Catholique students; in Strasbourg the exhibition 'Le vent de la Réforme: Luther 1517' and a viewing of Grunewald's Isenheim altarpiece at nearby Colmar; in Florence a visit to the Ospedale degli Innocenti, which Luther saw in 1510, and to the Ecumenical Centre for Art and Spirituality at Barga; at Yale a festive dinner for the speakers and the splendid campus setting; and, at the Community of Jesus monastery, liturgical celebrations, art workshops and an organ concert. The only one of these peripheral events specifically recalled in the present text is the performance given at Orleans by members of the community and professional soloists of Ralph Vaugh Williams's opera *The Pilgrim's Progress*, based on John Bunyan's 17th-century allegory of Christian life.

The papers published here are organized in six large groups, corresponding to key themes of the 2017 conference. Since many papers touch several themes, this grouping is somewhat arbitrary, and many essays could with equal reason appear in another section of the book. What is more, as normally occurs with collections of conference papers, conceptual development within individual groupings of papers is absent, each author defining and approaching the questions treated with considerable liberty.

The opening section of the book, *Art and Theology*, suggests the difficulty theologians often have in treating art (Villepellet and Theobald), the Old Testament background of a 'visualization' of the Divine (Joostens), the architectural solutions to the distinct theological articulations offered by Christian liturgies (Dianich), and the unique light which monastic life casts on art as an expression of theology (Verdon, Dyrness and Shannon).

The second section, *The Holy Spirit*, deepens the theological theme, reproducing the Paris meeting's emphasis on the Holy Spirit as the source of artistic creativity, a concept previously explored by a research group at the Institut Supérieur de Théologie des Arts through the figure of the bird/dove (Hétier). The biblical and theological implications of this idea are discussed (Cassingena, Souletie), its Medieval and Renaissance interpretations are summarized (Verdon) as is its incidence in contemporary visual art (Cottin) and in two influential artists of the early 20th century: Braque (Sautory) and Brâncuşi (Besançon and Grenier).

The third section of the volume, *Early Christian, Medieval and Renaissance Examples*, offers a synthetic panorama of art's capacity to 'incarnate' theological intuitions from the early Christian and Byzantine periods (Gazzola, Petrà) through the Middle Ages and early Renaissance (Verdon, Fortuna), up to Luther's still 'Catholic' experience of Florence in 1510 (Verdon).

Section four, *Reformation and Counter-Reformation Theology of Art*, reproduces the Strasbourg session of the 2017 event, with an overview of the influence of Reformed thought on art (Cottin), a discussion of the multiplication of printed images in Reformation Germany (Muller), a theological analysis of the biblical concept of 'likeness' in Reformation spirituality (Dyrness). There follows an overview of the Catholic reaction to the new ideas regarding art (Verdon) and a case study of the first major program of the Catholic Reform, that of the inner dome of Florence Cathedral (Cioli), with, finally, a return to the distinctive aesthetics and catechetical function of art in Protestant northern Europe (Föllmi).

Section five, *Theology in Modern and Contemporary Art*, considers the debt of the German Romantic painter Caspar David Friedrich, to the Rhennish mystic tradition as preserved in Lutheran thought (Valléjo), and the 19th-century rediscovery of the visual arts in Anglican Britain (Quash). Two papers study the art of Vincent van Gogh through the thought of Paul Ricoeur (Cottin) and of Romano Guardini (Dohna Schlobitten), while spirituality in today's monastic architecture (Cottin) and the struggle for a credible contemporary form of Greek Orthodox art (Marinis) suggest modern problems and solutions in the relationship between art and theology. A view of 20th- and 21st-century Christian art in the UK (Quash) and two American reflections on art as service (Sokolove), and on secularity as the new form of the sacred (Kosky), close the series of academic papers.

A 6th section, *The Artists Speak*, is devoted to the exhibition by Susan Kanaga and Filippo Rossi which was one of the constant elements of the five-part conference, 'Creator Spirit', with a theological reading (Verdon) and statements by the artists themselves on the meaning of ecumenical collaboration (Kanaga) and on art as a Christian calling (Rossi). This section, which offers a selection of images of the two installations – in Florence and in Orleans, Massachusetts –, concludes with a note on the performance of *The Pilgrim's Progress* in the

Community of Jesus's Church of the Transfiguration, in Orleans, with, again, a selection of images.

Section seven, the *Program of the Five-Part Conference*, furnishes the full roster of participants in the Paris, Strasbourg, Florence, Yale and Orleans meetings, and an *Appendix* gives essential information about each of the authors present here.

Illustrations

Where possible, authors' references to works of art are supported by illustrations. Unfortunately, the works of many 20th-century artists are available only at very high fees, which the budget of this publication could not cover. Readers will easily find most of the works mentioned online, however.

In the case of the illustrations provided by authors, the great differences in chromatic quality has made it preferable to reproduce in black and white.

Translations

A word is due on my translation of the French and Italian papers (with the exception of that by Yvonne Dohna Schlobitten, who herself furnished an English version). Translation is a thankless business, for nothing is ever really the same in another language and nuances are either lost or necessarily altered. Italians say 'traduttore traditore' – 'translator: traitor' –, and a naughty French quip holds that 'les traductions sont comme les femmes: plus elles sont belles, moins elles sont fidèles': 'translations are like women, the more beautiful, the less faithful'.

I have tried to be painstakingly faithful to the meaning and style of each of the authors whose text I translated, avoiding both slavish literalism and the temptation to 'interpret'. The authors were all asked to check my English version of their texts, and a few suggested corrections of terminology or style which were promptly made, even when – in the case of stylistic changes – this made the texts somewhat awkward. In the last analysis, it is worth translating important ideas even if something is lost in the process; the famous instance of course is the Bible, which down the centuries most believers and students have read in translation.

The language in which each paper was given is indicated in Part 7 of the volume, the *Program of the Five-Part Conference*, and the original French and Italian texts are available in the publications already indicated in our *Acknowledgments*: *La théologie au risque de la création artistique*, edited by Denis Hétier and Jérôme Cottin, Paris, 2018, and *Vivens homo, rivista di teologia e scienze religiose*, 28/2 (2017).

Contribution

Despite its inevitably fragmentary character, this collection represents an unprecedented attempt to bring Catholic, Protestant, Orthodox and Anglican artists, art historians and theologians together to discuss the arts. The exceptional quality of the scholars, and their different confessional, intellectual and cultural backgrounds, give the ensemble of texts a 'unity in diversity' appropriate to the ecumenical perspective which animated the 2017 event, and it is not unreasonable to hope that the appearance of such different points of view in a single publication may indeed favor future dialogue. Certainly, the efforts made here by artists and art historians to reason in theological terms, and by theologians to grasp the implications of artistic creation, are significant steps toward understanding how human beings created in the image of their Creator are *ipso facto* creative and define their relationship with God through acts which let them mirror his creativity. ▪

Part 1
Art and Theology

What Theology Risks in Artistic Creation

DENIS VILLEPELET

The arts in general claim the right of autonomy, in the name of their need for freedom and truth. The act of artistic creation is, in its free gesture, a quest for truth. The musician Modest Mussorgsky, writing to his friend Stassov, evoked this 'truth at point-blank range'. Artists look for flesh-and-blood truth, naked truth, stripped of all rhetoric or ornament. The arts come to grips with the real just as it is, and express fundamental anthropological questions. Yet that truth 'encloses us in immanence', vowing us to the world and only to the world. When, however, the arts give flesh to a strong presence of human vulnerability and finitude, they resound powerfully with the figure of the Crucified. The creative struggle with matter which produces musical compositions, paintings, architectural structures, videos or theater productions can 'direct people toward God'.

Between the quest for truth that takes flesh in the act of artistic creation, and truth's fulfillment in and through Jesus Christ, more than one significant echo resounds, in fact, and art and theology beckon to each other. Yet the union of these two words can pose a problem, for what in fact does creative artistic practice have in common with a discipline that is discursive and analytic?

Obviously the main danger to avoid is that of reducing art to a tool of theology – the idea that art is at the service of theology, remaining subordinate to the summons of theology, which itself risks nothing. According to that conception, theology certainly evolves, but in its own order and in complete autonomy, and Christian faith remains a permanent reality because transcendent, with theology preserving its integrity and enlightening its content. In that view, the arts do no more than extend the theologian's hand and are reduced to mere pedagogical tools, as Pope Gregory I affirmed long ago.

Such a view is insufficient. In reality the arts, at the very heart of the aesthetic experience which they propose, have their own specific field of comprehension and their own theoretical fecundity, being able to elaborate their own religious representation of the world. In that sense, they are truly able to put questions to theologians, and it is possible to establish an authentic dialogical relationship between the arts and theology.

If we preserve the distinctive original character of both the arts and theology, it seems to us that their dialogue is a two-way hermeneutical product: artistic creation can be considered a hermeneutic of Catholic faith 'in action', and theology a hermeneutic of art's expressions, for both speak of the Christian faith and are potential paths to God. ■

When a Theologian Meets the Work of Art

Epistemological Reflections

CHRISTOPH THEOBALD, S.J.

The inquiry into the relationship between art and theology was able to become an epistemological question only at the moment when the two fields effectively separated. That separation was the result of an historical process: the slow conquest, by the arts, of their autonomy, a development synonymous with modernity, achieved and signed by Kant in 1790 with his *Critique of Judgment.* If aesthetics traditionally signified the theory of sense perception – in his *Critique of Pure Reason* Kant speaks of "transcendental aesthetics" –, after Baumgarten (in his *Aesthetica*, published in 1750) this field also covered the 'science' of the beautiful and of art, sustained by the judgment of taste which, after some hesitation, the Königsberg philosopher would, in his final critique, succeed in sujecting to *a priori* principles. We have to remember that distinction between the theory of perception or fundamental aesthetics, on the one hand, and the criticism of art, on the other: a distinction that would remain decisive, even in the 20th century's great theological efforts to reflect upon aesthetic experience and the work of art. It was the fruit of a progressive autonomization of the sphere of the beautiful and of the 'fine arts', which in Hegel marked the *end* of the confusion art/religion (of which Greek statuary remains the unsurpassable paradigm) and the beginning of an inquiry into aesthetics,

which progressively forged its own categories of analysis and comprehension.[1]

Catholicism, which for the entire 19th century remained riveted to the Neo-Romanesque, Neo-Gothic and Neo-Byzantine styles, which were considered 'naturally religious', had difficulty integrating this development (as was also the case in other areas). The battle of the Dominicans Marie-Alain Couturier and Pie-Raymond Régamey, conducted between 1935 and 1969 in the journal *L'Art sacré* in favor of a new relationship with contemporary art, vividly illustrates the problem.[2] For, despite its autonomy – or perhaps because of it –, modern art remains and will always remain shot through with a vague apprehension about the 'sacred'. And this is true whether modern art takes the place of the religions and, with Heidegger, conceives their works as the ultimate *loci* of a 'revelation of truth'; or whether it returns to the perspectival system of Nietzsche, who saw artworks, tragedy in particular, as policing our fictions, allowing us to resist every form of consoling escape into a parallel world beyond appearances and to say 'Yes' to the creative game of life. And it is true when, with a Benjamin and an Adorno, modern art comes to arm us against all confusion between the beautiful and the sacred, underlining the messianic dimension of the artwork, which, due to the biblical interdiction of images, is reduced to being a sign pointing to a possible fulfillment. The obsession with the 'sacred' seems impossible to uproot, and, in the course of our development of the theme, we will have to return to that elementary typology. It at least shows that the modern separation between the Christian tradition and its theology, on the one hand, and art, on the other, has in no way entailed the disappearance of the 'spiritual' in the field of art but, on the contrary, has provoked its pluriform manifestation: that of a 'spiritual' which invites us to enter an 'ecumenical' relation with it.

That invitation can be understood in two senses, which we can express in the form of closely related questions. In what way does the effective encounter with an artwork modify theological discourse from within? And, when theology reflects on the Christian mystery and its 'tradition', what place should it assign today to aesthetic experience? Before treating these two sides of the same question (in the second and third parts of this paper), it will be useful to devote a moment to the 'aesthetic experience' itself and its inalienable autonomy, the challenge being to maintain its alterity in relation to theology right to the end.[3]

Respecting the autonomy of aesthetic experience

It is necessary to effectively penetrate the field of the 'sensible', which in its way is invested by art (as other papers in this publication suggest), in order to clarify what we call 'aesthetic experience'. Too often, in effect, we are satisfied to talk about art rather than let ourselves be touched, that is to say, transformed, by one or another work. Two facets of that experience, different but intimately tied to each other, should be briefly exemplified and reflected upon: its specificity as 'aesthetic' experience, and its proper place in 'the world of life'.

1. With regard to the experiential side, we can best approach the question through the notion of 'style', which is certainly applicable to every object, as suggested by the writings of Gilles-Gaston Granger (who speaks of a "stylistic of expression"),[4] but is particularly suited to *works* in so far as these are clues

which reflect an entire culture, proper to an individual and his era. When it is a question of *works of art*, style appears at the moment when the "utility of the object in question disappears" and its material becomes manifest, "exalted in its sensible density" (in Raymond Court's happy phrase), allowing its "luminescence" and "sonorescence" to also appear.[5] That suspension of a pragmatic or functional relation with reality automatically establishes another relation with the world, since the style of a work can be designated, according to Maurice Merleau-Ponty's phenomenological approach, as the "emblem of *a way of inhabiting the world*, of treating it, of interpreting it through the face or by clothing, by the agility of a gesture or by the body's *inertia*".[6] Citing Malraux, the philosopher specifies: "every style is the translation into form of elements of the world which allow us to orient it toward one of its essential parts". That operation of metamorphosis creates an *other* world, the world as the artist inhabits it. Let us note that the notion of style holds together (1) the creative singularity of the person who expresses, speaks, paints or composes, (2) the expression or the work itself, as it is described, and (3) the experience of the viewer or listener who understands a work's style only if he somehow installs himself, with the artist, in the creativity which the work of art and its style suppose – in other words, if he enters what Merleau-Ponty calls "the very operation of style".

It is precisely that operation that we may more simply call 'aesthetic experience'. This consists in *letting be* that which is other – the work, which, according to Merleau-Ponty, "bears in itself its own coherence, itself expressing the conditions under which it intends to be received and approved"[7] –, and thus overtake that which shows itself or lets itself be understood in its own springing forth, in the very place where the artist's *inspiration* or *individual genius* manifests itself (since the 18th century the latter has replaced the former).[8] Like all experience, what we term 'aesthetic' is thus multiform, but in every case it engages our senses and conducts them toward what, using terminology borrowed from Trinitarian theology, I call their 'circumincession', when it is given us to *see*, for an instant, a word listened to, or to *hear* that which we see. Two examples, in this decisive development of the theme, will offer the reader something more than my text, illustrating what it is that tips the argument toward another 'order'.

The first example is Caravaggio's *Calling of St Matthew* (fig. 1).[9] We know the story and perhaps the painting as well. "As Jesus was walking on from there, he saw a man named Matthew sitting at the tax office, and he said to him: 'Follow me'. And he got up and followed him" (Mt 9:9). I call your attention to only two remarkable stylistic features, the play of gestures which bind these two groups of people together, and the light. The painting lets us *see* a word that is *heard* and its gestural effect: Matthew indicates himself, as if to say: 'Me?'. Then the separation between the scene's actors and its viewers disappears, at the nodal point of the aesthetic experience, when our gaze upon the painting shifts us from external space to the space-temporal presence of the *hic et nunc*; when, in the flux of everyday life, a *moment* of truth supervenes for *a single person* (Matthew and each of us). That aesthetic event happens without any necessity, thanks to this mysterious ray of light, with Christ, and Peter, who reproduces Christ's speaking gesture, remaining in darkness.

The other example is musical, taken from Claude Debussy's *Piano Preludes*, the sixth of the first book, entitled *Steps on the Snow*.[10] If Caravaggio made us see the listening to a word, Debussy lets us understand what he sees. His space/time is fundamentally structured by the *rhythm* which, according to Henri Maldiney, is the axis of musical experience. Rhythm works on the listener's breathing to harmonize it, again in a unique way, with the 'founding instant of the rhythm', the silence which is *in* him and *in* nature.

Debussy, when he said of the prelude's rhythmic figure that 'this rhythm should have the sound value of a sad, icey landscape', indicated exactly the nodal moment of aesthetic experience: the circumincession of our senses somehow brought back to the essential rhythm of breathing, in the 'Open Space' where (according to Rilke[11]) every painter, musician and poet stands. That aesthetic experience – which we should qualify as "spiritual" in the broadest sense of the term – is extremely fragile, especially in the modern and contemporary era. For when – after the age of representation – painting broke away from mimesis of the world, and music suspended its tonal system thereby thwarting our search for an architectural framework, the auditive and visual capacities, or imagination, of the 'amateur' were either bypassed or called to what we term a 'conversion': called to live here and now and always before a given work. Simultaneously the non-necessity of that experience, its gratuitous and always surprising character, appeared (inspiration's suffering is the lot of every artist); and with it the need to install oneself, with the artist, in the very creativity which the work and its style induce (something that does not happen of itself). This 'dramatic' side of aesthetic experience, more present today than in the past, brings us to the other facet, the place that aesthetic experience has in 'the world of life'.

2. In our differentiated societies, artists in effect constitute and create a 'world' that is *other* and special: the world as they see it, hear it, etc. Now, that differentiation of 'worlds' has given rise to a new kind of actor – sometimes called 'art critic', sometimes 'commentator' (according to the emphasis we want to give) – who positions himself between 'the world of everyday life' and the 'fine arts' in their autonomy; I have just momentarily assumed that function.[12] It is precisely in the place where our approaches to the 'real' differentiate themselves and become specialized, that the work of the 'critic' – of the hermeneut, of the popularizer, or of those who call themselves initiators or 'ferrymen' – is situated. That terminology is particularly apt in the field of aesthetics, where the work of initiation pursues a double objective. It has the ambition of opening and of converting our bodily eyes and ears, to render possible an *aesthetic experience* to senses often anesthetized or atrophied by a strategic rationality; and it intervenes simultaneously and in an always detailed way in the *relationship of society with the beautiful*, offering the plurality of styles as so many ways of inhabiting the world. In effect, that relationship is exposed to the phenomenon

1. Michelangelo Merisi da Caravaggio, *Calling of St Matthew*, Rome, Church of San Luigi dei Francesi, Contarelli Chapel.

of seductive fashions, of economic exploitation and political manipulation, and yet remains the privileged place where – not without the techniques of communication – a common *ethos* can be formed, a manner of understanding one another at the level of feeling, and a way of understanding the question of sense.

And – to introduce what now follows – let us note that the somewhat rudimentary typology of 'spiritual positions' mentioned at the beginning of this paper occurs at just this point: the willingness of art to take the place of religion; a persistent apprehension of the 'sacred' (or, on the contrary, the desire to desacralize, that is to profane); or, again, emphasis upon the work's messianic dimension as the sign of an impossible completion, as, for example, in Adorno[13] and in Schönberg's *Moses and Aaron*. It is here that Christian tradition can and should position itself and insist upon the validity of its own conception, that of a Jesus-centered messianism – a particularly difficult task due to Christianity's very great aesthetic heritage.

What the theologian can learn from art and the aesthetic experience

In effect, in the ever-new situation of modern and contemporary autonomy of the aesthetic experience, the theologian and perhaps also the artist must undergo a veritable *apprenticeship*. In what way does the effective encounter with an artwork modify theological discourse from within? It is perhaps with that self-questioning that we should begin, for it has a bearing on the faith-experience, interrogated in its specificity by aesthetic experience, and with the place of theology and of the experience it claims for itself in the 'world of daily life'.

Let us begin with the analogy between aesthetic experience and the experience of faith. That analogy emerged as such as soon as the Church and the great 20th-century theologians – I think of Hans Urs von Balthasar and Karl Rahner[14] – encountered contemporary art and at the same time renounced an apologetic or strategic attitude in their way of conceiving the Christian mystery. The relationship which the 19th-century Church had had with art – with the Neo-Romanesque, the Neo-Gothic, the Neo-Byzantine – in effect showed an apologetic strategy. People thought that these styles, considered 'naturally' religious, favored a perception of the unity of the 'supernatural' and of that which was held to be indispensable by reason of its 'natural premises', the Church considering itself a *sign* or "great and perpetual motive of credibility and an irrefutable witness to its own divine mission".[15] But today, in acknowledging the gratuity of aesthetic experience, and its resistance manipulation, the theologian who confronts it sees himself invited to call attention to analogous characteristics at the heart of faith-experience. And that has led me to think of the Christian mystery in terms of style and manner of inhabiting the world which imply a specific relationship with the beautiful.

Two features of the faith-experience of encounter with Christ Jesus stand out then in a particular way. First, its coherence, the absolute concordance between its interiority, its words and its acts. Its form of life 'signifies itself' as being holy, in the sense of a real and astonishingly gratuitous presence, at once sensible and unfocused. We could apply to it the stylistic distinction articulated by Focillon, between "the *sign* which signifies" and the "*form* which signifies *itself*",[16] or to the characteristic of an artwork, which, according to Merleau-Ponty, "carries in itself its own coherence".[17]

On the condition, however, that the second feature of that experience of faith is respected, which is the transformation of the partner of the encounter. The partner is in no sense passive: although he allows Jesus Christ to be other, perceiving and understanding what he manifests of himself from the impulse of his *own* existence, the disciple really participates in this impulse, which tradition designates as being the work of the Spirit. Thus the encounter with Jesus Christ does not produce replicas but produces women and men inhabited by the Holy and Creator Spirit and inspired by him. In that way the three aspects of style specified above, in the first section, come to form a remarkable unity: (1) the singular presence of One who expresses himself in words and gestures, (2) his expression or 'work' reduced to

'nothing' since he has left us 'nothing', except his own life, his own body and blood, and (3) the experience of a witness who, listening and seeing, understands that work of Jesus Christ only if he himself enters that "operation of style" (as Merleau-Ponty would say) or enters into the creativity that the Messiah's 'work' and style suppose. To be sure, Scripture, as a work of the primitive community and of the Holy Spirit, maintains its textual autonomy; but it obeys its own stylistic canon only if it "effaces itself" and, in an ever new fashion, "inspires" the experience of encounter between the Messiah Jesus and his missionary disciples.[18]

On the basis of these brief indications, let us now return to the analogy between aesthetic experience and the experience of faith. It is important, first of all, to underline the decisive difference: Jesus Christ's involvement of his own existence for everyone, the "gift of himself" *usque ad mortem, mortem autem crucis*.[19] This gift stems from a logic of excess which defies all efforts to legislate in its regard; for it will always, here and now, turn out to be 'disproportionate', and yet, by grace, perfectly proportioned to this or that man or woman. It is precisely that difference between aesthetic experience and faith-experience which calls forth the notion of 'style', allowing us at the same time to conceive the 'singularizing structure' of Christian experience and thus its pluralization, and the pentecostal bond which ties together all these manifestations. In so far as it is an encounter with Jesus Christ and his witnesses, the faith-experience should not, therefore, be confused with aesthetic experience, but it has an aesthetic aspect and, for those who know how to see and hear, conveys a specific beauty. St Ignatius, for example, calls attention to it when, in the second week of his *Exercises*, he invites the retreatant to "consider *how Christ our Lord stands* in a vast camp near Jerusalem, *in a humble place, beautiful and gracious*".[20] Through its suspension of the tonal system and renunciation of mimesis of the world, modern and contemporary art is able to make us pay attention to certain aspects of style proper to the faith-experience. The *conversion* or *circumincession* of 'seeing' and 'hearing' (to say nothing of the other senses) is thus radicalised, preparing a 'seeing' and 'hearing' able to perceive the coherence of an unfocused 'presence', visible and radically discreet, that obeys a new kind of temporality and is guided by someone else or by the 'neighbor' who unexpectedly presents himself.

Like aesthetic experience, the experience of faith which situates itself at the heart of 'the world of daily life' requires an initiation, and therefore needs ferrymen, hermeneutes, critics. The theologian and theology can easily recognize themselves in what we said above about the position of this kind of actor at the heart of our differentiated societies. The science of faith, too, has allowed itself to be penetrated by the differentiation and specialization of its rationale, and today occupies a middle ground between believers' 'world of life' – their *sensus fidei* or *sensus Regni* –, and highly specialized theological disciplines such as exegesis, history, etc.

At the risk of over-simplifying the wealth of possible attitudes, let us distinguish at least two different positions. *Sometimes* the theologian-hermeneute will position himself more on the side of the 'works' of Christian tradition; all his culture will be invited to concur in a reading which, when it goes beyond the limits of the given work – as for example in biblical and patristic (that is systematic) theology –, presents itself as genuine recreation, capitalizing on its own faith-experience and that of its community and, by the beauty of its contents, leading the reader to forget the works which were its point of departure. *At other times* the commentator will situate himself more on the side of the recipient's fundamental aesthetic – his 'sense of the faith' –, summoning history, phenomenology or other arts, not to communicate information to the recipient, but to lead him to have a personal faith-experience, and thereby enter *hic et nunc* in the circumincession of its meanings: a "seesaw event", never predictable or strategically programmable, that is entrusted rather to everyone's freedom. At that point the commentator becomes a 'ferryman', destined to eclipse himself, leaving to the other – along with the Scriptures – only a musical score, a map or an exercise book with which to invent the itinerary of his own existence.

The theologian is then confronted with the plurality of forms of Christian life – Pope Francis recently spoke of its 'polyhedric pluralization'[21] –, and with the plurality of conceptions of the world or grammars of sense in our secularized lay societies, conceptions underlying the typology mentioned above. It is in this 'world of life', criss-crossed by numerous conflicts, that he attempts to give value to the 'dramaturgical behavior'[22] of God's Holy One and his disciples, knowing that the experience of faith and action certainly must be thought through, but depends entirely on the liberty of women and men who commit themselves at the heart of their daily life. Knowing that, the theologian can then pass from what he learned in his meeting with the artwork and, inverting his perspective, ask what place theology should today assign to art and to aesthetic experience when it reflects on the Christian mystery and its 'tradition'.

The artwork at the heart of the Christian mystery

That question is traditionally treated in discussions of liturgical space: of the church building, its furnishings, of the staging of liturgy, of the poetry of prayer and liturgical music, etc., all of those elements of sacred art being destined (if not 'manipulated') to render possible a sacramental kind of faith-experience at once ecclesial and individual. Without at all denying the importance of that approach, today it seems decisive to broaden it in light of what we have just said, in the direction of the pluriform manifestation of the 'spiritual' in art *and* of the pluriform manifestation of the Christian mystery. In effect, Vatican II situates the liturgy at the 'pinnacle' of an entire itinerary, and in turn makes this pinnacle the point of departure – 'the source' of Christian life in the very bosom of daily life and society.[23]

What is more, the Council recognizes the autonomy of art and artists, for "the Church has not adopted any particular style of art as her very own", according to the somewhat rapid statement of *Sacrosanctum concilium* (the *Constitution on the Holy Liturgy*).[24] Today that autonomy of art, and the fact that it is kept at a distance in relation to the religious world (as said above), allows it to participate, in its own way, in the biblical and Christian experience of holiness. On the itinerary laid out by the *Constitution on the Holy Liturgy*, we can situate the arts before and after the manifestation of holiness in our forms of life and in our liturgies. *Before*, first of all, because art works on our senses, at times baffling them by shifting their references, perhaps converting them and leading them toward their imaginary circumincession: an overall perception useful for seeing and hearing the others in the world in a different way. And *after*, because to suddenly discover the beauty of biblical holiness and of the Holy One of God can create and sharpen a spiritual sensibility made capable of perceiving – with the arts and beyond them – creation's sober beauty in the Open Space of a world without temples proclaimed in the Book of Revelation (21:22). That double and yet single perception is nonetheless sustained by an act of discernment which, in the perspective of Christian theology, intimately binds it to the work of the Holy Spirit – to the Spirit-mystagogue, one might say, bearing in mind that the perception in question is situated on a path. The necessity of discernment is moreover affirmed – in a somewhat abrupt way – by the *Constitution on the Holy Liturgy*,[25] and I must finally analyze it, briefly explaining the bond between art and the Holy Spirit, showing why we appeal to it, and drawing from it some criteria of authenticity.

1. In considering the pluriform manifestation of 'the spiritual' in art, and in observing the three parameters of the notion of style discussed in our first section, the Spirit's work in some way distributes itself throughout the creative act: on the result – that is, on the works – and on their recipients. The Spirit is invoked, first of all, for the artist's own *inspiration*, whatever his art be; the Spirit's work is then found in the *profusion of artworks*, precisely when a discernment is made, guided by Jesus-centered Christian messianism; and the Spirit's work manifests itself finally in that which the works arouse in women and men who, with them and thanks to them, have an aesthetic experience and perhaps a faith-experience as well.

A first consideration is that, in the presence of border-cases – lack of inspiration, doubts about the capacity to engender something new, the sterility of one or another tradition, violent opposition between traditions, etc. –, we should recall that the Spirit finds his first *raison d'être* in the bosom of an imploration, addressed by an individual or a group, to Him whom they believe to be at the level of their yearning. The Christian tradition's rare prayers to the Spirit are, in effect, hymns of supplication: *Veni creator spiritus, Veni sancte spiritus*. With these two texts we are in the apocalyptic climate of the 'end'; but the 'Come, Lord *Jesus*' pronounced on the last page of Revelation by the Spirit and the Bride, is here brought back to a more elementary and fundamental desire – 'Come, *Spirit*' –; as if those who so express themselves intuit that the unforeseeable coming from which their human history remains suspended also depends on their own spiritual state, as uncontrollable as the longed-for event itself is. The apostle Paul speaks of the 'groaning in labor pains' (Rm 8:22–3, 26) that every artist knows so well. In this context, to designate the Spirit as *creator* is to put him in the position of a 'water spring', and who would not seek that spring in himself to draw inspiration from it, when he desires to *express* or *recognize* the human in the flesh of artworks!

A second consideration: to link the Spirit and *holiness* – *Veni sancte Spiritus* –, is to indicate still more radically that the creativity required by the work of religious peacemaking and ecumenical reconciliation has its ultimate source in a way of opening oneself, at the price of one's own life, to another and to the universe: a way which, even as it exceeds our measure, can be desired as an effort possible to humanity: 'The Spirit looks forward to life and peace' (Rm 8:6).

The surprising profusion of artworks and styles is the precursory sign of that so desired and hoped-for ecumenicity. But it is also there – in the place where the conditions of such a pentecostal ecumenicity are at stake and where beauty and holiness touch each other – that the discernment mentioned above must penetrate our capacity of perception. We might be content to reduce the work of art to *appearance* (in the platonic sense of the term), but then we would lose its modern incarnation, as much in conformity with the phenomenology of a Merleau-Ponty as with a theology of the Incarnation. Now, that incarnational theology immediately stirs up two forms of contestation, widely attested in art history: the fascination exercised by the exaltation of the sensible, in its density and 'luminescence' and 'sonorescence', *and* the antidote that such fascination provokes, to wit: the fear and criticism of idolatry. The Christian itinerary – 'between' or 'by way of' these manifestations of the 'spiritual' – is fraught with danger and infinitely fragile, for in expressing itself in works of art, it should arrive at making possible a conversion of our senses capable of perceiving the humble beauty of a holiness that is communicative and communicating. Perhaps the term 'sacred art' runs the risk of concealing what is at stake, in maintaining a regrettable confusion between the 'sacred' (*sacrum*) and the 'holy' (*sanctum*).

Our third consideration is that, if we pass finally from the 'works' of art to their recipients, listeners or viewers, we discover a third reason for bringing the Holy Spirit into a theology of art: the proximity between beauty and holiness introduces into the work – *as* in the sacrament of the Eucharist – a movement of effacement. Here we can refer to Johannine phenomenology: the effacement of Christ Jesus in favor of the coming of the Paraclete (Jn 16:7, 13) is anticipated in his meeting with the Samaritan woman, when he promised her water that would become *in her* "a spring of water welling up" (Jn 4:14) and put her before the "hour" – and it is now – "when true worshipers will worship the Father in spirit and truth", no longer on a certain mountain or in a certain city... (Jn 4:21–4). In a Christian perspective, the work of art participates in this movement of effacement or interiorization which makes of the believer a listener and a seer in his daily life in a world without a temple, having *in* himself the 'water-spring' of his perception.

2. Three criteria of aesthetic authenticity can be singled out on this route which calls for

the intervention of the Spirit mystagogue or *hod-ägos* (see Jn 16:13). Out of a concern for precision, I will designate them with Greek terminology borrowed from the New Testament: *dynamis – krisis – metamorphôsis*.[26] The first criterion expresses the most elementary effect of an aesthetic experience open to the experience of faith, namely the communication of an 'energy' or 'force' – Paul Tillich speaks of the "courage to be" – which has a part in healing the subject and putting him 'on his feet' in his uniqueness. The second criterion adds necessary discernment and maintains the openness of beauty toward the holiness of Jesus Christ and his witnesses. Finally, the third criterion indicates the aim, that is the 'transfiguration' of the subjects in their bond among themselves and with the world, perceptible here and there, in a fugitive way, 'for an instant'. Aesthetic experience then anticipates an 'inversion' of perspective such as we find in the apostle Paul and in all the mystic tradition: "Now we see only reflections in a mirror, mere riddles, but then we shall be seeing face to face. Now, I can only know imperfectly; but then I shall know as fully as I am myself known" (1 Co 13:12). The authentic work of art has that spiritual capacity to shatter the mirrors in which we see ourselves or which send back echoes of our own voices, and to transform us into see-ers who are *seen* and heard people who *hear*.

Conclusion

In conclusion let us simply remark that the formal character of these three criteria is not an obstacle to our perception and discernment, put a 'plus' which maintains the ecumenical singularity and plurality of our aesthetic experiences open to the experience of faith. It is in fact to the concreteness of these experiences that the theology of art directs us, when it stops speaking... ∎

[Here Christoph Theobald invited his audience to listen to a few measures of Debussy's prelude *Des pas sur la neige*...]

1 See Raymond Court, *Le voir et la voix. Essai sur les voies esthétiques*, Paris, 1997, esp. pp. 15–42 ('L'art au défi de la modernité').

2 See Françoise Caussé, *La Revue "L'Art sacré". Le débat en France sur l'art et la religion 1945–1954*, Paris, 2010.

3 See Christoph Theobald, 'Le christianisme comme "style". Relecture du thème "Esthétique et théologie"', *Recherches de Science Religieuse*, 85/4(1997), pp. 589–600; Christoph Theobald, *Le christianisme comme style. Une manière de faire de la théologie en postmodernité*, 2 vols., Paris, 2007.

4 Gilles Gaston Granger, *Essai d'une philosophie du style*, Paris, 1988 (1st ed. Paris, 1968).

5 Raymond Court, 'Style esthétique et lieu théologique', *Recherches de Science Religieuse*, 85/4 (1997), pp. 537–56: 549.

6 Maurice Merleau-Ponty, *Signes*, Paris, 1960 (in particular chapter I: 'Le langage indirect et les voix du silence', and chapter II: 'Sur la phénoménologie du langage'). The development on style is at pp. 65–95.

7 Ibid., p. 79.

8 In his *Critique of Judgment* (1790), Kant recalls that the central term of modern aesthetics, 'genius', is "probably derived from *genius*, the spirit given a man for himself at birth, with the charge to protect and guide him, and which furnished the inspiration from which [his] original ideas emanate". Every genius's talent is a "natural gift", which consists in producing "that for which no single rule can be indicated", to wit: a product characterized by its originality and future exemplarity (§ 46).

9 See the commentary by Andrea Dall'Asta, 'L'image d'un Dieu qui passe. Lecture théologique de la Vocation de S. Matthieu de Caravage', *Recherches de Science Religieuse*, 85/3 (1997), pp. 331–4.

10 See Philippe Charru, *Quand le lointain se fait proche: La musique, une voie spirituelle*, Paris, 2011, pp. 217–33.

11 "Breathe, O invisible poem! / Pure exchange that never ceases between our own being / and the world's spaces. Counter-weight / in which I myself rhythmically happen, / unique wave of which I am the following sea". Rainer Maria Rilke, "Atmen", in *Die sonette an Orpheus*.

12 See Philippe Charru and Christoph Theobald, *La pensée musicale de Jean-Sébastien Bach: les chorals du Catéchisme luthérien dans la Clavie-Übung III*, Paris, 1993. See also Philippe Charru and Christoph Theobald, *Johann Sebastian Bach interprète des Évangiles de la Passion*, Paris, 2016.

13 Theodor W. Adorno, 'Sakrales Fragment. Über Schönbergs Moses und Aron', in *Musikalische Schriften. II. Quasi una fantasia*, Frankfurt, 1963.

14 Yves Tourenne, 'Amorce d'une esthétique théologique chez Karl Rahner?', *Recherches de Science Religieuse*, 85/3 (1997), pp. 383–418; Vincent Holzer, 'Esthétique théologique comme esthétique fondamentale chez Hans Urs von Balthasar', *Recherches de Science Religieuse*, 85/4 (1997), pp. 557–88.

15 Vatican I, Constitution on the Catholic Faith *Dei filius*, DH 3013.

16 Henri Focillon, *La vie des formes*, Paris, 1981, p. 7 (7th ed.; 1st ed. Paris, 1934).

17 See note 6.

18 See Christoph Theobald, 'La réception des Écritures inspirées', in «*Dans les traces…*» *de la Constitution "Dei verbum" du concile Vatican II. Bible, théologie et pratiques de lecture*, Paris, 2009, pp. 57–89.

19 Ph 2,8: '… even to accepting death, death on a cross'.

20 St Ignatius of Loyola, *Spiritual Exercises*, no. 144.

21 Pope Francis, Apostolic Exhortation *Evangelii gaudium*, §§ 234–7: 236.

22 See Jürgen Habermas, *Der philosophische Diskurs der Moderne. Zwölf Vorlesungen*, Frankfurt, 1985, p. 366.

23 *Sacrosanctum concilium*, 9 and 10.

24 Ibid., no. 123: "The Church as not adopted any particular style of art as her very own; she has admitted styles from every period according to the natural talents and circumstances of peoples, and the needs of the various rites. Thus, in the course of the centuries, she has brought into being a treasury of art which must be very carefully preserved. The art of our own days, coming from every race and region, shall also be given free scope…"

25 Ibid., no. 122, § 2: "The Church has, with good reason, always reserved to herself the right to pass judgment upon the arts, deciding which of the works of artists are in accordance with faith, piety and cherished traditional laws and thereby fitted for sacred use".

26 As to this tripartite division, see Christoph Theobald, 'L'expérience du "Maître intérieur"', in *Le christianisme comme style*, 2 vols., Paris, 2008, II, pp. 852–61.

The Visual Experience of God in the Hebrew Bible

JAN JOOSTEN

Introduction

The notion of 'seeing God' appears frequently in biblical discourse. Moses asks to see God, but God refuses, or at least gives in only up to a point: 'You cannot see my face … for man cannot see me and live'; but then God shows Moses his back! (Ex 33:13–23). Several other prophets claimed to have seen God: Isaiah saw him in the Jerusalem temple (Is 6) and Amos near a wall (Am 7:7), God showed himself to the patriarchs (Gn 17:1; 18:1; 26:2). The psalmist expressed his desire to see God (Ps 17:5; see 11:7; 42:3). The Bible texts do not invite us to take these references to a visual experience of God as metaphors. According to the New Testament, God is invisible (Col 1:15; 1 Tm 1:17; Heb 11:27), but one must not impose this viewpoint on the Old Testament. Recent research has underlined the corporeality of the God of the Bible: he "comes", he "descends", he can be found in specific places. With these characteristics, the Hebrew Bible is close to other ancient Near Eastern religious writings. The idea of 'seeing God' fits nicely in that cognitive framework.

We would like to know what psycho-physical experience these references to 'seeing God' imply: what did Abraham see when God showed himself to him? It is difficult to know. What we can do as modern readers of the Bible is to grasp the cultural, religious, social and political sense of these passages. That sense is complex, as we will see in the following pages.

Paying homage to the divine King

According to several legislative texts in the Pentateuch, Israelites have the obligation to 'see God' periodically.

> Three times a year all your menfolk must present themselves before the Lord Yahweh, the God of Israel (Ex 34:23; see Ex 23:17; Dt 16:16).

The English translation does not contain the verb 'to see', but the Hebrew text retains its sense. Literally the Hebrew text means: '…the men will let themselves be seen the Lord…'. The grammar of the phrase limps, which indicates a change in the textual tradition of the verse. The active voice has been transformed into a passive voice through a change in the way of speaking. In the beginning the Law commanded the men to Israel to see God, but out of respect for the Divine person the synagogue reading substituted the passive form. The same change affects other Bible texts:

> When the whole of Israel comes to look on the face of [alternative reading: present themselves

before] Yahweh your God in the place he chooses you must proclaim this Law in the hearing of all Israel (Dt 31:11).

When the child [Samuel] is weaned, I [Hannah] will bring him and we will see the face of [other reading: so that he may be presented to] Yahweh and he shall stay there forever (1 S 1:22).

All these texts make reference to a pilgrimage which the Israelites made, going to the central sanctuary. The phraseology is that of homage to a suzerain. To see God's face means: 'to be received by God in audience'.

The covenant binding Israel to its God, and which takes for granted the laws contained in Ex 21–3 and Dt 12–26, is conceived on a political model. The point of that conception is directed against earthly rulers: Israel should not be governed by an Israelite king or by a foreign sovereign. Her obedience is due exclusively to God. The temple plays the part of a royal palace, and the pilgrimage, as we said, corresponds to the courtesy-visit that a vassal makes to his suzerain.

To 'see God' is thus a duty, but a deeply-felt one, if we believe the Bible texts. The Psalms bear witness to the satisfaction which Israelites felt in visiting their God.

My soul thirsts for God, the God of life; when shall I go to see the face of God? (Ps 42:3).
For me the reward of virtue is to see your face, and, waking, to gaze my fill on your likeness (Ps 17:15).
Yahweh is righteous, he loves virtue, upright men will contemplate his face (Ps 11:7).

Here too it is a question of evocations of the pilgrimage undertaken on Israelite feasts: at the beginning and the end of sowing and after the wine harvest. In so far as the relationship with God is healthy, these periodic visits correspond to a real need. Before the earth gives its fruit, people come to implore the divine blessing, and after the harvest they feel a need to say thanks. Only in the case of alienation between the people and its God does the pattern become laborious:

When you come to see my face, who asked you to trample over my courts? (Is 1:12).

When the pilgrimage is divorced from genuine piety, which includes social justice, it becomes a mere rite. Then it can no longer play the role of celebrating the covenant and making the covenant live.

To a contemporary reader, a verse like that of Psalm 42, quoted above, may suggest a mystical vision. In the world of the Bible it is more natural to understand it, as we have done, as a reference to that recurrent religious act constituted by the long journey to the central sanctuary on the main national feasts. The core idea of the covenant structures Israelite religious experience, and, even if it remains hard to know to what exactly the vision of God evoked in the texts corresponds, that vision's religious-cultural role is clear. In periodically 'seeing God', Israel gave expression to its relationship with its heavenly Lord.

The danger of seeing God

In the texts listed above, the act of 'seeing God' is regular and commanded by the Law. Only Isaiah's text lets us glimpse the possibility that God may not appreciate being seen. This negative side also transpires in the texts where the fact of seeing God is judged to be dangerous. Manoah, Samson's future father, after seeing the angel who announces the birth of his son, exclaims:

We are certain to die, because we have seen God (Jg 13:22).

So too in the passage in which Moses asks, after the sin of the golden calf, to see God: God does not accede to the request and underlines that to see him carries with it a mortal risk.

The risk of seeing God does not seem to lie in a mortal irradiation emanated by the divine face. Like many other biblical personages, Manoah and Moses see God without dying. The analogy with the royal court furnishes a better explanation. The king's face should not be seen. Seeing the king is a privilege accorded to chosen individuals. Anyone who, contrary to custom, tries to see him becomes 'guilty'. Remember the case of Esther, who was the queen: after three days of fasting, she presented herself before the king in fear and trembling, risking her life. In the same way, to see God's face without having been invited to do so constitutes an act of *lèse-majesté*, punishable by death.

Those who see the face of God

The concept of the vision of God as a practically political act similarly explains another series of texts. In several passages the prophets affirm that they have been received by God or to have seen God. Balaam presents himself as one "who has had the vision of the All-Powerful" (Nb 24:4), Elijah as he who "stood before the Lord" (1 K 18:15). Micah Ben Yimla and Isaiah recount that they have seen God surrounded by his court:

> I have seen Yahweh seated on his throne; all the array of heaven stood in his presence, at his right and at his left (1 K 22:19).

> In the year of king Uzziah's death I saw the Lord Yahweh seated on a high throne; his train filled the sanctuary; above him stood seraphs, each one with six wings; two to cover its face, two to cover its feet and two for flying. And they cried out one to another in this way, 'Holy, holy, holy is Yahweh Sabaoth. His glory fills the whole earth!' (Is 6:1–3).

Ezechiel devotes an entire chapter to the vision of God which inaugurated his ministry (Ezk 1).

These prophetic claims make sense in light of what we said above. In the king's entourage there are privileged persons "who see the king's face" (2 K 25:19; Est 1:14). It is a question of close counselors, through whom anyone else who want the king's ear must pass. The same is true in the particular way of conceiving God as the king of his people. The prophets are, so to speak, "those who see the face of God". They are admitted to his throne room, received in audience. It is because they see God that they can claim to transmit words on his behalf and, still more important, to intercede with him for their fellow countrymen.

The theological value of the 'Seeing God' motif

Having rapidly explored these aspects of our theme, it is necessary to note that the vision of God, in the passages quoted, does not necessarily invite us to elaborate a theology of the arts. Seeing God is less an aesthetic experience than it is a rational act. In presenting itself before the Lord, in 'seeing his face', Israel gives concrete expression to the covenant which binds the people to its God. The danger is not situated in the object of the vision as such – no Steven Spielberg special effects – but in the exigencies that govern the relationship between the Israelites and their heavenly sovereign. *Lèse majesté* is punishable by death. And the prophets' privilege consists in the power to approach God, to see themselves given the authority to speak in his name and to intercede before him. What is important in this body of ideas is not what man sees when he sees God, but the very fact that he sees him.

The challenge of this theme is not immediately apparent. The hidden royal, or, rather, imperial background could put off a contemporary reader of the Bible: we prefer to think of the relationship with God in more democratic terms. The idea of an all-powerful God, surrounded by his heavenly court, who admits human beings to his presence provided they observe his law, can seem repressive. In that case it is important to put the conception in question back in its historical context. In the Bible, the image of God as a heavenly king, master of the universe who monopolizes power opposes, on the one hand, the thirst for power of Israel's earthly king and, on the other, the Assyrian, Babylonian or Persian imperialism of the surrounding world. If the God of Israel monopolizes power, it is to take it back from the world's power figures. The Bible rises up against these leaders to install another system. Despite its feudal airs, the biblical concept of a covenant puts human beings on equal footing. The challenge implied in the 'seeing God' motif belongs to the order of social justice and solidarity. ■

Christian Architectural Forms and Confessions

Differences, Contrapositions, Convergences

SEVERINO DIANICH

Across time, the architectural forms of the different churches throughout the world have differentiated themselves due to diverse geographical and cultural contexts, not because of confessional divisions. A particularly meaningful instance of spatial conception spontaneously formed within a particular cultural tradition is that of Ethiopian churches: their round shape, with an interior space reserved to the priests alone and an exterior ring for sacred ministers and singers, while lay participants remain outside the building, is the fruit of an absolutely singular convergence of Judeo-Christian liturgical customs with the ancestral myth of the Ethiopia's origins starting with the King Solomon's marriage to the Queen of Sheba, and with the tradition of the African hut (fig. 1).[1] What is more, even when dramatic divisions develop, there is often a persistence of earlier forms, for tradition has greater weight than doctrinal contrapositions, as is evident in all the architecture of the eastern churches and in a good part of Lutheran church architecture. It seems possible to say that only John Calvin's way of conceiving church space really determined a new way of projecting, building and occupying churches.

From meaning to form

Architecture is an art that creates works destined, not to be looked at and contemplated, as happens with painting and sculpture, but inhabited and 'lived'. It is thus natural that its forms be determined, in the various situations that call for buildings, by the meaning that the edifice has for those who project and by the way in which they want to inhabit it.

The first generations of Christians felt no need to construct sacred places in which to pray. Still fresh was the memory of Jesus's words: "When you pray, go to your private room and, when you have shut the door, pray to your Father who is in that secret place" (Mt: 6,6), and: "True worshipers will worship the Father in spirit and truth" (Jn 4:23–4). For Minutius Felix, in the 2nd century, Christians could take pride in having neither temples nor altars, because for them it was sufficient to present themselves to God with "a good soul, a pure mind and unstained sentiments".[2]

The *domus ecclesiae* ('house of the Church'), an original concept, was not the only possible solution to the community's problem of having a place of its own in periods of persecution but developed from the obvious pertinence of the home to the familial character of the Lord's Supper. As, gradually, the forms of the liturgy were enriched and the *domus* adapted to new ritual needs, and as the community also grew in size, the 'house of the Church' began to become 'a church'. The passage from familial liturgies to community-scale celebrations not only called for new dimensions but for new spatial arrangements as well. The growing complexity of the rites produced a need for a special space, characterized by an apse, for the altar, which was no longer the wood *trápeza* that could be mounted in a moment,[3] but a marble structure similar to a pagan *ara*. The organization of a special space around the altar, with an imposing chair for the bishop and stalls for the celebrants, enriched with a monumental ambo – a railed-off space, distinguished from that occupied by the laity – would gradually recreate, in Christian churches, the ancient sense of the 'sacred': of a dimension separate from 'profane' everyday reality.

The place of listening

Just as the Roman *domus* had offered its *triclinium* for the Eucharistic meal, so the Jewish synagogue inspired a spatial arrangement that allowed the community to gather around the *bema* (elevated platform) to hear the word of God. One of the most imposing testimonials to this feature comes, not surprisingly, from Syria, geographically near Galilee, where for a long time there was a flourishing Judeo-Christian community. In the Basilica of St Sergius at Resafa (fig. 2), in the center of the nave rises a majestic *bema*, on which the bishop and clergy could take their places and around which the people could gather near the pedestal of the lectern, above which, as above the altar, rose a high ciborium or baldachin. In Haghia Sophia in Constantinople too an ambo like "a tower splendid to see"[4] projected almost to the center of the church, under the dome, occupying a place in the midst of the people. In the West, by contrast, the ambo was generally attached to the area in which the altar stood and did not condition the overall spatial organization of the church. An exception to this rule is the church of San Clemente in Rome, where the central nave is in good part occupied by the

enclosed space destined for the cantors and with fully three ambos, from the small one for singing the psalms to the highest one for the proclamation of the Gospel.

The creation of magnificent ambos continued until the 14th century, when – the solemn character of the celebration of the Word having been lost – it finally ended.[5] The reading of Holy Scripture had assumed an insignificant ritual form, and the custom of delivering a homily had been lost. At that time the task of preaching was taken on by the friars of the new Mendicant orders, who created the form of the pulpit, originally a wooden platform that could be moved from one position to another inside the vast, unitary halls that Mendicant churches resembled. Such churches were without obstructing columns and thus suitable for listening to sermons, which had become independent both of the place in which delivered and of the moment of delivery, no longer necessarily within the liturgical celebration (fig. 3).

It is necessary to recall these phases of the historical development of spatial forms, since

1. Church of Kebran Gabriel, Bahar Dar (Ethiopia).

2. Basilica of St Sergius, Resafa (Siria).

3. Basilica of Santa Caterina d'Alessandria, XIII century, Pisa.

4. Haghia Sophia, Istanbul.

5. Cathedral of the Transfiguration of the Saviour, Suzdal (Russia).

the questions aggressively raised in the 16th century by the Reform would have much to do with the Word of God and with preaching.

The place of elsewhere

Beyond these variations, we should also observe that a component of Christian faith that has deeply affected the spatial organization of churches is the eschatological vision of life and history. The recurrent invocation of the Book of Revelation, "Come, lord Jesus", and his promise, "Yes, I will come soon!" (Rev 22:17–20), have determined an acute sense of the provisional nature of the present world, and have nourished the dream of the coming of God's kingdom. At the beginning of the 3rd century Origen wrote: "O Jew, if, arriving in the earthly city of Jerusalem, you find it destroyed, 'reduced to dust and ashes', do not weep … make no lament, but rather, in place of the earthly city, seek the heavenly one".[6]

In the East, especially, church spaces will offer the faithful the thrill of feeling themselves

already inhabitants of the heavenly Jerusalem (fig. 4). Paul the Silentiary, describing the uplifting joy of those who, at Constantinople, had first entered the magnificent basilica of Haghia Sophia, said that "the entire populace gave thanks and believed that it trod heaven's immaculate streets".[7] These sensations are one with the prevalently contemplative attitude of eastern spirituality, focused on the idea of redemption as the divinization of the human being, which in the liturgy is to be experienced in a sensory manner. To enter a church is like entering Paradise: beneath the 'heaven' of the dome, from whose apex the figure of the Pantokrator gleams, we are immersed in the light that comes from on high and from every side, in which, together with the angels and saints depicted on the church walls, we sing God's praises (fig. 5).[8] The liturgical action unfolds in good part behind the iconostasis, the mysterious threshold between the temporal and the eternal that conceals the liturgy's earthly actors, only to reveal – in the icons it presents to the

6. Basilica of Santa Maria Maggiore, Rome.

7. Basilica of Santi Cosma e Damiano, Rome.

devout gaze of the faithful – the true protagonists of the mystery taking place.[9]

Very different is the tradition of the Roman basilica. After assuming the model of the civil basilica with its multi-polar space, Christian architects transformed it into a one-directional hall, whose longitudinal organization inserts the faithful in a forward-moving journey rather than giving them the feeling of having already reached their destination. In fact, western spirituality is less marked by the contemplative spirit and more engaged with history, in the course of which, thanks to Christ's sacrifice, redemption is achieved and liberation from sin. The believer who enters a church has the impression of beginning the journey of conversion in order, at history's conclusion, to finally meet Christ (fig. 6). There is no lack of images of the Lord and the saints, gleaming in splendid mosaics, but – where in the East the Pantokrator attracts our gaze from the height of the dome – in the West he seems to wait in the shell of the apse for the faithful to reach him at the conclusion

of their journey, accompanied by saints who show the way, as is the case in the apse of the Roman church Basilica of Santi Cosma e Damiano (fig. 7). Two different forms of spatial organization thus developed, in the context of different cultural traditions: two worlds, that of the Christian East and West, which effectively represent two complementary aspects of the one faith.

Between listening and seeing

From the high Middle Ages on, the growing difficulty of the faithful in understanding what was read, and the progressive clericalization of the liturgy, slowly but surely reduced people's sense of being called to church to hear God's Word. The liturgical action tended to isolate itself behind high choral barriers – 'roodscreens' –, from which the faithful in the church nave remained excluded.[10] And so in the West, after the 14th century, ambos ceased to be erected, while the altars were enriched with splendid paintings, ever more magnificent and eye-attracting, arriving finally at the sumptuous retablos of Baroque churches (fig. 8). In the end, to allow people better to see and contemplate the images of Christ crucified, of the Virgin Mary and of the saints on the altar, many roodscreens were removed, thus restoring some participation on the part of the populace – a change in Christian liturgical experience that constituted an important

8. Misericordia Church, Braga (Portugal).

9. Reformierte Kirche, Wädenswil–Zürich (Switzerland).

10. Church of St Johannis, Castell (Kitzingen–Bavaria).

11. Lutheran church of Stykkishólmur, Stykkishólmur (Iceland).

anthropological change, the passage from listening and taking part, to seeing, watching and passively 'attending' Mass.

This shift of attention would prove emblematic of the reaction of Martin Luther, for whom "the only organs of a Christian are his ears".[11] For the Reformer, "the first and highest thing, from which everything else depends, is to teach God's Word. In fact, we teach with the Word, with the Word we bind and loose, we baptize with the Word, with the Word we sanctify and we judge everything by the Word".[12] The restored centrality of the Word of God and the recovery of the New Testament concept of the common priesthood of all the faithful determined new conceptions of church space. For Calvin the first thing to do was abandon the sense of 'sacrality of place', and he waxed ironic about "those who think God's ear is nearer in church than elsewhere", declaring: "They share the crude notions of the Jews and pagans". Churches, he said, are not places which "because of some hidden sanctity make prayer holy and the faithful worthier to be heard, but spaces in which to efficiently bring together the assembled faithful when they join in prayer, listen to preaching of the Word, receive the sacraments".[13] In Reformed churches, therefore, the spatial organization adopted was determined by the centrality of preaching, and thus of the pulpit, and by the need for a large space, preferably not longitudinal, suitable for an assembly of believers intent on listening (fig. 9). Yet Reformed churches do not restore the ambo tradition, with its solemn forms that exalt God's Word: in a liturgy suspicious of ceremonial, preaching dominates, rather than the ritualized reading or chant of the Gospel. The fact is that the power of the appeal to *sola Scriptura* in the name of the *sola fide* was able in very few years – more in some places, less in others – to determine a new conception of the spaces in which Christian communities gather.

Despite his lapidary 'ears only' principle, Luther did not disdain the function of the eyes in liturgical experience. Churches in the Lutheran tradition in fact, while not recovering the monumental ambo, have not failed to create spectacular pulpits. An interesting case is the tradition, developed especially in the 18th century, of the *Kanzelaltar*, an arrangement in which the pulpit occupies exactly the space that, in Catholic retablos, was reserved for the images of saints (fig. 10). Luther, in any case – differently from Calvin –, had not been immobilized in his estimate of images by the biblical prohibition,[14] and had developed a much more pragmatic view. The importance of preaching could, he believed, be enhanced by images, with which churches could continue to be adorned. In his Stadtkirche at Wittenberg one can still see a painting by the Cranachs put on the altar a year after Luther's death, in which he is represented among the apostles at the Last Supper, and, in the predella, is shown preaching to the people with, at the center, an image of the Crucifix.[15]

It was Calvin who could not resolve the conflict between word and image, listening and seeing. It would be unfair to think that he excluded the pleasure of sight from the experience of faith, but he held that only God's works, such as the beauties of nature, deserve to attract visual admiration, as – in the liturgy – only objects seen in the celebration of the sacraments merit "that our eyes fix their gaze upon them", since they are "living and very significant [images] which our Lord consecrated with his words".[16]

For oriental spirituality, on the other hand, such a conflict is simply unthinkable.[17] For Pavel Nikolaevich Evdokimov, "the image is as much a part of the essence of Christianity as the word",[18] not for its didactic function but for its revelatory value. According to Graziano Lingua, the icon was able to overcome slavery to idols, because it is "an empty space in which the presence of the invisible is perceived as self-emptying consummation, on the basis of the Son's *kenosis*".[19] Marie José Mondzain, studying Nicephorus's writings against the iconoclastic movement, sees in the graphic incised signs that an iconographer makes on a wall or wood panel a trace of the border between being, the uncontainable within the sign, and the empty space within the sign:

> The icon is not full of Christ. In any case its graphic limits have neither contained nor held prisoner the Word's essence … the brush stroke, this supporting mark which divides the panel in two, which cuts it, subjects us to the artifice of form without, for all that, attacking the essence of the model …the icon of Christ is empty of real carnal essence – which differentiates it radically from the Eucharist –, but is full of his absence.[20]

If that is the case, then for oriental spirituality it is evident that the walls inside churches should become, thanks to the icons painted there of saints, practically transparent. The figures that cover the walls, vaults and domes are not really representations of Christ, of angels or of saints: rather, their diaphanous figures are like the void of windows, and the window "is light, not 'similar' to light".[21] And, because "it is not so much a question of contemplating icons to see God's Son face to face as of letting ourselves be seen by Him – placed beneath a gaze that watches over us –, even though the faithful can see Him only with their human eyes"[22] church space can be felt as a place in which the eschaton is revealed. The architecture itself "announces and at the same time preaches" the new life to which the entire universe is destined.[23]

Ecumenical hybridization

Across time all the various architectural forms have never really been impermeable to each other, and in the last century, under the influence of the ecumenical movement, the process of hybridization significantly accelerated. Baroque taste did not remain confined in Catholic areas, and, in the East, the process of 'occidentalization' begun by Peter the Great in Russia, even if deprecated and in many respects correctly so,[24] has left traces which here and there live on. The wave of modernist architecture has led to a globalization of forms and consequent lessening not only of regional differences but of confessional ones as well, from which not even the Orthodox Church has escaped. The Moscow Patriarchate is realizing a program of two hundred new churches for the capital, among which several projects are highly innovative in their application of traditional canons.[25] And, while everyone knows that the Lutheran tradition conserved the taste

12. Fyodorovskaya Cathedral, the crypt, St Petersburg.

liturgy, and their attention to contemporary sensibilities. In St Petersburg, in the crypt of Fjodorovskaja Cathedral (fig. 12), they are experimenting with reforms of the Orthodox liturgy in a climate of lively ecumenism, favoring – with the removal of the iconostasis – the fuller participation of the faithful.[26]

In the Catholic Church the liturgical reform of the Second Vatican Council has promoted a renewed centrality of the Word of God and, in the spirit of a new awareness of the common priesthood of all the faithful, more widespread lay participation in the liturgy. Inevitably new architectural forms have developed, which in place of the totalizing longitudinal layouts of the past offer open plans and more welcoming spaces, with a new equilibrium between the ambo, the altar and the nave (fig. 13).

for images in churches, something new is clearly happening when oriental icons are exhibited or new churches are built, not with a pulpit on the main wall but a painting of the Virgin and Child (fig. 11). Even reformed communities have not been above placing images in their churches, albeit in the transparency of windows (see fig. 9).

Obviously, it is not only the ecumenism of architects that produces conspicuous borrowing by one confession from another, but the ever greater care taken by pastors in favoring the active participation of the faithful in the

The avenue of ecumenism – the way of *et et* rather than that of *aut aut* – has thus been opened at the level of artistic experience. The organization of church space has, today, an objective that all agree on: the fuller participation of the faithful, beyond the divisive dialectics of *listening* vs. *seeing*, *preaching* vs. *celebration*, *pulpit* vs. *altar*. To architecture too one can now apply Jérôme Cottin's observation on the visual arts:

13. Church of Santa Maria Madre di Dio, Calenzano (Florence).

Art cannot be enclosed in any single category: in its creativity it constitutes a universal language more inclined to serve than to combat ecumenism … An artistic language which the churches begin to discover once they discover ecumenism.[27] ∎

1   See Osvaldo Raineri, 'I cristiani d'Etiopia', in *Popoli e chiese dell'Oriente cristiano*, edited by Aldo Ferrari, Rome, 2008, pp. 61–99.

2   Minutius Felix, *Octavius* XXXII,13.

3   Apparently this was the case in old St Peter's Basilica before a great marble altar was put over the Apostle's funerary monument; see Timothy Verdon, *La basilica di San Pietro: i papi e gli artisti*, Milan, 2005, p. 30.

4   That is how Paul the Silentiary describes it in his *Ekphrasis* composed for the consecration: Maria Luigia Fobelli, *Un tempio per Giustiniano. Santa Sofia di Costantinopoli e la Descrizione di Paolo Silenziario*, Rome, 2005, pp. 101, 113.

5   Severino Dianich, 'L'ambone: ascoltare e vedere la Parola di Dio', in *E la Parola si fece bellezza*, proceedings of the symposium (Barga, 19–28 May 2016), edited by Timothy Verdon and Giovanni Serafini, Florence, 2017, pp. 115–23.

6   Origen (185–254 AD), *Homiliae in librum Jesu Nave* XVII, I (SC 71,372). John Chrysostom spoke of churches as "the dwelling of the angels and archangels, the royal palace of God, heaven itself": *Homiliae in Epistula I ad Corinthios* 36, 5–6 (PG 61, col. 313s).

7   Fobelli 2005, op. cit., p. 55.

8   See Basilio Petrà, *La Chiesa dei Padri. Breve introduzione all'Ortodossia*, Bologna, 1998, pp. 49–66.

9   See Pavel Florenskij, *Ikonostas* [1921–2], Italian ed. with the title *Le porte regali: saggio sull'icona*, Milan, 1977.

10   In 1215 the Fathers of the Fourth Lateran Council, deploring the fact that some priests, "when they take part in a celebration, break the silence appropriate to the sanctuary and begin to discuss other subjects with laypeople present", tell us what happened in the nave while in the sanctuary others were celebrating in a devout way. See *Conciliorum oecumenicorum decreta*, edited by Giuseppe Alberigo et al., Bologna, 1973, p. 243 (2nd ed.; 1st ed. Bologna, 1962).

11   "Solae aures sunt organa Christiani hominis": Martin Luther, *Vorlesung über den Hebräerbrief nach der vatikanischen Handschrift*, edited by Emanuel Hirsch and Hanns Rückert, Berlin–Leipzig, 1929, p. 250.

12   Martin Luther, *Werke*, ed. Weimar, 1883–90, XII, p. 180.

13   John Calvin, *Christianae Religionis Institutio* [1536], in *Opera quae supersunt omnia*. I, Brunsvigae, 1864, 1st book, chapter 3, col. 87.

14   See Jérôme Cottin, 'D'un art confessionnel à un œcuménisme par l'art', *Positions luthériennes - Théologie - Histoire - Spiritualité*, 64/2 (2016), pp. 177–96: 196.

15   Jérôme Cottin, 'L'image dans la tradition protestante. Origines et actualité', in *Ratio imaginis. Esperienza teologica, esperienza artistica*, proceedings of the symposium (Florence, 26–8 September 2000) Bologna, 2001, pp. 150–81: 165.

16   John Calvin, *Institutionis Christianae Religionis* [1559], in *Opera quae supersunt omnia*. II, Brunsvigae, 1864, 1st book, chapter 11, col. 84. See also Jérôme Cottin, *Le regard et la parole. Une théologie protestante de l'image*, Geneva, 1994, p. 221, and the author's contributions to the present volume.

17   The Christian East has known and suffered from the iconoclast crisis, but not with the perception of a possible conflict between images and the Word.

18   Pavel Nicolaevic Evdokimov, *L'art de l'icône. Théologie de la beauté*, Bruges, 1972 (2a ed.; 1a ed. Brussels, 1970), p. 37.

19   Graziano Lingua, *L'icona, l'idolo e la guerra delle immagini: questioni di teoria ed etica dell'immagine nel cristianesimo*, Milan, 2006, p. 39.

20   Marie José Mondzain, *Image, icône, économie. Les sources byzantines de l'imaginaire contemporain*, Paris, 1996, pp. 121–3.

21   Ibid., p. 61.

22   Jean-Jacques Wunenburger, *Filosofia delle immagini*, Turin, 1999, p. 223.

23   Evgenij Nikolaevich Trubeckoj, *Tri ocerka o russkoj ikone*, Moscow, 1916; reference ed. *Contemplazione nel colore: tre studi sull'icona russa*, Milan, 1977, p. 24.

24   For Evgenij Trubeckoj this was "the death of a great religious art" (ibid., p. 78).

25   I thank Father Andrey Yurevich of the Patriarchate of Moscow, who gave me the opportunity of observing several projects. On the website of a group of architects with the significant name "Quadratura Circuli" (http://inrussia.com/churches-for-big-cities) it is possible to see several very significant examples of new studies and experiments.

26   I thank Stefano Parenti of the Pointifical Athenaeum "Anselmianum" of Rome, who provided me with much useful information.

27   Cottin 2016, op. cit., p. 196.

Monastic Life and Artistic Creativity

TIMOTHY VERDON

It is not difficult to suggest affinities between the monastic commitment to live entirely for God and the creative act that produces art.[1]

The principal text used by Christian monks, the Bible, opens with an account of how God created the world and human beings. In that account, the creative acts all spring from God's word: "God said: 'Let there be light', and there was light" (Gn 1:3). For the Bible, creation thus stems from God's word, and when the New Testament identifies Jesus Christ as the eternal word of God, it logically insists that "not one thing came into being except through him" (Jn 1:3; cf. Jn 1:14). In biblical terms, all creativity comes from God's word.

To be effective, however, a word must be heard, and precisely this has been an objective of Western monasticism. St Benedict's *Rule for Monks* begins with the admonition to "listen". "*Obsculta, o fili, praecepta magistri…*", "Listen carefully, my son, to the master's instructions…" (RB Prologue 1).[2] The monastery is a place where women and men listen: to the 'master' who imparts wisdom, to the tradition which shapes the master's teaching, and above all to God and his Spirit. Speaking of God, Benedict exhorts monks with the words of

a psalm: "If you hear his voice today, do not harden your hearts…" (RB Prologue 10, see Ps 95[94]:8). In Benedict's view those who embrace monastic life must, indeed, "attend with the ear of your heart", accepting with docility what God's Spirit tells them (RB Prologue 1). Summing up, we can say that monastic life is a place of listening to and reception of a creative word, with an ear that bends toward it and a heart that remains permeable. Sight is involved too, and St Benedict's Rule makes it a part of the monk's response: "Let us open our eyes to the light that comes from God, and our ears to the voice from heaven that every day calls out this charge: 'If you hear his voice today, do not harden your hearts'". Benedict's insistence on full sensory involvement echoes the first letter of St John, whose Author speaks of "something which has existed since the beginning, which we have heard, which we have seen with our own eyes, which we have watched and touched with our own hands", and which he calls "the Word of life", claiming that in Christ "life was made visible" and adding that he and others saw it and bear witness to it (1 Jn 1:1–2). St John's Gospel adds that the life present in the Word Christ is "the light of men": the real light that illumines every human being (Jn 1:3–4 and 9), and thus Benedict can speak of 'light that comes from God'.

St Benedict says that the Almighty admonishes us "every day", *cotidie*, and in the psalm he quotes we find the term "today", *hodie*. The full psalm verse quoted, "If only you would listen to [God] today, do not harden your hearts as at Meribah, as you did that day at Massah in the wilderness", juxtaposes the reader's 'today' with the distant past of the Exodus, when Israel rebelled against God and his servant Moses (Nm 14:1–35), for, in the Bible and in monastic life, the past, often recalled, is important since we can learn from it. That notwithstanding, however, what really counts is 'today': "No need to recall the past, no need to think about what was done before", Yahweh tells his people through the prophet Isaiah: "See, I am doing a new deed, even now it comes to light; can you not see it?" (Is 43:18–19a).

Our real theme is this "new deed" taking shape in each of us today: so gradual, so subtle, that we must strain to perceive it. Human creativity is in fact a response to this on-going creative act of God, as monks, who are commanded to listen daily to God's admonishments, know, and it is not surprising that Benedict saw the monastery as a "workshop" (*officina*) in which, with sisters and brothers who have the same calling, monks become artisans, skilled in using what he calls the "tools of the spiritual craft", *instrumenta artis spiritalis* (RB 4:75–8). Benedict's meaning was obviously figurative: what he calls 'tools' are not painters' brushes or sculptors' chisels but the spiritual and moral precepts of Christian life.

In time however the figures of speech became literal truths. Monasteries developed into centers of architecture, sculpture, painting, work in gold and silver, music, theater and so on, as if an atmosphere of creativity in people's inner life naturally promoted their creative activity *ad extra*.[3] It is no exaggeration to say that the achievements of monks in the arts between the 7th and the 13th centuries molded the cultural consciousness of post-antique Europe, just as the monastic life itself, perceived as a creative social choice, touched the Western imagination.

For, indeed, monastic life is a question of imagination – of faith, of course. Those drawn to monastic life imagine that its rigors will favor an eventual flowering, as Benedict assures his readers, admitting that the road "is bound to be narrow at the outset" but promising that, "as we progress in the way of life and in faith, we shall run on the path of God's commandments, our hearts overflowing with the inexpressible delight of love" (RB Prologue, 48–9). And those who take the saint at his word, and join monastic communities, need long-term imagination to persevere in believing "things that no eye has seen and no ear has heard, things beyond the mind of man, all that God has prepared for those who love him" (1 Co 2:9).

Historically, monastic life has called for a similar effort from those who do *not* embrace it, but who, across the centuries, have opted to consider monks sages and seers rather than threatening dissidents. From the thousands who went out to the Egyptian desert to ask Abba Anthony for "a word", to the millions who today read Thomas Merton, Enzo Bianchi and other monastic authors, ordinary people have chosen to believe that reclusion does not signify rejection, and that monastic silence is bright with God's wisdom for all. Moving in its simplicity, this conviction points toward the monastery's deepest function in the imaginative life of society, as symbol, investing everything in its purlieus with holiness. Perceived as "listeners" in whom a "new deed" is ever taking shape, monks have come to exemplify existential authenticity.

This paradigmatic dignity, found in all faiths that have monastic life-forms, is particularly strong in Christianity, where monks are traditionally deemed the "professionals" of religious life. Not only because their life makes them 'experts' in liturgy and in the arts which accompany it, but because, 'making profession', they solemnly commit themselves to live the principles and practices of Christian life in a more integral way. Theoretically everyone may run or sing or write, but only a few are designated 'professionals'; only a few devote their lives to these activities on the basis of a psychic identification with the skills themselves, an irresistible attraction which they interpret as a 'vocation'. Yet monks chart a course that remains accessible to ordinary Christians, and this special role in a shared endeavor explains the symbolic power their life has for others. "Listeners" who do not harden their hearts, they show that it is possible to exclude ambient noise to better hear the word which even now is creating in us a "new deed": life in Christ.

The Community of Jesus, which has promoted the present symposium, illustrates both the attraction exerted by monastic life and its creative consequences. Simple Christians who wanted to pray and work together in the spirit described in chapter 2 of the Acts of the Apostles, at a certain point these women and men discovered the ancient monastic tradition of the Church and concluded that the Spirit was inviting them to become part of it. Drawn by the beauty of monastic music and art, they accepted these creative means as components of the invitation, forms in which they could express the 'new deed' taking form in them, and through which they could in turn draw others to Christ. Most Community members being protestants, this attraction required them to overcome both the suspicion of monastic life that colored the 16th-century Reform and the refusal of the visual arts characteristic of reformed worship. And so, listening to the God who said, "Now I am making the whole of creation new" (Rv 21:5), they left the past behind and entered his "today", building a basilica and filling it with images, gladdening their eyes with Scripture not only read but seen, and their ears with Scriptures sung in an archaic language to ancient tones. Hearing Benedict's call to incline the heart's ear, they lifted their gaze to a Christ who is "the same today as he was yesterday and will be forever" (Heb 13:8), "Beauty ever ancient, ever new".[4]

In this way a Protestant community reached the Catholic conclusion that art serves a purpose in worship. Children of the Reform, they reached this certainty by reading the Bible, which confirms that art was part of God's plan of old, informing us that "the artists whom the Lord had blessed with wisdom and intelligence so that they might execute the works required for the construction of the sanctuary" were guided by Moses himself to make "everything just as the Lord had commanded" (Ex 36:1). The passage from the book of Exodus in which these words appear suggests the theological rationale of art in the service of worship, situating the calling of the first artists and the building of the sanctuary in the context of the chosen people's flight from slavery in Egypt toward freedom in a promised land. In Exodus, the calling of the artists and their work for the sanctuary are in fact conclusive acts in a series of events crucial for the identity of God's people – events which it will be useful to briefly recall.[5]

While Moses on the mountain received the tablets of the Law with the ten commandments, at the mountain's foot his people lost confidence, fashioning a golden calf and adoring it (Ex 32:1–6). When Moses came down, offended at the Israelites' faithlessness he shattered the tablets, obliging the people to choose between Yahweh and their idol with the words, "Those who are with the Lord follow me!" (Ex 32:15–28). Praying, Moses obtained pardon for the people's sin and a promise that the Lord would walk in their midst.

When then he asked the personal privilege of seeing God, Yahweh answered: "You cannot see my face, for no human being may see me and remain alive" (Ex 33:20). Yet God made a concession to his friend: "Behold a place near me. You will stand on the rock and when my glory passes before you, I will place you in the cavity of the rock and cover you with my hand until I have passed. Then I will remove my hand and you will see my back. But you may not see my face" (Ex 33:21–3). Moses then ascended the mountain again and beheld, in this partial way, Yahweh who, as he passed, identified himself as "merciful and compassionate, slow to anger and rich in faithfulness". God then established an alliance with Israel and the ten commandments were rewritten on other tablets (Ex 34:1–28).

It was at this point that, descending the mountain a second time, Moses persuaded the people to make a "voluntary contribution" of all that was required for the liturgy and summoned the first of the artists, Bezaleel, declaring that Yahweh himself had "filled him with the spirit of God so that he might have wisdom, intelligence and knowledge in every kind of work, in order to conceive and realize projects in gold, silver, brass; in cutting and setting stones; in carving wood and in every sort of ingenious work" (Ex 35:31–3).

In this sequence of events, which opens with the golden calf and closes with the ornaments of the sanctuary, it is perfectly clear that art in the service of worship is related to *sin* and *forgiveness*, becoming indeed the sign of a radical choice made by people and of God's own promise to 'walk in their midst'. Art in the service of worship prolongs the partial revelation of divine glory (God's back seen by Moses) and manifests the Israelites' willingness to contribute with their own means to realizing a 'place near to God' whose architect in any case is God himself, who furnished the plan and endowed the artists with talent. The "voluntary contribution" required of the people in fact is an earnest of their repentance for the sin of idolatry, just as the resulting beauty of the sanctuary signals the alliance offered by Him who is "merciful and compassionate, slow to anger and rich in faithfulness, who conserves his favor for a thousand generations and pardons the offense, the transgression and the sin" (Ex 34:6–7). As presented in the Old Testament, that is, art becomes a privileged sign of alliance between sinful man and the God who, pardoning sin, walks with his people; it is practically a 'sacrament' of the presence and salvation He offers.

These functions, which in ancient Israel were concentrated first in the moveable sanctuary which Moses built and then in the Jerusalem temple, might seem destined to lose significance in the new alliance instituted by Christ. Speaking to a woman of Samaria, Jesus in fact stated that neither the Samaritans' sacred mountain nor the Israelites' Temple was any longer necessary, because "the time has come – and it is now – when true worshipers will worship the Father in spirit and truth, for the Father seeks such worshipers. God is spirit", Jesus continued, "and those who worship him must do so in spirit and in truth" (Jn 4:21–4).

In much the same vein, one day when he was preaching, hearing people speak "of the Temple and of the beautiful stonework and votive gifts which adorned it", Jesus said: "Days are coming in which, of all that you admire here, not a single stone will escape destruction" (Lk 21:5–6). And, on another occasion, he used clearly provocative language to re-dimension Israel's liturgical-artistic faith, when – after expelling moneychangers and merchants from the outer courtyard – he justified his action by promising: "Destroy this Temple and in three days I will make it rise again" (Jn 2:19).

The key to such passages is provided by the evangelist John in the verses following this assertion. Noting the astonishment of Jesus's listeners – "This Temple took 46 years to build and you will make it rise again in three days?", they exclaim –, John specifies that Christ "was speaking of his body", and that "when he later rose from the dead, his disciples remembered his having said this, and believed in the Scriptures and in Jesus's words (Jn 2:20–2). For Christian theology in fact, the new 'temple' – the 'place near to God' where believers contemplate the Father's glory – is Christ himself.

In the New as in the Old Testament, man may not in fact see Yahweh in person, and the fourth gospel insists that "no one has ever seen God" (Jn 1:17). The gospel adds however that the only-begotten Son who dwells in the Father's bosom has revealed Him (Jn 1:18). This assertion goes back to Christ himself, who, when the apostle Philip asked to see God, answered: "He who has seen me, has seen the Father" (Jn 14:9). In the same spirit, a Pauline text asserts that Christ "is the image [εικων, icon] of the unseen God" (Col 1:15).

But if Christ is the incarnate 'icon' of the invisible Father – the irradiation of that glory which Moses yearned to see and could not –, it follows that the role of images in the new alliance is ultimately not *less* but *more* important than in the old! The most richly decorated area of the Jerusalem Temple (as, earlier, of the 'Dwelling' or 'Tabernacle' fashioned by Bezaleel) was the inner cell that hosted the arc in which God's ten words were preserved on stone tablets: its walls of precious cedar carved with bunches of flowers alluded to the importance of God's words (see 1 K 6:14–18). In Jesus Christ, however, not 'ten words' but *the* Word – the Logos or *Verbum* – became flesh. He was not hidden in an arc in an inaccessible chamber, but made manifest to all, as the first letter of St John insists:

> That which was from the beginning, that which we have seen with our own eyes, that which we have contemplated and which our hands have touched – the Word of life (for life has become visible, we have seen it and bear witness to it and proclaim this eternal life which was with the Father but now has become visible to us) –: that which we have seen and heard, we proclaim to you, so that you too may be in communion with us (1 Jn 1:1–3).

In the new alliance, art in fact will be a form of proclamation, meant to engender communion, of "that which was from the beginning" and which some have now experienced in sensory fashion – have "seen", "contemplated", "heard" and even "touched" –:

the Word incarnate, eternal life which, becoming visible, elicits the joyful testimony of those who see it. In fact, the concluding phrase of the passage just cited is: "We write these things to you so that our *joy* may be complete" (1 Jn 1:4).

In the life of the Church the designated place for expressing joy – the typical context of witnessing and communion – is the liturgy. Art made in its service thus automatically becomes part of a *proclamation* that is also an *encounter*, in direct analogy with the sacraments, the signs of salvation and new life instituted by Christ. It is in fact from the sacramental liturgy that sacred images draw their 'power', their 'presence', their 'reality'. Monks themselves are sacraments – living signs – of Christ's transforming power, and the art they produce is simply an expression of the creative "new deed" in act in their lives. ■

1   See *Monasticism and the Arts*, edited by Timothy Verdon and John Dally, Syracuse, New York, 1984.
2   *RB 1980. The Rule of St Benedict in English*, edited by Timothy Fry, Collegeville, MN, 1982, p. 15.
3   Timothy Verdon, 'Introduction: Monasticism and Christian Culture', in *Monasticism and the Arts* 1984, op. cit., pp. 1–27.
4   Augustine [of Hippo], *Confessions* X, 38: "pulchritudo tam antiqua et tam nova".
5   Timothy Verdon, 'Art and the Liturgy', in *The Ecumenism of Beauty*, edited by Timothy Verdon, Brewster, MA, 2017, pp. 85–113.

The Monastery as Laboratory of the Arts

The Case of the Community of Jesus

WILLIAM DYRNESS & MARTIN SHANNON

MARTIN SHANNON. The materials for this year's symposium introduce the Community of Jesus as an "ecumenical Benedictine monastery". These are helpful terms for presenting a fuller picture.

As a monastery – albeit a "non-traditional" monastery, in that we gather a variety of vocations under one roof: celibate men and women "religious", single adults, married couples, and families with children – we place a premium on the value of our *common life*, and upon all of those values and practices that both secure and foster that life: mutual acceptance and forgiveness, the pursuit of truth and honesty, the sharing of homes and possessions – those things that both express and teach us the meaning of *sacrificial love* – preferring the other; serving one another; honestly settling differences; pursuing and requiring what is best for individuals and community alike; admitting when we are wrong; submitting one's own will for the sake of the common good. The vocation to *live* together in a monastery means dying and rising together.

As a Benedictine monastery, our own *Rule of Life* draws deeply from the Rule of St Benedict, a guide for monastic life that has stood the test of time, under some of the most severe circumstances, by some of the most difficult people imaginable! – the pursuit of God;

prayer; daily work; governance by a superior; hospitality, "cherishing Christ above all". In connection with this symposium, there are two other values to note. First, in chapter four of his Rule, Benedict describes the monastery as the "workshop" in which all of the "instruments of the spiritual craft (*artis spiritalis*)" are put to use. The monastery is the "studio" in which human lives are re-made in the image of God. Second, when art also is made in the monastery – and, for that matter, when even the most mundane of jobs are done, or the simplest of tools are used – all is to be done in such a way *that God may be glorified*. For Benedict, this is the supreme goal of even the meanest task.

As an ecumenical Benedictine monastery, our membership comes from a wide array of Christian traditions, including Reformed, Lutheran, Anglican, Catholic, and Pentecostal. In fact, the majority of our number comes from various Protestant backgrounds, even as our evolution has led us to embrace a growing number of Catholic sensibilities and practices. Perhaps this is most clearly evident in the prominent place in our life of *both* Word and Sacrament. Not surprisingly, in the context of a predominantly Protestant community, I can speak of the *centrality of the Scriptures* in our liturgical, corporate and individual lives. But I can just as easily speak of the *centrality of the*

1. Designed by Andreas Göser OSB, *Christ Pantokrator*, Glees (Germany), Maria Laach Abbey, mosaic apse.

2. *Christ in Majesty*, Florence, church of San Miniato al Monte, mosaic apse.

Eucharist as our "daily bread" and of Baptism as the foundation of our monastic vows. In fact, we have come to view life more and more through the lens of sacramentality.

Two other points must be made, both of which say something about the roots as well as the on-going life of this community. First, it is important to understand that we did not come here to create art – we came to be 'recreated' ourselves. "Since its founding," we state in the Prologue of our Rule, "the Community of Jesus has cherished the inherited conviction that human lives can be changed – converted and re-formed by the burnishing hand of the Holy Spirit – and made to reflect more clearly the life of their Maker and Lord". The message of our founders, and the lives of the founding generation, have made our own transformation the singular goal for our being here together. Anything else that we are or that we do is and must always be firmly rooted in this primary soil.

Second, such transformation has always been seen as intimately connected with the actual "stuff" of life – with "what we *do* with what we *have*". One of our founders in particular was a lover of beauty in whatever form she encountered it (this was already evident in her work as the owner of Bethany Retreat House when it was a New England Bed & Breakfast). She believed that living to the glory of God was as much a part of planting a garden or setting

a table as it was for preaching the Gospel or praying for one's neighbor. God deserves the *best* we can offer of ourselves – *every* aspect of ourselves. This is the only fitting response to the best that God has already offered to us. Beauty, therefore, was as essential as goodness and as indispensable as truth.

The making of art found a place, therefore, very early in the life of this community. As a predominantly Protestant community, for example, hymn singing was a vital part of our worship. Learning to do it well eventually led to the formation of a choir, led to *Gloriæ Dei Cantores*, which eventually led to the quality of music, both vocal and instrumental, for which the Community of Jesus is known. The same can be said for learning Gregorian chant, a less "Protestant activity" perhaps, but surely fitting for, and eventually central to, the worship life of this ecumenical monastery.

Some learned how to craft small pieces of stained glass – crosses, crèches, and other religious symbols. Making banners was an early art-form – simple burlap and felt with phrases from the words of Scripture and of our founders.

Designing and printing community newsletters, greeting cards and eventually small magazines – all essentially for "in-house" use – eventually led to the creation of Paraclete Press and the publishing of books and music.

3. Designed by Helen McLean, mosaic by Alessandrea Caprara, *Christ in Glory*, mosaic apse.

And theater began as a way of entertaining and celebrating – small productions, to which high standards of excellence and beauty in set, costume, music and text were already being applied. Today, *Elements Theater Company* carries forward that vision.

These and other artistic endeavors – always rooted in the vocation to holiness and the pursuit of excellence – are now the invisible foundation stones that sit under the Church of the Transfiguration and all that has further been "built" because of it. Planning the church included the formation of art guilds and other craft groups – in mosaic, stone-carving, fresco, wood-carving, metal work, calligraphy.

Virtually every aspect of art in the church is the result of some kind of collaboration between the hired artists and members of this community, who sometimes apprenticed, sometimes designed, and sometimes fabricated.

The Church of the Transfiguration was dedicated in June of 2000. Ten years later, when the bells were hung in the tower and the final fresco was painted, the church was completed and the vision for the art program was fulfilled. We do and will continue to make art in this community, even as we do and continue to be re-made ourselves. Now, in 2017, we reflect on the art that we helped to form, and that now forms us – on the role, the place, and the meaning of art that has been created *in*, *by*, *for*, and *through* this particular "ecumenical Benedictine monastery".

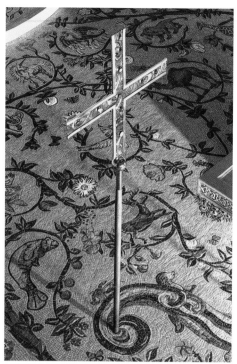

4. Designed by The Community of Jesus, fabrication by Robert Jordan, processional cross.

WILLIAM DYRNESS. It is altogether fitting that we take the opportunity of being on this lovely campus to reflect on the possible role of an "Ecumenical monastery" in creating works of art that express deeply held religious convictions. To begin I want to linger on the idea of an ecumenical community creating works of art. Up until the last generation of scholarship, it would have been common to believe (and develop in scholarly ways) that only the Orthodox and Catholic traditions, with the possible addition of the Anglican version of this, would have a fixed and identifiable "tradition of sacred art". Other traditions may have contributed in other ways – educational, political or even (*pace* Weber) economic – but they have made no substantial inroads in developing aesthetic and artistic habits and institutions. We now know the mistake in these assumptions, which often simply amounted to religious (or sometimes even class) prejudice, though they are nevertheless assumptions that are still widely operative.

To begin then, I may be permitted to address, and gently correct, such assumptions. I cannot claim to know all that might be mentioned as contributions of these various Christian groups, but I might be allowed very briefly to suggest what these gifts to the larger Christian world might be in order to clarify what we might intend by the term "Ecumenical". The Eastern Orthodox tradition, arguably the original Christian tradition (the imagination reigning when Benedict shaped his rule), already in the 6th century, was coming to the conviction that the presence of heaven – or the realm of *aletheia*, truth as they understood it – was the most significant site for beauty. In particular this was to be embodied in images of Holy personages, or icons, which would provide an opening, or window to that other heavenly world; these images represented both an offering to God and God's descent in our midst. As the Council of Nicea put this in 787 CE: "For the more often [holy persons] are seen in their pictorial representations, the more the beholder is excited to the recollection and desire of the ones represented and to offer them greeting and reverent worship". Beauty then was associated with particular sites that conveyed this spiritual and other worldly reality. Interestingly, though Martin Shannon does not mention this tradition as having representatives in the community, it has clearly had a deep impact on both the aesthetics of the worship space and the practices promoted in the community – specifically in the writing of icons.

The second obvious influence – to most observers connected with Benedictine spirituality – is the Roman Catholic (Monastic) Tradition. Like the Orthodox tradition from which it came, it too identified specific places and objects where God's presence could be seen and felt, though this included a wider variety of objects within sacred spaces. As Andrew Martindale comments: By 1200 CE, "it was not possible to stand in a church and look in any direction without finding some detail of architecture, some image, or indeed some ceremony which did not inform one about the Church as an institution, of the means of salvation which she afforded, and of the vision of heaven beyond". Believers were instructed to see through

5. Designed by Helen McLean, mosaic by Alessandra Caprara, mosaic floor: font, processional path, medallions.

these sites, and the beauty that always adorned them, to their source in God. Indeed, they were not only signs of that other reality, but media to be used, as Augustine put it, in believers' journey to God. The focus on the "Paschal Mystery" speaks of the theological ground of this aesthetic in the Incarnation – God became part of the created order in the person of Christ, in order to restore its beauty – a reality the Catholic tradition believes to be literally embodied and celebrated in the Eucharist. While the centrality of the incarnation emphasizes the presence of Christ in the elements of the Eucharist, it is not restricted to this. This Catholic background commitment disposes worshipers to see the persons and objects of their world as potential mediators of grace. It encourages a wide variety meditative and visual practices that tend to 'read' images and events as signs of this Presence – the world for the Catholic, as Andrew Greeley says, is enchanted.

But I want to argue that Protestants, despite their sometimes bewildering diversity, have developed worship practices with their own unique aesthetic potential. At the risk of oversimplifying a complex tradition, I think one can argue Protestant worship practices move in two directions – each with particular implications for the practice of art. For some both personal and corporate practices encourage

6. Designed by Gabriele Wilpers, fabrication by Derix Glass Studios, west wall architectural glass sculpture, Transfiguration.

an intense inward focus on the believer's relationship with God in Christ, and for others worship is meant to promote a concern with God's work of salvation in the world in which they are called to participate – the first more the concern of those called Evangelicals, the other the focus of more mainline Protestant believers. Though these emphases once prompted observers to see aesthetics as unimportant, we now see that they can embody a more capacious sense of God's working – not only in preaching and teaching of Scripture which is central, but in singing, and in various forms of media both inside and outside the church. This is true even if these artifacts and practices are used more often for catechesis than contemplation. My own research has shown, surprisingly, that this openness to media has led to the proliferation (and experimentation) with a wider variety of aesthetic practices both inside and outside the space of the church than is evident in the other two major traditions.

Let me develop these two emphases of Protestant spirituality a bit. To believe the inclination to deeply personal spirituality and the movement into the larger world which the Reformation encouraged have no aesthetic significance, as is common, simply recycles the longstanding prejudices that I mentioned earlier. In fact I believe one can point to two particular areas of artistic development that owe something to these Reformation values – the role of language and the realism of landscape, portraits, and architecture. While I cannot develop these in any detail here, their enumeration might serve to signal what a Protestant contribution to Ecumenical art might be.

First it is incontrovertible that Protestant emphasis on language – in preaching, teaching, and the promotion of printed materials – as the privileged carrier of spiritual values opened up a potential site of new aesthetic forms. This impulse had its origin in the hearing, reading and teaching of the Scripture – newly translated into the vernacular – which the Reformers championed. But the spread of these Scriptural practices were to have profound aesthetic implications. This can be seen, I would argue, in the rich development of English literature, especially in the flowering of spiritual poetry, in 16th and 17th century England. Much of this lyrical poetry amounted to widely admired devotional models that also influenced the spiritual manuals produced during this period. All of this highlighted the Protestant call to the personal experience of God's grace, often interpreted by poets like George Herbert or John Donne as a dramatic struggle of the soul with its sin. Even the suspicion of imagery played a role in the artistic development of this period. For since the imagining power of the mind was tainted by pride and sensuality these writers realized that the word could serve as bulwark of the spirit against the enticements of the image (cf. Ernest Gilman, *Iconoclasm and Poetry*). In all this poets and writers sought to reflect the unique aesthetic style of Scripture that Protestants increasingly read, studied and memorized, and which was beginning to form a uniquely Protestant imagination.

A parallel aesthetic influence resulted from Reformers call to extend the drama of salvation

7. Church of the Transfiguration, view of east end.

out into the larger world. The world, Calvin famously argued, was a grand theater in which the glory of God could be seen and played out. There is a growing consensus that the habits of thought birthed in the Calvinist side of the Reformation played some role in the emergence of Renaissance theater – seen in particular in the works of Shakespeare. As I have implied the dramatic structure of the preached narrative of Christ's death and resurrection – which for Protestants had come to supplant the Eucharist as the focus of worship – lent to everyday life a new dramatic character that playwrights sought to explore in their dramatic productions. This impulse surely played some role in the rise of realistic theater in the 16th century and subsequently. As Regina Schwartz has argued, even if "the theater cannot *do* anything to other humans [or] *offer* anything to God", it can awaken our longing for redemption and forgiveness (*Sacramental Poetics*, p. 42). Shakespeare and his contemporaries were able to exploit this larger dramatic vision while pre-senting a secularized version of the medieval religious ritual – now being played out through the whole of life.

Many have argued that this dramatic impulse played an important role in the evolution of landscape painting and portraiture in England and Holland; and in the development of neoclassical architecture in France. In Holland painters like Jacob von Ruisdael sought to portray the world of nature in the narrative terms provided by Reformed theology. That is, they sought – both in landscape and portraits – to portray the world in terms of a "selected naturalism" (Svetlana Alpers), that is in terms of the narrative of sin and salvation. Meanwhile in France, the Huguenot (Calvinist) architects employed the newly rediscovered classical styles to create a reordered world, which they understood in their Calvinist terms as a recovery of Eden. Notice all these forms of art-making reflect a particular theological tradition in aesthetic forms, but they are characteristically artwork outside the space of the Church. And while the impulses of this tradition no doubt continue to influence artists up to the present, until very recently there was little or no attention paid to creating art to decorate the space of worship – what we are calling sacred art. And this lacuna forms part of the heritage of the Community of Jesus [hereafter: COJ] itself, something I will comment on below.

What do we make of these differences and how might they be reflected in the Community of Jesus? To what extent do these varying visual practices encourage, or impede ecumenical exchange and conversation? When one reflects on the creative expressions that have emerged in COJ, the marvelous proliferation of sacred art encourages one to think that this environment might in fact be a model that others can follow. But in making such a judgment, certain clarifications suggest themselves. First of all, it is not traditions that create works of arts, but artists and – more importantly – communities that do this. This community has of course commissioned works of art that they have envisioned and wanted for their corporate refashioning of themselves. But more importantly, they have done this by forming smaller craft groups – in mosaic, stone-carving, fresco, wood-carving, metal work, calligraphy. These various groups, or we might call them "studios" (like medieval workshops), have served as creative spaces for art to emerge. And the splendid productions of Paraclete Press have provided a forum for rich ecumenical exchange. And the impetus for all of this is the call to serve the community as they pursue their corporate life together – even if their ministries, of music, playmaking and publishing, extend beyond this.

But the question persists: what does the *ecumenical* nature of the community contribute to the art as art? Surely there are examples of artwork that would be more directly traced to one or another tradition I have sketched, but there is also the sense, at least to this observer, that the Orthodox and Catholic models of artmaking have carried more weight. Is it not the case that the Benedictine practice of praying the hours has overshadowed, for example, the Presbyterian focus on preaching and teaching?

One way of pursuing, and perhaps allaying, this concern is to focus on the sacred space that this community has formed for itself. Martin Shannon describes COJ as an Ecumenical Benedictine Monastery. Quoting Benedict, he points out that the monastery is the "workshop" in which all of the "instruments of the spiritual craft (*artis spiritalis*)" are developed and practiced. Now of course, famously, the Protestant reformers insisted that all monasteries should be closed. And while this response was – then and now – considered overly radical, there was a critical point being made in this decision. For both Luther and Calvin, the spiritual arts, the *artes spiritales*, were emphatically *not* to be practiced only by those living in cloistered communities; they were also to be practiced in the home and out in the world. These "arts" were to shed their glow over all of life – the plowman, and washerwoman in their workshop and kitchen were performing spiritual arts.

Against this history, this group of Christians decided to form not simply a community but a monastery; but it is a monastery, I think, with a particular Protestant flavor to it. Recall that all these 16th and 17th century art forms sought to develop a particular style that imitated the narrative of Scripture. But equally important they sought to model in their artmaking the need to paint themselves into the picture, that is to become yourself part of the artwork that they were creating. This recalls the central point that members of the COJ came together not to create art, but to be recreated themselves. In this respect they were following the impetus that Benedict laid out in his rule, but they were also perhaps expressing a particular Protestant version of this. Martin Shannon notes that they came together seeking conversion, that is the transformation of their lives under the creative power of the Holy Spirit; in pursuit of this, they sang hymns and they studied the Scripture. But he notes further they were seeking to be transformed by using the stuff of their daily lives – "what we *do* with what we *have*". That is, they were consciously seeking to see their lives as the *locus* where this burnishing of the Spirit would take place, seeing this drama in their everyday world. And they pursued these goals largely as Protestants – though Catholics and Orthodox were later welcomed.

In coming together to be themselves recreated, under the influence of their leadership they also sought to shape devotional and worship spaces that were places of beauty. When I heard this history, I asked myself: where, in the 1970s when the community was forming, could they look for resources by which to pursue this worthy goal? Well they could not look at very many Protestant churches or communities as models for shaping sacred art, no such models existed at the time. Understandably, then, they turned to the larger Christian tradition, in its Catholic and Orthodox forms, for inspiration, even if they did this as Protestants.

In my research with contemporary believers from Christian traditions, I often regretted that our protocol did not allow respondents to listen in on one another. If they had, it is certain they would have found a surprising overlap in the purposes and impact of their worship experiences. Even when, say, Protestant worshipers expressed unease for the way Catholics use images, one had the feeling that if they actually heard Catholics express the meaning these objects had for them, they would feel differently. Enthusiasm for good worship crossed all the boundaries and resulted in expressions that, despite the variety of form, resonated with a common faith. A careful review of these responses indicates that there might be an emerging *sensus fidelium*, a sense of the faithful, with respect to worship, even when this common core takes a variety of forms. And it might just be this emerging *sensus fidelium*, that the Community of Jesus may be modeling for us.

One case in point of this mutual influence is the place of music in the community. Clearly this does represent, as Martin Shannon reminds us, the protestant contribution to the community aesthetics. And indeed he reports that early on hymn singing was a characteristic practice. But he also notes the appropriation of Gregorian chant also seemed a valid spiritual practice. Indeed, the visitor might be forgiven for thinking the latter has become the dominant musical practice. And singing the services of the hours evokes monks praying in Latin – the religious called to live in cloisters, rather than the congregational singing in the vernacular, which Luther and Calvin instituted. Clearly such congregational singing has come to characterize the growth and development of Protestant worship – from the Genevan Psalter, through the hymns of Isaac Watts, to contemporary praise choruses. And there is no doubt this wider Protestant heritage lies behind the gifted choirs and instrumentalists of COJ who tour the world, as they display together musical gifts from various Christian traditions, even if the Protestant heritage itself is recessive rather than dominant. As Protestants they were pioneering a retrieval of the broader aesthetic heritage that their co-religionists had mostly left behind. But perhaps they have not done as much as we might like in promoting a uniquely Protestant contribution to the ecumenical process of artmaking.

Here is where I think it is possible to say that the COJ can serve as a model laboratory for ecumenical efforts in creating sacred art. That is, they do this not simply as the site of the chapel, press and singing and playing groups they have formed. But also in the itinerary they have followed in seeking to become a place where one can seek to remake oneself in an environment of beauty. But I think we can say more than this: their journey reflects, and offers an instance, of the quest of the Christian Church over the last fifty years to come together and share all the riches of its various member traditions. In this they have been encouraged I'm sure by the example the Second Vatican Council (1961–5) as it sought to distill the decades-long process of liturgical renewal and to open itself to the modern world and to other parts of its faith tradition. The mutual learning that has taken place since then has enriched us all, even if, as James White put it, we have sometimes passed each other going in opposite directions. The Community of Jesus then might well be one of the few places where we can see progress being made toward the aesthetic *sensus fidelium* we all seek, and that God has in mind for us. ∎

Part 2

The Holy Spirit

Artistic Creation
and Theology of the Holy Spirit

From First Appearance to Flight

DENIS HÉTIER

As developed in a research seminar of the Institut Supérieur de Théologie des Arts (ISTA) of the Institut Catholique of Paris, the theme indicated in the title of this brief text led first to a concentration on biblical and artistic expressions of breathing and then, progressively, to an investigation of the figure of the bird, which, far from being a simple image, expresses, as we came to see, the very act of artistic and poetic creation, and does so in an intimate and essential way.

Gaston Bachelard, in his essay *L'air et les songes*,[1] remarks that what first attracts us in birds is their flight. He shows that the image of a bird in full flight is an original, primary image expressing a fundamental symbolic force: lightness, vivacity, youth, purity, sweetness, freedom. The bird in flight is made of the air which bears it and of the movement which bears it away. The "world of the bird" – that this creature evokes existentially – is before all else desire for flight, song which makes itself heard and which beckons, conversion toward the light and transformation, intimate communion, a new space to reach. But the "world of the bird" also and equally reminds us of the solidity and opacity of the body and of matter, of its finitude and of the limits of those who, understandably, dream of birds, hear them, look at and recognize them.

This "world of the bird", in its interiority and creative dynamic, in its dimension at once of inauguration and completion, in all its deepest and most paradoxical resonances, has never ceased to inspire numerous artists at the very heart of their creative experience, to the point that it could become an essential expression of that experience.

The approaches of ISTA professors and students to this "world of the bird" in relation to the arts and artistic creation immediately made manifest and evident, in a deep and intimate manner, what is implied in the use of the dove as a metaphorical figure of the Holy Spirit. We should recall that in the biblical texts that recount Jesus's baptism, it is not so much a question of a dove as of something "like a dove", just as in the account of Pentecost the disciples hear a noise "like" a violent wind, and see flames "as if of fire". The exegete Jean Radermakers notes that the account of Jesus's baptism does not indicate the appearance of a dove as much as it does the way in which the Holy Spirit acted in Jesus.[2] These all too brief observations nonetheless confirm the hypothesis that a study of the "world of the bird" in the arts can contribute, in some measure, to a deeper understanding of a theology of the Holy Spirit, especially as far as his creative and sanctifying action is concerned. ■

1   Gaston Bachelard, *L'air et les songes. Essai sur l'imagination du mouvement*, Paris, 1943, p. 83.

2   Jean Radermakers, *Au fil de l'évangile selon saint Matthieu. II. Lecture continue*, Brussels, 1974 (1st ed. Heverlee–Louvain, 1972), p. 62.

Who Will Give Me Wings like a Dove? (Psalm 54:7)

FRANÇOIS CASSINGENA

People talk about artists. The world talks about them – at least about the ones it knows. It talks about them with admiration or with amusement. But also at times with a sort of commiseration, as if artists did not count much in all that serious and muscular machinery which takes pride in making the world turn: in all that arsenal of pulling, striking and moving forces which converts its conquests into numbers, in that general business of official trades whose efficiency is maximum, whose success is the salary and whose subordination of matter (if not of humanity itself) is the ultimate horizon. As if artists were exceptions in the great animal kingdom of human society, due to some indefinable quality of superfluousness, evanescence, decoration such as one attributes to birds. People talk about artists, therefore. But artists, in general, do not talk a lot. In any case they don't like to talk about themselves. Above all they refuse to talk about themselves as artists. Their extreme sensitivity tells them that if they were to autonomously declare themselves as such, even in the most modest way imaginable, they would immediately cease to be so, losing their state of grace. That beginning of noise about their own person, that incipient calling attention to their identity, would be enough to put the bird to flight – the mysterious bird of paradise of which artists are more the captives than the keepers. Deep in themselves, artists know very well that they are homeless in their own condition, since that condition requires precisely that they possess nothing and install themselves in nothing. In a word, contrary to what many people believe (and to what certain artists may invite us to believe), artists never use the first person singular. In their estimate no work which they produce either authorizes them to do so or establishes them in a comfortably seated position. Poetry wants us to never rest in it, at least never in the manner of a proprietor or potentate making a satisfying inventory of his real estate holdings.

> My soul, you have many good things laid by for many years to come: take it easy, eat, drink, have a good time (Lk 12:19).

– which is to say, behave in a way exactly opposite that of the birds:

> Look at the birds in the sky. They do not sow or reap or gather into barns; yet your heavenly Father feeds them! (Mt 6:26).

Artists thus experience a strong repulsion at the idea of claiming for themselves the title of artists, as if divining in such a claim all the makings of a sacrilege. That being the case, should we really be astonished that artists do not very much like to chat about their art: to respond in a reasonable way, that is, to what people ask them? To be sure, artists have no difficulty giving detailed explanations about their materials, their tools, their techniques – they do so happily and freely. But for all the rest it is another story. "Where did the man get all this?", people ask; "What is this wisdom that has been granted him, and these miracles that his hands work?" (Mk 6:2). To be sure, the hands are where the miracles come from, but hands cannot be explained: they can be looked at: we can follow their flight with our gaze, like a pianist's hands on the keys, or those of the potter at his wheel. Yet despite our efforts, hands cannot be comprehended in their rapid to-and-fro movements, in the free course of their agility. And there are men like that, who seem to have birds in the place of hands, or trees. Hands that, incomprehensibly, grow, spread, branch out – fingers that weave things astonishingly alive and autonomous:

When he was a child five years of age, Jesus was playing near the ford of a stream, from which he directed a trickle of water toward a puddle, in order to make it limpid. Then he drew soft clay from the basin and fashioned twelve birds. It was the Sabbath and many children were playing with him ... Joseph arrived and reprimanded Jesus saying: 'Why are you doing what it is not allowed to do on the Sabbath?' But, hearing these words, Jesus clapped his hands and made the sparrows fly away, saying: 'Go on, fly away and remember me, you who are living'. And the sparrows flew away chirping.[1]

While St Francis was saying these words, all the birds began to open their beaks, to stretch their necks, to spread their wings... Finally, when the sermon ended, St Francis made the sign of the cross over them and gave them leave to go; and all those birds rose together into the air with wonderful songs, then they divided into four groups, following the cross which St Francis had traced above them in the air: one group flew to the East, another to the West, the third South and the fourth North, and each group went off singing marvelously.[2]

Imagine for a moment human hands constituting not a cage for birds, as they usually do, but the nest – not a trap but a perch.

An artist, we said, talks willingly about accessories but keeps quiet about his deep *doing*, about his verb *to do*, whether active or passive (as if one could distinguish!): all chit-chat on that subject strikes him as indecent, without counting its negative impact on the process which is unfolding within him, which is truly at ease only with his reticence. Without any doubt he knows something about how he does what he does. But he knows nothing at all about how *that* is done. The difference may seem subtle, even specious, but it is actually considerable. For beneath what *he* does – in the very stuff, in the grain, in the interval, between the lines, in the pauses, the sighs, the silences of what the artist does – is *what* is being done, which decidedly escapes him. Before he starts to work, suddenly measuring the precariousness of his resources, the artist may for a moment ask himself: "How can this come about?" (readers will recognize one of the Gospel's most dramatic questions). And the answer arrives, often without the artist's hearing or knowing anything of the annunciation made to him: "The Holy spirit will come upon you, and the power of the Most High will cover you with its shadow" (Lk 1:34–5). For it is certain that the most licentious poets, the most damnable, are in a state of virginity when – through what they do with the mineral, verbal or sonorous material familiar to them – some sort of *what* is *done* – I mean a kind of epiphany, a kind of incarnation. And the virginity that is theirs in those creative hours makes them enter the Kingdom straightaway. On every artist a shadow passes. In every artwork a shadow remains. A shadow without which it would not be what it is. Without which it would not be so profound. A shadow which cannot be explained and on which light can never be fully thrown. Once the work is finished, the artist asks himself: "How did that get done?" For he really doesn't know. *What* has been done exceeds what he did, and it is precisely that presence of an *event* – (*verbum caro*) *factum est* – that lies at the heart of *doing*, that excess of *event* is over-*doing* which identifies an authentic work of art. A work of art is a work in which something has happened and in which something never stops happening.

And so there is a shadow. The shadow of the *dove* (Mt 3:16; Jn 1:32), since in the end that shadow has an origin and one must really give a name to our bird. The shadow is brought. Brought although one brings it above oneself (the mystery of the epiclesis); brought because one brings it in oneself (the mystery of inhabitation). *Spiritus Sanctus superveniet in te* (Lk 1:35). The dove's gesture appears very detailed here, and all its movements call for our consideration. *Superveniet in te...* Have you really understood? It "will come upon you". It comes over (*super*), and it dwells in (*in*). It covers at the same time as it impregnates. It hatches at the same time as it encloses. So much for the shadow, its role in the business is clear. But, if you want, we can also speak of fire and its role, since the dove is also fire. "And there appeared to them tongues as of of fire; these separated and came to rest on the head of each of them. They were all filled..." (Ac 2:3–4). With the fire, you see, it is the same as with the bird: it comes to rest upon and it fills within. *Superveniet in te...* An unusual fire, which overshadows that on which it comes to rest: a shadow that is not only beneficent but *dulce refrigerium*, as the Pentecost liturgy says of it.[3] But now our fire-bird is beginning to fly on its own, inviting us to explore its charms... It is time to return to the artist.

There is the shadow, we said. But the shadow does not do everything. It is not exactly its role to *do*. It passes *over*, it passes *within* that which is in the process of being done, in that which is done, but it doesn't do. It operates but does not do. It passes, it operates. Sometimes, at least, not always. The artist is not nicely seated in the shade, just so, without doing anything, waiting for the shadow to pass, for the bird to pass. "Why have you been standing here idle all day?" (Mt 20:6). On the

other hand, the bird doesn't like to frequent people who do nothing. "For the holy spirit of instruction flees deceitfulness" (Ws 1:5). Laziness too. For his part, the artist distrusts ecstasies, enthusiasms, illuminated discourses, naive imaginations, aggressive mediatic, ideological or mystical bidding for inspiration and genius.

He knows only his own work, from which the dove's possible passage does not dispense him and from which he takes no holidays. This work is his ordinary domain, the only continent of which he is sure and of which he can speak with competence and honesty. Distrustful of all mythology, of all spiritualism, of all easy, hasty, indiscreet, intrusive and 'colonialist' theologization of the artistic craft, he will obstinately put the accent on its laborious aspect and will try to discourage mystification. It does not bother him, after all, to be taken for a positivist, a materialist, a boor. He knows that if childlike poetry precedes the positivist moment, poetry equally pure and true follows it, provided one accepts this inevitable phase of life's history as a trial by fire. He takes pleasure in disenchanting imaginations too blessed, too innocent, to have estimated the incomparable price of an art that has survived disenchantment. Skeptical about every etiological convocation of the supernatural, the artist concentrates his attention on – and draws that of others to – a mystery immanent in his work itself and emanating from it. For beyond all the prestige that people attribute him, and all the miracles which they believe he performs and the emotional transports to which they think him accustomed, his artistic creation remains something very modest, very fragile, very fallible. "I went down to the potter's house, and there he was, working at the wheel. But the vessel he was making came out wrong, as may happen with clay when a potter is at work. So he began again and shaped it into another vessel..." (Jr 18:4). Of his art (of which he is the first and the perpetual apprentice), the artist sees only, and across time knows only, the dimension of hard work, which he would be sad, to say the least, to have people forget due to careless promotion of dilettantish creativity. He cloisters himself in his unpredictable and obscure work, sinks into it, annihilates himself:

this moment of body-to-body confrontation with matter, of perdition in matter (we always get a bloody nose from matter, we and the figure we thought we could impose upon it), is – still more than a moment of dialectic negativity, like that of Hegelian antithesis –, a paschal moment of death and resurrection. For we never do anything good without dying a bit – without something of ourselves dying in what we do, at the very least that idea of the work which we had conceived and which matter's index of refraction always somehow disfigures, to make possible the advent – laborious this time – of another form. It happens that, in the course of this painful loss-of-self in work, and while great waters submerge the first idea that all at once begins to seem far-off, the worker, like the dove of the ark, *finds nowhere to perch* (Gn 8:9); or, feeling the disproportion between his own clumsiness, his stiffness, and the grand general impulse which he would like both to assist and reveal, he utters a groan: "Who will give me wings like a dove, to fly away and find rest?" (Ps 54:7). Amid the torments of work he yearns for ease, and summons the presence of the bird. The presence of the Dove whose effect is evoked in the liturgical poem cited above: *In labore requies… "*In labor, repose…". Special suffering attaches to the artist's fundamental *desire to say*, inseparable, in his case, from the *desire to live*, since his motto is more or less: "I must either create or die". Hard as it is to 'drop a calf' it must, obviously, be done at a certain altitude.

One must start, as we have seen, very far down. It is down below that *that* happens. The artwork is in no sense a figment of fantasy, a *coup de théâtre*, a *deus ex machina*. It is a try, an effort, an offering. The most airy birds themselves do not fall like rain one fine day from heaven's heights: they are born from mud, between modeling fingers. The word made flesh is not the product of a parthenogenesis, but the bud that sprouts from a laborious genealogy. The *doing*, in this case, is conjugated with the *Let it be done to me* of Luke 1:38, and work becomes God's cradle. A man of flesh harnessed to a work of flesh, the artist exposes himself unreservedly to the pollens that reach him from the superabundant field of the

1. François Cassingena, *Oiseau de feu.*

real – from the rarest of perfumes and wildest of herbs –, in a grand 'good day' of light and wind. To call him an aesthete is to say little and to put it badly: in truth he is a 'pan-aesthete', that is to say he feels *everything*, he ascetically exerts himself in order to feel everything, he enters – fraternally, cosmically, ecumenically – into the fundamental gratitude of all that exists. At his door every morning he receives a delivery of matter: of his matter, always first in his view because of the mystery inherent in him, so inherent that he himself is its filigree and *basso continuo*. He does not undertake to put up anything whatsoever – neither poem nor melody nor vase nor building – which he does not first of all and ceaselessly let rise around him, with him and in him: all that he puts his hand to, all that is wrung from that which people believe as immobile as stone. He does not undertake what he has not set himself to learn, listening to all the covert words which rise from this world, in order to conduct them to the sonorous full daylight of an *Amen* or of a cry. "A shoot will spring from the stock… on him will rest the Spirit" (Is 11:1–2). That bird suspended above a stalk: a motif extremely purified, fit to tempt the pen of some Chinese painter, moist with a single drop of ink, like black sun. The bough, the reed, make the effort to rise, despite the fact that the bird does the favor of descending. "*Superveniet in te…*" (that story of annunciation again). The assent is one with the offering, the consensus with the trial, the answer with the question, the recompense with the thought. And it is all of that together:

the concommitance of these two movements, from below to above and from above to below, the conspiracy between the above and the below, which – a bit at a time, a step at a time –, create the work and then forever "work" in the finished piece. For something happens, and in silence something comes to rest on every instant of time in which the artist is at work. The tacit benediction whose friendship he attracts is not external to his work, the last act following what he has done, but is rather the soul contemporary with all that he has done, immanent in all that he has done. The bird is not superfluous to the rising bough: the bough would not grow at all if the bird did not light upon it.

The artist in his atelier makes the work in the recollection and reclusion of his act, at once nuptial and agonistic in nature, as much embrace as combat. In this laboratory, in this austere confinement, he does not dream of pleasing anyone at all, neither patron nor public nor (must we say it?) himself. He must give a rigorous accounting. He stands before the mystery and majesty of the real, in a solitude with no possible reprieve or dispensation, which he takes care to honor with exactitude. He will have no peace unless he finds, among a thousand facile approximations, that precise equation of words, of sounds, of rhythms, of colors, of forms, which answers the question which the mystery puts to him – a mystery which now lies entirely in his own responsibility as artist. Perhaps that too is the meaning of the words: "I was born for this, I came into the world for this, to bear witness to the truth" (Jn 18:37). The artist does his work, and it is enough. But at the very heart of *doing*, in the hollow of *doing*, a *verb* appears. It takes hold, clots, coagulates: it is very humble, very vulnerable, very low. And it is that which is properly "theological", even before all the patented theologies take it on as an object of speculation. For the "theological" or "spiritual" is not an ingredient, a seasoning, a decoration, an extrinsic value, a heterogeneous given, but rather a walled peak, a terminal sprout that has grown patiently, a roof substantially one with the structure which dignifies and bears it. As much as he is condescending ("*superveniet in*

te…"), the Spirit is intrusive, pushing his way up from the depths of the earth like those liquid rocks which congeal as mountains, pulling transfigured matter in their wake, making of matter's affinities, of matter's underlying intentions,[4] the vector of their own epic. Whether verbal, musical, pictorial or mineral, the artist's matter – his dear matter, his dear half – is always conductive matter and consequently conducted, constructed, erected, elaborated, carried to the step which is uppermost, the level glowing with presence. To such a level of presence, indeed, that the matter becomes, without demonstrative declarations, a presence of the Spirit. Péguy the Christian and Valéry the agnostic both said just that, experiencing it each in his own way in the background of different "illuminations":

C'est l'épi le plus dur qui soit jamais monté
Vers un ciel de clémence et de sérénité…[5]

[It is the hardest stalk that ever rose
Toward a heaven of clemency and calm…]

Patience, patience,
Patience dans l'azur!
Chaque atome de silence
Est la chance d'un fruit mûr![6]

[Patience, patience,
Patience in the azure sky!
Each atom of silence
Is the luck of mature fruit!]

What "sweats through" or "has sweated through" the work – the presence of the Spirit – can in effect be said through images of a stalk or of fruit, the one and the other sharing the same substantial concentration, the same patience of the process which makes them grow, opening them to the biological future of a new fecundity. The Spirit is in subtle, vertiginous, acrobatic and fleeting interface with the effort and the gift of germination and of rain; he supervenes at noon, when fatigue is forgotten in dance, in that region of encounter where the banquet can be generously shared. The artist, in a concrete language of which he is expert, resumes – as much as he assumes –

the diffuse and exigent impression he has received from the universal mystery, the great worldly "sacrament". An exigent impression, we can say, because the impression pressures artist himself more than anyone else to pluck it from the subjective realm and give it expression, an objective form susceptible of becoming common property and thus of entering human commerce. From that moment, in a very special way, the artist becomes that active cell or universal impression in humanity's sensible body and in the social body of all who exchange news about the world (never ceasing to interrogate it in the time in which they live): a pan-aesthetic experience, condensed and precipitate. In him and in his work a sort of photosynthesis is realized, without the artist having to furnish an explanation (such analytic work would take him from his proper domain and restrict him, beyond doubt delaying his true work). He converts the illumination to which he has generously exposed himself into living tissue (words, sounds, colors, forms, volumes), as he likes or rather by his grace, bringing mundane reality to its point of incandescence, and with astonishment seeing the new matter – his own work – become in turn the principle of an indefinitely expansive gathering of interpersonal relations. An artwork in fact gives others the chance to speak, a masterpiece becomes their capital city.

Theologians, by contrast, remain wisely silent before the potter or the poet: they are not personally involved in this kind of thing, and do not, by natural temperament, live in the pan-aesthetic dimension, their habit of rational construction (albeit respectful of the mystery) makes them somewhat forget the fecundity of approaches at once practical and more passive. They keep a fraternal distance from this brother who, basically sharing the same search (and the same uneasiness) as themselves, nonetheless chooses a different path. They look at him, they listen to him, and they wait until something "theological" takes shape. They will underestimate the birds born of clay. They will have the good taste to avoid precipitate dogmatization of what they see and hear in the artist's workshop, and will try to hold on to the lesson of taciturnity that is quietly suggested. For around

the artist, in the artist, in his work, there is always silence, much silence. And silence should always maintain its advantage over information. On his side, the artist does not become the vassal of any apologetic program or follow any prefabricated theology: an autochthonous theology (one is tempted to add: self-taught) imperceptibly makes itself visible with the forms – in the forms – of which it is the origin. The aesthetic way is in no sense subaltern to other ways that are held to be more serious, more competent: it has its own consistency and full legitimacy. It is not enough to say that there are different ways leading to ideal Beauty (only prudently and at the end of our essay do we evoke this intimidating term, so as not to be disheartened), for humble 'beauty-in-the-process-of being-made' is itself a way. It has the innocence, the artlessness of a question to which there is no answer and which never ends. The artwork, always a blessing, situates itself in the human landscape as a question mark, with the same character of urgent vitality as a water source. And if it happens that the artist (who refuses to call himself such) is also a bit theologian (even while refusing that title too), his theology will present itself, even in a university environment, exclusively in the livery of art, instinctively espousing the dynamism of his usual art-form. Can the artist do otherwise, or can we expect something different of him? "Poetry" is not a distraction from everyday life, a department of the intellectual faculties, an episodic confection of anodyne forms: it is, at least for some (probably for all, although most people do not know it and do not want to know it) the *a priori* form, the form which encompasses all of existence. One is a poet not because of a position one has learned or conquered, but because of an 'original' disposition: "Yahweh God planted a garden... and there he put the man he had fashioned" (Gn 2:8). The artist is a theologian, therefore, but in a way that is empirical, empathetic, intuitive, clandestine, truant, unusual and at times insolent. Placed in the incomprehensible space that at times seems a garden, at times only ill-defined terrain, artists look, listen, touch, meditate. Their almost professional involvement in the fleshy and material mediations, and their fully voluntary immersion in them, establish them in a privileged complicity with the Word and with the Word's great adventure. Still better, it inserts them in a fellow-worker relationship that makes them "comrades" in the term's fullest sense. They know something about this story of incarnation. Of the artist we can also say – but prudently (for in speaking of man we need many adverbs modifying the verbs) – "What is in him comes from the Holy Spirit" (cf. Mt 1:20). Artists take their place more spontaneously on the side of the gestation than of the kerygma. A gestation of which, once again, they hesitate to speak, fearful of divulging its mystery. They try, above all, to keep themselves daily, modestly, obscurely, under the fiery plumage of the Dove who draws and prods them, and whose well-beloved they hesitates to call themselves. Sometimes (Oh sometimes!), like children, they hold the dove in their hands, murmuring in a low voice this prayer:

Veni, creator Spiritus…
Fons vivus, ignis, caritas…

Come, sovereign Authority,
Come, Magnitude great as the sea,
Holy lust proportioned to desire,
You who trouble the surface and calm the depths,
Rapacious for sweetness.
Come, Waterspring whose flow keeps malleable in our hands
Every possibility.
Come, Flame whose trial gives form and force and makes what is fragile endure.
Come, Love without whom no good is done,
And without whom, when the work is done, we see nothing good.
Model a bird from my clay,
A bird
Which far from my ark will bring peace. ■

1   Infancy Gospel of Thomas 2,1–4.
2   St Francis of Assisi, *Little Flowers*, part I, chapter 16.
3   See the sequence *Veni, Sancte Spiritus* (Mass of Pentecost).
4   Like the veining of wood and the ductility of metal, there is also a musicality latent in words, a potential friendship of colors: it is with all that – with all that 'evangelical' preparation of matter – that the artist enters into confidence, or, if one prefers,

it is all that he obeys. He seeks to promote matter, not to domesticate it. He accompanies it in its intentionality, he orients it toward the finished expression (even if it is never 'finished') of his implicit 'I meant to say'.
5   Charles Peguy, 'Présentation de la Beauce à Notre-Dame de Chartres', in *Œuvres poétiques complètes*, Paris, 1975, p. 898.
6   Paul Valéry, 'Charmes (Palme)', in *Œuvres. 1*, Paris, 1957, p. 155.

The Spirit Who Gives Flesh

JEAN-LOUIS SOULETIE

The theology of the Spirit no longer develops its reflection on the sole basis of the third Person of the Trinity's hypostasis and procession from the Father, as in medieval metaphysics. Today it begins with Scripture, going over the way the Bible speaks of the Spirit of God. The starting-point for exploring the question of the Spirit is the mystery of Christ's death and resurrection, in order to show that the Spirit who raised Jesus is the same one who is also communicated to men and women. It is the Spirit who gives them flesh, just as the same Spirit came to Mary so that the Word of God might be born (Lk 1:35).

The Spirit between singularity and universalism
The Spirit of the risen Christ
Jesus rose from the dead giving the Spirit. This is of course the meaning of Pentecost; but in St John, the crucified Jesus already exhales the Spirit of Life as he bows his head in death. Despite this gift, however, history's violence carries on, and the coming of the Kingdom seems delayed. The earlier part of the Acts of the Apostles gives numerous examples of the Spirit's actions, but later they seem to fade out. The Holy Spirit's interventions show how little inclined were the witnesses, including Paul, to face the new categories of people they had

to meet. Chapter 10, recounting the exchange between Peter and Cornelius, attests to this. Thus, if there was a continuity in apostolic witnessing, paradoxically it consisted in always going toward others, as Paul's journeys show. The universalization of the message was diffracted in communities founded on the outskirts of the empire. The Spirit universalized by differentiating, giving flesh to the new communities the apostles gave birth to.

The Spirit and the tensions of the world
The Spirit who was promised as the Paraclete recalls to us all that Jesus did and said. For the apostles, that anamnesis happened in historical time, a time of violence and contradiction, also a time of pluralism in Christian communities. The exegete Claude Tassin has shown that:

Luke does not sow the idea of ecclesial witnessing as one of comfortable unanimity. The richness of witnessing depends on the diversity of persons and the socio-cultural mix of individuals and of groups. The 'Hellenists' will never become 'Hebrews' (Ac 6:1 ff.). The witness of the Church consists in the sometimes stormy confrontation of experiences. Peter agrees to explain his conduct in the Cornelius episode (Ac 11:1–18), and the Antioch missionaries are willing to submit their freedom to discussion by other Christian currents (Ac 15).[1]

The gift of the Spirit thus underlines the present incompleteness of history as it remains the prey of the world's violence and of the complexity of communities of disciples as they struggle to come to terms with their own history. Paul speaks of the inexpressible groans of creation as it is brought to completion, comparable to the disciples who have received the Spirit's first fruits and await adoption (Rm 8:20–3). The Spirit given and rejected in humanity's spiritual combat attests to the gap between the Resurrected Christ in whom everything is already accomplished, and the definitive realization of the Kingdom within humanity.

A hermeneutic of danger

In that active waiting, that hermeneutic of danger, as the German theologian Johann Baptist Metz calls it, the Spirit is given to configure the disciple to Christ, to his words and acts. Tassin again remarks:

> When, with Stephen's boldness, the witness advances along paths new to him, where will he find assurance that he will not betray the continuity of a witness that must make Christ present here and now? Luke's answer is simple: whether it is the apostles or Stephen or Paul, they are not content with words; they pay with their life the witness they bear to Jesus. To be sure, Acts tells the story of matchless heroes, and does not push readers either to martyrdom or to fanaticism. The book simply recalls that there is no witnessing unless there is also coherence between the words one speaks and the way one lives.[2]

The gift of the Spirit attests to the resistance to the disenchantment with the world that afflicts our societies. This disenchantment is rooted in the optimistic modernity characteristic of post-war reconstruction. In that period Christian preaching dialogued with the different forms of Marxism, whose hope was immanent to history, as well as with Jewish post-Holocaust thought (Jürgen Moltmann, Johann Baptist Metz, Nicholas Lash). The tragedy of political messianism called Christian hope into question, and this hope finally turned anew toward the Messiah's cross. The hope of the 1960s, initially won over to the ideology of progress and an expanding western economy, buoyed by the independence of various countries from former colonial powers, collided all the more violently with the disillusion provoked by the failure of the dominant political utopias. Effervescent hope gave way to a hermeneutic of danger, spurred on by biblical apocalyptic. The future continued to provoke human projects, but it was a dark future full of threats. By now, for Christian faith the future was to be found in the cross of Christ crucified whose promised coming would be for God's eschatological judgment. There he will be the advocate of that Creation for which he gave his life because of his love for the Father's work for humanity and the cosmos.

The Spirit does not crush the fragment beneath the weight of totality

That history of violence attests to the Spirit as the one who brings about the dangerous adequation between saying and doing, and thus reconfigures Christian existence as *sequela Christi*. Like prophets, the witnesses of the Acts of the Apostles are not above history but in it. The witness follows Christ and is obliged to reflect on events, belatedly discovering the presence of the Spirit; and that discovery, the fruit of prayer, reorients the witness's life. That is what Luke did as he wrote the story; and it is thus that the book of the Acts constitutes a testimony.

Not only does the Spirit attest that human history is full of this unutterable groaning, this combat against resistance to the action of the Spirit, but this same Spirit also attests to the wisdom of the Cross. The Spirit awakens a creative imagination with which today we must import Christian convictions into the institutional and political realm, as it were translating them into a historical body, as in a corpus. The objective is to get beyond the modern alternative between the divinities of polytheism (Max Weber), who anesthetize responsibility, and the therapeutic God of well-being who does not challenge us by demanding radical conversion. The Christian practice of following Christ has always been opposed to the dionysiac idea of existence. The *sequela Christi* imposes a politics of peace born from the *memoria passionis*, from concern for the Other's misfortune. That ethic of the following of Christ increases the imaginative capacity of Christians, allowing them better to meet the world with which and in which Paul VI (*Ecclesiam suam*) urged them to converse. In that way the Church can be that school of virtue which takes part in the public dialogue that different rational systems conduct among themselves. Do not those who suffer possess in reality the authority of the weak, the authority of those who lack everything, even recognition of their suffering? Their authority as those who suffer invites us to think of human dignity otherwise than as simply rooted in the history of the species. That authority may seem fragile but it is in fact strong, for it alone can resist the cultural amnesia of the victors. The Spirit revives the memory of those defeated by history and prevents the fragment from being crushed by the totality of the State, of power, of culture, of globalization, etc. – by all these ways of thinking of Unity which cannot tolerate either divergence or difference.

The Gospel thus gives value to the fragment in the name of the wisdom of the Cross. The Man-God, the central figure of creation, as Hans Urs von Balthasar writes, cannot be conceived as an isolated grandeur (*isolierte Grösse*), deprived of all historical context (*geschichtlich zusammenhanglose*) – that was the viewpoint of Gnosticism, which believed it could consider him a sort of aerolite. On the contrary, he must be a figure of authentic union with human history (*echte Gesamtgestalt*) and be comprehensible as such: that was the position of Irenaeus of Lyon against Gnosticism. But the Man-God can be part of that unity (*Einheit*) only through the interpretation of history (*qualifizierten Geschichte*), and not with the theologically amorphous mass of 'pagans'. The history

with which he can form a single figure has to be detached (*herausgehoben*) from general history, and what is more, it must, starting with him, be identified as oriented toward him.

The Spirit in history resurrects the body in the very place where the rootedness of human existences is eroded and lost. The Spirit is prophetic in the very place where the dignity of persons is denied even in their bodily existence (health, housing, nourishment).

There is a universalism of the *theologia crucis*, otherwise known as the 'Wisdom of the Cross'. The encyclical *Fides et Ratio* explains it in this way:

> Reason cannot eliminate the mystery of love which the Cross represents, while the Cross can give to reason the ultimate answer which it seeks. It is not the wisdom of words, but the Word of Wisdom which Saint Paul offers as the criterion of both truth and salvation. The wisdom of the Cross, therefore, breaks free of all cultural limitations which seek to contain it and insists upon an openness to the universality of the truth which it bears. What a challenge this is to our reason, and how great the gain for reason if it yields to this wisdom! (*Fides et Ratio*, § 23).

The Spirit who brings to mind Christ's action is the Spirit of life. The Spirit prevents the particular from being crushed by the universal. For this is the same Spirit who comes from the dead body of the crucified Lord. The Pentecostal outpouring of the Spirit demonstrates that the Spirit is not a prisoner of historic and institutional references and works towards unity in accord with the Wisdom of the Crucified, a scandal for the Jews and folly for the pagans (1 Co 1:23). So we are able to formulate our thesis: the Spirit in the world does the same thing as he did in Jesus, throughout Jesus's life, passion and resurrection.

Drawn from the Crucified, the Spirit gives body to the Word
The Spirit of the Crucified

According to what we read in Scripture, the Father emitted the Spirit from the body of the crucified Jesus in order to give it to the disciples. The Spirit is not present to the body of the disciples as an object might be, but as breath, in accord with the first chapter of Genesis taken up again in the New Testament. The third Person of the Trinity gives everyone the unity of the Father and the Son, and in Pauline theology makes the baptized become adoptive children. The Spirit brings this unity to the level of Creation, so that if "Christ died for all and the human being's ultimate vocation is truly unique (that is, divine), we should hold that the Holy Spirit offers to all, in a way that only God knows, the possibility of being associated with the paschal mystery".[3]

According to St John, Jesus told his disciples: "It is for your own good that I am going, because unless I go, the Paraclete will not come to you; but if I go I will send him to you" (Jn 16:7). Jesus thus established a very clear relationship between his departure – that is to say his elevation on the cross – and the gift of the Holy Spirit. In that way, as Joseph Moingt writes:

> John (19:34) shows the piercing of Jesus's side with the lance ... from which flow water and blood. And when Jesus gives the Spirit to his disciples at the moment of leaving them in Jn 20:21–3, he shows them the wound in his side to tell them whence comes the Spirit which he breathes upon them. So the Spirit comes out of a dead body, and comes thence as a source of life which has conquered death and, more exactly, which has even nourished itself on death, turning death into life. The Spirit comes out of death as from nothingness, but comes as a seed of life able to animate other bodies, able to form other Christs (Karl Rahner) who will continue Jesus's mission. And we see the Spirit distance the disciples from the empty tomb, sending them forward. It is the Spirit who prevents them from staying to wander about near the empty tomb, and so separates the past from the present, allowing the present to be and allowing the disciples to exist in Jesus's present and not only in his past. The Spirit opens the future to them, and that is the beginning of a new history.[4]

For John (Jn 5:26–9), the Spirit flowed from Christ's body:

> For as the Father has life in himself, so he has granted the Son also to have life in himself, and, because he is the Son of Man, has granted him power to give judgment. Do not be surprised at this, for the hour is coming when the dead will leave their graves at the sound of his voice: those who did good will come forth to life; and those who did evil will come forth to judgment.

Jesus's mission was to give this life, his Spirit, that is, his own breath of life, the breath of life of his body, the Spirit of God mixed with his breath of life and also capable of animating our bodies. This announcement of the resurrection of the body is the Gospel's central message, the promise of the victory of life over death whose cosmic meaning is universal. To show that Jesus's work is to free life from the shackles of death is the full meaning of the Gospel, inasmuch as it points toward the paschal event and the gift of the Spirit.

It is important here to situate the Holy Spirit in relation to God's project of creation and salvation as this is attested in the Scriptures. From Genesis on, the Spirit and the Word act together as God's two hands (Irenaeus). Their common action is to draw the world forth from nothingness and to give it an order so that it becomes habitable by creatures similar to God himself and able to live his eternal life. The Holy Spirit is thus at work in the world, summoning animal life to rise up to attain spiritual life, to the freedom and power of love.

The gestation of this world takes place in the pains of childbirth (Rm 8) and is the work of the Spirit. Human beings oppose this birth of a new flesh (Rm 6:1–11), the flesh that clothes the New Man (2 Co 5:16–18 *kaïnê ktisis*). The New Man is configured to Christ risen from the dead. When Jesus gives his breath back to God, he is reborn in God through the very act of offering himself to die for all. To use Irenaeus' expression, in Jesus God became accustomed to living our human life, in order to raise our human life to communion with himself. Jesus's resurrection, says Joseph Moingt, "is thus also truly the act by which Jesus, raised to the Father, delivers to humanity the Spirit of his own body, which has become immortal by passing through death. The New Man is someone who has been transformed by Easter, in his very flesh... That is what redemption is: liberation from sin and death".[5] From sin: from everything that refuses the corporal reality of the Spirit's life through an idolatry of the flesh that does not recognize the Spirit's mediation through that flesh and the relationship which that mediation serves. And liberation from death: because the Spirit makes it possible to live in the freedom of Jesus, who did not take heed for himself, and so took on the responsibility of dangerous speech, one that is never concerned with itself, but is destined to give life even to those who refuse to accept it.

What Christianity calls redemption is therefore brought to completion "in the gift of the Spirit, that is in the gift of life. It is completed in the mission given to the Holy Spirit... And so Jesus's work was to give his life to God in order to bear witness that God is love for all of humanity, excluding no one. And he delivered this witness to us by the gift his Spirit, who will make the same faith and love grow in us".[6]

Opening to the Spirit
In a very Pauline vein, one could say that as Moses gave the tables of the Law, so in and through Jesus the Father gives us his Spirit. The Father thus teaches humanity to behave like Jesus, that is, like his children, as St Luke's parable attests (Lk 15). The Spirit kindles the same freedom in humanity as in Jesus. According to Luke 4, in the temptation in the wilderness, the Spirit exposed Jesus to the desert – to recognition of God's Word, that is, inasmuch it is not a lying word like Satan's. Replicating the opening scene of Genesis, Jesus had the task of discerning the voice of justice where Adam had confused it with the voice of the deceitful serpent. The Spirit gives access to a filial liberty whose authority is nothing less than the call of God the Father to action. This liberty is fraught with risk, as in the episode

of the adulteress in St John (Jn 8:1–11), but thwarts every perversion of the Law whose meaning is to love God and your neighbor as yourself. According to Moingt:

> If we answer the Spirit's call, the Spirit enters us without doing us any violence. He mixes with our spirit, grafting us onto Christ, and thus with Christ we form a single body animated by the same breath of life which is Jesus's own. In that way we become members of the body of Christ. But this insertion is realized in the universal communion of fraternal love. That is why it is done within the Church.[7]

In Mary the Spirit gave a body to God's Word. The Spirit again gave a body to the apostolic group scattered by the Messiah's death. The Spirit elicited a body of writings (the Bible) which calls to mind God's work of salvation. The Spirit brings about the sacramental body of Christ in the Eucharist. The Spirit makes the Church an ecclesial body and, in the works of culture, gives the world flesh.

The Church is a work of the Spirit, as Peter's meeting with Cornelius in Acts 10 attests, with the baptism of the whole household. As an open society, and in proportion to its own conversion, the Church takes the place of societies closed by clan barriers:

> Do not forget... that you were at that time separate from Christ and excluded from membership of Israel, aliens with no part in the covenants of the Promise, limited to this world without hope and without God. But now in Christ Jesus, you that used to be so far off, have been brought close by the blood of Christ. For he is the peace between us and has made the two into one entity and broken down the barrier which used to keep them apart, by destroying in his own person the hostility, that is, the Law of commandments with its decrees. His purpose in this was, by restoring peace, to create a single New Man out of the two of them, and through the cross to reconcile them both to God in one body; in his own person he killed the hostility. He came to bring the good news of peace to you who

were far off and peace to those who were near. Through him, then, we both in the one Spirit have free access to the Father (Ep 2:12–18).

The Spirit makes a new humanity spring forth; that is the mission of the Spirit in history: "It does not concern only our passage from earth to heaven, but the renewal of history and its opening to the universality of the Kingdom of God".[8]

Conclusion

Nothing forms a limit for the Spirit of God, constituted as the source of spiritual life by virtue of Christ's resurrection. This does not mean that the Spirit is evanescent. The Spirit gives body and life to all its works: the historic body of Jesus of Nazareth, the scriptural body of the Bible, the sacramental and ecclesial body.[9] It is because he is a spiritual body that the Risen Christ can declare that he will

be with us until the world's end (Mt 28:20). And it is because Christ is with us until the end of the world that he gives himself an infinity of visible bodies in the Church spread throughout the world and history. The goal of the Spirit's creative activity uses the Church to gather humanity in unity. Beginning with the Church, the Spirit "spreads throughout the world the same spirit as is in the Church, that is the evangelical message of unity and brotherhood, the same message that we find in the Eucharist, the self-offering of each for the other. The way of salvation is that of bodies offered for others (Jn 15:12–13).[10] So it becomes clear how fundamental it is for Christianity that the Spirit be intimately bound to the body. Even when the body is reduced to a trace as in Christian Boltansky and Yves Klein, or a support in Olaf Breuning, or mere matter in Ousmane Sow, the Spirit's fleshly mediation still remains. ■

1   Claude Tassin, 'Saint Paul, homme de prière: originalité d'une prière d'apôtre', *Sedos Bulletin*, 28/11 (1996), pp. 290–4: 294.

2   Ibid.

3   See the *Gaudium et Spes*, 22 § 5.

4   Unpublished text of a lecture in the parish of Saint-Germain-l'Auxerrois at Châtenay-Malabry, Joseph Moingt, *L'Esprit Saint*, March 1995: <http://www.saint.germain.free.fr/conferences/conferences98/moingesp.htm>, accessed 30th May 2019. (For the theological argumentaion, see Joseph Moingt, *Dieu qui vient à l'homme. I. Du deuil au dévoilement de Dieu*, Paris, 2002; *Dieu qui vient à l'homme. II. De l'apparition à la naissance de Dieu*,

Paris, 2005–6; *Croire au Dieu qui vient. I. De la croyance à la foi critique*, Paris, 2014 and *Croire au Dieu qui vient. II. Esprit, Église et monde: de la foi critique à la foi qui agit*, Paris, 2016.

5   Moingt 1995, op. cit.

6   Ibid.

7   Ibid.

8   Ibid.

9   See Henry de Lubac, *Oeuvres complètes. XV. Corpus mysticum. L'Eucharistie et l'Église au Moyen Âge. Étude historique*, edited by Éric de Moulins-Beaufort, Paris, 2009, section 5.

10   Moingt 1995, op. cit.

Creator Spiritus
The Holy Spirit in Florentine Art

TIMOTHY VERDON

In Florence, as elsewhere, the iconography of the Holy Spirit normally illustrates relevant biblical texts, especially the second verse of the Book of Genesis, which states that at the beginning, when God created the heavens and the earth, the earth was a formless void, there was darkness over the deep and God's wind hovered over the water (Gn 1:2). In the Latin of the Vulgate, "wind" corresponds to *spiritus*, 'spirit', and since the text speaks of a 'wind of God', in patristic readings the 'spirit' is qualified as 'Holy Spirit'. Artists usually visualized the Spirit in the form suggested by the New Testament, that of a dove, as one sees in the Creation scene of first important series of images realized in Florence, the cycle of mosaics inside the Baptistery, dateable to the mid-1200s (fig. 1).[1]

The same cycle has an illustration of another text relative to the Holy Spirit, the passage in the Gospel of Luke narrating the Annunciation and the assurance given Mary, troubled by the angel's words about motherhood (apparently impossible due to her virginal condition): "The Holy Spirit will come upon you...and the power of the Most High will cover you with its shadow. And so the child will be holy and will be called Son of God" (Lk 1:35; cf. Mt 1:20: fig. 2).[2] The iconography of the Annunciation will always be important in this city whose identity is communicated by a flower, the lily or iris, and which until the 18th century opened its civil new year on March 25, the feast of the Annunciation and thus also of the conception of Christ.

These two examples make clear that in Florence, as in all of Christendom, the idea and image of the Holy Spirit were associated both with the primordial act of creation and with the conception of the Savior, an event of special interest in a city characterized by intense Marian spirituality and with two large sanctuaries dedicated to the Blessed Virgin: Santissima Annunziata and Orsanmichele. We can add moreover that, from a very early period, the implications of these two biblical incidents tend to converge, as in a small relief beside one of the side doors of the Cathedral: an *Annunciation* with a symbolic domed structure between Gabriel and the Virgin, which the dove representing the Holy Spirit has penetrated. The angel's words written below the dove – *Ave gratia plena*, "Hail, full of grace" – make it clear that the domed building alludes to Mary's body, which at that very moment was 'penetrated' and 'filled' with God's grace – with his Word, that is, who in her became flesh (fig. 3).

The relief evokes Mary's body with an architectural structure because the relief was carved between 1290 and 1310: in the very years, that

1. Salerno di Coppo (?), *Creation of the World*, Florence, Baptistery of San Giovanni.

2. Francesco (Master of the Crucifix of San Miniato), *Annunciation*, Florence, Baptistery of San Giovanni.

3. Anonymous sculptor, *Annunciation*, Florence, Cathedral of Santa Maria del Fiore, exterior.

is, in which the city began to construct its new cathedral dedicated to the Virgin, Santa Maria del Fiore. In fact a more refined version of the same subject in the Victoria and Albert Museum in London is attributed to Arnolfo di Cambio, first architect of the cathedral, and so there was probably a link between the rising building and the iconography of the relief.[3] Arnolfo's project for the church probably included a dome – smaller than the one finally built by Filippo Brunelleschi but in any case a dominant architectural feature –, and this further reinforces the likelihood that the domed structure in the relief alludes to the just-begun new cathedral. It also suggests that the Holy Spirit shown inside the small temple, in the relief, was seen as the ideal architect of the future cathedral, which – like Mary at the *Annunciation* – had the function of housing Christ's body, the *Corpus Mysticum* constituted by the Florentine Christian community. The Spirit, therefore – the same one who "hovered over the water" of the formless void – was imagined as One who *creates*, *gives form*, *organizes space*, *builds*.

This idea was perhaps in the mind of the sculptor who, a few decades later, *c.* 1340, in one of the reliefs at the base of the Bell Tower showing Florentine arts and crafts, depicted an architect leaning over his work table, 'inspired' and almost in ecstasy, as if possessed by the Spirit (fig. 4) – as, indeed, in the same series, the painter and the sculptor are also represented. It was a biblical way of depicting the impulse toward artistic creation: as an expression of divine Wisdom, within which is

> a spirit intelligent, holy, unique, manifold, subtle, active, incisive, unsullied, lucid, invulnerable, benevolent, sharp, irresistible, beneficent, loving to man, steadfast, dependable, unperturbed, almighty, all-surveying, penetrating all intelligent, pure, and most subtle spirits… a breath of the power of God, pure emanation of the glory of the Almighty (Ws 22:5).

It was in this 'sapiential' sense that Vasari would later call Michelangelo "divine".

Still another New Testament event is fundamental for the iconography of the Holy Spirit, the baptism of Christ, when the vision of the Spirit descending on the Savior confirmed Jesus's condition as Son of God. Especially important for Florentines, whose patron saint is John the Baptist, was the account given in the fourth Gospel, where the Precursor himself sees

and explains the sense of this vision: "I saw the Spirit coming down on [Christ] from heaven like a dove and resting on him. I did not know him myself, but he who had sent me to baptize with water had said to me, 'The man on whom you see the Spirit come down and rest is the one who is going to baptize with the Holy Spirit'. Yes, I have seen and am the witness that he is the Chosen One of God" (Jn 1:32–4). The most beautiful painting of this scene – the *Baptism of Christ* by Piero della Francesca, an artist formed in Florence – helps us grasp the epiphanic dimension of the Precursor's words (fig. 5). The Spirit *reveals* Christ: John the Baptist recognizes Jesus as the Chosen One because he sees the Spirit descend and rest upon him. The Spirit is the promised sign through which the Father identifies Jesus as his Son.

Of great interest in that sense is the central position given the Spirit in the funerary chapel of an aristocratic young prelate, the Cardinal of Portugal, in the Florentine church of San Miniato al Monte.[4] The uncle of the deceased, Alphonse V, King of Portugal, ordered a sumptuous chapel to be built to commemorate his nephew, Cardinal James of Coimbra, who had died in Florence in 1459 at barely 25 years of age: a chapel with a marble tomb and facing

4. Andrea Pisano and assistant, *Architecture*, detail, Florence, Museo dell'Opera del Duomo.

5. Piero della Francesca, *Baptism of Christ*, detail, London, National Gallery.

6. Luca della Robbia, *The Holy Spirit and the Seven Gifts*, Florence, San Miniato al Monte, Chapel of the Cardinal of Portugal, ceiling.

7. Anonymous miniature painter, *Savonarola, inspired by the Holy Spirit, disputes with Eastern sages*, woodcut in Girolamo Savonarola, *Dialogo della verita prophetica*, Florence, Biblioteca Nazionale Centrale, Cust. F.7.

episcopal throne carved by Bernardo and Antonio Rossellino, an altarpiece painted by Antonio and Piero Pollaiolo, and a ceiling in glazed terracotta by Luca della Robbia. And at the center of the ceiling, dominating the entire chapel, is the Holy Spirit distributing his gifts, symbolized by seven candlesticks (fig. 6). This iconographic choice, which clearly insists upon the young cardinal's sanctity, also illustrates the Florentine conviction that the outpouring of the Spirit is not limited to the Only-begotten Son, Jesus, but meant for all God's children.

This indeed is the universal pneumatic vocation described by the prophet Joel and remembered by St Peter at the first Pentecost, when he quoted the words Joel attributed to God: "I will pour out my spirit on all mankind. Your sons and daughters shall prophesy, your old men shall dream dreams, and your young men see visions. Even on the slaves, men and women, will I pour out my spirit in those days" (Jl 3:1–5; Ac 2:17–18). "Your sons and daughters shall prophesy, your old men shall dream dreams, and your young men see visions": From the early 15th century onwards, the prophetic potential of human beings – their capacity to abandon themselves to God's Spirit, letting themselves be invaded by Him – was one of the themes of Florentine art, a privileged line of theological and anthropological research. In Donatello and Fra Angelico, as later in Botticelli and Michelangelo, the inward gaze, the transfigured visage, together with the head turned up to God, bear witness to the desire to visualize an inner *movement* that is perfect *stillness*, a *music* that is absolute *silence*.

In confirmation of this tendency, at the end of the 15th century Savonarola dedicated a printed pamphlet to the gift of prophecy, and the illustration that accompanies his text – a woodcut by an unknown artist – shows the Dominican friar in conversation with other learned men under the influence of the Holy Spirit, just outside the city whose skyline is dominated by Brunelleschi's dome (fig. 7).[5] The woodcut recalls the pneumatic reading of intellectual activity frequent among the Greek Fathers: in chapter 9 of St Basil's *Treatise on the Holy Spirit*, for example, which insists that

8-9. Piero di Cosimo, *Immaculate Conception with Saints*, whole and detail,
Florence, Gallerie degli Uffizi, Galleria delle Statue e delle Pitture.

souls bearing the Spirit and illuminated by him become themselves spiritual and shed their grace on others. From that derives the prevision of future events, the understanding of mysteries, the comprehension of hidden things, the distribution of spiritual gifts, heavenly citizenship, the dance with angels, endless joy, dwelling in God, the resemblance to Him, and the greatest thing man can desire: to become God (PG 32, cols. 107–10).

The Savonarola woodcut 'anticipates' a very surprising 16th-century work illustrating the Spirit: the large altarpiece by Piero di Cosimo for the Servite friars of the Marian sanctuary of Santissima Annunziata, painted *c.* 1505 and today at the Uffizi (fig. 8).[6] The image, which shows Mary on a pedestal amid saints, places her directly beneath the Holy Spirit, toward whom she lifts her joy-filled face. The painting's subject, often erroneously identified as the Immaculate Conception, is the Conception of Jesus – the moment, that is, when, beneath the Spirit's luminous shadow, Mary conceived the child, as suggested here by the gesture of her right hand, caressing a womb visibly enlarged. On the ground below the pedestal (fig. 9) an open book reminds us that at this moment the

Word of God became flesh, and that the God who previously "spoke to our fathers through the prophets" now "has spoken to us through his Son" who is also the son of Mary (cf. Heb 1:1–2).

The abandoned book of the Scriptures dramatizes Mary's intense relationship with the Spirit here, confirming that Piero di Cosimo was attempting to create a new, completely original, iconographic formula for the event implied in the Annunciation account. He in fact depicts the *Annunciation* in the relief carved on Mary's pedestal, an allusion to the church for which the painting was destined, dedicated to "the most holy Mary Annunciate". In that context the abandoned book he shows would have reminded viewers of a famous fresco in Santissima Annunziata, a 14th-century *Annunciation* held to be miraculous, in which a Bible appears, open to the words of Isaiah: "Et virgo concipiet".

But, with extraordinary boldness, Piero di Cosimo's own painting replaced the traditional iconographic formula of the Annunciation, allusive but unspecific, with one that concentrated attention on the event's theological content, which is: human nature made fecund and filled with life through direct contact with God's

10. Michelangelo Buonarroti, *Doni Tondo*,
Florence, Gallerie degli Uffizi, Galleria delle Statue e delle Pitture.

Spirit. The artist involves the other historic episodes of Mary's and Christ's life depicted here – the *Nativity*, in the left background, and the *Flight into Egypt*, in the analogous position at the right – in the same pneumatic logic, as if insisting that, beyond historical details, what really counts is the eternal present of the human being's relationship with God.

The same subject – the transfiguring relationship of the human being with God – is elaborated by Michelangelo in the same years, in a circular painting done for the Florentine patron Agnolo Doni and known as the *Doni Tondo* (fig. 10).[7] Rich in mysterious details such as the nude youths in the middle distance, this painting, destined for the bed chamber of Doni and his wife Maddalena Strozzi, again speaks of Christ's conception, showing Mary's abdomen – her womb – accented with silver highlights at the center of the composition, and, between her legs, the book of the Scriptures abandoned because the Word is about to become flesh. Mary

lifts herself, turning toward the Son who comes from his Father's bosom and prepares to descend; the Child's left leg rests on the Father's thigh, while his right leg finds support on his mother's arm. The infant maintains his equilibrium by gripping Mary's hair.

Vasari says that Doni, who had commissioned the work, initially refused to accept it because of the high price Michelangelo asked. But perhaps the real reason for the refusal was Michelangelo's unconventional, even shocking iconography. Doni and his wife had ordered a *Holy Family*, and the painting in fact is usually identified with that title, even though, as with Piero di Cosimo's work, such a conventional title is misleading. In the *Doni Tondo* there are too many troubling novelties: the muscled ephebes embracing in the middle distance; the physical intimacy between the old man and Mary, seated between his legs with her right arm resting on his knee (whereas 'Holy Family' scenes normally separated Mary, Jesus's mother, from the child's putative father, Joseph). Above all Michelangelo's figure of Mary here is unique in all the history of Christian art: without a veil, her body in energetic movement, her athletic arms fully visible!

Mary is the central figure of this composition designed to show her response to God. The force with which she lifts herself from the ground (she is also a 'Madonna of Humility') is animated by the ardent yearning for the Absolute visible in her visage. In humanist Florence, dominated by Marsilio Ficino's platonic and Plotinian thought, to which the young Michelangelo was exposed in the Medici household, desire – 'desiderio', or, as Florentines then said, 'desio' – was the beginning of a spiritual journey which, beginning with external beauty, led by ascending steps toward supreme and unchanging Beauty, God. Ficino, like many of the Florentine humanists, was a cleric, and 'desire' in his theology has a function similar to that which St Paul attributed to the Holy Spirit when he said:

> The Spirit… comes to help us in our weakness. For when we cannot choose words in order to pray properly, the Spirit himself expresses our plea in a way that could never be put into words, and God, who knows everything in our hearts, knows perfectly well what he means… (Rm 8:26–7).

Mary's upturned face in Michelangelo's painting, touched by a light that comes from on high, recalls a text written by the most 'platonic' of the Latin Church Fathers, Augustine of Hippo, who imagined the human gaze ravished by divine illumination. And, as we call to mind Augustine's words, we should also remember that at the beginning of his career Michelangelo was befriended by the prior of the Augustinian Convent in Florence, for whom he realized a large, polychrome wood crucifix, and that the Convent, where the artist in fact lived for a period of time, is dedicated to the Holy Spirit, 'Santo Spirito'.

The text is famous: Augustine, in his *Confessions*, describes an experience analogous to what Michelangelo attributes to Mary in the *Doni Tondo*. Speaking to God, the saint says:

I entered into my own depths, with you as guide; and I was able to do it because you were my helper. I entered and, with the eye of my soul, such as it was, I saw your unchangeable light shining over that same eye of my soul, over my mind. It was not the light of every day that the eye of flesh can see, nor some greater light of the same order, such as might be if the brightness of our daily light should be seen shining with a more intense brightness and filling all things with its greatness. Your light was not that, but other, altogether other than all such lights. Nor was it above my mind, as oil above the water it floats on, nor as the sky is above the earth; it was above because it made me, and I was below because made by it. He who knows the truth knows that light, and he that knows that light knows eternity. Love knows it. O eternal truth and true love and beloved eternity! You are my God, I sigh to you by day and by night. When first I knew you, you lifted me up so that I might see that there was something to see, but that I was not yet the man to see it. And you beat back the weakness of my gaze, blazing upon me too strongly, and I was shaken with love and with dread… (VII, 10).

In the *Doni Tondo* the Spirit is not represented in the customary form of a dove but as divine attraction acting on a human being's heart and body, visible in her gaze and feelings. In Mary's case especially, St Paul's words to the Christians of Rome apply: "the Spirit of God has made his home in you… and if the Spirit of him who raised Jesus from the dead is living in you, then he who raised Jesus from the dead will give life to your own mortal bodies through his Spirit living in you" (Rm 8:9–11).

I want to conclude with a contemporary image, a triptych by Filippo Rossi, a Florentine artist of our time and a participant in the present symposium (fig. 11): a work today in the United States, in the monastery of the Community of Jesus, the ecumenical religious community supporting the symposium generally and hosting its final session at their house on Cape Cod, Massachusetts.[8] Rossi's stylistic abstraction is only apparent, though, for the title he gave this work, *Magnificat*, evokes in

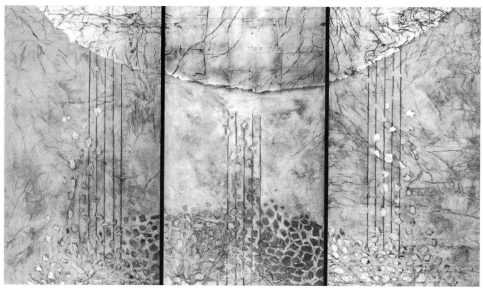

11. Filippo Rossi, *Magnificat*, Orleans, MA, Church of the Transfiguration.

a clear way its narrative meaning, Mary's joy rising like music, like chant, toward Him who is light, the light of which Augustine wrote, above our inner eye, above our intelligence – "unchanging light". Aspiring to reach this light, Mary herself becomes luminous as she says: "My soul proclaims the greatness of the Lord and my spirit exults in God my Savior" (Lk 1:46).

This has been a theme of Florentine art for more than seven hundred years: the Holy Spirit indwelling human flesh, overwhelming women and men with gifts, working in their minds and hearts to fuse the desires of created beings with the Love which God is, Father, Son and Holy Spirit. ■

1   See Miklós Boskovits, *A Critical and Historical Corpus of Florentine Painting. I. The Thirteenth Century. II. The Mosaics of the Baptistery of Florence*, Florence, 2007, pp. 11–26.

2   Ibid., p. 385.

3   E. Neri Lusanna, in *Arnolfo. Alle origini del Rinascimento fiorentino*, exhibition catalogue (Florence, Museo dell'Opera del Duomo, 2005–6), Florence, 2005, pp. 366–8.

4   Giancarlo Gentilini, *I della Robbia: la scultura invetriata nel Rinascimento*, 2 vols., II, Florence, 1992, p. 77.

5   See *Immagini e azione riformatrice. Le xilografie degli incunaboli savonaroliani nella Biblioteca Nazionale di Firenze*, edited by Elisabetta Turelli, Florence, 1985, pp. 73–4.

6   See Timothy Verdon, *Mary in Western Art*, New York, 2005, p. 55.

7   Ibid., pp. 217–23.

8   See Timothy Verdon, *Art and Prayer: the Beauty of Turning to God*, Brewster, MA, 2014, pp. 53–5.

The Holy Spirit and Contemporary Visual Art

Toward an Artistic Pneumatology

JÉRÔME COTTIN

The Holy Spirit and contemporary visual art. *A priori*, these two themes could not be farther apart, and it seems incongruous to bring them together. The Bible has no 'image' to designate the strong theological notion which the Holy Spirit represents, and which subsequently, in the course of the reflections of the councils of the first centuries, became the "third Person" of the Trinity. To be sure, the Bible speaks of a dove (Mk 1:10; Mt 3:16; Lk 3:22; Jn 1:32) and of tongues of fire (Ac 2:3), yet these are not images but simple metaphors ("like"). The only biblical account that allows us to visualize the gift of the Spirit is that of Pentecost (Ac 2:1–13); but after having been abundantly represented in the course of centuries it does not much inspire today's artists.

In the history of Christian art, the numerous efforts of artists who have tried to give a visual equivalent for the Holy Spirit, whether as a single figure or as part of the Trinity, could be thought of as the history of a prolonged defeat: representations of the Trinity with three human forms – or two, with a dove between them –, fail to communicate the very thing they seek to indicate.[1]

The thesis that I will defend here is that there is indeed a relationship between the Holy Spirit and contemporary art creation (in both directions: the Spirit toward the arts

and the arts toward the Spirit). But to identify it we must free ourselves of a double conditioning, no longer aligning ourselves with "Christian iconography", which in any case is no longer pertinent to the contemporary era, after the end of "Christian art": today when artists realize a dove (like Braque's doves or Picasso's), it is a symbol of peace, not of the Holy Spirit. And as for fire, it usually signifies destruction, not the coming of the Spirit. The other necessary change of viewpoint consists in no longer understanding the Holy Spirit as a primarily dogmatic notion, but rather as biblical. A brief return to the biblical notion of the Spirit is thus useful.

Biblical notes on the Spirit (*Ruach* and *Pneuma*)

The Holy Spirit, or simply the Spirit, is one of the most frequent words in both Testaments: it is designated by the Hebrew word *Ruach*,[2] and by the Greek word *Pneuma*.[3] It is important to note that in Hebrew the Spirit, *Ruach*, is feminine. If the Spirit is a part of God, there is thus femininity in God, and we are already far from dogmatic systems of thought! It is beyond the scope of the present reflection to propose a biblical theology of the Holy Spirit, however, and in any case others have already done so.[4] We will simply retain a few elements, important for our theme.

- In the Bible the Spirit is a term with several meanings, which sometimes oscillate between 'breath' and 'wind'. We can sum up by saying that there are three kinds of Spirit. The Spirit of God (or of Christ), the Spirit of Man, the Spirit of God (or of Christ) in Man. Sometimes these three notions of the Spirit are separate, but sometimes they are intimately linked, as is clear in the chapter dedicated to the Spirit in the Letter to the Romans (chapter 8).

- It would be a mistake, and un-biblical, to interpret these notions of the Spirit through Greek philosophical categories and opposing it to the body, or more broadly to earthly material reality. The exegete Gerd Theissen, in his *Psychology of the Early Christians*, has effectively demonstrated that in St Paul the notion of the Spirit comes to inhabit the human being touched by grace and becomes an anthropological reality which gives man the force of a renewed action, of creativity, of a *creation*. What is more, despite the running opposition between flesh and spirit which Paul uses, his anthropology is in no sense dualist, precisely because, for the Apostle, the Spirit designates what Theissen calls an "anthropological outfitting".[5] On the subject of Pauline anthropology, Theissen goes on to say:

> From birth, every human being possesses a 'spirit' alongside his body and soul. But at the same time the Spirit indicates a divine force, irrational, which seizes the human being from without, making him capable of extraordinary experiences and actions. On its own side, that spirit given to man in part inhabits the Christian (in an inhabitual manner) and in part lays hold of him (in an actual manner), but only in particular situations. The three meanings come together in Romans 8,14–16.[6]

- The Spirit is not a person or a state but rather a dynamic, a power of transformation. Interior and exterior transformation. It transforms the human being's heart: "You ... live ... by the spirit, since the Spirit of God has made a home in you" (Rm 8:9). The theme of the inhabitation of the Spirit is constantly underlined by Paul, who frequently uses the expression

"The Spirit dwells in you" (1 Co 3:16; 6:19; 2 Co 6:16; Rm 8:9, 11).

- But the Spirit transforms creation as well. Thus Ps 33:6 says that the Spirit participates in the work of creation: "By the word of Yahweh the heavens were made, by the breath of his mouth all their array. He collects the waters of the sea like a dam". Or again, in Ps 104:29–30, which indicates the ensemble of living beings: "Take back their breath and they die and revert to dust. Send out your breath and life begins; you renew the face of the earth". This transformation of creation by the power of the Spirit, of which we possess only the first fruits, reaches its apotheosis in Rm 8:19–22.

- With the manifestation of the Spirit, the invisible becomes visible. That is especially underlined by the evangelist Luke, who spoke above all to Greeks: for him the Spirit, the *pneuma*, makes itself manifest in visible and palpable reality. For the author of the third gospel and of Acts, the two words *dunamis* and *pneuma* are almost synonyms. Thus in Ac 19,2 every baptized person possesses the Spirit in such a way that it is visible and sensible to him.

- The Spirit is more than the actual presence of Christ among us and in us, the Christ proclaimed and living in the midst of the assembled community. To be sure, the resurrected Christ is one of the manifestations of the Spirit, and that is particularly underlined by Luke (Acts) and by Paul; but the Spirit also acts independently of Christ, in the Church and in the world.[7] There is a parallel between the works of the Lord and the work of the Spirit, without it being necessary to identify each with the other.

After having insisted on this "theo-anthropological" notion which the Spirit is in the Bible, we must see in what way the Spirit can lead us indirectly to artistic creation. I will make three remarks on this subject.

The Bible certainly does not establish a direct link between the Spirit and artistic creation. But it suggests this link, and even makes it possible, in the measure in which the Spirit of God makes the human being capable of acting better, or differently, or in any case otherwise: capable of going beyond his capacities, of overstepping his limits, of inventing a different and better world. In Ga 5,25 Paul says it explicitly: "Since we are living by the Spirit, let our actions be guided by the Spirit". Those actions can include interior images, and is that not the genesis of the art work? Is that not the sense of the words of the prophet Joel (3,1), about the Spirit creating visions? "I shall pour out my Spirit on all humanity. Your sons and daughters shall prophesy, your old people shall dream dreams, and your young people see visions". We could continue to illustrate this capacity of the Spirit to create new things in and through man citing Lk 4,18: "The Spirit of the Lord is on me … He has sent me to proclaim liberty to captives, sight to the blind". In that citation it is amazing that it is precisely the sense of sight to be restored, not that of hearing. In the gospels of Mark and Matthew, where the Spirit is little discussed, the Spirit is – as in the Old Testament – synonymous with God's power which allows people to speak and act beyond their normal human capacities.

Paul moreover puts the manifestation of the Spirit in direct relation with the 'image' (*eikon*), but with an image *still to come*, not yet achieved: that of the unveiling of God in all things and in everyone. Let us reread 2 Co 3,13–18, where, thanks to the Spirit, it is a question of unveiling: in Christ, the veil which impeded Moses from seeing God is removed, and as a result "all of us, with our unveiled faces, like mirrors reflecting the glory of the Lord, are being transformed into the image that we reflect in brighter and brighter glory; this is the working of the Lord who is the Spirit" (verse 18). At the heart of this passage in which visual metaphors abound (unveiling, face, transformation, glory, image), we find a double notion of the Spirit: "This is the working of the Lord who is the Spirit".

What is more, twice in the Bible we find a link between the gift of the Spirit and artistic creation. The Spirit of God is compared to a work of art. Thus in Ex 28,3–6, God tells Moses: "You will instruct all the skilled men whom I have endowed with a spirit (*ruach*) of wisdom…". And concludes: "The work of an artist". (Ex 39:8). God's Spirit can also render man capable of creating beautiful things. That is the case for Bezalel, the only artist named in the

Bible: "Look, Yahweh has singled out Bezalel son of Uri, son of Hur, and has filled him with the spirit (*ruach*) of God, in wisdom, knowledge and skill in every kind of craft" (Ex 35:30–1).

These biblical passages on the Spirit (*ruach/ pneuma*) are sufficiently numerous and central to lead us to conclude that a biblical comprehension of the Holy Spirit can very well constitute the base on which to found a theology open to artistic creation, seen as openness to all that is possible.

What can we now say from the artists' point of view, and – more exactly – from the point of view of contemporary artists? If the Bible (indirectly) links the Holy Spirit to artistic creation, do artists themselves make a link between their creation and the Spirit of God?

Several examples will show that contemporary artists, without doubt more effectively than their predecessors in 'Christian art', can express – by their forms and colors more than by subject matter and visual motifs – the reality of the Holy Spirit both as the subject of their works and as the 'motor' (inspirer) of their art. We will see that in looking at various contemporary (20th- and 21st-century) artistic realities.

New expressions in liturgical art

Let us begin with what is most identifiable: contemporary artistic creations in a liturgical context, which make reference to the manifestation of the Spirit in places of worship – that is to say in relation to the liturgy and the proclamation of the Word. I will briefly comment on four contemporary realizations of significant quality.

One of the most beautiful examples is the immense stained-glass window by Alfred Manessier (1911–93), entitled *The Pentecost Window*, which is the central window of the Lutheran church of *Unser Lieben Frauen* at Bremen, 1964–79. The French artist, who when he converted to Christianity adopted a non-figurative style, has expressed in glass the intensity of the Pentecost event (the irruption of the Holy Spirit). In what we perceive as flames, we think we make out a human form. The intensity of the warm colors becomes less and less lively as the eye moves toward the bottom, where cold colors dominate. The central position of the window in the depth of the choir-area is a hymn to the manifestation of the Spirit who founds the Church. The window is not an illustration of the Pentecost account (it is non-figurative), but rather a visual equivalent. On the two sides of this central window are two others with theological themes, the Incarnation (or Christmas) window, at the left, and the Preaching window at the right. But the biggest of the three is the Spirit window, which unquestionably is also the most successful and which transmits the strongest visual impression.

Another place, another creation. For the French Reformed church in Berne, the Swiss typographer Adrian Frutiger realized a wall hanging entitled *Pentecost*; it is part of his *Christian Liturgical Cycle*.[8] Red forms evoke with equal effectiveness both flames and the flow of blood in the veins, with this commentary: "The ceaselessly renewed force of the Spirit".

The same liturgical idea guided Marie-Luise Frey's installation entitled simply *Rot* (red), and which is part of her *Six-color Project* (*Sechs-Farben-Projekt*) realized in 2010 in the Stadtkirche of Darmstadt.[9] This specialist in *paramentique* – liturgical textiles for altars, ambos and pulpits – wanted to celebrate the 120th anniversary of this atelier of liturgical weaving linked to the *Elisabethenstift*. Each installation adorned the interior of the church during the different liturgical times. For the time of Pentecost, threads of wool and fabrics in different tints of red descended from the keystone of the church's vaulting, giving the impression of a sudden irruption of something from outside. In this case it was the color red alone, with all its variants of tint and nuance, which symbolized the irruption of the Holy Spirit. And, as if to signify that this ecclesial event could have social repercussions, in the same period the church bell tower, visible to all and everywhere, was floodlit in red.

Thus, to designate the Spirit's manifestation in the contemporary era, the color (red), more than the form or subject, is plastically meaningful.[10]

The third realization is of an entirely different kind. We are in the Benedictine Abbey of Melk, in Austria. That prestigious abbey overlooking the Danube also affords the occasion for several contemporary artistic creations in the park which surrounds it. Our gaze is drawn by a sculpture in marble evoking the Trinity, with a human form that can, from a certain angle, become three forms (fig. 1).

The inscription below the sculpture tells us that it is a work of Laurus Edelbacher, dated 2014 and entitled *Der Vater, der Sohn, die Geist* (The Father, the Son, *the* Spirit [n.b., the article *die*, used for the Spirit, is feminine, not the usual masculine article *der*]). In changing the gender of the word 'Spirit' (which in German is masculine), the artist, who without doubt is also conversant with the Bible, thus wanted to make evident the Spirit's femininity, totally forgotten or denied by the Church, and thus to make God's own femininity evident.

These four examples show that their artists were very creative in representing not the Spirit as such but the Spirit's effectiveness, its creativity, in the measure in which, like Christ

1. Laurus Edelbacher, *The Father, the Son, the Spirit*, Gardens of the Benedictine Abbey of Melk, Austria.

and in him, the Spirit makes all things new (2 Co 5:17). In these examples, artistic gesture and theological conviction are perfectly met.

The contribution of non-Western art

To leave old iconographic patterns in order to better represent the Holy Spirit or the dynamic which it suggests is doubtless easier for non-Western artists, for at least two reasons: they are not marked by Western Christianity's rather rigid iconographic tradition of representation of the Spirit/the Trinity; and they come from cultures for which non-rational realities (like the Holy Spirit) do not pose problems. It is not therefore astonishing that non-Western artists feel inspired by a visual translation of the Holy Spirit.

I will give two examples of Indian artists who speak to us of the Holy Spirit in a renewed way.

In 1987, Reginald Pavamani, an Indian artist living in Paris, realized a large work, *Pentecost* (acrylic on canvas), which he donated on the occasion of the construction of the Protestant church of Corbeil-Essonnes: fire, air (heaven) and a crowd mix, forming a mosaic colored with tones that are essentially red, orange and blue. In his rather figurative work we clearly see flames, but they represent vivifying fire, not conflagration. The construction of the image, marked by a style that we could define as 'naïf', owes nothing to the traditional iconography of the Pentecost account. Children are in particular evidence, as well as a mix between the interior and the exterior: at the end we do not know if we are inside or outside, if it is a question of intimacy or of a public event.

Another Indian artist, Frank Wesley (1923–2002), did a picture in gouache entitled *The Holy Spirit*, (undated, Swain Collection), referring to the promise of the Spirit-Paraclete in the Gospel of John (14:14–17; fig. 2).[11]

We can consider his work a *hapax*: it is the only time the Holy Spirit is represented with a human feminine face. The face of that woman-Spirit, with delicate features of the Indian type, is meditative. Her eyes are closed and her broad brow – the seat of wisdom in Indian anthropology – is enlightened by a halo

2. Frank Wesley, *The Holy Spirit*, Swain Collection.

of bright, diffuse light. She has long red hair, which seems to be of fire, in which the symbols of the four evangelists are discretely evoked (a bull, an eagle, a lion and a man).

All the examples mentioned up to this point present contemporary artistic realizations inspired by the theme of the Spirit, but done in a Christian and liturgical context. The artists mentioned, of whom some are internationally known – Manessier,[12] Frutiger,[13] Wesley[14] – were nourished by a Christian faith personally lived, anchored in Church tradition. But can we go further and say that some artists, unsupported by Christian faith, culture or tradition, have 'grasped' by their art what the Bible means when it speaks of the Holy Spirit? Would they be able to rediscover the Holy Spirit, not as a 'divine person' or a dogma, but as a mysterious force investing man and making him capable of creating something new? Without being able to give a definitive answer, we may suppose that this is possible.

The Holy Spirit outside christianity

If we wanted to explore this theme more fully, it would be necessary to return to the book/program of Wassily Kandinsky, the 'inventor' of non-figurative art: *The Spiritual in Art*.[15] In that work continually republished for more than a century, it is often a question of the Spirit and of artistic creation. To be sure, the Spirit of which Kandinsky speaks does not correspond, *stricto sensu*, to the biblical Holy Spirit: it is a matter rather of the spirit of the artist-creator. Kandinsky, the artist and theoretician of art, certainly had a good understanding of religion and the Bible, but was also nourished by numerous other influences, philosophical and theosophical. Yet for the Russian-born artist who had emigrated to Munich, these references were not mutually exclusive. We know that his art borrows from the tradition of Russian icons, which are supported by a theology of the Spirit typical of the Orthodox tradition. In *The Spiritual in Art* we find phrases such as:

> The spiritual life to which art also belongs, and of which it is one of the most powerful agents, is translated by a movement forward and upward, complex yet clear, and which can be reduced to a simple element. It is the clear movement of knowledge.[16]

The artist was firmly convinced that art opens us to the spiritual, which permits a deepened knowledge of reality under the form of anticipation. We could say the same thing of the Holy Spirit.

I will give two examples of artists working outside of Christianity, who have nonetheless created works that perfectly evoke the Spirit of God, works which could therefore enter into dialogue with a Christian pneumatology.

The first is Yves Klein (1928–62), a contemporary of Manessier and also known at world level, thanks to the color blue which he invented and 'labeled' under the name 'International Klein Blue'. Moreover it was the artist himself, an esoteric and eccentric personage, who put his 'ultramarine' blue and the *pneuma*, the Spirit, in relation. His biographer, Hanna Weitemeier, says:

> Yves Klein always remembered the profound shock that his first encounter with the frescoes of the basilcia of St Francis at Assisi had been for him – when for the first time he perceived the intensity of the blue in Giotto's frescoes. It was the blue of Assisi that gave him the certitude that the blueness of blue was without dimensions.[17]

At the origin of Klein's blue there was thus an aesthetic shock, which occurred however in a religious context. In Giotto, we suspect, artistic expression and Christian spirituality cannot be separated. Klein's biographer continues:

> His words, in fact, concerned a quality of the spiritual potential of art … In Klein, our gaze progressively dissolves in the optic of a cosmic awareness: first there was diversity of colors, then a concentration on the color blue alone, and finally, in logical consequence, on the concept of 'void'. It was not a question of the vacuity of airless space, but of a free and invisible quality of energetic space. If this void is certainly invisible, its structural component, more basic than air itself – the 'pneuma', that is –, is what creates energy in the empty space.

The commentary which follows becomes still more theological. Weitmeier calls attention to a discovery made by the French artist: the spiritual is not opposed to the material, nor the spirit to the body. On the contrary, the spiritual seeks to deepen the material, in the degree in which it internally traverses it to make it another reality, proclaimer of a new world:

> If the 'blue period' depended on the Western conception of a spiritualization of the body, with his 'pneumatic period' Yves Klein took the opposite path, that of the incarnation of the spirit as it manifests itself in real, everyday life.[18]

Now that is exactly what a biblical theology of the Holy Spirit says, but through the mediation of Christ incarnate, which implies at one and the same time an acceptance and a transformation of matter, of the body, of the flesh. It remains to understand if there is not something Christic in Klein's artistic act. We could moreover ask whether his *Anthropométries*, the blue traces left on a canvas by blue-painted female bodies, might not symbolize the femininity of the Spirit-*Ruach*.

The second example is more recent and less eccentric. We owe it to the Swiss photographer Olivier Christinat. In his cycle *Apocryphal Photographs*, inspired by metaphorized biblical accounts and figures,[19] we find an intriguing photo entitled *The Offering* (1998).

A simple subject, a rectangular white table on which, at the center, is a bunch of grapes. Why do we have the impression that it is something more than a simple still-life, and that, behind the banal representation, something else is hidden? Surely because the table has no legs (they were erased in a reworking of the photographic negative). It levitates, 'floats' in the air between heaven and earth. All at once this table and grapes evoke another table, other grapes: the communion table and the wine of the Last Supper, offered by God in Christ for gathered humanity. The work could symbolize the presence of the Spirit (the epiclesis) at the 'offering' of bread and wine at the Last Supper (here, the individual grapes). In this photograph there is almost nothing, but at the same time there is everything: the image becomes sign, and the sign symbol, in the sense that it puts in contact with each other contradictory realities: heaven and earth, the visible and the invisible, absence and presence. Confronted with this interpretation, the artist – agnostic but with a biblical culture – did not deny it. Indirectly, therefore, the photo evokes the active presence of the Holy Spirit, who transforms modest realities – bread, grapes, wine, the cup – into a veritable Christic presence.

Contemporary creations in church contexts

I will conclude this discovery of contemporary art's creative capacities in 'representing' (it would be better to say 'staging') the Holy Spirit with three works made for church contexts. Differently from those discussed above, these are not liturgical representations, but in their own way speak of the Holy Spirit in the Church and in the world.

The first realization – an installation – could almost seem shocking (fig. 3). It is an installation by the Belgian artist Fred Eerdekens, *Holy Spirit Come Home* (glass table, packages, lighting, 248 × 125 × 105 cm). It was presented in 2008 in Brussels Cathedral, as part of the exhibition *Septiformis*, organized for the 75th birthday of Cardinal Danneels.[20] In the foreground we see big white letters forming the words 'HOLY SPIRIT', placed on a glass table.

3. Fred Eerdekens, *Holy Spirit Come Home*, installation in the Cathedral of St Michael and St Gudula (Brussels), 2008.

Behind the letters, a pile of food boxes pulled out of the cupboard to provision a kitchen: we make out boxes of corn flakes, pasta, biscuits, etc. What relationship can there be between the word written in the foreground and these piled-up objects? The artist certainly wanted to express above all that the Holy Spirit is a vivifying and creative force which invests the sphere of our most ordinary daily life. The Spirit does not breathe only on the Eucharistic transformation, but on every repast we take, and on the occasion of every meeting. The Holy Spirit is not in the first place a theological concept, but a life-force that makes us live.

Alain Arnould's commentary on the work confirms this theological reading:

> It is however through everyday life [the life of a consumer society] that the light makes legible the letters "Holy Spirit". Light, God's first creation, is the source of life. It makes its way through our habits and our routine to offer us that divine presence and also a design and a hope. Divine light traverses our everyday experience. In sharing our reality, and incarnating itself in it, it projects life in our reality. That vivifying and creative force receives the name of Holy Spirit… which is written on the ground we tread and on the floor of the cathedral where men and women come to meet God.[21]

The entire exhibit, moreover, was placed under the authority of the Holy Creator Spirit, by its title and by the text of Rabanus Maurus (776–856) that introduced it: "You are the Spirit of the seven gifts, the Father's finger, the Spirit of truth promised by the Father, it is you who inspire our words".[22] 'Words' which can take the form of objects, of three-dimensional creations, of artistic realizations.

The second artist, Sylvie Tschiember, realised an installation/performance as part of the collective exhibition 'The Breath, the Spirit', which brought artists together at the Protestant Theology Institute of Paris in May 2016.

We see a black square (70 × 70 cm) hung on a wall, on which a text in white letters is written in a circle. Below, placed on the ground, is a heap of feathers. These feathers are not static. They fly, fly away, being stirred up by an

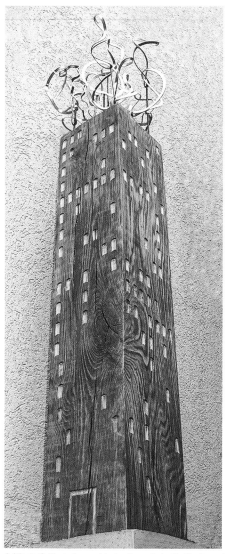

4. Marie Odile Lafosse-Marin, *From Babel to Pentecost*, private property of the artist.

invisible hair dryer which, blowing air, transforms the pile of feathers into a rising rain of feathers, which twist and turn before the black square. The installation at that point became performance. Let us listen to what the artist wanted to say about her work:

> I work on the hidden-revealed and every time the Word is hidden, torn apart, confused, crossed out, indecipherable. The figure of a

circle in a square: the *circle*, symbol of water, in the *square*, a symbol of the Earth, is the dynamic image of a dialectic between the heavenly transcendent to which man naturally aspires, and the earthly context in which he is presently situated. The circle combined with the square evokes movement, change. The *feather* has a symbolic role, and means writing. In numerous symbolic systems based on the theory of the four elements (earth, air, water, fire), the feather is linked to air, or to breath, which in turn is the symbol of life. The feather is the symbol of the divine word's expression delivered by writing.[23]

More theologically, we could understand Tschiember's installation/performance as a metaphor of the central theological idea that Scripture – the written word of the Bible – becomes the Word of God thanks to the action of the Holy Spirit, symbolized by the feathers rising in flight. A sort of visual translation of Paul's phrase, "The letter kills, but the Spirit gives life" (2 Co 3:6).

The last work I will present is a sculpture by Marie Odile Lafosse-Marin, entitled *From Babel to Pentecost* (2007: fig. 4), exhibited on various occasions and in different places. The artist – who is also a former student of the Institut Supérieur de Théologie des Arts (ISTA) of the Institut Catholique of Paris – connects the biblical theme of the gift of the Spirit with the day of Pentecost, interpreting it however in light of the Babel story (Gn 11:1–9). Her combination of the two accounts – of Babel and Pentecost – is completely coherent with

the exegesis of the Pentecost text, which offers itself as an inverted version of the Babel story. In effect, where in Genesis 11:7 God brings it about that human beings speak different languages and no longer understand each other, in Acts 2:7–8 and 11 God's Spirit allows them to communicate and comprehend one another despite their different and unknown languages. Our artist has symbolized Babel with a tower – an oak beam – which can also be seen as a modern dwelling, a skyscraper, on which are curved copper forms soldered to twelve elements in reinforced concrete. The copper forms symbolize the flames of the spirit in the Pentecost account. We have a minimalist sculpture – more a sign than a representation – which conjugates pairs of contraries: fire and matter, curved lines and straight, the weight of the beam and the lightness of the iron shafts, God (the Spirit) and the Human, ascending movement and descending movement.

In conclusion, despite the paucity of illustrations[24] I have tried to show the potential of contemporary art and its capacity to treat the theme of the Spirit from a point of view that is not only philosophical but also biblical. Indeed, there is more than mere analogy between the Holy Spirit's capacity to create new things, and artists' ability to create art works that break free of aesthetic rules and traditional iconography. Art works can be – at one and the same time or separately, according to how we read the situation – the fruit of artistic genius, the work of the Holy Spirit, or the testimony of convictions rooted in faith. ■

1 This is what emerges from the images of the Trinity analyzed from the point of view of their iconography by François Boespflug, *Dieu et ses images. Une histoire de l'Éternel dans l'art*, Montrouge, 2008, pp. 197–242, (chap. VII, 'Les Trinités européennes'). See also *Trinity and Salvation. Theological, Spiritual and Aesthetic Perspectives*, edited by Declan Marmion and Gesa Theissen, Oxford–Bern–Berlin–Brussels, 2009.

2 29 occurrences in the Old Testament.

3 350 occurrences in the New Testament.

4 Max Alain Chevallier, *Souffle de Dieu. Le Saint-Esprit dans le Nouveau Testament*, Paris, 1978 (I), 1990 (II; the first volume includes an important section on the Holy Spirit in the Old Testament, pp. 19–82). For a more systematic approach, see Pierre Gisel, *La subversion de l'Esprit. Réflexion théologique sur l'accomplissement de l'homme*, Geneva, 1993.

5 Gerd Theissen, *Psychologie des premiers chrétiens: héritages et ruptures*, Geneva, 2011, pp. 53–118.

6   Ibid., p. 102.

7   This perspective has been underlined especially by the reformer John Calvin.

8   Adrian Frutiger, *Freie Formen – Formes libres – Free Forms*, Bern, 2013, p. 207.

9   Marie-Luise Frey, *Sechs-Farben-Projekt*, Darmstadt, 2010.

10   This was the proposition of an article in the journal *Arts Sacrés*, no. 36, 2017, pp. 48–87.

11   Naomi Wray, *Frank Wesley. Exploring Faith with a Brush*, Auckland, 1993, pp. 122–3.

12   Alfred Manessier was one of the best-known French artists of the second half of the 20th century. He represented France in the 31st edition of the Venice Biennale in 1962.

13   Adrian Frutiger created an internationally known typography: the characters Univers and Frutiger, as well as numerous systems of signs (among which those in the Paris metro and at Charles De Gaulle airport). Several schools in Germanic and English-speaking countries bear his name.

14   Frank Wesley worked and lived in India, Japan, the USA and in Australia. He was chosen by his country to design the urn which contains the ashes of Mahatma Gandhi.

15   Wassily Kandinsky, *Über das Geistige in der Kunst: insbesondere in der Malerei*, München, 1912.

16   Ibid., p. 9.

17   Hannah Weitemeier, *Yves Klein, 1928-1962. International Klein Blue*, Koln, 2002, pp. 34, 39.

18   Ibid., p. 33.

19   Olivier Christinat, *Photographies apocryphes*, Paris, 2000.

20   *SeptiFORMIS-Ars in Cathedrali*, exhibition catalogue (Brussels, Cathédrale St-Michel-et-Gudule, 2008), edited by Alain Arnould and Mark Delrue, Halewijn, 2008, p. 34.

21   Ibid.

22   Ibid.

23   A commentary written by the artist and addressed to Jérôme Cottin.

24   The oral communication in the context of the conference was accompanied by a PowerPoint presentation. The reader will find many of the works mentioned here in Internet.

Georges Braque: From Palette to Bird

MARTINE SAUTORY

Relentlessly we run after our destiny,
Sensation. Revelation
Georges Braque[1]

Georges Braque, an avant-garde painter of the beginning of the 20th century, born in 1882, is as well known for his invention of cubism, together with the solar Picasso in 1908, as he is for his multiple and magnificent representations of the bird. The main theme of his last years, the bird which Braque considered "a kind of résumé of his art",[2] traverses, accompanies, flies over, illuminates and penetrates his works[3] in an obsessive way.

A rapid inventory gives a first idea of the breadth of this motif and the way it impregnates Braque's entire œuvre: five wall decorations, one a stained glass window; seven plaster casts; two sculptures and a vase; four Ligugé enamels; plus thirty canvases with their preparatory works (the incomplete *catalogue raisonné* of Braque's painted works[4] does not allow us to finish the inventory), but above all more than one hundred and forty graphic works in every technique: etchings, lithographs, prints, water colors and drawings used to illustrate twenty some odd collections of poems, without counting his mosaics, jewelry and unfinished projects.

Already present some fifteen years before the artist's death in 1963, the bird occupies a place

at one and the same time central and subliminal in Braque's œuvre: "central [we have seen] for the proliferation and diversity of its representations"; "subliminal for the powerful symbolic reverberation which it carries with itself, even when Braque refused every notion of symbol".[5]

The bird of the gods – born of a gesture

The bird makes its true entry[6] in the painter's iconographic repertory during his preparatory work for the illustration of Hesiod's *Theogony*, a subject that Braque proposed to his dealer, Ambroise Vollard, who in 1931 asked him for engravings for a book.

The artist's source of inspiration, the beach at Varengeville-sur-Mer (Seine-Maritime), where Braque lived in the summer, became the cradle of a new mythology. Through this account devoted to the birth of the universe and the origin of the gods, Braque re-established a bond with archaic Greek art and Etruscan art, of which he was particularly fond.

In dialogue with the monumental cliffs, a new Olympus, Braque carved bits of chalk he took from the beach and reinterpreted, on bits of plaster and smoke-blackened reinforced cement,[7] figures of the ancient gods. It is with

Zelos[8] or *Héraclès*[9] that the birds appear, born of a gouging movement with the point of his knife, their features supple and fluid. Perched on the god's hand, the bird is a privileged interlocutor, winged ally of the mythological divinity.

Vollard's project was not completed, interrupted by the dealer's death. Only in 1955 would it be taken up again by Aimé Maeght, Braque's gallery dealer and editor.

The geometric bird: from serpent to bird

In counterpoint with the nicely rounded bird we must also mention the presence of the *geometric bird*,[10] "inspired by the decoration of a Boeotian bowl in the Louvre museum".[11]

Given to the painter as a model by *Le modèle*[12] itself, this planar bird, *the geometric bird*, turns out to be the development of a straight line between two points, which then is curved before becoming a bird. Represented in this way, these schematic forms suggest a symbolic passage from serpent to bird in which their symbols of the heavenly and earthly world[13] speak to each other. The poet Saint-John Perse,[14] author of the treatise *L'ordre des oiseaux* which Braque illustrated when he was eighty-four years old, doubtlessly intuited that primordial purity when he wrote: "[The birds] preserve in our midst something of the dream of creation".[15]

Braque would regularly repeat the motif of the symbolic bird, at once skeleton and cage,[16] even in the jewelry he made in the evening of his life.[17]

The emergence of the bird –
And everything becomes bird

On his return from the First World War, in which he had been wounded, Braque would abandon with the cubist style that had distinguished him from his contemporaries to devote himself to still-life subjects, progessively eschewing the living model to the point of abandoning it.

Often Braque's canvases portray sideboards, pedestal tables, tables laden with ready-to-hand objects, since for him "if a still life is not within arm's reach, it seems no longer to be a still life and to move me".[18] It is through these objects arranged in an organized jumble that the bird

reappears and durably impregnates the artist's iconographic vocabulary.[19] "In any case, we knew Braque's bird long before it was recognized and described as such", writes art critic Pierre Descargues. "We saw its long neck as a bottle,[20] or the sleeve of a mandolin.[21] The body hollowed out for the beginning of the wing".[22] Everything becomes the beginning of a wing or of a bird.

The bird: 'metaphor of the palette with inspired wings'

A particular object made its way into Braque's numerous representations of interiors: the palette, a creative instrument indispensable to the painter, who puts his paint on it and mixes his colors. The artist's first space, where all his options are concentrated, beneath his brush the palette is by turns ordered and disordered. Traversed by his finger, it prolongs his hand and becomes a limb to the point of extending the painter's self.

In front of the model in *The Painter and His Model*,[23] the palette belongs to the shadow. Like every painter, Braque maintained a close relationship with his palette, even if he reached the point of preferring paint-pots in order to avoid mixing colors, as we can see in the photograph where Braque in a velvet outfit, with an elegant palette in his hand, corrects the large canvas of his decoration for the Louvre.[24]

Poised like a bird in the branches of a palette tree[25] "made into a house", in Braque's canvases it is sometimes square, sometimes round, left on the table in *Studio with a Black Vase*,[26] then shorter, reduced to a measuring instrument under a draughtman's square in *Still Life and the Palette*, 1939, abandoned near the stove in *The Stove*,[27] bicolor and traversed by long brushes on the edge of a table ready to fall off in the *Large Interior With Palette*.[28]

Slowly we see Braque's palette, which opens to a new space, a space of creation and of flight, fly off and never again stop flapping its wings. A progressive development, this slippage of the palette toward the bird, which the art historian Jean Leymarie called a "metaphor of the palette with inspired wings",[29] draws us into an imaginary world where the bird-palette, bird-reflection, becomes – more than a bird – a mirror of unconscious answers.

The founder bird: the rose colored bird of *The Atelier* (1939)

In this period of maturation, a picture of 1939, *The Atelier*,[30] reveals the particular bond uniting palette, painter and the bird. This scene, from which the painter is absent, although represented by the stool, emphasizes the dialogue between the airy palette poised on the table and the rose-colored bird emerging from its frame. In that *mise en abyme*, the bird remains in place while the painter has flown off. Jean Leymarie,[31] once again, sees in this bird "born of painting"[32] the appearance of Braque's founder bird, ten years before the artist would return to the theme.

The Bird, Phantom of the Atelier – The bird of the *Ateliers*

The construction of Braque's large workshop at Varengeville[33] allowed the artist to undertake the very personal work of his series *Ateliers I à IX*, from which between 1949 and 1956 would get eight large canvases (Atelier VII does not exist). He saw this series as "a homage to the mystery of artistic creation".[34]

The autobiographical series[35] presents identifiable objects among ambiguous forms, poetically mixed together in spaces which let themselves be crossed by phantomatic figures of majestic birds, long cranes that seem to rise from the shadow.

In *Atelier V*,[36] the palette and the bird respond to each other. In the foreground, the palette, like a mirror, reflects the objects and the sky. Above, the bird, striped with vertical rays, stretches out, pushing back the shadows projected by the prefabricated structure of the atelier, which the painter's imagination has easily transformed into a cage. Braque will later recognize that this exercise was difficult, "for the objects suddenly began to live their own life, each different from the others",[37] but the bird who magnifies the space, with his pacifying presence also harmonizes it and gives it air. Breaking out of pictorial confinement, the bird opens the painting to an elsewhere.

The surprise of song

While the realization of this work was a vital liberation for Braque, whose creative progress now passed from impregnation to a hallucination which could reach the level of obsession,[38] it was not for all that a foregone conclusion. For "the painter, who, according to Braque, thinks in form and colors",[39] in painterliness, there was also the literary surprise of drawing.

So it is that he was astonished to see the white bird of *Atelier VI*[40] come and perch naturally on top of an easel. Upright like his later *Ibis*,[41] the sacred bird of the Egyptians executed in bronze during the Second World War, this white bird illuminates the canvas. To the poet André Verdet, who asked him if it "doesn't monopolize the attention … being so very true", Braque answered: "But it is the shock of song … I want everything to irradiate from this bird … First one sees only him … then the gaze broadens to take in his light …The song of his light innundates the picture. The picture ends up becoming song".[42] Braque, first witness of the bird's appearing in his picture, was preceded by the work he was putting together. His dispossession[43] allowed him to be astonished by the surprise and kenotic dimension of the future, and allowed the heightened light around the bird to resound with another dimension. It becomes a song of creation whose symbolic power, like a bullet, breaks out of the picture space and reorganizes the painter's universe with its musicality.

Atelier IX: coming out of the Atelier

In the last picture of the series, *Atelier IX*,[44] the bird, burst into pieces, escapes from the atelier.

Inhabiting the space of heaven – the Louvre ceiling

We find it again on the ceiling of the biggest French museum, where it truly takes flight. This decoration commissioned of Braque when he was seventy years old revealed his interest in the bird to a numerous public and at the same time gave him the chance to leave a testimonial accessible to all.[45]

At the Louvre Braque had to find his place amid the heavy gold decorations of the Etruscan room.[46] His large black birds[47] with white rings close the space of the ceiling, opening it to a sky the color of the night. Beyond doubt it was that particular situation that gave the artist the possibility to effectively translate his search for a new space – the space which he had felt coming since his cubist period, when he had rejected Euclidian space and every notion of perspective. Without earthly points of reference, his birds dance in the sky. Created to be united, they rise in order to better separate from each other, vying in a certain "tension which gives life"[48] to the work.

Asked about his interest in the bird, Braque, in interviews with journalists, often recalled his visit to an ornithological reserve in May in 1955.

> A few weeks ago I was in the Camargue.[49] Above the ponds I saw large birds pass. From that vision I drew airy forms. The birds inspired me, and I tried to extract the best profit for my drawing and painting. Yet I had to bury the memory of their natural function as birds … in order to approach what essentially interests me: the construction of a pictorial reality.[50]

Recounted two years after his realization of the Louvre ceiling, that experience sounds all the more like a justification for his fascination with the bird rather than as a genuine discovery.

The bird, a universal figure of space

Alone,[51] with a companion[52] or in squadron,[53] "Braque's succinct bird is hardly a mere motif",[54] as Saint-John Perse wrote. It is made to fly and to travel. The bird discovers shadow, night, the forest; it traverses the clouds and plays with the stars. Intent upon its destination, it is also "the bow and the arrow of flight";[55] running toward the sun, it "stabs the sky",[56] as Braque said, citing Reverdy. Ever in flight, Braque's bird has lost its materiality. It is universal and does not belong to any identifiable species. "People imagine that every bird should be a dove",[57] Braque noted. A spontaneous spurt of creation, it is not symbolic,[58] it is "inallusive … and innocent … of any memory",[59] the poet says. Ever in movement, it is nonetheless always immobile. Belonging to

heaven and earth, the bird is a "pretext for painting the space"[60] it inhabits and a response to the artist's deepest "spiritual aspirations".[61]

Two major works in a flurry of wings, and the bird and his nest

Among these various experiences, two pictures that still fascinate us today are echoes of each other: *The Flurry of Wings*,[62] reworked by the artist until 1961, and *The Bird and Its Nest*.[63]

The flurry of wings

Two-toned on a pale blue background, an "aerodynamic bird hits the black target with his flight".[64] John Richardson, an English journalist and art historian, says:

> I will always remember seeing Braque paint *The Flurry of Wings*. During days and weeks he kept adding greyish, liquid paint, coat after coat, until the canvas was so encrusted with pigment that one could barely put it on or take it off the easel. The result is a sky that has an astonishing cumulus quality and seems more tangible than the bird – a typical Braque paradox.[65]

The Flurry of Wings, a transcendent canvas, comes back to earth thanks to the weight of its pigment, a mixture of oil and sand.[66] It was finished only in 1961.[67] Braque explained to the poet and journalist André Verdet:

> It was finished, as harmonious as I could want. After four months of observing it every day, of living it, I realized it had become too much a matter of habit. A great comfort for my eye. I decided therefore to create a rupture, painting another bird [the duck] in the picture's lower left … At times one needs these effects of surprise. They prevents routine from setting in…[68]

A feeling of the infinite and of eternity seems to hover in the canvas. Never will the bird reach the target. One of Braque's aphorisms, "Relentlessly we run after our destiny", followed by the two juxtaposed words, "Sensation. Revelation"[69] – two faces of the same coin –, seems to translate the inaccessible quest for truth of the painter standing before his easel. But also the unattainable goal toward which all of us are tending.

The Bird and Its Nest has been defined "the résumé of his art"[70]

> The testimony of Mariette Lachaud [his faithful assistant] allows us to situate the beginning of the picture's execution on Easter morning 1955, when Braque laid the work out on the basis of a preliminary study. He would finish it in three months, and liked it so much that he chose it to represent him at the Brussels Exposition Universelle … he would keep it until his death, carrying it [on the roof of his car] in his transferrals between Varengeville and Paris.[71]

It was placed above a sideboard.[72]

> Braque, Marcelle [his wife] and Mariette sat in front of the fire and looked at the painting as people look at a television. Mariette never saw the master express more joy than when he was communing with this picture.[73]

The vegetation is dead but the nest is fecundated by Easter eggs, the promise of a future life. Life is born again from an animal.

> "And since he considered the great bird as the résumé of his art", as the artist told Liberman, who visited him in his studio, Braque obstinately refused to sell it. "It is endowed with a hypnotic power", Liberman said. And Braque quickly added: "That's exactly so. One believes one can hear the beat of the wings.[74]

At the end of his life, Braque would often return to this particular way of depicting the great motif of the bird – to the precise formal and thematic relationship of the animal and its nest, that is. After a long journey, the bird came back to earth and found shelter in a new space: the vegetation. That is how it dies in the crepuscular light of Braque's last stained glass window, *White Bird on a Violet Backdrop*,[75] of 1962, at the Fondation Marguerite et Aimé Maeght at Saint-Paul-de-Vence.

The bird, witness of a metamorphosis

As we have seen, the bird, a true point of crystallization, was reworked by Braque in every sense. Its almost obsessive multiplication in his œuvre comes to signify something of the force of a bird which is not a drawing of a bird. It comes to touch something very deep, disclosing the bird's *totalizing* presence. Laying hold of the bird was, for Braque, a way of perpetuating the industrious bird in himself and in his palette: the bird "who, invisible, has never ceased to watch over its nest where straw and grain, bark and musk have been amassed".[76] "It is not a theme which he served, developed. The bird is an element of a larger way of saying the world: the form most laden with meaning, with the greatest concentration of options".[77] Braque let himself be led by the bird much more than he could have led it. He let himself be borne by the breath of inspiration. "The Eternal One makes himself known in the breeze, which [Braque's] bird meets in its flight".[78] ∎

1   Georges Braque, *Cahier* [1956], ed. Paris, 1994, p. 115.

2   Alexander Liberman, *Maîtres et ateliers*, Paris, 1989, p. 122.

3   Braque's works being still subject to ADAGP rights, it is impossible to reproduce them here. The reader is directed to the illustrations in *Georges Braque 1882-1963*, exhibition catalogue (Paris, Grand Palais, 2013–14; Houston, The Museum of Fine Arts, 2014), edited by Brigitte Leal, Paris, 2013.

4   *Catalogue de l'œuvre de Georges Braque*, edited by Nicole Worms de Romilly Mangin, 7 vols., Paris 1959–82.

5   Henry-Claude Cousseau, 'Entre ciel et Terre, les dernières peintures de Braque', in *Georges Braque 2013*, op. cit., pp. 214–49: 217.

6   As Braque himself says, the bird is present in his work as early as 1910, integrated in still life paintings that have certainly been destroyed. See Jean Leymarie, 'Georges Braque, L'Oiseau et son nid', *Quadrum*, no. 5 (1958), pp. 72–3.

7   See Georges-Paul Collet, *Correspondance Jacques-Emile Blanche - Maurice Denis (1901-1939)*, Geneva, 1989, p. 246.

8   *Zelos*, 1931, Saint-Paul-de-Vence, collection Adrien Maeght, in *Georges Braque 2013*, p. 163.

9   *Héraclès*, 1931, Saint-Paul-de-Vence, Fondation Marguerite et Aimé Maeght, photo *Georges Braque 2013*, p. 164.

10 See Mariette Lachaud, *Dessins et reliefs photographiés dans l'atelier de Georges Braque à Varengeville-sur-Mer*, 1939, photograph, Paris, Centre Pompidou, Musée national d'art moderne (MNAM), Bibliothèque Kandinsky, in *Georges Braque 2013*, p. 159.

11 Sophie Bowness, 'La Théogonie et les muses de Braque dans les années 1930', in *Braque-Laurens, un dialogue. Autour des collections du Centre Pompidou, Musée National d'Art Moderne et du Musée des Beaux-Arts de Lyon*, exhibition catalogue (Lyon, Musée des Beaux-Arts, 2005–6), edited by Isabelle Monod-Fontaine and Sylvie Lecoq-Ramond, Paris, 2005, pp. 36–46. On the collections of the Centre Georges Pompidou, Musée national d'Art Moderne, and of the Musée des Beaux-Arts de Lyon, see the abovementioned exhibition catalogue, also cited by Cousseau 2013, op. cit., p. 217.

12 See <http://www.christies.com/lotfinder/Lot/georges-braque-1882-1963-le-modele-5790366-details.aspx>, accessed 30th May 2019.

13 See *Dictionnaire des symboles. Mythes, rêves, coutumes, gestes, formes, figures, couleurs, nombres*, edited by Jean Chevalier and Alain Gheerbrant, Paris, 1969, p. 695.

14 Saint-John Perse makes a magnificent contribution to this theme with thirteen poems, the manuscript of which was the subject of an exhibit with Braque's engravings at the Bibliothèque nationale de Paris: *L'Ordre des oiseaux, Saint-John Perse, Georges Braque*, from 17 December 1962 to 17 January 1963.

15 Saint-John Perse, *Oiseaux*, Paris, 1963, p. 34.

16 Id. Preceding photo, in *Georges Braque 2013*, p. 158.

17 See photo: <http://www.oab.fr/Georges-BRAQUE/asteria.htm>, accessed 30th May 2019.

18 Jacques Lassaigne, 'Un entretien avec Georges Braque', *Vingtième siècle*, 41 (1973), pp. 3–9: 6.

19 See photos in *Georges Braque 2013*, pp. 132–3.

20 See *La nappe rose*, 1933.

21 See *Nature morte à la mandoline*, 1938, Coll. M. et Mme Leigh B. Block (I am uncertain whether the painting still belongs to this collection) and *Nature morte à la nappe rouge*, 1934, coll. part., photo *Georges Braque 2013*, p. 170.

22 Pierre Descargues, 'Georges Braque en un tableau', *Plaisir de France*, November 1973, no pag.

23 *The Painter and His Model*, 1939, New York, collection Mr. Walter P. Chrysler (I am uncertain if the work is still in this collection).

24 See photo, Studio Routhier, 1953, *Georges Braque 2013*, p. 289.

25 See photo, Archives Laurens in Alex Danchev, *Georges Braque le défi silencieux*, Paris, 2013, p. 185.

26 *Studio with a Black Vase*, 1938, Washington D.C., The Kreeger Museum, see photo: <https://www.kreegermuseum.org/about-us/collection/painting/Georges-Braque_Studio-with-Black-Vase-Latelier-au-vase-noir>, accessed 30th May 2019.

27 *The Stove*, 1942–3, New Haven, Yale University Art Gallery, in *Georges Braque 2013*, p. 194.

28 *Large Interior with Palette*, 1942, Houston, The Menil Collection, photo *Georges Braque 2013*, p. 190.

29 Jean Leymarie, *Georges Braque. L'Oiseau et son nid*, Bruxelles–München, 1958, p. 72.

30 New York, Metropolitan Museum, see photo <http://www.metmuseum.org/art/collection/search/486270>, accessed 30th May 2019.

31 Jean Leymarie, *Braque*, Geneva, 1961, p. 91.

32 *Œuvres de Georges Braque (1882-1963)*, exhibition catalogue (Paris, Centre Georges Pompidou, 1982), edited by Nadine Pouillon, Paris, 1982, p. 151.

33 See photo *Georges Braque 2013*, p. 282.

34 Ibid., p. 153.

35 See *Atelier II*, 1949, private collection, and *Atelier IV*, 1949, photos *Georges Braque 2013*, pp. 224 and 226.

36 1949, New York, The Museum of Modern Art, photo *Georges Braque 2013*, p. 227.

37 André Verdet, *Entretiens. Notes et écrits sur la peinture. Braque, Léger, Matisse, Picasso*, Paris, 1978, pp. 13–14.

38 "Si je devais chercher à voir quel est le chemin de mes tableaux, je dirais qu'il y a d'abord imprégnation suivie d'une hallucination – le mot ne me plaît pas, mais il touche la vérité – qui devient à son tour une obsession et pour se libérer de l'obsession, il faut faire

le tableau sans ça on ne peut pas vivre…", words of the artist collected by Dora Vallier, 'Braque, la peinture et nous', *Cahiers d'Art*, 29 (1954), pp. 13–24: 24.

39 Ibid., p. 19.

40 1950–1, Saint-Paul-de-Vence, Fondation Marguerite et Aimé Maeght, photo *Georges Braque* 2013, p. 228.

41 1942–3, Paris, Centre Georges Pompidou, MNAM, photo *Georges Braque* 2013, p. 174. *Ibis* is part of a bronze bestiary with motives taken from Antiquity. It joins the horse and the fish.

42 André Verdet, 'Avec Georges Braque', *Vingtième siècle*, supplement 18 (1962), p. 22.

43 Deborah Jenner, 'Sagesses orientales', in *Traces du sacré*, exhibition catalogue (Paris, Centre Georges Pompidou, 2008), edited by Mark Alizart, Paris, 2008, pp. 385–7: 386: "As Daisetz Teitaro Suzuki [in *Essays in zen Buddhism*] remarks, 'If a logical pattern or a thought slides between the brush and the paper, the whole effect is lost'" ("Comme le fait remarquer Daisetz Teitaro Suzuki [dans Essays in zen Buddhism], 'si une logique ou une pensée vient se glisser entre le pinceau et le papier, tout l'eff et est perdu'").

44 1952–6, Paris, Centre Georges Pompidou, MNAM, photo *Georges Braque* 2013, p. 230.

45 See photos *Georges Braque* 2013, pp. 218–19.

46 Photo: <http://www.panoramadelart.com/georges-braque-les-oiseaux>, accessed 30th May 2019.

47 Of which "an etching for a text of René Char, … is the prototype": Danchev 2013, op. cit., p. 244.

48 "Tension qui, précisément est entretenue par le conflit de l'idée poursuivie et du tableau qui s'affirme. Je crois que c'est cette tension qui donne la vie au tableau. Héraclite parle de "la tension de la lyre". Pour qu'une corde vibre, il faut qu'elle soit tendue. En peinture, c'est la même chose. Il faut arriver à une certaine tension. Si le tableau s'accomplissait sans résistance, il serait sans portée", sayings of Georges Braque collected by Georges Charbonnier, Interview, 'Georges Braque parle: Le talent sert à masquer les choses …', *L'Express*, 2 July 1959, p. 32, reprinted in Georges Charbonnier, *Le monologue du peintre*, Neuilly-sur-Seine, 1980, pp. 25–6.

49 "Par une journée grise de mai 1955, [Braque] visite la Tour du Valat, station ornithologique dirigée par son ami Lukas Hoffmann, fils et héritier de la fortune des Hoffmann-Laroche, mécènes de Braque depuis longtemps", Danchev 2013, op. cit., p. 240.

50 André Verdet, *Georges Braque*, Geneva, 1956, p. 10.

51 See Guillaume Apollinaire, *Si je mourais là-bas*, Paris, 1962, illustrated by Georges Braque. See *Georges Braque* 2013, p. 95.

52 See *Les oiseaux noirs*, 1956–7, Saint-Paul-de-Vence, coll. Adrien Maeght, photo *Georges Braque* 2013, p. 240.

53 See *Le billard*, 1947–9, Caracas, Museo de Arte Contemporaneo, <http://mac.fmn.gob.ve/node/459>,

accessed 30th May 2019, and Studio Lipnitski, *Georges Braque dans son atelier*, photo *Georges Braque* 2013, p. 198.

54 Perse 1963, op. cit., p. 152.

55 Ibid., p. 160: "Pour l'oiseau … quel privilège déjà, sur la page du ciel, d'être à soi-même, l'arc et la flèche du vol! Le thème et le propos!" See *Les oiseaux*, 1954–62, Belfort, Musées de Belfort, photo *Georges Braque* 2013, p. 236.

56 Pierre Reverdy: "Une hirondelle poignarde le ciel", quoted by Alex Danchev, in Danchev 2013, op. cit., p. 242.

57 Ibid., p. 240. Of course we think of Picasso's *Colombe de la paix* but also of Max Ernst's nightmare birds.

58 One can nonetheless question the symbolism of the crane often used by Braque. The crane is the immortal bird of Taoism.

59 In the plural in the texts, see Perse 1963, op. cit., p. 161.

60 "But merely another pretext for painting space": John Richardson, *Georges Braque*, Harmondsworth, 1959, p. 29.

61 Cousseau 2013, op. cit., p. 217, note 9, p. 302. See Marielle Tabart, 'Brancusi et l'oiseau', in *Traces du sacré* 2008, op. cit., pp. 156–8: 156, retaken and developed in *Constantin Brancusi, l'esprit de l'oiseau* (château de Fontainebleau, festival d'histoire de l'art, 10th edition, 2012), extracted from *Midi*, 30 (2012). We also think of Gaston Bachelard and his *Poétique de l'espace* (1957).

62 1956–61, Paris, Centre Georges Pompidou, MNAM, photo *Georges Braque* 2013, p. 241.

63 1955, Paris, Centre Georges Pompidou, MNAM, photo *Georges Braque* 2013, p. 235.

64 Verdet 1956, op. cit., p. 8.

65 Cited by Léonard Gianadda in his preface to *Georges Braque*, exhibition catalogue (Fondation Pierre Gianadda, Martigny, 1992), edited by Jean-Louis Prat, Martigny, 1992, p. 27.

66 "Une présence, un poids de réalité presque hallucinants. Braque y travaille des mois, entasse des kilos de peinture. Mariette [Lachaud, sa fidèle assistante] en descendant: 'N'est-ce pas? C'est trop. C'est presque insoutenable'", Jean Bazaine, 'Braque: Un enrichissement de l'espace', *La Cité*, no. 19 (1964), p. 52.

67 The canvas was presented in the exhibition *L'Atelier de Braque* at the Louvre, 15th November 1961, extended to 26 February 1962.

68 Verdet 1962, op. cit., pp. 21–2, reprinted in Verdet 1978, op. cit., p. 13.

69 *Georges Braque* 2013, op. cit., p. 115.

70 Liberman 1989, op. cit., p. 122.

71 *Braque, Œuvres* 1982, op. cit., p. 142.

72 See photo by Mariette Lachaud, *L'oiseau et son nid (1955) dans la salle à manger de Braque à Varengeville*, after 1955. Silver gelatine proof. Archives Quentin Laurens, *Georges Braque* 2013, p. 292.

73   Danchev 2013, op. cit., p. 240.

74   Liberman 1989, op. cit., p. 122.

75   See photo: <http://www.fondation-maeght.com/fr/collection/morceaux-choisis/3/georges-braque>, accessed 30th May 2019.

76   Gaëtan Picon, cited in the unsigned text in [certainly by Marius David]: "C'était en septembre 1963, Varengeville, en présence de nombreuses personnalités dont Malraux, a fait à Braque d'émouvantes funérailles", reprinted in *Connaissance de Dieppe et de sa région*, 81 (1991), p. 4; 1st ed. of *Paris-Normandie* or *Informations Dieppoises* (date uncertain), September 1963.

77   Pierre Descargues, *Georges Braque 1973*, op. cit., no pag.

78   Marie-Madeleine Davy, *L'Oiseau et sa symbolique* [1992], in Ead., *La nature et sa symbolique*, [posthoumous ed.], Paris, 2015, p. 50.

Flight in the Art
of Constantin Brâncuşi

MARIELLE BESANÇON, MARTINE GRENIER

Why write about my sculptures?
Why not simply show their photos?
Constantin Brâncuşi

These few words of Constantin Brâncuşi express his confidence in the revelatory power of photography, and urge us to use it to approach his *oeuvre*. Photography became an early companion of his work, but, not recognizing his sculptures in photographs made by others, Brâncuşi decided to become their sole photographer. In the 1920s he invested in good equipment and built a dark room in his studio. Today more than five hundred negatives and a thousand two hundred prints survive, revealing the artist's way of looking at his own work. They make clear what interested him and what he sought to do as a sculptor.

"In all my life I have sought only the essence of flight", he said.[1] He sought how, from the heaviness of sculpted, cut or sometimes cast matter, to render palpable the ascensional dynamic of flight leading from the ground toward the infinite, the spiritual.

That way of imagining was inspired by his ancestral origins. Constantin Brâncuşi was born in 1876 in Rumenia, in a village in the Carpathians, in the heart of a rural and archaic world. He left his family early to learn sculpture at the School of Arts and Crafts of Cracow, then at the Fine Arts School of Bucharest. After long wanderings, in good part on foot, he arrived in Paris in July of 1904, where he pursued his formation at the École des Beaux-Arts. A strong personality, he worked very briefly for Rodin, from whom he would always seek to distinguish himself, for, according to him: "Nothing grows in the shadow of big trees".[2]

In view of this ensemble of elements, in order to explore the dream of flight which Brâncuşi's whole œuvre implies, we have chosen to base our essay on ten photographs, all taken by him.[3]

Self-Portrait in his studio[4] (1933–4)

Brâncuşi invites us to enter his studio in Impasse Ronsin in the 15th Arrondissement (fig. 1). The sculptor, with the release mechanism in hand, occupies the stage in the bright, luminous space; above his head, completely centered, rises one of his *Endless Columns*.

Beginning in the 1920s, his studio became the place where he presented his work, a complete work of art in itself which he ceaselessly renewed. In effect, Brâncuşi modified the arrangement of his works almost daily, and photography allowed him to render these ephemeral *mises-en-scène* perennial. Passionately interested in his works' relation to space in the continually changing sunlight, he made his studio a living and coherent world, the microcosm of his universe.

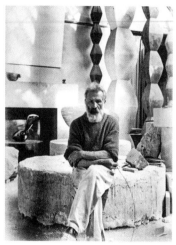

1. Constantin Brâncuşi, *Self-Portrait in his studio*, c. 1933–4.

Bird in Space in white marble[5] (1923)

This is his first bird called 'in space' (fig. 2). Installed on a base, its pure form gushes vertically from a pyramidal chaos. This photograph shows Brâncuşi's passion for elevation. He said: "Everything that is in the process of raising itself intoxicates me".[6] In the way it occupies the stage, the bird carved of heavy marble offers itself here as a luminous presence.

Brâncuşi does not try to represent his sculpture. The photographic space offers an environment in which it can hold out, persist; a space to unveil its dynamics. In the play of light, the bird becomes a palpitating flame of life, whose form is projected on the wall in a cast shadow.

On the ground the pile of ugly stones recalls his relationship with matter: marked by the Rumenian wood-cutting tradition, Brâncuşi practiced the direct cut, a technique which particularly differentiated him from Rodin, as did the fact of not claiming for himself the role of creator, but rather of intercessor, able to reveal what he called "the cosmic essence of the material",[7] which can be translated thanks to its deep link to the whole universe.

Wood, marble, stone, plaster, metal – of all these materials he would say: "Every material has its own language, which it is not my aim to suppress and replace with my language. My aim is simply to make the matter say in its own language what I think, what I see".[8]

La Maïastra[9] (1910–12)

This is one of the oldest photos of his first bird, the *Maïastra* (fig. 3). In Rumenian *pasàra maïastra* means magic bird, and *pasàra*, bird, is a feminine noun. Many Rumenian legends make reference to this magic bird. Two in particular inspired Brâncuşi: in the first the *pasàra maïastra* has the double nature of a bird and of a hidden princess, a bird-fairy who guides prince charming through various trials, helping him defeat magic spells with the goal of freeing his true love; the second legend is linked to the Rumenian custom of the *Bird of the soul*: at burials people put on the tomb a sort of funerary pole carved with geometric motifs and surmounted by a wood bird which symbolized the soul of the dead person and had to remain for forty days, the supposed duration of the soul's elevation to heaven. Brâncuşi had moreover decided, before giving the idea up, to install such a bird on top of his *Endless Column* at Târgu Jiu, in as much as it is a funerary monument. Here the *Maïastra* is raised on a

2. Constantin Brâncuşi, *White Marble Bird in Space* (1923), photo by his author.

triple socle, but it is above all the staging which makes it dominate its space. Authoritative, like a totem, it looms over other sculptures, among which two white, ovoid forms, from which it seems to come forth, are particularly evident. It emerges from its somber socle toward a sky which belongs to it.

Brâncuşi realized several *Maïastra* and many other birds of which he would say: "I worked on the enchanted bird from 1909 on and have not yet finished it. I would like to represent imponderability in a concrete form. Enchanted birds have bewitched me and I have never broken free. It is flight which has kept me busy all my life".[10]

The photographic image allowed Brâncuşi to explore in depth the paradox of a sculpture without weight.

The Golden Bird[11] (1919)

Although very close to the greatest photographers of his time, Alfred Stieglitz (1864–1946), Edward Steichen (1879–1976), and Man Ray (1890–1976), Brâncuşi persisted in not following their technical advice. Man Ray attests: "He showed me his photos. They were

3. Constantin Brâncuşi, *Maïastra* (1910–12), photo by his author.

out of focus, over- or under-exposed, streaked or stained. This, he said, was how his works should be reproduced. Perhaps he was right: one of his golden birds had been taken under a ray of sun, so that it irradiated light as if it had a halo, which gave that work an explosive character".[12]

Brâncuşi set himself to polishing his sculptures in search of surface perfection, purity of form. The polishing of bronze in particular changes the appearance of the material, which becomes a mirror. In reflecting the surrounding space, the material appears immaterial, almost transparent. The goal pursued by the sculptor was to let the essence of the material shine through the surface.

"Flight effaces the bird",[13] Bachelard would later write in *L'air et les songes*.

In the photographic act, Brâncuşi succeeded in leaving the last word to light. It is light on his sculpture that creates the event, that engraves it on the sensitive plate. The negatives permit him to capture the metamorphoses which light produces on the polished bronze, with shadows projected on the background. The heavy sculpture transformed into light renders visible that which he said he was seeking in his work: the bird's spark, the essence of flight. Not that of winged flight, but of a direct union with the sun. Brâncuşi willingly cited the mystic Milarepa – a Tibetan buddhist ascetic of the 11th century – of whom it is said that he could move from place to place by splitting a sunbeam.[14]

The yearning for flight which impregnates Brâncuşi's sculpture is apparent in the deep complicity with light which he cultivated – with sunlight, which organizes his universe.

Shadows[15] (1922)

Brâncuşi experimented with, and got around, technical procedures, allowing himself to be taken by surprise by accidental situations, at the phase of the negative or of its development (fig. 4). He welcomed and calculated, as he did when cutting stone, allowing form to take shape in the photographic matter, depending on the light. And thus he let his sculptures get away.

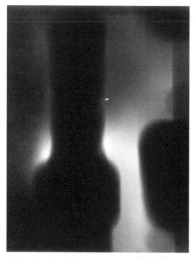

4. Constantin Brâncuşi, shadows (1922), photo by his author.

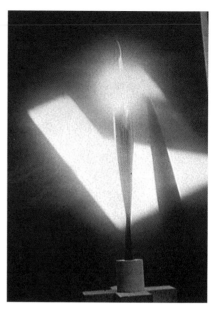

Polished Bronze Bird in Space[16] and *White Marble Bird in Space*[17] (1927)

His photographic compositions are *stagings of his works in light*, often done in series; they offer new life to his sculptures.

It was not a matter of reproducing the bird, but of letting it fly off. "It is not birds that I sculpture, but flight", he said.[18]

The fact of capturing the same work at different moments of the day shows the importance which the artist gave to sunlight and to its impact on his sculpture. We should note that the times of day when he permitted visits to his studio were determined by its greater or lesser sun-lighting in those moments.

These serial shots are similar to cinematographic experiences, his studio becoming at one and the same time a filming location.

The bird's form is stretched in the verticality of ascension, the upper extremity cut in an open angle. About thirty versions of the *Bird in Space* would be realized in marble and bronze.

Through the magical play of light and shade, the staging and illumination of these birds allows them to assume the flight that was Brâncuşi's dream for them.

5a-b. Constantin Brâncuşi, *Polished Bronze Bird in Space* (1927), photos by his author.

Black Marble Bird in Space[19] (1936)

Mixing matter, form and light, he tried to produce 'a pure impulse'. The bond tying the bird to earth – the socle – is so tenuous that it seems ready to yield to the impulse of the luminous spark that rises in the black marble (fig. 6). This

6. Constantin Brâncuşi, *Black Marble Bird in Space* (1936), photo by his author.

7. Constantin Brâncuşi, *White Marble Bird in Space* (1927), photo by his author.

8. Constantin Brâncuşi, *White Marble Bird in Space* (1936), photo by his author.

Bird in Space seems worked by the blacksmith's fire. Brâncuşi in fact forged his own tools in his studio.

White Marble Bird in Space[20] (1936)

In this photograph (fig. 7), Brâncuşi's art has worked a miracle. The translucent white marble has concentrated the light at its point, which becomes incandescent, and the sculpture (figs. 5a–b) lifts itself from its socle. The bird rises!

This *Bird in Space* is photographed in front of a dark hanging attached to the studio wall (fig. 8), held at left and right by two people (at the right we recognize Brâncuşi). The bird appears on the black rectangle speckled with small white stains, deliberately preserved in this print, since there exists another version, without stains.[21]

The stained backdrop was maintained to enhance the sculpture. The backdrop becomes a heaven, a cosmos favorable to the bird's flight. It is not the sculpture alone that is captured by the objective, but its metamorphosis in the studio, photographed as we photograph an installation, a performance.

The Gallic Cock[22] (1923)

This wood sculpture is the first in Brâncuşi's series of cocks (fig. 9). Other versions would follow, in plaster, ever more monumental, one of which would be cast in bronze and polished.

As with his other birds, Brâncuşi does not try to make us see a cock in a figurative way. He himself said: "It is not the exterior form which is real, but the essence of things".[23] Here again, verticality and elevation, but the cock-animal does not fly. Birds fly, the cock crows. It is his song which lifts itself up and occupies the space, a powerful and abrupt cock-a-doodle-do, here directed toward the light.

Endless Column – Bird in Space[24] (1926)

To the compositions of socles and sculptures which he photographed in his studio Brâncuşi gave the name "mobile groups". This mobile group bears the name of its two principal sculptures, the *Endless Column* and the *Bird in Space*, which he brings into dialogue (fig. 10).

The endless column theme will occupy him for about forty years. The rhomboid – a truncated double pyramid – is a simple element cut

9. Constantin Brâncuşi, *The Gallic Cock* (1923), photo by his author.

10. Constantin Brâncuşi, *Endless Column–Bird in Space* (1926), photo by his author.

11. Constantin Brâncuşi, *The Endless Column*, Târgu Jiu (1938).

in wood, loaned to Rumenian rural architecture: an element that he first used as a socle. The same motif would later be repeated several times vertically. It was beginning with three rhomboids that Brâncuşi called these works *Endless Columns*, carving them as works in their own right.

Here the column has a central position, stretching toward the studio ceiling, as if to hold it up. And the tip of the bird seems to dart toward the exterior, through the open window: the bird is ready to fly out of the enclosed space.

The Endless Column of Târgu Jiu[25] (1938)

Numerous *Endless Columns* would be made, of different sizes and materials. In 1926 Brâncuşi, in his desire to work in a more monumental manner, carved one of a single piece, more than seven meters high, for the garden of his friend Steichen.

Beginning in 1937 he worked on a sculptural ensemble composed of the *Table of Silence*, the *Door of the Kiss* and this *Endless Column* (fig. 11). This ensemble of works was commissioned for the site of Târgu Jiu in Rumenia, in memory of the young Rumenians who had

died in the First World War. The column measures more than thirty meters in height. The structure is in cast iron covered with brass. It is composed of sixteen modules. Did Brâncuşi know that in India the number sixteen corresponds to totality? To tell the whole story, even today, following Vedic tradition, Indians say 'sixteen sixteenths':[26] a totality open to the infinite, since serial forms are not closed at their extremities.

The work rises like a great socle binding the ground to the sky, the earthly to the spiritual, and, as Brâncuşi wished, it becomes a pillar sustaining the heavenly vault, a veritable *Axis Mundi* – an archetypal notion analyzed by Mircea Eliade who defined the *Axis Mundi* as the center of the world, binding earth to heaven, sacred above all other things, which every inhabited region, every microcosm, possesses. Eliade also showed that that axis is an integral part of the symbolism of ascension, of flight and of transcendence.[27]

The ascension that rhythms the overlay of rhomboidal forms and flight toward an infinite space – the same space that attracts birds – represents the transcendence that animates the human condition.

An axis whose stability and perennial duration are reinforced here by the mobility of the clouds.

In his inaugural discourse, Brâncuşi said he considered the *Endless Column* of Târgu Jiu unfinished, and hoped it would be prolonged to an even greater height. He also dreamed of raising a hundred-and-twenty meter column at Chicago, the top of which would be out of sight.

When Brâncuşi photographed his sculpture, he made visible the desire which motivates his work. These negatives – in their use of the frame to fix light and shade modulations, as well as in their ephemeral and at times fortuitous staging – crystallize the fugitive impulsions of his creative intuition. They make the imagination play, provoking *almost* alchemical transformations of matter and in that way prolonging his work as sculptor. Constantin Brâncuşi's photographs are artistic acts in themselves. They disclose what his sculpture demanded to fully exist in his eyes, the access to the world's cosmic order which his desire for flight suggests. ■

1   In Pierre Schneider, *Un moment donné, Brancusi et la photographie*, Paris, 2007, p. 35.

2   Pierre Cabanne, *Constantin Brancusi*, Paris, 2002, p. 14.

3   To facilitate the reader's task, internet references are provided for the works discussed.

4   <http://mediation.centrepompidou.fr/education/ressources/ENS-brancusi/popup02.html>, accessed 30th May 2019.

5   The third photo in <http://felicecalchi.blogspot.fr/2012/04/constantin-brancusi-dans-son-atelier.html>, accessed 30th May 2019.

6   In Schneider 2007, op. cit., p. 46.

7   Conversation with Petre Pandrea, Catalogue of the 1925 New York exhibition.

8   Schneider 2007, op. cit., p. 21.

9   The third photo in <https://historyofourworld.wordpress.com/2009/10/09/constantin-brancusi-the-hermit-of-montparnasse/>, accessed 30th May 2019.

10   Marielle Tabart, *Brancusi, L'inventeur de la sculpture moderne*, Paris, 1995, p. 119.

11   <http://www.metmuseum.org/art/collection/search/265431>, accessed 30th May 2019.

12   Schneider 2007, op. cit.,p. 103.

13   Gaston Bachelard, *L'air et les songes, Essai sur l'imagination*, Paris, 1943, p. 85.

14   See Jacques Vigne, *La mystique du silence*, Paris, 2003, p. 227.

15   The second photo in <http://www.paperblog.fr/4686706/pourquoi-ecrire-brancusi-photographe/>, accessed 30th May 2019.

16   <https://www.centrepompidou.fr/cpv/resource/cRbkRk/rGBjpLp>, accessed 30th May 2019.

17   <https://www.photo-arago.fr/Archive/L%27Oiseau-dans-l%27espace,-marbre-blanc-(oct.-1927)-2C6NU0VKSWC1.html>, accessed 30th May 2019.

18   In Cabanne 2002, op. cit., p. 35.

19   <http://art.rmngp.fr/fr/library/artworks/constantin-brancusi_l-oiseau-dans-l-espace-marbre-noir-1931-1936_epreuve-gelatino-argentique>, accessed 30th May 2019.

20   <https://www.photo.rmn.fr/C.aspx?VP3=SearchResult&IID=2C6NU0P62UTY>, accessed 30th May 2019.

21   The two prints are visible in Schneider 2007, op. cit., pp. 92–3.

22   <http://art.rmngp.fr/fr/library/artworks/constantin-brancusi_vue-d-atelier-l-oiseau-dans-l-espace-marbre-blanc-1923-le-coq-gaulois-projet-disparu-1922-1923_epreuve-gelatino-argentique>, accessed 30th May 2019.

23   In Schneider 2007, op. cit., p. 33.

24   <http://mediation.centrepompidou.fr/education/ressources/ENS-brancusi/popup03.html>, accessed 30th May 2019.

25   <http://mediation.centrepompidou.fr/education/ressources/ENS-brancusi/popup18.html>, accessed 30th May 2019.

26   Charles Malamoud, *Cuire le monde, rite et pensée dans l'Inde ancienne*, Paris, 1989, p. 139.

27   Tabart 1995, op. cit., p. 117.

Part 3

Early Christian, Medieval
and Renaissance Examples

Life and the Spirit in the Ancient Church (2nd–3rd Centuries)

ISAÏA GAZZOLA, O. CIST.

Introduction

One might perhaps think that to treat the question of the theology of the Holy Spirit "in the ancient Church" – and, what is more, in the limited sense that I am about to propose – is to attempt the impossible. But isn't that the case for every theological act daring to explain the mystery of God as professed by faith in worship – *in medio ecclesiæ*, that is –, "at the division of the joints from the marrow" of the ecclesial body convoked by the Word to proclaim and celebrate God's grace?

Thus, in the manner of an agreement established with the readers, I will first take the liberty of more exactly specifying my theme, beginning with the title of this paper: *Life and the Spirit in the Ancient Church (2nd–3rd Centuries)*. The expression 'ancient Church', in itself rather comprehensive, refers to the very first centuries of Christianity. It is generally to that period that historians and Patristic scholars make reference in order to treat and explore questions related to their disciplines. For myself, I propose to use the Council of Nicea (325) as the *terminus ad quem* of my observations. In effect, as has been noted elsewhere,[1] the pre-Nicene period offers a privileged viewpoint for grasping the evolution of practices and language characteristic of the life of the churches. It is therefore in the heart of that period that I will treat the question of the theology of the Holy Spirit.

And I should at once note that, in the theological reflection of the Church, especially during the period to which I refer, the theology of the Holy Spirit can at first seem insufficiently articulated, in respect to its later development. Thus, to fully grasp that theology, in this paper I propose to privilege an approach of the symbolic kind – cosmological and anthropological, that is –: the approach characteristic of theological reflection on the Holy Spirit in the era here considered. In effect, the pneumatology of the 2nd and 3rd centuries does not offer explicit affirmations like those formulated by the conciliar debate of successive periods, but emerges in the broader context of the faith transmitted and expressed in the very bosom of living and diversified ecclesial practices.

We can therefore pose the following problem in the form of a hypothesis: if the pre-Nicene period does not explicitly articulate a theology of the Holy Spirit, this is because it still expressed itself in an inchoative way. Its theology sprang from the very heart of human existence, in response to life's fundamental questions – God and the cosmos, man and his destiny. What is more, intimately bound to the constitutive passages of the human condition – birth, growth, death – that theology would highlight the body and its ritualization.

To better define the problem thus enunciated, in this paper I propose to somehow decode the pneumatology of the 2nd and 3rd centuries beginning with the way in which human existence was understood in that period, and to do so in relation to the fundamental questions and constitutive passages just mentioned.

Since reflection on the subject of the *Pneûma* illustrated by church writers and practices in that period is rather vast and complex, it seems wise to limit the field of observation. I will therefore refer especially to Irenaeus of Lyon, who devoted himself with great firmness to offering a vision of the economy of salvation that was at once harmonious, unified and original. His thought also bears witness to the development and richness of theology in Asia Minor toward the end of the 2nd century. As far as practices are concerned, I will take into account, on the one hand, the acts of worship with greatest importance – Baptism and the Eucharist –, and, on the other, the very first examples of artistic expression in the Christian world – painting, sculpture, epigraphy –, which appeared around the second half of the 3rd century and in the first decades of the 4th. Scriptural interpretation, worship and the figurative arts in fact show themselves, in that era, to be fundamental *loci* of verification, formulation and celebration of the Church's faith. One can also affirm that paleo-Christian art is, properly speaking, a *locus theologicus*, because of the bond it has with gesture and the Word, with reality and corporeality.

On the basis of this formulation of the problem, I will decline my argument in three moments, with attention to the constitutive passages of the human condition: coming into the world, growing, dying. In the first, I will sketch in a synthetic way the essential lines of a theology of the Spirit, in light of the protology which characterizes the thought of Irenaeus of Lyon. It is at the heart of that overall vision of the cosmos and of man that, in a second moment, we will have to situate the sacramental economy, which is itself understood within a dynamic of growth under the Spirit's action. Finally, in a third moment, I will limit myself to sketching how nascent Christian artistic expression, for which the human condition's last breath was the matrix, represents a theology of the Holy Spirit.

Coming into the world.
The modeling of man

In the face of Gnostic currents which not only deformed a correct vision of God, of the world and of revelation, but also departed from a true and positive conception of man and his salvation, Irenaeus of Lyon took position, refuting the Gnostics' ideas and engaging in a debate with them, in order to defend and re-establish the truth on the subject of the Christian faith, from both the anthropological and the soteriological points of view.[2]

Situating himself in continuity with the Pauline doctrine of salvation, Irenaeus underlined the unity of God's "benevolent design" (Ep 1:9–10). There is but a single divine economy in regard to the human species, a sole overall plan of salvation history encompassing everything: creation and redemption, Old and New Testaments, the world and humanity. The unity of God, and that of the Son who recapitulates all things in himself, are the basis of the unity of that universal economy.[3]

At the heart of this divine plan, it is humanity in its entirety – man and his salvation – which is highlighted.[4] Although basing himself on the well-known tripartite distinction of the human being – "spirit" (*pneûma*), "soul" (*psuché*), "body" (*sōma*)[5] – Irenaeus develops his own vision of the "spiritual" and "perfect" man, whom he always considers as the "man of flesh" (*homo-caro*),[6] mortal and corruptible, who must assume immortality and incorruptibility.[7] The salvation of which he speaks, in other words, is salvation of the flesh (*salus carnis*).[8] Following that vision, which does not separate anthropology from the divine economy, God created man to "deposit in him all his benefits"[9] and to give him "life, incorruptibility and eternal glory".[10]

In that act of creation, the unity of God – "the only God, the Omnipotent and only Father"[11] –, is intrinsically tied to the indivisible unicity of the Creator God who, without any need for the angels as intermediaries,[12] is author of the creation of the whole universe. Thus, in describing the creation of man, Irenaeus makes reference to two verses of Genesis (1,26 and 2,7),[13] in which he perceives "the order, the rhythm and the movement" – "fabrication" (*poíēsis*) and "fashioning" (*plásis*) – by which man "became a being made in the image and likeness of the uncreated God".[14] A unique creative process,[15] manifesting the care which God has for man – "made" and "fashioned" (whereas the other creatures are only "made") –, as well as the beauty and dignity of the human body modeled by God and "clothed with his own features".[16]

In this unitary vision of creation, man's body is at once "made" and "fashioned" by the Father, the Creator God, assisted as he is by "the Word and Wisdom, the Son and the Spirit",[17] whose presence and action at the very heart of creation are metaphorically described as being those of "the hands of the Father".[18] That image allows Irenaeus, on the one hand, to interpret the "Let us make" of Genesis 1, 26[19] as the moment in which God convokes the Son and the Spirit to the ministry[20] of "fabricating" man, and, on the other, to show that the creation is a shared work, realized by the Father, the Son and the Spirit.

In "the rhythm and movement"[21] of this shared work, we can distinguish different functions: "The Father decides and commands, the Son executes and models, the Spirit nourishes and gives growth, man progresses and lifts himself toward perfection".[22] Thus the "fashioning" of man is perceived by Irenaeus as a work which is pursued for the full duration of the economy of salvation, "from the beginning to the end",[23] up to the moment when "Adam becomes a being in the image and likeness of God".[24] It is the Spirit's function to prepare and "put everything in order",[25] to "coordinate",[26] to "give form to the things he has put in order",[27] to "work",[28] to "mourish and give growth",[29] to "form man in the likeness of God".[30]

The "hands of the Father" metaphor thus makes it possible to establish, at the very heart of the economy of salvation, a bond between creation and redemption. In effect, it was after he used "his hands" to fashion man of earth "pure and fine"[31] that God "clothed the work so-modeled with his own features, in order that even what appeared to human eyes would be divine in form".[32] Now, according to Irenaeus, the image thus traced upon Adam's modeled flesh – the image of God – was that of the "Son of God, in whose likeness man was made",[33] and it was after having breathed upon his face a breath of life[34] that, "both by virtue of the breath and according to the work that had been modeled, man was similar to God".[35]

It is therefore only at the moment of his incarnation that the Word of God manifests "the image in all its truth, in becoming himself the very thing his image was".[36] That paradoxical "reciprocity of images"[37] – the incarnate Word revealing to man "in whose image he had been made"[38] – allows us to better understand the relationship between image and likeness. From the very beginning, man was not created as a perfect being[39] but in a state of constitutive fragility – he is made of flesh – which Irenaeus compares to that of a new-born infant.[40] Not yet having "mature judgment",[41] Adam sins through inexperience, losing the likeness to God but not the image written in his flesh. Thus, God's Word, becoming flesh, "made the image appear…[and] re-established the likeness in a stable fashion, making man fully similar to the invisible Father by means of the Word, who now became visible".[42]

Growing. The "water come from heaven" and the "bread of immortality"

If "life, incorruptibility and eternal glory"[43] constitute the end for which God created man, participation in this gift is prepared in a progressive way, by a maturation-pursued through one's entire existence[44] – in which man is called to exercise his freedom, a constitutive dimension of his being.[45] Thus Irenaeus puts the creation of man in relation both to "eternal glory" and to salvation history[46] – that is, with the time during which God, "like an architect designs the structure of salvation (*fabricatio salutis*)"[47] and disposes "the human race in view of the symphony of salvation (*consonantia salutis*)".[48] These images characterize this time and allow us to grasp it as an "economy" (*oikonomía/dispositio*) – in the sense of a 'plan', a 'design' – by which God puts everything to work in order to lead man to salvation.[49] Man thus becomes accustomed to "following God",[50] to "bearing him",[51] to "entering into communion with him",[52] to seeing the "glory"[53] promised at the beginning.

In the plan of God, who wants to recapitulate everything in the Word – as in his "symphony" which rings through the time of creation and of salvation –, this process of habituation[54] is two-fold. On the one hand, man must learn to enter into communion with God,[55] and, on the other hand, God himself must become used to dwelling with man. That "double habituation"[56] follows the stages of salvation history on the one side and the other. In the "order, rhythm and movement"[57] of a fashioning which goes forward "from the beginning to the end",[58] man "progresses a little at a time and lifts himself toward perfection".[59] Thus it is that, in Paradise, 'infant' Adam receives in germ, as it were, the Spirit who gets bigger in him and makes man grow with him. The Spirit, whose function is to "nourish and give growth",[60] makes man grow and shapes him "in the likeness of God".[61] The Spirit himself gives immortal life as nourishment for man, who through his disobedience had lost immortality and incorruptibility.

That growth is also realized through incorporation in Christ through Baptism[62] and the Eucharist.[63] In effect, since Christ's own flesh had to be anointed and filled with the Spirit, his baptism in the Jordan becomes the model of the baptism of believers. Baptism is thus at once a bath that purifies the soul and the body and a bath of regeneration which operates a new modeling, a 'new birth' of man. There are, therefore, three 'births' or 'generations' of man: that of Creation, that of Baptism, and that of Resurrection. Through Baptism man becomes God's 'dwelling' and recovers communion with him. That baptismal generation is brought about by the Holy Spirit, "Water come from heaven", "generous rain", "God's dew",[64] which transforms the believer himself into a "spring of water welling up".

As far as the Eucharist is concerned,[65] Irenaeus cannot understand it without underlining its relation to the creation, from which are drawn the bread and wine that become the body and blood of Christ, or apart from its fruit in those who receive it: the Eucharist is food for eternal life and a pledge of the resurrection of the flesh. There are thus three levels tied each to the other – creation, the Eucharist,

and the resurrection of the body –, in each of which a transformation is effected. It is the Spirit, "bread of immortality," who is given as nourishment in the Eucharist.[66] According to Irenaeus, the figure of that growth is the grain of wheat[67] which must first be laid in the earth and rot before it springs up, multiplied by the Spirit; it is then harvested and put in the barn, after a winnowing that separates wheat from chaff. In the same way, our bodies must dissolve in the earth after death but have already, in the Eucharist, received the seed of the Spirit, the germ of eternal life and earnest of incorruptibility procured by the Father.

Final Repose. Living in the Spirit

Irenaeus's thought and overall perception of salvation history offer a unified vision of the world, of human existence and of the faith. In that vision, Christian life – structured as it is by the great stages of existence: birth, growth, death – appears as extended between the economy of creation and that of salvation. God reveals his goodness and does not stop bending over his creature, fashioning it, breathing upon it, accustoming it to enter into communion with him. And the water come from heaven and the bread of immortality are thus ceaselessly offered so that man can enter into that communion. In this vision, everything is unified and brought into relationship like a 'symphony': the beginning and the end, Adam and Christ, the Old and New Testaments, heaven and earth, past and future, life and death. The same hands of the Father that were active in forming the 'man of flesh' now work at his salvation; the Word itself has become a "man of flesh" and the Spirit vivifies the corruptible and mortal flesh by giving it the gift of incorruptibility and immortality.

Irenaeus of Lyon did not leave death out of this picture, considering it, first, in the economy of creation, as the expression and consequence of Adam's disobedience,[68] provoked by the serpent's lie and jealousy.[69] But if, in the first economy, Adam's disobedience had introduced death, in the economy of salvation Christ's obedience is a source of life;[70] if a tree of wood engendered death, it is by obedience on the wood of another tree that Christ destroyed death.[71] We too are, at the same time, disobedient and dead in Adam and "obedient unto death" in Jesus Christ, for death possesses a double value: even if it was introduced by sin, it puts an end to sin.[72]

Thus, Irenaeus retains physical death as a dissolution of the flesh: "[death] is to lose the way of being proper to the living, to become without breath, without life, without movement, to be dissolved in the elements from which we received the beginning of our existence".[73] Neither the soul nor the Spirit undergo death, but the flesh, which "once the soul leaves… becomes breathless and lifeless and bit by bit dissolves in the earth from which it was drawn".[74] The flesh thus decomposes because deprived of the life of the Spirit – "the life of those who partake of Him"[75] – and of the life of the soul – "the breath of life".[76]

It is on the horizon of this unified vision of God and man, of man's destiny and of the economy of salvation, that we are going to explore the ultimate stage of all human existence, that of death. We will do so by observing how the Christian artistic expression born at the turn of the late 3rd and very early 4th centuries apprehended the moment of death. In particular, as indicated in our introduction, on the basis of this nascent Christian art expressed in the bosom of ecclesial communities, we are going to try to make out how a theology of the Holy Spirit might be formulated.

This observation will be limited to a *corpus* whose components present the following characteristics: the works all come from Rome; they are dateable to the 3rd (4th) century; they are works of funerary art; they represent two artistic expressions: painting and epigraphy.

This *corpus* has been assembled in light of the present symposium's theme and, more specifically, for this essay on the representation of the Holy Spirit in the pre-Nicene age. It is the result of research made possible thanks to the repertory of the Pontificia Commissione di Archeologia Sacra[77] and of the Epigraphic Database Bari,[78] both available on line.

Since analysis of the *corpus* can only be sketched here, I propose to pursue this theme more thoroughly in a future study.

The *Baptism of Jesus*

That the Holy Spirit be represented in the form of a dove at the moment of Jesus's emergence from the water is completely natural, in that the evangelical account of Christ's baptism constitutes the scriptural archetype of the subject's iconographic representation. Yet the fact that this scene is used in nascent Christian funerary art obliges us to ask what its theological scope/meaning was.

This scene can be considered virtually paradigmatic of Christian funerary art as we find it in the catacombs. That art, in effect, appears as an analepsis of human existence and, most especially, of the existence of the person buried – a sort of cinematic flashback of the believer's life. Indeed, in evoking the original moment of Christian experience, the representation of the baptism of Christ binds the deceased person himself to this original moment.

The image of the baptism of Christ – a theophany *par excellence* – sums up the deceased person's destiny, his hope of a new creation such as Christ's baptism had launched – a new creation announcing the resurrection of the flesh, for – as Irenaeus stresses – in manifesting himself in the flesh, the Word showed humankind what it truly is and what is its destiny.

A *Baptism of Christ* in the Catacomb of Callixtus (fig. 1), among the most ancient, assumes typological value as an experience of living and saving waters. One can thus relate it to other personages who, in the economy of salvation, have born witness to the presence and action of God at the heart of death's peril. Let us review some of these images in the following pages.

The Samaritan Woman

This mural (fig. 2), whose interpretation is debated, shows a woman (the Samaritan?) drawing water from a well. The waters appear to be overflowing and gushing and can be interpreted as an announcement of the life offered and inaugurated by the baptism which the Spirit vivifies.

Noah emerging from the ark

A scene of Noah emerging from the ark (fig. 3), his arms raised as he acclaims his salvation

1. *Baptism of Christ: Jesus Emerging from the Water,*
Rome, Catacomb of Callixtus, level 2, hypogeum a,
cubiculum 1 (x), north wall.

2. *Christ and the Samaritan Woman,*
Rome, Catacomb of Callixtus, Crypt of the Sacraments,
cubiculum A3, entry wall, at the left.

3. *Noah emerging from the ark,*
Rome, Catacomb of Priscilla, Greek Chapel.

The three young men in the furnace

This image (fig. 4) shows the three young men in the furnace. They are upright in the middle of the fire (as mortal a peril as were the rising flood waters), with their hands lifted to heaven beneath the epicletic presence of the dove, which is like the dew sent by God mentioned in the biblical text.

A woman in prayer

The prayerful posture of the preceding Old Testament personages invites us to interpret in the same way the figure of a woman in prayer that we find in an important position in the Catacomb of Priscilla (fig. 5). Even without the representation of a dove, the prayerful position translates this believer's faith and her certitude of divine salvation. Thus her *orans* gesture is not a "plea" for salvation, but the sign that salvation has been well and truly realized, and that the believer somehow gives thanks to God.

Funerary inscriptions

In the research I undertook based on Christian epigraphic evidence, it is interesting to note that a first inquiry into the corpus of inscriptions has made it possible to confirm that the

after the deluge, bears witness to God's promise realized after the trial of death. It is interesting to compare this image with that of Christ's baptism, in the sense that Noah appears as its prefiguration. The dove is represented on three occasions: in the scene of baptism, in that of Noah and in that of the three young men in the furnace, they too shown in a posture of prayer.

4. *Three Young Men in the Furnace*, Rome, Catacomb of Priscilla.

5. *The Veiled Woman*, Rome, Catacomb of Priscilla, cubiculum of the 'Velata', far wall.

expression "Holy Spirit" is generally tied to a wish for life or for repose.

The most meaningful expressions are "May you live in the Holy Spirit" (fig. 6) or "Here… reposes in the Holy Spirit" (fig. 7). That invites us to consider the Christian's death as being the condition for acceding to the true life which the Spirit gives as a first payment.

Among the epigraphic examples I have been able to find, and which seem significant to me,

there is also the funerary inscription of Licinia Amias (fig. 8). This, while neither representing nor naming the Spirit, includes the representation of two fish accompanied by the inscription "fish of the living", which here again suggests a baptismal and pneumatological interpretation.

Finally, let us note a last inscription (fig. 9), dateable to the turn of the 3rd–4th century, that is at the end of the period to which my study refers. This inscription, in briefly citing a

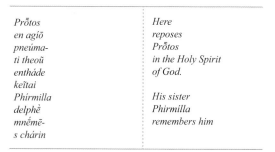

Car(---) Kyriaco [---]	*Car(---) Kyriaco [---]*
Most sweet child [---]	*fil(io) dulcissimo [---]*
May you live in the Holy Spirit	*vibas <i>n spirito sa[ncto]*

6. Author's transcription of the funerary inscription of Kyriacus, Rome, Catacomb of Callixtus.

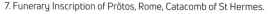

Prŏtos	*Here*
en agiō	*reposes*
pneúma-	*Prŏtos*
ti theoũ	*in the Holy Spirit*
entháde	*of God.*
keĩtai	
Phírmilla	*His sister*
delphḕ	*Phirmílla*
mnémē-	*remembers him*
s chárin	

7. Funerary Inscription of Prŏtos, Rome, Catacomb of St Hermes.

concise version of the Trinitarian formula in an abridgment of the Creed, truly seems to inaugurate a new theological reflection born with the ecumenical councils, and which from this time forward announces a new pneumatology.

Conclusion

At the end of this itinerary, which proposed to explore the theology of the Holy Spirit in the ancient Church, I must now conclude. As noted at the outset, the challenges were considerable, since it was necessary, for the period chosen, to give an account of a theology that had not yet been formulated in a systematic manner, and to interpret an artistic production at the first stage of its birth.

Nonetheless, the two sources of information to which I referred – Irenaeus of Lyon's theological vision and paleo-Christian art – seem to converge around a notion that I believe funda-

mental for a theology of the Holy Spirit: that of experience, which moreover is the characteristic trait of all theological reflection in the course of the pre-Nicene era.

One can thus state that, in pre-Nicene reflection, Christian life was a living experience of the Spirit which got translated into the confessions of faith, the Church's liturgical life and its artistic production, taking body in the very existence of the believer – stretched between his coming into the world and his final rest –, and tracing the horizon of his destiny.

An experience of the Spirit, therefore, which theological formulation and art expressed in a symphonic way as a presence of the Spirit not 'in front of' but 'within': at the heart of man's creation and coming into the world, of his life and existence – a principle of life and immortality right down to earth's depths. ■

d(is) m(anibus) ((corona))	DM (*«Dis manibus»* (garland))
ichthùs zṓvtōn	Fish of the living
((piscis)) ((ancora)) ((piscis))	(fish) (anchor) (fish)
Liciniae Amiati benemerenti	To Licinia Amias who fully deserves it,
vixit	She lived
------	

8. Funerary Inscription of Licinia Amias, Vatican City, Cemetery near St Peter's Basilica.

(Lazarus) Aedesius neofitus	*(Lazarus) Ædesius, néophyte,*
	a eunuch
	from Armenia,
qui credidit	believed in the Father,
in patre et filio	in the Son
et spiritu sancto	and in the Holy Spirit.
natione armenius	He lived
eunuchus	25 years
qui vixit annis	and rests
XXV et quievit	in peace
in pace pr(idie) kal(endas)	
octob(res) ((folium))	September 30

9. Funerary Inscription of Ædesius, Rome, Catacomb of St Sebastian.

1   See Michel Fédou, 'La théologie anténicéenne. Quelles ressources pour la christologie?', in *De Jésus à Jésus-Christ. II. Christ dans l'Histoire*, proceedings of the symposium (Paris, 24–5 March 2011), edited by Vincent Holzer and Jean-Louis Souletie, Paris, 2011, pp. 189–207.

2   For a presentation of Irenaeus of Lyon, his œuvre, his theology and the context in which his thought was born, see (in chronological order) Albert Houssiau, *La christologie de saint Irénée*, Louvain, 1955; Ysabel de Andia, *Homo vivens. Incorruptibilité et divinisation de l'homme selon Irénée de Lyon*, Paris, 1986; Jacques Fantino, *La théologie d'Irénée. Lecture des Écritures en réponse à l'exégèse gnostique. Une approche trinitaire*, Paris, 1994; Robert M. Grant, *Irenaeus of Lyons*, London–New York, 1997; Rodrigo Polanco Fernandois, *El concepto de profecía en la teología de san Ireneo*, Madrid, 1999; Bernard Sesboüé, *Tout récapituler dans le Christ. Christologie et sotériologie d'Irénée de Lyon*, Paris, 2000; Eric Osborn, *Irenaeus of Lyons*, Cambridge–New York, 2001; Michel Fédou, *La voie du Christ. Genèses de la christologie*

dans le contexte religieux de l'Antiquité du IIe siècle au début du IVe siècle, Paris, 2006, pp. 169–215. As far as Irenaeus of Lyon's works are concerned, I will mainly refer here to *Adversus hæreses* (*Contre les hérésies* = CH) and to the *Demonstratio apostolicae praedicationis* (*Démonstration de la prédication apostolique* = Dém), in the edition of Adelin Rousseau [AR], Louis Doutreleau [LD], Charles Mercier [CM], in the collection "Sources chrétiennes" (=SC) published by the Editions du Cerf, Paris: Irénée de Lyon [Irenaeus of Lyon], CH, vol. I, book I, edited by AR and LD, SC 263, 1979; Id., CH, vol. I, book II, edited by AR and LD, SC 264, 1979; Id., CH, vol. II, book I, edited by AR and LD, SC 293, 1982; Id., CH, vol. II, book II, edited by AR and LD, SC 294, 1982; Id., CH, vol. III, book I, edited by AR and LD, SC 210, 1974; Id., CH, vol. III, book II, edited by AR and LD, SC 211, 1974; Id., CH, vol. IV, book I, edited by AR, SC 100, 1965; Id., CH, vol. IV, book II, edited by AR, SC 100, 1965; Id., CH, vol. V, book I, edited by AR, LD, CM, SC 152, 1969; Id., CH, vol. V, book II, edited by AR, LD, CM, SC 153, 1969; Id., Dém, edited by AR, SC 406, 1995.

3   CH III–II, 16, 6, pp. 312–15: "There is thus but one God, the Father, as we have shown, and a single Christ Jesus, our Lord, who has come through all the 'economy' and who has recapitulated everything in himself. In this 'everything' man too is included, that work modeled by God: Christ has thus recapitualted man in himself, from invisible becoming visible, from unreachable, reachable, from impassible, subject to suffering, from Word, man". The theme of "recapitulation" is fully treated by Sesboüé 2000, op. cit., pp. 125–63.

4   CH IV–II, 22, 2, pp. 688–9: "For Christ has not come only for those who, from the time of the emperor Tiberius, have believed in him; and the Father has not exercised his providence in favor only of the men of our time, but in favor of all men without exception who, from the beginning, according to their capacity and in their periods, have feared and loved God, have practiced justice and goodness toward their neighbor, have desired to see Christ and hear his voice".

5   According to the order of 1 Th 5:23. Irenaeus, on his side, speaks of "three things [...which] constitute the perfect man: the flesh (*caro*), the soul (*anima*) and the Spirit (*spiritus*)"; see CH V–II, 9, 1, pp. 106–7.

6   CH IV–II, Preface 4, pp. 390–1: "For man is a mix of soul and flesh, and of a flesh formed according to the likeness with God...".

7   CH V–II, 13, 3, pp. 170–1: "These words [1 Corinthians xv, 53–5] will be said with all justice when this mortal and corruptible flesh, destined to die, crushed beneath death's domination, will mount toward life and be clothed in incorruptibility and immortality...".

8   Ibid., 2, 2, pp. 30–1: "Vain in every way are those who reject all God's 'economy', denying the salvation of the flesh, despising its regeneration, by declaring that it cannot receive incorruptibility".

9   CH IV–II, 14, 1, pp. 538–9.

10   Ibid., pp. 540–1.

11   CH II–II, 30, 9, pp. 318–19.

12   CH IV–II, 7, 4, pp. 462–5.

13   "God said: 'Let us make (*poiésōmen*) man in our own image, in the likeness of ourselves, and let them be masters of the fish of the sea, the birds of heaven, the cattle, all the wild beasts and all the reptiles that crawl upon the earth' (Gn 1:26); God fashioned (*éplasen*) man of dust from the soil. Then he breathed into his nostrils a breath of life, and thus man became a living being" (Genesis 2, 7). The biblical text used here is *La Bible d'Alexandrie. I. La genèse*, edited by Marguerite Harl, Paris, 1986.

14   CH IV–II, 38, 3, pp. 954–5.

15   In commenting upon the creation of man, Irenaeus refers, simultaneously and without distinction, to the double account to which the book of Genesis bears witness, which he cites in the following order: Gn 11:7 and Gn 1:26. See ibid., 20, 1, pp. 624–7.

What is more, following the usage of the Septuagint, Irenaeus does not oppose the two verbs: "make" (*poiéō*) and "fashion" (*plássō*); see *La Bible d'Alexandrie* 1986, op. cit., p. 100, notes 2–7.

16   Dém, 11, pp. 98–9.

17   CH IV–II, 20, 1, pp. 626–7.

18   Ibid., 7, 4, pp. 464–5; CH V–II, 1, 3, pp. 28–9; 6, 1, pp. 72–3; Dém 11, pp. 98–9. On the subject of the "hands of God" see Jean Mambrino, 'Les deux mains de Dieu dans l'œuvre de saint Irénée', *Nouvelle revue théologique*, 79 (1957), 4, pp. 355–70; De Andia 1986, op. cit., pp. 64–7; Fantino 1994, op. cit., pp. 306–9; Sesboüé 2000, op. cit., pp. 183–90.

19   CH IV–II, Preface 4, pp. 390–1; 20, 1, pp. 626–7; CH V–II, 1, 3, pp. 28–9; 15, 4, pp. 210–11. Prior to Irenaeus, Theophilus of Antioch offers one of the first examples of this interpretation: "As if he needed help, God takes to sayiing 'Let us make man in our image and likeness'. He did not say 'let us make' to anyone other than to his Word and his Wisdom". See Theophilus Antiochenus [Théophile d'Antioche], *Ad Autolycum libri tres*, French ed. with the title *Trois livres à Autolycus*, by G. Bardy, Paris, 1948, II, 188, pp. 144–7.

20   This "ministry of an inexpressible richness" is neither foreign nor exterior to the Father, for the Son and the Spirit who assist him are "at once his Progeny and his Hands"; see CH IV–II, 7, 4, pp. 464–5; CH IV–I, pp. 212–19. On the "ministry" of the Word and the Spirit in the creation of man see De Andia 1986, op. cit., pp. 65–7.

21   CH IV–II, 38, 3, pp. 954–5.

22   Ibid., pp. 954–7.

23   CH V–II, 16, 1, pp. 214–15. According to De Andia 1986, op. cit., see p. 68: "The metaphor of the imprint of the hands of God on the work which they never cease to model, right to the end, indicates the constant relationship between the hands of God and the image and likeness in man and consequently the eschatological sense of the image and likeness".

24   CH V–II, 1, 3, pp. 28–9.

25   CH II–II, 30, 9, pp. 318–21. The Latin translation is: *omnia aptavit et disposuit*.

26   CH III–II, 24, 2, pp. 476–7.

27   CH IV–II, 20, 1, pp. 626–7.

28   Ibid., 20, 6, pp. 644–5.

29   Ibid., 38, 3, pp. 954–5.

30   Dém 5, pp. 90–1.

31   Dém 11, pp. 98–9.

32   On this subject, Ysabel de Andia correctly notes that "The image is not only an imprint, graven once and for all, but 'fingerprints' which adhere to the soft earth. It thus acquires a dynamic sense, pratically a 'plastic' one"; see De Andia 1986, op. cit., p. 68.

33   Dém 22, pp. 114–15.

34   Dém 11, pp. 98–9.

35   Ibid. "earth", "divine power", "features of the form", "breath of life" constitute the four elements

of the fashioning of man. See the development in De Andia 1986, op. cit., pp. 75–9.

36   CH V–II, 16, 2, pp. 216–17.

37   The expression is that of Sesboüé 2000, op. cit., p. 148.

38   CH V–II, 16, 2, pp. 216–17.

39   CH IV–II, 38, 1, pp. 942–7.

40   Dém 12, pp. 100–1: "Having thus made man the master of the earth and all it held, God secretly established him also as master of the servants who were there. These however were in their adult age, whereas the master, that is man, was quite small, for he was as yet only a child, and man had, as he grew, to reach adult condition". Theophilus of Antioch also develops the theme of the infancy of Adam: see Théophile d'Antioche, *Ad Autolycum*, ed. 1948, op. cit., II, 25, pp. 160–1.

41   Ibid.

42   CH V–II, 16, 2, pp. 216–17.

43   CH IV–II, 14, 1, pp. 540–1.

44   Ibid., 11, 1–2, pp. 498–501: "[God] modeled [man] in view of a growth and a maturity, according to the word of Scripture: 'Grow and multiply'. It is precisely in this that God differs from man: God makes, while man is made. He who makes is always the same, whereas that which is made necessarily receives a beginning, an intermediate state and a mature condition".

45   Ibid., 37, 1, pp. 918–21: "...God made [man] free, with an autonomy of his own right from the start, just as he has his own soul, to make use of God's counsel voluntarily and without being constrained by God". Irenaeus develops this theme of "liberty" in important chapters of his work (CH III–II, 20–3, pp. 382–469; CH IV–II, 37–9, pp. 918–73; CH V–II, 29, 1–2, pp. 362–71). On this subject see the thought-provoking remarks of Joseph Caillot, 'La grâce de l'union selon saint Irénée', in *Penser la foi. Recherches en théologie aujourd'hui. Mélanges offerts à Joseph Moingt*, edited by Joseph Doré and Christoph Theobald, Paris, 1993, pp. 391–412.

46   Salvation history is thus stretched out between the beginning (creation) and the end (Incarnation / coming of the Kingdom). Irenaeus establishes a link between "the beginning" when God models man "in view of his gifts" and the history of the distribution of these gifts, which he reconstructs at length; see CH IV–II, 14, 2, pp. 542–3.

47   Ibid., pp. 544–55.

48   Ibid.

49   On the notion of "economy" in Irenaeus, see De Andia 1986, op. cit., pp. 88–9; Fantino 1994, op. cit., pp. 85–98.

50   CH IV–II, 14, 2, pp. 542–3.

51   CH III–II, 16, 3, pp. 298–9; CH IV–II, 14, 2, pp. 542–3; 20, 6, pp. 642–3; 38, 1, pp. 946–7; CH V–II, 8, 1, pp. 92–3.

52   CH IV–II, 13, 1, pp. 526–7. On the subject of union and communion with God, see De Andia 1986, op. cit., pp. 161–9.

53   CH IV–II, 38, 3, pp. 956–7: "...It is God who must be seen one day, and the vision of God procures incorruptibility, 'and incorruptibility makes us be with God'".

54   CH III–II, 20, 2, pp. 392–3: "...the Word of God who dwelt in man and became Son of Man to accustom man to understand God and to accustom God to dwell in man, according to the Father's good pleasure".

55   CH IV–II, 14, 2, pp. 542–5.

56   See Sesboüé 2000, op. cit., p. 152, who developes this notion.

57   CH IV–II, 38, 3, pp. 954–7.

58   CH V–II, 16, 1, pp. 214–15.

59   CH IV–II, 38, 3, pp. 954–7.

60   Ibid., 38, 3, pp. 954–5.

61   Dém 5, pp. 90–1.

62   CH, III, 17, 2, pp. 330–5; V, 15, 3, pp. 206–11; 32, 2, pp. 398–405.

63   CH IV–II, 18, 4–5, pp. 606–13; 33, 2, pp. 804–9.

64   CH III, 17, 3, pp. 334–7.

65   On the subject of the Eucharist, see De Andia 1986, op. cit., pp. 244–54, whose development I follow here.

66   CH IV–II, 38, 1, pp. 942–9.

67   CH IV–II, 18, 5, pp. 610–13.

68   CH V–II, 23, 1, pp. 290–1.

69   CH III–II, 23, 1, pp. 444–7.

70   CH V–II, 21, 1, pp. 260–5.

71   CH V–II, 16, 3, pp. 218–21.

72   CH III–II, 23, 6, pp. 460–3.

73   CH V–II, 7, 1, pp. 86–7.

74   Ibid., pp. 88–9.

75   Ibid.

76   Ibid., pp. 86–7.

77   <http://www.archeologiasacra.net/pcas-web/home>, accessed 30 May 2019.

78   <http://www.edb.uniba.it/about>, accessed 30 May 2019.

Spirit and Matter, the Hand of Man and the Faith of the Church

The Sacramental Character of the Icon in Eastern Theology

BASILIO PETRÀ

The object of the following considerations is a particular aspect of the theology of icons: the question whether these do or do not have a sacramental character.

To treat the theme adequately we should first say something of the meaning attributable to the word 'sacrament'. The term, of Latin origin, initially indicated a reality or act or value that was sacral in nature – for example the soldier's oath that generated a sacred bond. In Christian Latin the term was progressively used to translate *mysterion*, the Greek word indicating a rite or initiation, used to designate in particular the Christian initiatory rites of Baptism and the Eucharist. The hermeneutics of sacramental discourse, like the determination of the number of the sacraments, have a long history, with notable differences between the Greek East and the Latin West, but for the purposes of this essay it is unnecessary to rehearse this in detail. Here it suffices to recall that there is at least one essential feature attributed to any liturgical reality indicated as a 'sacrament' or a 'sacramental mystery', and that is the presence of a sensory reality through which 'passes' or 'is communicated' something supernatural, divine grace, in a way that is objectively efficacious for the sanctification/salvation of the believer.

To speak of the sacramental character of the icon is therefore to speak of the sanctifying relationship presumed to exist between the sensible reality – the icon – and the person of the believer. Since however the icon is a sensible reality representing a prototype – Christ[1] or a personage who participates in Christ's holiness – it follows that to speak of the icon's sacramentality is to speak of the sanctifying relationship between the prototype, the material reality of the icon, and the person of the believer.

As is well known, during the iconoclast controversy the chief accusation against the iconodules was that the veneration of icons was an idolatrous act and that the sacramental comprehension of the icon favored idolatry. Nor can it be denied that the main exponent of the iconodule position, St John of Damascus (676–749), precisely for his sacramental comprehension of the presence of the prototype in the icon, in some texts ran serious risks in that sense. For St John of Damascus, in fact, God himself "has become matter for me, and has deigned to inhabit matter and to operate my salvation through matter".[2]

On this subject Egon Sendler writes:

He [St John of Damascus] sustained that the icon is, 'filled, as it were, with energy and grace'. Such an expression, not free of ambiguity and of the danger of fetishism, in a metaphoric way says that the body of Christ communicates its holiness to the matter on which it is painted. The icon would thus become real participation in Christ's body and would be near the sacraments. In practice, some iconodule fanatics considered icons superior to sacraments, and went so far as to add fragments of icons to the Eucharistic species![3]

Certainly less exposed to these risks was St Theodore the Studite (758–826), who did not think of the presence of the prototype in the image as energy able to sanctify the sign even in its material givenness, but rather as a hypostatic resemblance of the icon to the prototype represented. The example he used to illustrate this idea is well known:

Let us take as example a ring on which the emperor's image is incised: one impresses the image in wax, pitch or clay. The seal remains immutably the same in each of these materials, which, themselves, on the contrary, are different each from the other. The seal would not remain the same in the different material substances if it participated in some way in the various kinds of matter. In effect it is separate from these and remains on the ring. In an analogous way the likeness of Christ, even if impressed on a material support, is not in communion with the matter in which it finds expression, but remains in the hypostasis of Christ, to which it belongs.[4]

In St Theodore's view the prototype's presence in the icon is not, therefore, an almost physical presence which, uniting the icon to itself like a material extension, in that way transmits to the image its own energy, but rather a hypostatic kind of presence: the iconic image in some way reproduces the lineaments or characteristic features – hypostatic and therefore personal – of the prototype.

I recall these two names for a good reason: they may be considered to represent the two interpretive modalities of the relationship between prototype and icon that not only typified several centuries of the first millennium but that have traveled through history. It is indeed possible to say that these two modalities are, *aliquo modo*, still present in the context of eastern theology, and that their contraposition is still unresolved.

An interesting demonstration is the to some extent conflictual thought of two great Orthodox theologians, both belonging to the Theological Institute of St Sergius in Paris: Boris Bobrinskoy (1925–), still alive, and Olivier Clément (1921–2009).

The first authored an important essay, which appeared in 1987, published in various places and translated in many languages. In the original English version which I recall here the essay is entitled: *The Icon: Sacrament of the Kingdom.*[5]

This title, chosen with great care, was inspired by a fundamental work of Alexander Schmemann (*Eucharist: Sacrament of the Kingdom*), and sought from the first page to invite readers to see the icon as "the sacrament of the self-revelation and self-communication of God's Beauty and Glory" and to suggest a "dynamic concept of the icon as sacrament, or as a particular expression of the radically sacramental character of the Church".

Thus for Bobrinskoy the icon's sacramentality is indubitable. To be sure, that becomes clear only if, renouncing a view that Bobrinskoy calls the "familiar atomistic and materialistic conception of the sacraments", one returns to the Mystery of the Church as the "sole and self-sufficient sacrament of the salvation communicated by the Trinity's Love through the redemptive work of the incarnate Word and of the Holy Spirit". Obviously a fetishistic approach to icons must be avoided, but (he observes) neither can one fall into the error of a platonic dualism that sees salvation as the negation of matter and in that way voids Christ's incarnation of sense.

The sacramental value of the icon must be safeguarded because it "represents [such] a gift of sacramental fullness" that without it "Orthodoxy would be seriously diminished". In fact, the living experience that the Church has of itself – that "primordial and pre-theological" experience that furnishes the original given of church life – imparts a radical awareness that "the icon is truly a sacrament, a way of presence and of communion of Christ's human-divine nature",[6] intimately connected with the reality of the incarnation itself. Not by chance, Bobrinskoy here cites the words of St John of Damascus: "By virtue of the fact that God has now been seen in human flesh and has lived among men, I represent that which is visible of God",[7] to attest to the intimate bond between the icon and the incarnation: the icon is possible only because the incarnation is true.

The icon should not be seen only in relation to the prototype, Christ, but also in relation to man himself – in relation to man's inner reality: man in fact was originally made in the image and likeness of God in Christ. That means that, if, on the one hand, the icon is a way of communion-presence of Christ, who is the Father's perfect image, on the other, precisely for this reason, it is also a way of communion-presence that deeply calls forth the interior image in every man. What is more, in the economy of Christianity, first for the fact of creation and then for that of redemption in Christ, we bear his image carved in our heart: his image is the very sense of our life. Man is interiorly iconic, Bobrinskoy says, and "the purpose of our life is to manifest this inner icon. The role of our spiritual fathers and mothers – our 'pedagogues' in the Church – is to lead us to just such a manifestation: 'My children, I am going through the pain of giving birth to you all over again, until Christ is formed in you' (Ga 4:19)".[8]

This explains Bobrinskoy's peculiar formulation and description of the icon's sacramentality:

On the basis of the correspondence that exists between the painted icon and the image of God in the human heart, we can return to the notion of the icon's sacramentality. With that we mean, on the one side, the icon's property and function of transmitting the sanctifying presence of Christ and his saints, and on the other its capacity to elevate to God both the prayer of the Church and personal prayer. That means that the icon possesses sacramen-

tal value and functions of diverse degrees and kinds. And I would like to distinguish three aspects of this sacramentality: its *making*, its *permanence* and its *mediation*.[9]

In its *making* the icon is born from the iconographer's purified heart, a heart in which the Spirit has worked, that is, to reproduce both within the iconographer and through his brush "the interior and eternal image". As a result, "from the icon's first conception to its completion, He, the Lord Christ, must increase and the painter decrease. At the end of his crucifying effort the iconographer must bow down, prostrate himself and erase himself before Him who transcends and judges all".

What happens in the icon's *permanence*?

The icon acquires a sacramental existence that is autonomous, objective, permanent and true for every person in every moment and everywhere. The icon not only reflects the glory of the Trinity's Kingdom which we are called to inherit; it actually contains the life-giving energy of that Kingdom. In St John of Damascus words, it is "full of divine energy and grace" (*De imaginibus*, I,16). That is: the icon is full of the Holy Spirit. It is not only an object and one of the means of contemplation, and therefore of prayer; it is truly a means, a channel, of human sanctification, due to the inseparable presence of grace and divine energy within it. This 'energetic' or sanctifying (because pneumatological) function of the icon is one of the fundamental characteristics of Orthodoxy's veneration of sacred images, and at the same time perhaps the only aspect of Orthodox icon-piety that Catholic theology has some difficulty accepting.[10]

From this line of reasoning Bobrinskoy then draws rather particular conclusions:

We should therefore conclude that in Orthodox theological awareness as in Orthodox piety, every icon is ontologically 'miraculous', overflowing with the life-giving energy of Christ's Spirit. Here too the Church's doctrine on the 'objective' sanctity of the sacraments (*ex opere operato*) and the openness of the sacrament's celebrant to God's Grace (*ex opere operantis*) should be totally applied to the icon as a place of divine presence and an instrument of divine grace. If every icon is 'miraculous' by virtue of its sacramental nature, some icons nonetheless manifest God's presence in a more tangible way.[11]

A third order or level of the sacramental nature of the icon – the reason for which it was made – is its function of 'mediation' in the context of profound personal prayer. Man, by his very nature, is a sacramental being; he is an 'iconic' creature, "an animal who has received the order to become a god", as St Basil says. He therefore needs a particular tool for the sacraments and symbols of his faith, in order to obtain the vision of and communion with the One who is invisible and indescribable. Through meditation on the icon, a truly personal relationship is established between the believer and the 'mystery' of the person represented. Orthodoxy never forgets the role of the icon (and of the sacraments) as 'deacons': to serve the coming of the Trinity's Kingdom in this world through the sanctification of the human heart.[12]

Insisting on the objective character of the icon's sanctifying energy, and on its 'miraculous' character, Bobrinskoy is definitely in continuity with the great theologians of the Russian diaspora to Paris. I refer especially to Sergej N. Bulgakov (1871–1944) and to the pages he wrote in 1932 on the icon and its veneration.[13] Warning against all inadequate perceptions of the icon,[14] Bulgakov underlined that the sacramental sense of the icon is tied in a particular way to its ecclesiastical consecration, linking even the icon's miraculous sense to this:

The veneration of icons is founded not only on the figures or events which these represent, but also on the faith in this presence of grace that the Church gives for the power of *sanctification* of icons. It is a sacramental act that justly establishes a *bond* between the prototype and the image, that which is figured and the figure itself. By means of this

sanctification, the icon of Christ becomes the mysterious place of an encounter between the person praying and Christ. The same is true for images of the Mother of God and of the saints, who, by means of this mediation, continue as it were their earthly lives in their manifestation (the veneration of holy relics has an analogous sense). By virtue of this presence of grace, by means of the icon a help can be communicated, as if it came from those who are represented in the icon. In this sense, and as a matter of principle, every icon that has been empowered – that is, blessed –, is miraculous.[15]

I also refer to Pavel Evdokimov (1901–70), to whom we owe masterful pages on the icon. Let it suffice to recall what he said in a famous introduction to Orthodoxy which he wrote:

Let us say only what is essential: for the East the icon is one of the sacramentals of presence, and the rite of consecration confers upon it a miraculous character: "channels of grace from the sanctifying power" (St John of Damascus, *Discourse on Sacred Images* I,16) – a place of 'epiphanies'. The Seventh Council very explicitly declares: "Both with the contemplation of Scripture and with the representation of the icon... we recall all the prototypes and *are brought into their company*" (Mansi, t.13, col. 482).[16]

And a little further on Evdokimov adds:

With its sacramental character the icon breaks open the triangle[17] and its immanentism, affirms its own freedom from both the artist and the spectator, and elicits not emotion but the coming of a fourth element in relation to the triangle: the advent of the transcendent *to whose presence the icon bears witness*. The artist disappears behind the tradition which speaks, the artwork becomes an outpouring of the presence, a theophany before which it is not possible to remain a mere spectator but we must bow down in an act of adoration and of prayer.[18]

A truly and remarkably different way of conceiving the relationship between prototype, icon and believer characterizes a text published in 1998, about ten years after Bobrinskoy's, by Olivier Clément, and similarly translated in various languages, entitled *Small Introduction to the Theology of the Icon*. In it appear several expressions that seem written in explicit opposition to Bobrinskoy's ideas:

Icon theologians have clearly distinguished icons from idols, underlining that the icon in no way pretends to grasp him (or her) whom it represents: an 'artificial image', the icon is in no sense of the same nature as its model. It does not belong to the magic order of possession but to the properly Christian order of communion. It is not part of the category of sacrament, in which matter receives a sanctifying force, but steers us to the category of relationship, of interpersonal encounter. The prototype – the divine-human (Christ) or the deified human (a saint) – eludes all opacity, every separation. On the contrary, it becomes present and welcoming in the image that represents its 'likeness'. The iconic presence is therefore a personal transparency "according to the likeness of hypostasis" (Theodore the Studite, *Antirrheticus* II, 3,1) – that is, the transparency of a person at once unique and in communion. The icon permits a meeting of gazes (from which derives the importance of the pupil of the eye[19] as the point of transcendence), in which, rather than watch, I am watched. I am watched by a gaze of sanctity, a gaze beyond death that powerfully draws me toward that beyond. The gaze of One who has risen from the dead, which awakens my own resurrection and God's image in me as a call to freedom and to love. The inscription of the Name on the icon (*épigraphé*) underlines this relationship with the person represented. And so St Theodore the Studite can affirm that the icon of Christ is Christ, without the least magical confusion: "The image of Christ according to relationship" (*Antirrheticus* 1,11).[20]

That Clément's words have a polemic tone *vis-à-vis* Bobrinskoy – or in any case in respect to the use of sacramental theology in reference to icons – is made clear by an indicator of some relevance. In his famous presentation

of the Orthodox Church, published in a first edition in Paris in 1961,[21] and then in several re-editions and translations,[22] a central term used to present the icon is *mysterion*:

The value of the icon is not only pedagogical but also *mysteric*. Divine grace reposes in [*dans*] the icon. This is the most essential and most mysterious point of icon theology: the 'likeness' with the prototype and the prototype's 'name' constitute the objective sanctity of the image: "The icon is sanctified by the name of God and the name of God's friends, the saints, that is, and it is for this reason that it receives the grace of the divine Spirit" (St John of Damascus: PG 94, col. 1300).[23]

This language of 1961 does not reappear in the *Small Introduction* of 1998, indeed there is no room in the later publication for the idea of a divine grace that reposes *in the icon*. There, even though Clément recalls a certain *mysteric* value of the icon, he modifies its sense. What he in fact says is: "The icon does not have a merely pedagogical value but a 'mysteric' one as well, disclosing a benediction given by the Church".[24]

Clément was probably influenced in this by Jean-Luc Marion's warning to take care in using the term 'sacrament' for icons. In fact we should not forget that the French philosopher, basing his argument especially on Theodore the Studite's interpretation of the icon, precisely in the icon's non-sacramental character saw its difference from the Eucharist. "Whence the importance", he wrote, "of not qualifying the icon with the title of sacrament. The icon is closely bound to its paradoxical legitimacy as *typos*: sign and not nature of the invisible – a distant figure of the invisible, precisely because the invisible is universal … the icon declares itself to be the useless servant of a veneration that does not touch it, but before which the icon disappears to the point of transparency".[25] Clément's attention to the young Marion's reflections is beyond doubt,[26] even if his perception of the category of 'likeness' is different and more effectively recovers Theodore the Studite's line of reasoning. Marion in fact criticizes a certain ethical reading of the icon.[27]

We should not exaggerate this interpretive tension between Bobrinskoy and Clément, since it remains true for both that the icon opens to believers a relationship and communion with the prototype. Yet there is a difference that should not be underestimated: in Olivier Clément's view matter does not receive a sanctifying force, a divine energy. It would be really difficult to argue that such an interpretation of the icon corresponds to the Church's experience of the veneration of sacred icons and of their miraculous character.

After 1300 years, therefore, the St John of Damascus/Theodore Studite duality still marks Orthodoxy. I wish to conclude with a curiosity: precisely in the period when Clément showed such reticence in using the term sacrament for icons, John Paul II, writing his *Letter to Artists* of 1999, citing Pavel Florenskij went so far as to say of the Middle Ages:

> The centuries that followed bore witness to a great development of Christian art. In the East

the art of icons continued to flourish, tied to significant theological and aesthetic canons and sustained by the conviction that the icon is, in a certain sense, a sacrament: in analogy with what happens in the sacraments, in fact, the icon renders the mystery of the Incarnation present in both of its aspects. Precisely for this the icon's beauty can best be appreciated in a church with burning lamps that call forth from the penumbra infinite reflections of light. On this experience Pavel Florenskij writes: "Gold, barbarous, heavy, futile in broad daylight, in flickering lamplight or in the light of candles comes alive, gleaming with myriad sparks, now here, now there, letting us intuit other kinds of light, not terrestrial, that fill the space of heaven".[28]

In this passage, John Paul II somehow paid homage to the Orthodox idea of the sacramentality of the icon, precisely at the moment when an authoritative Orthodox theologian like Clément called for caution in the use of that term. ▪

---

1 The icon of Christ is the first of icons; all the others are such only in as much as they represent the saints *in Christo.*

2 St John of Damascus, *De imaginibus,* I,16 (PG 94, col. 1245).

3 Egon Sendler, *L'icône, image de l'invisible,* Paris, 1981, p. 47.

4 Theodore the Studite, *Epistola ad Platonem* (PG 99, cols. 504–5).

5 The English text of Boris Bobrinskoy 'The Icon: Sacrament of the Kingdom' is available in <http://www.apostoliki-diakonia.gr/en_main/catehism/theologia_zoi/themata.asp?cat=leit&NF=1&contents=contents.asp&main=texts&file=6.htm>, accessed 30th May 2019. That digital version reproduces the original English text published with the abovementioned title in *Saint Vladimir's Theological Quarterly,*

31 (1987), pp. 287–96. For an Italian translation see Boris Bobrinskoy, *Il mistero della presenza*, Qigajon, 2000, esp. pp. 17–27.

6 Bobrinskoy 1987, op. cit.

7 St John of Damascus, *De Imaginibus* I,16 (PG 94, col. 1245).

8 Bobrinskoy 1987, op. cit.

9 Ibid.

10 Ibid.

11 Ibid.

12 Ibid.

13 Père Serge Boulgakov, *L'Orthodoxie. Essai sur la doctrine de l'Eglise*, translated from Russian by Constantin Andronikof, Lausanne, 1980, pp. 155–60. It should be remembered that a first, shorter version of this work was published by Alcan (Paris) in 1932.

14 Ibid., p. 157: "The Orthodox Christian prays before an icon of Christ as if before Christ himself, but the image, which is the place of this presence, remains an object and in no way becomes an idol or a fetish".

15 Ibid.

16 Paul Evdokimov, *L'Orthodoxie*, Paris, 1959.

17 From the context it appears that the 'triangle' is that which connects the artist, the work and the spectator.

18 Ibid., p. 322.

19 A strange coincidence: Guillaume Apollinaire, in the poem *Zone* at the beginning of the collection *Alcools* writes: "Christ, pupil of the eye".

20 Olivier Clément, 'Petite introduction à la théologie de l'icône', *Contacts*, no. 181 (1998), pp. 25–32.

21 Olivier Clément, *L'Église orthodoxe*, Paris, 1961.

22 See the Italian translation of the 7th French edition: Olivier Clément, *La Chiesa ortodossa*, Brescia, 2005.

23 Ibid., p. 115.

24 Clément 2001, op. cit., p. 59.

25 In 1986 Jean-Luc Marion was invited to speak in the international conference *Nicée II* held at the Collège de France on 2–4 October. He read a paper entitled "Le prototype de l'image", later published with the title "Le prototype et l'image", in *La croisée du visible*, Paris, 1991. The volume has been re-published by PUF in Paris in 1996, where the essay occupies pages 117–54. My quotation is at p. 138: "D'ou

l'importance de ne pas qualifier l'icône commune du titre de sacrement. L'icône s'en tient donc strictement à sa légitimité paradoxale de tupos: signe et non nature de l'invisible – figure à distance de l'invisible, précisément parce que l'invisible la marque de part en part … l'icône se proclame elle-même serviteur inutile d'une vénération qu'elle ne touche pas, mais devant laquelle elle s'efface jusqu'à la transparence".

26 Cfr. Jean-Pierre Rosa, 'L'arte contemporanea e il religioso (intervista con Olivier Clément)', *Nuova umanità*, no. 67, 12 (1990), pp. 75–83. At p. 82, after recalling von Balthasar on different themes, Clément mentions Marion with these words: "E c'è anche in qualcuno come Jean Luc Marion, che è molto più giovane, una riflessione estremamente acuta sull'icona".

27 Cfr. Jean-Luc Marion, *La croisée du visible*, Paris, 2007, pp. 136–7: "L'iconoclasme critique la dérive idolâtrique supposée des icônes, parce qu'il s'obstine à les interpréter selon la logique de la similitude et de la rivalité mimétique, sans jamais soupçonner – ou accepter – quel le typos ait rompu sans retour avec l'imitation d'un original".

28 Cfr. <http://w2.vatican.va/content/john-paul-ii/it/letters/1999/documents/hf_jp-ii_let_23041999_artists.html>, accessed 30 May 2019. The citation, found in number 8 of John Paul II's *Letter*, is from Pavel Florenskij, *Reverse perspective* [1919–20], Italian ed. with the title *La prospettiva rovesciata ed altri scritti*, Rome, 1984, p. 63.

Florence and the Theological Vocation of Art from Arnolfo and Giotto to Michelangelo

TIMOTHY VERDON

Florentines, refined art connoisseurs, have long considered themselves competent judges of talent. In his *Purgatorio*, Dante Alighieri confirms that his contemporaries thought they knew who was better, who worse, and – commenting on a change of taste in his time that would prove fundamental for later art –, says: "Credette Cimabue ne la pittura / tener lo campo, e ora ha Giotto il grido, / sì che la fama di colui è scura" – "In painting Cimabue thought he held the field, but now Giotto is acclaimed and the older artist's fame grows dim" (XI, 94–6).

In the context of the present symposium it is useful to ask *why* people of Dante's time preferred Giotto (fig. 1) to the older Cimabue (fig. 2). Centuries of art historical studies, from Vasari's *Lives* and pre-Vasarian sources on, have explained the formal and cultural reasons for this choice – greater plasticity, new naturalism, the rediscovery of Graeco-Roman sculpture –, but only recently have scholars begun to discuss its theological meaning: the peculiar capacity of Giotto's style to express the then new Franciscan spirituality focused on the human body and emotions, and thus to take Western art beyond the Byzantine aesthetic of sacral alterity.[1]

My point is that, if Dante's generation preferred Giotto to Cimabue, it was because Giot-to's style satisfied needs that were not only aesthetic but religious and, indeed, theological, visually translating the new incarnational emphasis of Western spirituality and articulating an anthropological model coherent with the period's nascent humanism. While preserving the Byzantine conviction of the sacramental force of images, Florentine art in Giotto's time responded to the vocation assigned by the Bible to all created things, to speak of God, perfecting new languages in which to communicate his mystery. From Arnolfo di Cambio, author of the early 14th-century *Madonna and Child* carved for the main door of the rising cathedral (fig. 3), to Giotto and his school, to Masaccio and Donatello, and finally to Michelangelo and other 16th-century masters, the overall development of Florentine art implies a response to this expressive 'calling'.

Within this general orientation there are, moreover, episodes of specific theological reflection, such as the series of reliefs realized for Giotto's Bell Tower by one of his collaborators, the sculptor Andrea Pisano together with his workshop in the 1340s, with scenes illustrating the arts, crafts and scientific occupations of Florence at that time: a series in which Antonio Paolucci correctly recognized a "theology of human work"[2] – an intuition perhaps derived from Lorenzo Ghiberti, who

1. Giotto di Bondone, *Madonna Enthroned* (*Ognissanti Madonna*), Florence, Gallerie degli Uffizi, Galleria delle Statue e delle Pitture.

2. Cimabue, *Rucellai Madonna*, Florence, Gallerie degli Uffizi, Galleria delle Statue e delle Pitture.

in his *Commentari* described the personages shown in the reliefs as "the inventors of art". From the first relief in the series on, the cycle in fact speaks of *creativity*: of human beings who, fashioned in the image and likeness of the Creator, are naturally 'creative' in their relationship with the world. The seven reliefs of the main front of the Bell Tower narrate first God's creative activity, then that of early humankind, moving from *God Creating Adam* to *The Creation of Eve* and to *Adam and Eve Working*, he with a hoe, she with the distaff.[3] The story line then proceeds to Jabal, inventor of the art of herding (Gn 4:20), and Jubal, father of those who play musical instruments (Gn 4:21; fig. 4), to Tubalkain, an artisan of works in copper and iron (Gn 4:22; fig. 5), and finally to Noah, who, since he planted a vineyard after the Flood (Gn 10:20), represents the tradition of winemaking.

This choice of Biblical subjects is actually rather conventional: we often find the same steps of Creation illustrated on French cathedrals – at Chartres, Laon, Auxerre, Bourges and Lyon for example. Whoever planned the series of reliefs for the Florentine Bell Tower wanted simply to satisfy a need common to large European churches, therefore. But he did it in an absolutely unusual way, leaving out of the Adam and Eve story their temptation and expulsion from Paradise, in order to arrive straightaway at their work, which is thus not presented as a punishment for sin but as a direct consequence of having been made in the likeness of a *Deus Artifex*, an Artisan God.

Such exaltation of creative activities, among which the fine arts of painting, sculpture, architecture, mirrors the ideas of a well-known Florentine theologian of that time, Fra Remigio de' Girolami, a Dominican friar who, after studying with St Thomas Aquinas at Naples or Paris, began a school of theology for Florentine laymen, among whose pupils was Dante himself, at least according to tradition. In a treatise probably published in the early 14th century, *Contra falsos ecclesiae professores*, Fra Remigio elaborated the theory that the Church 're-news' the disciplines of human learning, giving them sense and illuminating their function as mirrors of the multiform perfection of Christ.[4] He speaks in these terms of many of the occupations illustrated in the Bell Tower reliefs: of *lanificium*, for example, the making of wool cloth; of *navigatio*, the art of traveling and transporting merchandise by water; of *agricultura*, agriculture (fig. 6), which leads him to ponder man's contemplative instinct, and the solitude of forests and fields where, far from the city, man works with only family and domestic animals for company.

For all their interest, however, the Bell Tower reliefs have a merely ancillary function, illustrating ideas articulated by Fra Remigio or other theologians of that time. Completely different is the contribution of a monumental fresco executed by Masaccio eighty years later, in the conventual Dominican church of Santa Maria

4. Andrea Pisano, *Jubal, the beginning of the art of music*, detail, Florence, Museo dell'Opera del Duomo.

5. Andrea Pisano, *Tubalkain, the beginning of metalwork*, detail, Florence, Museo dell'Opera del Duomo.

3. Arnolfo di Cambio, *Madonna 'with Glass Eyes'*, Florence, Museo dell'Opera del Duomo.

6. Andrea Pisano, *Agriculture*, detail, Florence, Museo dell'Opera del Duomo.

Novella, depicting the *Holy Trinity the Virgin, St John and Donors*, whose theological content is conveyed by purely artistic means: figural composition, anatomy, perspective, architecture and location (fig. 7).[5] The artist, to whom we suppose the friars explained the subject's meaning, found solutions that not only 'illustrated' but also commented upon trinitarian theology, offering a visualization that is also catechesis. Masaccio situates the Divine Persons in relation to the human beings shown, using perspective to suggest spiritual 'depth'

7. Masaccio, *The Holy Trinity with the Virgin, St John and Donors*, Florence, Basilica of Santa Maria Novella.

and ancient architecture to evoke 'eternity'. His artistic means are connatural to his message, that is – the horizontal skeleton below the main scene balances the vertical Christ figure surmounted by the Holy Spirit and the Father, summing up in abstract but clear terms the work's paschal message, just as the location of the fresco opposite a door leading from the church graveyard suggests that Christian death admits believers to the space of the Father, Son and Spirit. In Masaccio, I mean, the formal organization of the image's components offers an original commentary upon the theme, revealing the artist *as* theologian.

In another early 15th-century Florentine master, the Dominican friar John of Fiesole, known as Fra Angelico, we find a veritable interpenetration of the professions of 'painter' and 'theologian', in works that are at once icons and mystical dissertations.[6] An eloquent example of Angelico's theological/pictorial art is his fresco at the Friary of San Marco depicting the *Transfiguration* (fig. 8), in which the gazes and gestures of the protagonists accurately interpret the New Testament event. Angelico knows that this vision of the Savior's glory was accorded to Peter, James and John in view of the imminent Passion, as St Leo the Great affirmed, insisting that "the Transfiguration without doubt served to remove from the disciples' soul the scandal of the cross, so that the humiliation of the Passion, accepted voluntarily, might not shake faith of these men to whom the sublimity of Christ's hidden dignity had been revealed".[7] And to express all this Angelico has invented a compositional formula of enormous iconic force, making of the sign of Jesus's humiliating death the decisive component of his glorious vitality: Christ's raised and outstretched arms in fact express willingness, freedom – they are a natural development of his corporeal contrapposto, clearly legible despite the Savior's long, white robes.[8] They communicate what St Leo called Christ's "hidden dignity".

Angelico realized this fresco in the cell of a brother friar, who, like himself, was a member of the Order of Preachers and possessed with the interpretive tools needed to decipher it. But even laymen of that time appreciated the theological nuances of such images, as we deduce from the words of a contemporary, the self-taught goldsmith Marco di Bartolomeo Rustici, whose account of a journey to the Holy Land uses terminology remarkably similar to the pictorial language of Angelico's *Transfiguration*. Speaking to a reader whose capacity to understand he takes for granted, Rustici exclaims:

> Oh, how glorious it would be, and gently consoling, to behold in heaven the glorious and yearned-for face of Jesus Christ, who is more beautiful than all the sons of men. My child, I do not mean that we should see him despised, reviled, without the beauty in which his most sweet mother clothed his humanity [–]: not beaten, whipped, mistreated, despised and crucified [–], but rather, I say again, clothed with the stole of immortality and crowned with that glory which his eternal Father gave him on the day of his holy resurrection – on the day, that is, when Holy Church sings, Hec est dies quam fecit dominus exultemus et lettemur inea, which means 'This is the day which the Lord has made, let us sing and rejoice in it'. And think: in that vision will be the repletion of which the holy prophet speaks when he says: Satiabor domine cum aparverit grolia tua; to wit: 'Lord, I will be replete when your glory shows forth in my soul'.[9]

These words, written around 1447, powerfully express the mystic aspiration to which Angelico's painting appealed: a yearning for the Divine then widespread, veined with biblical and liturgical allusions and perceived as an experience of inner transformation.

The 16th century the heir to this tradition of exegetical iconography, and of the theo-poetic identity of Florentine artists, was Michelangelo Buonarroti, who, with an older brother, Lionardo, a friar at San Marco, must have known the art of Fra Angelico, of which he in fact preserved the luminosity and spiritual ardor.[10] Michelangelo's theological use of biblical sources is treated in the third and fourth volumes of my recent study of the Sistine Chapel,[11] his interest in Resurrection theology in an essay I wrote for the 2017 London exhibition on Mi-

8. Fra Angelico, *Transfiguration of Christ*, Florence, Museo di San Marco.

chelangelo and Sebastiano del Piombo,[12] and his extraordinarily deep meditation on Christ's death is the theme of another essay, dedicated to the Florence *Pietà*.[13]

In that sculpture (fig. 9) – the artist's penultimate work, carved for his own tomb and showing Michelangelo 'as' Nicodemus, holding Christ's dead body –, there is a virtual symbiosis, practically a fusion of the two male figures, so that our eye has difficulty distinguishing where Christ's body ends and Michelangelo's begins. Particularly if we imagine an upward-angled view for this work probably meant to stand above an altar – the view of the priest celebrating Mass, or of the kneeling faithful – it is clear that the figure looming above Christ constitutes a physical and psychological extension of the Savior. Or, to put it differently, Jesus's youthful torso, powerful even in death, is seen as flowing from the hunched form above it, the old man tensed in his effort to bear Christ's weight.

The theological implications of this extraordinary melding of forms – of old and young, living and dead – must be sought in the same Gospel of John which recounts Nicodemus' visit to Christ by night. Two passages in

9. Michelangelo Buonarroti, *Pietà Bandini*, Florence, Museo dell'Opera del Duomo.

particular, related to the Nicodemus episode but not dependent on it, suggest what Michelangelo wanted to convey in marrying his own figure with that of Christ in such a way as to render them indistinguishable: passages explicitly relating the believer's (and Nicodemus') hope for rebirth after death with the mystery of the Holy Eucharist. In John 6, where Jesus deeply troubles his listeners by insisting that he, Christ, is the 'bread of life' and whoever eats this bread will live forever, he finally states:

My flesh is real food and my blood is real drink. He who eats my flesh and drinks my blood lives in me and I in him. As I, who am sent by the living Father, draw life from the Father, so whoever eats me will draw life from me. This is the bread come down from heaven; not like the bread our ancestors ate: they are dead, but anyone who eats this bread will live forever (Jn 6:55–8).

The second passage is the farewell discourse which Jesus pronounces at the Last Supper, the recurrent theme of which is the perfect communion of life between Christ and his heavenly Father which, as he prepares to die, Jesus extends to his disciples. 'Do you not believe that

I am in the Father and the Father is in me?', he asks at the beginning of this long monologue (Jn 14:10), and then, presenting his relationship to his followers as that of a vine to its branches, he tells them: 'whoever remains in me, with me in him, bears fruit in plenty' (Jn 15:5). He teaches them these things, he says, 'so that my own joy may be in you and your joy be complete' (Jn 15:11), and 'so that you may find peace in me' (Jn 16:33). Finally, for these followers who in him will find joy and peace, Christ asks his Father:

> May they be one in us as you are in me and I am in you ... With me in them and you in me ... so that the love with which you loved me may be in them, and so that I may be in them. (Jn 17:21, 23, 26).

These passages describe a physical as well as spiritual communion of life in which, eating Christ's body and drinking his blood, we live in him and he in us: we draw life from him as he himself draws life from God his Father. Part of the meaning of Michelangelo's composition in the *Pietà* – the aging body fused with the youthful one, a man facing death supporting the God who would rise from the dead – has to do with this 'communion' made present in the Eucharist.

There is a further dimension to this relationship of total union, which perhaps sheds light on the formal genesis of the Florence *Pietà*. St Gregory of Nyssa, reflecting on the passage in Ecclesiastes: "There is a time for everything ... a time for giving birth, a time for dying" (Qo 3:1–2), says:

> we are ourselves in a certain sense fathers of ourselves, when, by our good intentions and our free choice, we conceive and give birth to ourselves and bring ourselves to the light.[14]

The saint then specifies that a believer's 'self-fathering' consists in allowing "the form of Christ" to be produced in him: this is the 'time to be born'. And the 'time to die' is not in contrast with such spiritual birth, but its necessary complement: the believer "who never lives to sin, who mortifies continually the limbs of his flesh, and bears about in his body the dying of the body of Christ, who is always being crucified with Christ, who never lives to himself but has Christ living within himself" experiences, according to Gregory of Nyssa, 'a timely death which has produced true life'.[15]

Now if, with Michelangelo scholar Charles De Tolnay, we see the Florence *Pietà* as developed from the composition of a black chalk drawing made for Vittoria Colonna, depicting the body of Christ deposed from the cross and placed between the spread legs of Mary, his mother,[16] then Gregory of Nyssa's metaphor of the believer's 'parenting' of Christ suddenly has remarkable force. In the sculpture intended for his own tomb, Michelangelo puts himself in place of Mary: not as 'mother' but as 'father' of Christ, who is 'born' from the artist's aging body upon the altar. Michelangelo the penitent 'produces' the form of Christ in his own flesh, for indeed, as St Ambrose teaches:

> Every soul who has believed conceives and generates the Word of God ... According to the flesh, one woman is the mother of Christ, but according to faith Christ is the fruit of all men.[17]

Thus, to Nicodemus' question, as to how a man already old could be born again, the Florence *Pietà* answers, in the spirit of St Cyril of Alexandria, that:

> the body of Christ gives life to those who share with him. By being one with those who must suffer death, Christ's body drives death out; by bringing forth in itself a principle capable of utterly destroying corruption, his body expels corruption.[18]

In this work intended for the tomb in which Michelangelo expected his own body to be laid, this response gives eloquent expression to the artist's theological hope for the 'new birth' of resurrection. ■

1   On this subject see Caroline Bynum, 'Franciscan Spirituality: Two Approaches', *Medievalia et Humanistica*, new series, 7 (1976), pp. 195–7; Hans Belting, *Die Oberkirche von San Francesco in Assisi. Ihre Dekoration als Aufgabe und die Genese einer neuen Wandmalerei*, Berlin, 1977; Henry Thode, *Franz von Assisi und die Anfänge der Kunst der Renaissance in Italien*, Berlin, 1885; Chiara Frugoni, *Francesco e l'invenzione delle stimmate. Una storia per immagini fino a Bonaventura e Giotto*, Turin, 1993; Ewert H. Cousins, 'Francis of Assisi. Christian Mysticism at the Crossroads', in *Mysticism and Religious Traditions*, edited by Steven T. Katz, New York, 1983, pp. 163–90; Giulio Renzi, O.F.M., *Piero della Francesca: pittore teologo nella Basilica di San Francesco ad Arezzo*, Siena, 1990, pp. 17–18; Timothy Verdon, '*Verbum caro factum*. Teologia, spiritualità ed iconografia del pulpito istoriato', in *Pulpiti medievali toscani*, edited by Daniela Lamberini, Florence, 1999, pp. 17–29; Timothy Verdon, *L'arte sacra in Italia. L'immaginazione religiosa dal paleocristiano al postmoderno*, Milan, 2001, pp. 76–89; Timothy Verdon, *The Story of St Francis of Assisi in Twenty-Eight Scenes*, Brewster, MA, and Barga, 2015, pp. XI–XXX.

2   Antonio Paolucci, 'Intorno alle sculture del Campanile: la statua e il suo doppio', in *Il Campanile di Giotto*, edited by Timothy Verdon, Florence, 1994, pp. 41–58.

3   See Timothy Verdon, '"Alza la voce con forza". L'iconografia del Campanile e l'annuncio cristiano', in *Il Campanile di Giotto* 1994, op. cit., pp. 85–115.

4   Emilio Panella, O.P., 'Per lo studio di Fra Remigio de' Girolami', *Memorie domenicane*, new series, no. 10 (1979), pp. 19–308: 109–74.

5   See Joseph Polzer, 'The Anatomy of Masaccio's Holy Trinity', *Jahrbuch der Berliner Museen*, 13 (1971), pp. 18–59; Edgar Hertlein, *Masaccios Trinitat: Kunst, Geschichte und Politik der Fruhrenaissance in Florenz*, Florence, 1979; Alexander Perrig, 'Masaccios "Trinità" und der Sinn der Zentralperspektive', *Marburger Handbuch für Kunstwissenschaft*, 21 (1986), pp. 11–43, and W. Kemp, 'Masaccios "Trinitat" im Kontext', *ibid.*, pp. 45–72; Ursula Schlegel, 'Observations on Masaccio's Trinity in Santa Maria Novella', *The Art Bulletin*, 45 (1963), pp. 19–33; Otto von Simson, 'Uber die Bedeutung von Masaccios Trinitatfresko in Santa Maria Novella', *Jahrbuch der Berliner Museen*, 8 (1966), pp. 119–59; Rona Goffen, 'Masaccio's Trinity and the Letter to the Hebrews', *Memorie domenicane*, new series, 11 (1980), pp. 489–504; Charles Dempsey, 'Masaccio's *Trinity*: Altarpiece or Tomb?', *The Art Bulletin*, 54 (1972), pp. 279–81; Timothy Verdon, 'Rappresentazioni della Santissima Trinità', *Ratio imaginis. Esperienza teologica, esperienza artistica* (a special number of the review *Vivens homo*, of the Facoltà Teologica dell'Italia Centrale), Bologna, 2001, pp. 207–15; Timothy Verdon, 'Masaccio's Trinity. Theological, Social and Civic Meanings', in *The Cambridge Companion to Masaccio*, edited by Diane Cole Ahl, Cambridge, 2002, pp. 158–76; Timothy Verdon, 'L'amore, la famiglia, la città: la *Trinità* del Masaccio in contesto', in *La Trinità del Masaccio. Arte e teologia*, edited by Severino Dianich and Timothy Verdon (special number of the review *Vivens homo*), Bologna, 15 (2004), pp. 127–43.

6   See Timothy Verdon, *Beato Angelico*, Milan, 2015, passim.

7   *Sermo LI*, in *Sermones et epistolae*, PL, 54, cols. 310–11.

8   See Verdon 2015, op. cit., pp. 10–13.

9   *Codice Rustici. Dimostrazione dell'andata o viaggio al Santo Sepolcro e al monte Sinai di Marco di Bartolomeo Rustici*, edited by Kathleen Olive and Nerida Newbigen, Florence, 2015, fol. 59v.

10   Timothy Verdon, *Michelangelo teologo. Fede e creatività tra Rinascimento e Controriforma*, Milan, 2005, pp. 18–22 and passim. See also Charles De Tolnay, *The Art and Thought of Michelangelo*, New York, 1964: particularly chapter 3, 'Michelangelo's Religious Outlook', pp. 58–62.

11   Timothy Verdon, *La Cappella Sistina. Cuore e simbolo della Chiesa*, 4 vols., Vatican City, 2017.

12   Timothy Verdon, 'Birth, Death, rebirth. The Infancy, Passion and Resurrection of Christ in Michelangelo', in *Michelangelo and Sebastiano*, catalogue of the exhibition (London, National Gallery, 2017), edited by Matthias Wivel, London, 2017, pp. 53–64.

13   Timothy Verdon, 'Michelangelo and the Body of Christ. Religious Meaning in the Florence *Pietà*', in *Michelangelo's Florence Pietà*, edited by Jack Wasserman, Princeton, 2003, pp. 127–48.

14   PG, 44, cols. 702–5 (Homily 6).

15   *Ibid.*

16   Charles De Tolnay, *Michelangelo. The Final Period*, Princeton, 1971 (2nd ed.; 1st ed. Princeton, 1960), p. 151.

17   PL, 15, cols. 1635–42 (Expositio in Lucam).

18   Commentary on the Gospel of St John, Book 4,2. PG, 73, cols. 563–6 (Commentary on the Gospel of St John).

Gates of the Kingdom

A Narratological Reading of Lorenzo Ghiberti's Projects for the Florence Baptistery Doors

AGNESE MARIA FORTUNA

In the fifty years in which Lorenzo Ghiberti worked on the doors of the Florentine Baptistery (fig. 1), and which roughly coincided with the first half of the 15th century, there was widespread acceptance of that new mind-set which we usually call Renaissance humanism. It was a genuine cultural revolution that was born and that flourished in republican Florence, a city whose prosperity and mercantile and political enterprise found programmatic expression in a season of artistic and intellectual activity destined to mark indelibly not only the city's physiognomy but that of Europe in general. The Florentine chancery and the cultivated circle that frequented it directly or indirectly formed generations of functionaries and political figures destined to be active at Italian and European courts for several decades. In the popular imagination, humanist Florence became the concrete ideal of civil life, a lived and living expression of that ideal of *eudaimonia* – or human flourishing[1] – which found in ancient source texts, studied from this moment on with particular philological respect and care, its examples, measure, and rationale.

The time's innovative character, of which its actors were well aware, had many aspects.

This essay will consider how this character is found to reverberate in the change in narrative method which Ghiberti introduced in conceiving and realizing the Door of Paradise with respect to the door he had realized for the Baptistery twenty years earlier, the so-called 'North Door'.[2]

Beyond metaphor

The character of an era can also be considered as a particular narrative or interpretive style: every age has its own way of reading events and recounting them, and this is especially true for all that regards foundation myths and the accounts in which a given culture recognizes and expresses itself. By choice the substantially homogeneous society of medieval Christendom preferred the metaphorical forms of typology and allegory.

The intelligibility of metaphor, which works according to the logic of an assumed similitude or of an analogical relationship, in fact relies on a reference to a further level of meaning beyond the literal narrative. That in turn takes for granted not only the same broadly shared universe of sense, but also an implicit devaluation of the inherent worth of the literal level. In the case of works of religious character such as the doors of the Florence Baptistery, the dynamics of translation from the contingent level (the history of the people of Israel, of John the Baptist, and of Jesus right up to the founding of the Church) to the transcendent level (the divine plan for salvation) are perfectly explicit.

With the changing times, shaken by the political and religious crises that hit Italy in particular, and afflicted by terrible outbreaks of the Black Plague, the last of which decimated Florence on the eve of the 15th century, religious, political and social uncertainty finally led to a radical rethinking of the ideal balances that had sustained the preceding era. The universe of sense remained firmly Christian, but the reference to transcendence could no longer be declined as in earlier times, nor could earthly existence be considered merely a dolorous parenthesis to be patiently supported in obedient expectation of an other-worldly prize. Before the practically daily reality of death, people began to re-evaluate life.

1. Baptistery of San Giovanni, Florence, view of the East front showing the Door of Paradise.

The dimension of the present with its urgent demands, the decisive role of human behavior – in short the exercise of individual freedom in the collective task of giving concrete expression to human and Christian flourishing –, tended now to be understood as signs of the presence or absence of God's Kingdom in the here and now of every aspect of the city's life. An attempt to answer the religious crisis was the reunification project that led to the Council which began its final session in Florence in 1439. Prior to the Council, there had been renewed interest in Greek culture which had led to a rediscovery of the eastern patristic tradition, encouraged and shaped by the philological fervor that guided studies and research.

One thinks, for example, of how crucial the brief role played by Manual Chrysolorus was, after he was summoned by Coluccio Salutati[3] to teach in the Studio Fiorentino in 1397. Even more relevant, as far as theology goes, was the arrival of Greek scholars for the Council and the role of Ambrogio Traversari, indicated by Richard Krautheimer as the effective author of the iconographic project of the Ghiberti door known as 'of Paradise', inspired by Ambrogio's writings.[4]

As is known, the question of the paternity of the iconographic project of the Gates of Paradise has long been debated.[5] Opposing Krautheimer's hypothesis, Frederick Hartt, a former Krautheimer pupil, indicated St Antonino Pierozzi, undoubted inspirer and director of many Florentine iconographic projects, as the author.[6] More recently, first Sharon Dale and then Amy Bloch, while not absolutely excluding the presence of a director, underline the role of Ghiberti himself in defining the work's doctrinal point of view – a seemingly daring hypothesis given the complex contents of the panels.[7]

Therefore various events and factors led people to abandon the privileged vision of an earlier age. In the city squares, or, rather, in intellectual circles, the other's point of view returned, bearing with it the appeal of an ancient but half-forgotten tradition. The vision *sub specie aeternitatis*, that up to that time had structured the imagination, gave way to the perspective vision of human ocular experience in the works of the artists then engaged in illustrating the changing times on the walls and doors of Florentine religious and civil buildings. This resulted in the proliferation of possible visions or interpretations, with their full weight of uncertainty and fallibility, as well as in the involvement of the viewer as an eye-witness of the events narrated, which the perspective implied.[8]

The narrative system of the North Door

The North Door (fig. 2), realized by Ghiberti between 1403 and 1424, sums up the New Testament in twenty quatrefoils going from the Annunciation to Pentecost and proceeds from the lower left to the upper right, above two rows of panels with 'witnesses': four doctors of the Latin church (from the left Ambrose, Gregory, Jérome and Augustine) and the evangelists (from the left John, Matthew, Luke and Mark). The elegant sobriety of the narration draws upon 14th-century models, endowing them with new pathos.

The North Door's relationship with the South Door (fig. 3), devoted to the life of John the Baptist and realized by Andrea Pisano from 1329 to 1336,[9] is not only one of form and style. In both we note the same relevance given to the chronological sequence composing a narrative in separate scenes: a sequence faithful to Gospel sources and divided into two parts corresponding to the sequence of preaching/martyrdom, even if the reading order of the two doors is different.

In Pisano's work the order in fact develops from top to bottom and from left to right, and the bipartition is articulated as in a diptych, with the first part on the valve to the viewer's left and the second part to the right.[10] In both doors, moreover, in the two lowest registers

2. Lorenzo Ghiberti, North Door, Florence, Museo dell'Opera del Duomo.

3. Andrea Pisano, South Door, Florence, Museo dell'Opera del Duomo.

certain personages are portrayed: in Pisano's case the seven traditional virtues to which Humility is added (an opportune addition for the city to which Dante, in the 16th Canto of his Inferno, had attributed measureless pride).[11]

As in the South Door the history of St John the Baptist emerges from the combination of a section dedicated to the saint's preaching followed and completed by a section dedicated to his martyrdom, so in the North Door the first ten historiated panels, in the lower part, narrate events preceding Jesus's entry into Jerusalem, and the ten upper panels events following it. Some iconographic patterns are significantly repeated: compare, for example, the panel illustrating the *Annunciation* and that showing the *Temptation of Christ*, or the *Last Supper* panel and that depicting *Pentecost*.

The hermeneutic key of Ghiberti's entire program, which culminates significantly with the foundation of the Church, is pneumatic and incarnational. It is worthy of note that the only miracles represented are *Jesus Walking on the Waters and Saving St Peter* (fig. 4) and the *Resurrection of Lazarus*.

Although the scenes should certainly be read in light of the baptismal function of the building for which the doors were made, it is not

out of place to hypothesize a reading that links some of the episodes, and the way in which they are represented, to the sad historical moment of the Great Western Schism.

In particular the scene of *Jesus walking on the waters and saving Peter*, based on the Gospel account in Matthew (14,24–33), in the foreground – in front of the boat with its cruciform mast and gathered canvas (a symbol of the Church navigating in stormy seas) – shows Peter sinking but saved by Christ, who then reproves him for his lack of faith – as if alluding to the dramatic crisis of the papacy of that time and exhorting to hope in a salvation that could come from Christ alone.

The narrative system of the Gates of Paradise

As is well known, the original iconographic program drawn up in 1424 by Leonardo Bruni, which has reached us in a transcription contained in a letter from Bruni to Niccolò da Uzzano and the other members of a deputation created by the Calimala Guild to decide the program and artist of the new Baptistery door, declines the history of salvation in a series of exemplary episodes, according to the typological mechanism (NT<–OT).[12] In Bruni's program each scene followed the logic of metaphor, that is, with that translation from the contingent level to the transcendent one described above. Despite the presence of a chronological reading (moving from the 'effects', as Ghiberti calls them in his *Commentari*: from the Creation to Solomon's Judgment), the interpretive key was in fact typological. Every scene would have presented a personage or event whose *exemplar* is Christ seen in his soteriological function, according to the extremely rich patristic tradition. From the point of view of the door's narrative logic, every episode should therefore have repeated the same paradigmatic schema.

Given this typological mechanism, which takes for granted but does not illustrate the history of salvation, resuming it in representative symbolic codes, the result would have been an accentuation of the effect of translation: in all probability the contingent element would have been completely 'transubstantiat-

4. Lorenzo Ghiberti, *Jesus Walking on the Waters and Saving St Peter*, Florence, Museo dell'Opera del Duomo, North Door.

5. Coppo di Marcovaldo (?), *Christ as Pantokrator*, Florence, Baptistery of San Giovanni, vault.

ing in each a unique narrative system, with a variation of narrative patterns at the limit of virtuosity. That notwithstanding, it maintains the metaphoric system as well and, in a certain sense, doubles it. We thus have stories inserted in the history of salvation – or, rather, episodes inserted in stories inserted in the history of salvation.

The first impression, even for viewers unfamiliar with the stories illustrated, is that of a juxtaposition or dislocation of representations of events based on the shared space they occupy. Even if knowledgeable viewers may sometimes note 'causal connections' among the episodes of each panel, giving the sense of chronological contiguity (in the *Creation of Adam and Eve* scene, for example, where there is also the account of Original Sin, or in the panel with the *Stories of Abraham*, fig. 7), at other times the story becomes, as it were,

ed', so to speak, with events and personages appearing literally abstract, and the tension toward transcendence would have been much more marked (one thinks for example of the second relief pilaster on the façade of Orvieto Cathedral, realized by Lorenzo Maitani and his workshop more or less between 1300 and 1330).[13]

Making it all intelligible was the supposition, necessary and taken for granted, of a shared universe of sense – specifically the supposed knowledge of, and rootedness in, the foundation myth of Christian identity understood in mysteric terms. In the position where the door was mounted this would have offered itself as a catechetical tool (making the 'mysteries' clear), implicitly turned toward the image of Christ enthroned inside the Baptistery (fig. 5) and thus illuminated by the door.

In as much as baptism in the building's font virtually admitted the baptizand to Florentine citizenship, one can plausibly imagine a link between the Florentine humanist ideal of individual flourishing and the relation of Bruni's iconographic project to the Baptistery's interior decoration.[14]

Ghiberti's finished work, realized between 1425 and 1452[15] (fig. 6), diminishes the number but expands the size of the panels, insert-

6. Lorenzo Ghiberti, Door of Paradise, Florence, Museo dell'Opera del Duomo.

liquid, losing all sense of consequentiality (as in the panel with the *Stories of Esau and Jacob*, see fig. 9).

In other words, in some cases temporal sequence is expressed through spatial contiguity, in others it is sacrificed and all that remains is spatial contiguity, with a disorienting effect on the viewer. In these cases, the loss of a time sequence seems to bring the various episodes, there assembled, out of the panel's single surface in a kind of estranging contemporaneity, and factual details emerge in a therefore disconnected way as if they were coming from the plural memory of those who witness the event.

There is a kind of paradox here: the panels where this occurs ought to narrate stories but do not. Rather they tell their stories in fragmentary form, practically challenging every effort at univocal interpretation, both for those who do not know the stories and still more for those who do. The facts emerge, in short, in all their enigmatic elusiveness: they are represented, and therefore speak to the viewer, but become meaningful only if, once again, they are subsumed within the logic of metaphor that refers them to a higher plane and presupposes one shared universe of sense.

That notwithstanding, it remains true that the narration, without losing its paradigmatic function at least for those who share the universe of Christian meaning, in as much as it is now a history of stories and no longer of types, tends to acquire concreteness and dynamism: to come down to earth, as it were, becoming narration of experiences, with the level of indecipherability that is often an effect of considering our own or other people's experience. Indecipherability also means precariousness and a heightened sense of contingency, and these sentiments are typical of societies in transition from a sure and homogeneous world that has disappeared to the world in the process of becoming and substantially unknown that is announced by the questioning presence of the other.

Precisely as a history of stories and not of types, the narration no longer activates only a mechanism of reference to transcendence (the Christian mysteries of salvation often linked according to the implacable pedagogy of the

7. Lorenzo Ghiberti, *Stories of Abraham*, Florence, Museo dell'Opera del Duomo, Door of Paradise.

Last Things), but also a comparison with the present and with the contingent.[16] And while the relationship with the Christ of the Baptistery mosaics remains the ultimately illuminating reference, the stories told on the door offer and receive light from the present also. They are oriented towards today, the here and now of all who let the stories interrogate them.

Contiguity

Just as the dislocation of stories in a single space – their contiguity, which is repeated in the panels themselves and in all the door – declares that the various episodes in every panel belong to the same history, so the act of becoming Christians and belonging to the same community is declared by sharing the same event and place of salvation, and of becoming citizens by virtue of sharing the same public, religious and civil space.

In the logic of metaphor, the sharing which is at the basis of citizenship tends toward homologation. By contrast the situation and the dynamics of contiguity safeguard heterogeneity: each is, for others, the 'other', with the result that all are radically distinct but in the same situation. Civic life is perceived as inscribed in the logic of the Kingdom in so far as it is encounter, welcome, confrontation.

8. Lorenzo Ghiberti, *The Encounter of Solomon and the Queen of Sheba*, Florence, Museo dell'Opera del Duomo, Door of Paradise.

9. Lorenzo Ghiberti, *Stories of Jacob and Esau*, Florence, Museo dell'Opera del Duomo, Door of Paradise.

In this perspective particular significance can be attached to the change of episode in the Solomon story: David's son is not presented as the judge between contending mothers, as in Bruni's program, but as a Hebrew king who welcomes a gentile queen, in a relationship of perfect difference but also of perfect equality (fig. 8) – an episode that Krautheimer explained in light of its implicit ecclesiological meaning, linking it to the almost contemporary Council of Florence.[17]

Among the most complex panels from the narratological point of view is that with the *Stories of Jacob and Esau* (fig. 9), fragmented into episodes dislocated in space on the basis of a compositional logic apparently quite unconcerned with chronological consequentiality.

The story of Jacob's election certainly evokes the mystery of divine grace which shows preference without regard for rules; it can also, however, seem to be a kind of apology for human shrewdness. The reference to the reality of Florentine life in the time of Cosimo de' Medici must have seemed particularly clear to contemporaries, conscious of being sinners but confident in divine mercy because persuaded that they had done well by the city, even if, not infrequently, through a dishonest use of wealth and other stratagems. One thinks of the rebuilding and enlargement of the conventual buildings of San Marco, entrusted in 1437 to Michelozzo by Cosimo de' Medici to overcome his remorse for some rather questionably acquired wealth, in response to a suggestion by Pope Eugenius IV.[18]

Fragmentedness and contingency

If this approach may seem slightly, but perhaps not unduly, forced, a possible conclusion would be that the fascination which Ghiberti's narrative experiments in the Door of Paradise exerts on us is perhaps due to a fundamentally congenial link between his bold style and 20th-century experimentalism. We could further acknowledge that the sense of disorientation that some of his panels transmit is something we recognize as part of our everyday experience: the fragmentation of memory and of sense, the tendency to give greater weight to spatial contiguity than to chronological sequence; in fact the feeling of contingency and of imponderable becoming also characterizes our period of "precarious communities"[19] which force us to live together as far-from-home orphans of dissimilar traditions – communities certainly very far from the substantially homogeneous human climate that found expression in the great season of medieval allegory.[20]

10. Lorenzo Ghiberti, *The Encounter of Solomon and the Queen of Sheba*, detail, Florence, Museo dell'Opera del Duomo, Door of Paradise.

To be sure, the evolving society of Renaissance Florence enjoyed a rootedness in the universe of Christian sense that was still vital, a condition that our society no longer knows. Beyond the failure to which the attempt at union was destined, the point of view of the Council fathers was more complementary than reciprocally estranged, as it was then held to be. Despite the differences, it was enough to restore a sense of multiple possibilities of interpretation of the Christian mystery and of the biblical sources, just as the rediscovery of the great schools of ancient western thought offered a various repertory, on which all might ideally agree, of the ideal of human flourishing of which the *civitas* should have been, as it were, the incarnation.

In this sense, the last panel's image of the meeting between Solomon and the Queen of Sheba (fig. 10), represented as a wedding solemnly celebrated in an architectural space that recalls both the interior of Florence Cathedral and an ideal *agorà*, with the two main figures that seal a pact of reciprocity on the open threshold of an enclosure that is not a barrier, could be considered a splendid icon of the hoped-for union and of a convergence without loss of identity. ∎

1   Also translated as "happiness", *eudamonia* is Aristotle's term for human good, or living and doing well (see *Nicomachean Ethics*, 1095a, 15–22). The long lasting fortune of *Nicomachean Ethics* in the Florentine culture is variously attested, from Dante's mention in the *Divine Comedy* (Inferno XI, 79–84) to Leonardo Bruni's translation (1417–18); see David A. Lines, 'Humanistic and Scholastic Ethics', in *The Cambridge Companion to Renaissance Philosophy*, edited by James Hankins, Cambridge, 2007, pp. 304–18. On translating *eudaimonia* as "flourishing" see John Milton Cooper, *Reason and Human Good in Aristotle*, Cambridge, MA, 1975, p. 89.

2   See, with a different point of view, Amy R. Bloch, 'The Evolution of Lorenzo Ghiberti's Approach to the Narrative Relief', in *Depth of Field:*

Relief Sculpture in Renaissance Italy, edited by Donal Cooper and Marika Leino, Oxford et al., 2007, pp. 125–48.

3   "In 1453 the Turks conquered Byzantium: yet, if the empire was lost, it new a kind of salvation in Byzantine culture. A key personage in this process was Manual Chrysolorus, who taught for three years in Florence, from 2 February 1397 through 10 March 1400, invited to teach Greek at the Studio by the Republic's Chancellor, Coluccio Salutati (1331–1406). Chrysolorus's Florentine years marked the clear beginning of the process of rebirth of Greek literature in the West, after centuries of absence. Among those who learned Greek from him were, with others, those who would become the first great translators of Humanism: for example Jacopo Angeli da Scarperia (*c.*

1360–1410/11) and Leonardo Bruni (1370–1444). What is more, the search for Greek manuscripts in the West was begun, both by Coluccio and by other personages" (David Speranzi, 'L'eredità di Bisanzio nelle biblioteche dei Medici', in *Voci dell'Oriente: miniature e testi classici da Bisanzio alla Biblioteca Medicea Laureziana*, edited by Massimo Bernabò, Florence, 2011, pp. 193–209: 193).

4 Richard Krautheimer, *Lorenzo Ghiberti*, in collaboration with Trude Krauthmeir-Hess, Princeton, 1982, pp. 177–9 [1st ed. Princeton, 1956].

5 For a succinct but effective *status questionis* see Amy Bloch, *Lorenzo Ghiberti's Gates of Paradise: Humanism, History, and Artistic Philosophy in the Italian Renaissance*, Cambridge, 2016, p. 4.

6 See Frederick Hartt, 'Lucerna ardens et lucens: il significato della porta del Paradiso', in *Lorenzo Ghiberti nel suo tempo*, proceedings of the symposium (Florence, 18–21 October 1978), 2 vols., Florence, 1980, I, pp. 26–57.

7 See Sharon Dale, 'Ghiberti's Gates of Paradise: An Old Testament Typology', *Rivista d'arte*, 5th series, 4 (2014), pp. 13–29; Bloch 2016, op. cit., pp. 1–9.

8 On Ghiberti's perspective studies see Corrado Maltese, 'Ghiberti teorico: i problemi ottico prospettici', in *Lorenzo Ghiberti* 1980, op. cit., II, pp. 407–19; Luigi Vagnetti, 'Ghiberti prospettico', ibid., II, pp. 421–34.

9 On the chronology of the two doors' realization and the complex question of their location, see the doctoral thesis of Amy Bloch, *The Sculpture of Lorenzo Ghiberti and Ritual Performance in Renaissance Florence*, Ph.D. Diss., New Brunswick, The State University of New Jersey, 2004, pp. 188–206.

10 See Antonio Paolucci, *Le porte del Battistero di Firenze alle origini del Rinascimento*, Modena, 1996, p. 27.

11 On the era's contradictory imagination in regard to the character of the city see Christian Bec, 'Il mito di Firenze da Dante al Ghiberti', in *Lorenzo Ghiberti* 1980, op. cit., I, pp. 3–26.

12 Timothy Verdon, 'La porta del Paradiso e la fede dei fiorentini', *La porta d'oro del Ghiberti*, pro-

ceedings of the symposium (Florence, 20 November 2012–4 June 2013), edited by Timothy Verdon, Florence, 2014, pp. 19–42: 39.

13 See Gianni Cioli, Agnese Maria Fortuna, 'Tra timore e speranza: temi escatologici nei rilievi della facciata e nei cicli pittorici del duomo di Orvieto', in *Spazi e immagini dell'eucaristia: il caso di Orvieto*, edited by Gianni Cioli, Severino Dianich and Valerio Mauro, Bologna, 2007, pp. 131–68.

14 See Verdon 2014, op. cit., pp. 19–42: 19–25.

15 On the door's chronology and the sources for its realization see Bloch 2016, op. cit., pp. 9–13.

16 Amy Bloch argues that her reading of the Gates of Paradise demonstrates "Ghiberti's profound engagement with the meaning of the stories, and not just, or even primarily, with their traditional theological significance. For centuries before his time, Christian writers, preachers and liturgists had understood the events of the Old Testament as typological precedents of occurrences recounted in the New Testament. Ghiberti, however, also connected them to a range of topics of special interest to him and his contemporaries, fashioning original interpretations of biblical stories that the reliefs conveyed to both the viewing public and members of his artistic and intellectual circles ... Ghiberti ... through his selection, imaginative reading, and knitting together of moments from the Bible and his examination of ancient and medieval sources (visual and textual), created images that function not merely as didactic representations but as multitextured narratives exploring the drama of the human condition and commenting on the social, political, philosophical, historical, and artistic issues of his days"(Bloch 2016, op. cit., pp. 3–4).

17 Krautheimer 1982, op. cit., pp. 181–7.

18 See Piero Bargellini, *Vedere e capire Firenze: guida storico artistica*, Florence, 1951, p. 203.

19 See Zygmunt Bauman, *Community: Seeking Safety in an Insecure World*, Cambridge, 2001.

20 On the mutual dependence of rhetorical forms and social structures, see especially *The Common Growl: Toward a Poetics of Precarious Community*, edited by Thomas Claviez, New York, 2016.

A German Friar
in Renaissance Florence

Martin Luther at the Ospedale degli Innocenti

TIMOTHY VERDON

In 1510, seven years before he published his 95 theses, the Augustinian friar Martin Luther came to Italy for a study trip authorized by his superiors. In addition to Rome, Luther also visited Florence, cradle of the Renaissance, where – among other things – he seems to have seen the large orphanage or 'Founding Hospital' – the Ospedale degli Innocenti (fig. 1) – which years later he would remember with enthusiasm, saying:

> In Florence I saw how carefully the hospitals are kept ... So too the houses for abandoned children, where these are lodged, fed and educated in a very excellent way; they are all dressed in the same way, in clothes of the same color, and are looked after in a very paternal manner.[1]

The Ospedale degli Innocenti, designed by the greatest architect of the early Renaissance, Filippo Brunelleschi, was thus known to the 16th-century Reformer and part of his direct experience: a site rich in art, which by 1510 already had Andrea Della Robbia's glazed terracotta roundels depicting the Holy Innocents on its exterior (fig. 2), and, on the altar of its church, the monumental *Adoration of the Magi*

by Domenico and Ridolfo Ghirlandaio (fig. 3), as well as many other of the works today visible in the Ospedale's museum installation.

These facts raise the question of a possible influence of Florence on the future reformer. Did what later emerged as Luther's moderate attitude toward art preserve traces of his brief Florentine experience? Obviously no definite answer is possible, since Luther's writings on art never mention specific works. Today, however, when many Protestant communities are rediscovering the function of art in places of worship, even an oblique answer – not 'definite' but at least evocative – may be helpful.

Luther's writings regarding art, all dating from many years after his brief Florentine visit, do in fact suggest a response to our query. In the 50th of his 95 theses, the friar emphasized that the new Vatican Basilica, to pay for which the indulgence was emanated whose preaching in Germany caused grave scandal, was being built at the cost of the flesh and bone of the Pope's flock.[2] And in his *Explanations of the Theses* published in 1518, Luther would say that the principal good work that Christians must perform is to succor the poor and aid those in need, and that assistance should be given in these cases even if that meant interrupt-

1. Raffaello Petrini, *Veduta della Catena* (*Chain Map*), detail with the Ospedale degli Innocenti, Florence, Museo di Palazzo Vecchio.

2. Andrea della Robbia, *Roundel with a Holy Innocent*, Florence, Ospedale degli Innocenti, exterior façade.

ing the building of churches or the collection of funds for the purchase of liturgical objects and ecclesiastical furnishings.[3] The following year, in his *Sermon on Usury*, Luther would again condemn wasteful expenditure for the adornment of churches, even though in the same text he underlined his belief that some elements of what he calls 'the visible Church' are necessary and legitimate. He insisted however that "we ought to draw a boundary line and see to it that the worship is pure rather than costly…", adding: "It would be better if we gave less to the churches and altars … and more to the needy".[4]

These words are significant, because – if in Rome, in the colossal size of the rising St Peter's Basilica (begun only four years before his journey but already imaginable from the foundations and bases of the gigantic crossing piers), Luther had been scandalized by what he considered waste –, in Florence he was perhaps edified by the typical Tuscan sobriety and more human proportions of the Ospedale degli Innocenti (fig. 4). The friar must have appreciated the fact that Florentine art was called to celebrate charitable assistance given to the needy: to the abandoned children welcomed as 'Holy Innocents' in the structure created for them by the Silk Guild, who are depicted both in Andrea della Robbia's roundels and in Do-

menico Ghirlandaio's altarpiece. In Florence, that is, he might have grasped art's potential in shaping the conscience of Christians called to form a *societas perfecta*. His brief Florentine visit may have reinforced Luther's sense that in any case art has a function in the life of the Church.

Born in 1483, in 1510 Luther was 27 years old and still happily Catholic.[5] He was at the beginning of what could have been an important ecclesiastical career, with five years of experience as an Augustinian friar, three as a priest, and two as instructor at the recently founded Wittenberg University, where he taught dialectics and physics, reading and commenting Aristotle's *Nichomachean Ethics*, the work Raphael puts in Aristotle's hands in his *School of Athens*, which was in course of execution when Luther visited Rome (fig. 5). In the fields of architecture and painting, the young professor must have known the churches of the cities in which he had lived: Magdeburg, where his father had sent him in 1497 to attend the school of the Brethren of the Common Life; Erfurt, where he had taken his university degree and then become a friar; and Wittenberg, where he had joined the faculty of the new university. Of course nothing in the decoration of these still medieval buildings prepared him for the novelty of Italian Renaissance art, even

3. Domenico and Ridolfo Ghiralandaio, *Adoration of the Magi*, Florence, Ospedale degli Innocenti.

though it is unclear whether he took particular notice of the stylistic differences between what he had seen in his fatherland and what he saw in Rome and Florence. His clear sensitivity to the messages that art transmits does not necessarily signify an aesthetic position but rather Luther's traditional concern for the moral content of Christian activity. His insistence that money is better spent to help the poor than to adorn churches in fact echoes St John Chrysostom's advice to wealthy believers desirous of embellishing churches with art:

> Give God the honor he asks for, that is give your money generously to the poor. God has no need of golden vessels but of golden hearts. I am not saying you should not give golden altar vessels and so on, but I am insisting that nothing can take the place of almsgiving. The Lord will not refuse to accept the first kind of

gift, but he prefers the second, and quite naturally, because in the first case only the donor benefits, in the second case the poor get the benefit. The gift of a chalice may be ostentatious, almsgiving is pure benevolence. What is the use of loading Christ's table with gold cups while he himself is starving? Feed the hungry, and then if you have any money left over, spend it on the altar table.[6]

Luther's reservations on the subject of church art also reflected the moralism of the Brethren of the Common Life and the austere spirituality of the *Devotio moderna* which they promoted.[7] In the school run by the Brethren at Magdeburg it is in fact very likely that young Martin read the movement's manual, *The Imitation of Christ*, attributed to the Augustinian Canon Thomas à Kempis, in the first chapter of which we find the biblical source of Luther's attitude toward art, there where the author, evoking the Book of Qoheleth (Ecclesiastes), insists that:

It is vanity to search for wealth destined to end, and to put our hopes in it. Vain too is ambition for honors and ascent to high position. Vanity it is to follow our carnal desires and aspire to things for which we shall later be severely punished; vanity to want to live long, giving little though to living well. It is vanity to occupy oneself only with the present life and not to look toward the future. It is vanity to love what rapidly passes and not hasten there where eternal joy endures. Call to mind often the proverb, 'The eye is never satisfied with seeing, nor the ear with hearing'. Behave, therefore, in a way that detaches your heart from the visible things of this world, lifting you to the things of heaven, which we cannot see.[8]

The refusal of ostentation typical of the *Devotio moderna* explains, moreover, the role which, from 1520 onwards, Luther assigns to art in what he calls *Werkheiligkeit*, 'Justification based on good works'.[9] He condemns indulgences – and, with these, the taste

4. Filippo Brunelleschi, the courtyard of the Ospedale degli Innocenti.

for collecting relics and the custom of commissioning paintings and statues for churches – as expressions of the notion that by such acts it is possible to acquire credit with God and thus 'merit' salvation, which in the friar's view springs from faith alone, not from works, however 'meritorious'. In a homily on 'Good Works' he would say that adorning churches with artistic masterpieces means relying on art to buy access to heaven, and insisted that the root of the cult of images is this manipulative impulse (not adoration of the images themselves, which he does not ascribe to his contemporaries). "I have so often spoken out against such works [i.e., the commissioning of art for churches]", he states, "since among a thousand faithful it is hard to find even one who did not place his hope in this, who did not want to earn the grace of God in this way".[10]

That said, however, we must add that Luther did not share the iconoclastic fury of 16th-century contemporaries such as Andreas Bodenstein von Karlstadt and Gabriel Zwilling, who was also an Augustinian, or of violent movements like the one which in 1521 occupied Wittenberg's monasteries and on December 3 destroyed the altar of the city's Franciscan church.[11] On Christmas eve of that year the parish church and that of the castle were occupied, and on January 10th, 1522, the Wittenberg Augustinians destroyed the images in their church and conventual buildings. A week later, on 17th January 1522, Karlstadt finished his treatise on 'The Removal of Images', and a print made a few years later illustrates this

5. Raffaello, *School of Athens*, detail showing Aristotle, Vatican City, Apostolic Palace, Stanza della Segnatura.

very process, showing men with axes and pikes destroying statues in a church, while – on the viewers right, in the lower corner – another man burns these images (fig. 6).[12] The print, realized at Nurnberg between 1530–40, documents another phenomenon as well: the stockpiling of some images in a structure adjacent to the despoiled church, in view of their future res-

6. Erhard Schön (?), *Klagrede der armen verfolgten Götzen und Tempelbilder*, c. 1530, woodcut.

7. Henrikus Füllmaurer, *Mömpelgarder Altar*, Vienna, Kunsthistorisches Museum.

titution to the patrons or perhaps of their sale. The artist, perhaps Erhard Schön, in the upper right in fact shows a rich man directing the whole operation and, behind him, a container brimming with coins. From this man's eye a large beam grows – a reference to well-known Gospel passages (Mt 7:3, Lc 6:42) –, and this detail apparently condemns both the 'business' of church spoliation and the hypocrisy of those who practiced it claiming to extirpate idolatry. The text accompanying the print, written by Hans Sachs, the poet of the Lutheran reform, is entitled *Klagrede der armen verfolgten Götzen und Tempelbilder* ("Lament of the poor, persecuted images"), and has the popular irony characteristic of German literature of that time.

Luther too was skeptical, and in February 1522, with the complicity of the Elector of Saxony, sought refuge in the Castle of Wartburg under the false name of 'Junker Jorg', 'Sir George'. He distanced himself from the iconoclasts and, returning to Wittenberg, in March 1522 preached publicly against the forced im-

position of new ideas upon a population still tied to the rites, practices and art of the centuries-old Catholic tradition. These are his *Lenten sermons* or *Invocavitpredigten*, in which, recalling the Byzantine debate on the same question, Luther concluded that both iconoclasts and iconodules were wrong, since human liberty cannot be coerced.[13] For him, that is, art remained an acceptable option, and Lutheranism would continue to produce paintings for churches for catechetical purposes, such as the enormous *Wandaltar* or cupboard altarpiece by Heinrich Füllmaurer, today in Vienna, with more than 150 New Testament scenes, each with the relative Gospel text clearly inscribed upon the image (fig. 7).[14]

All this happened many years later, however. In Florence in 1510 our friar had not yet worked out the questions he would treat in sermons and writings of the 1520s and 1530s. Without wanting to reduce him to the status of a modern tourist, we must suppose that he visited the city's main churches: the Baptistery with its three sets of bronze doors illustrating biblical themes, the Cathedral with its marble singing galleries by Luca della Robbia and Donatello; and the majestic basilicas of the mendicant orders, among which that of his own Augustinian Order, Santo Spirito, designed by Brunelleschi. In Santo Spirito he could have seen the deeply moving crucifix carved by the young Michelangelo, but also Cosimo Rosselli's popular *Madonna of Succor*. If he was interested in scandal, at the Servite basilica of the Santissima Annunziata he could have read the inscription next to Michelozzo's marble ciborium in which Piero de' Medici, who commissioned the work, published its cost, while in the neighboring chapel he could admire the cupboard containing gold and silver *ex voto* images, its exterior decorated with New Testament scenes painted by Fra Angelico. None of these masterpieces would have surprised him, in any case, since German churches like those of the rest of Europe had works that were identical in function, although different in style.

What was Luther's reaction to revolutionary works such as Michelangelo's *David*, for which nothing in Germany can have prepared him? Or to bold efforts to reinvent traditional iconography, such as Piero di Cosimo's *Madonna of the Incarnation*, as the work should

be called, then on an altar in the Santissima Annunziata?[15] Did people speak to him of Savonarola, burnt at the stake twelve years earlier, who had reproved artists for depicting Mary dressed luxuriously, as if she were a lady of high society or a stylish prostitute?[16] We do not know, just as we do not know how long he remained in Florence.

Luther probably never saw several works destined to become icons of our modern notion of Renaissance art – Botticelli's *Primavera* and *Birth of Venus*, for example, then in private hands. But he did see two big Florentine hospitals, Santa Maria Nuova and the Ospedale degli Innocenti, and was struck both by their efficiency and by the moral 'elegance' of these institutions. In Florence he grasped that art could place itself in the service of Christian charity, calling the attention of God's people to the 'little ones', just as later the artist closest to him, Lucas Cranach the Elder, would remind contemporaries that the Lord Jesus, against the advice of his disciples, had welcomed and caressed children.

Arguably Luther's brief Florentine experience helped confirm him in the traditional Catholic understanding of artistic talent as a 'vocation': a call to speak, through the eyes of believers, to the heart of the Church. ■

1 From Luther's "Table discourses", 1 August 1538. See Attilio Piccini, 'Gli Innocenti: arte e storia', in *Spedale e museo degli Innocenti*, Florence, 1977, pp. 5–16. See also Luca Rinaldi, 'Architettura e assistenza nella Firenze granducale (secc. XVI–XVII)', in *Storia della solidarietà a Firenze*, proceedings of the symposium (Florence, Spring 1984), Florence, 1985, pp. 56–63, and Timothy Verdon, 'La Piazza e la carità: gli istituti di aiuto fraterno intorno al Duomo', in *I tesori di Piazza del Duomo*, Florence, 1997, pp. 9–40.

2 See Sergiusz Michalski, *The Reformation and the Visual Arts. The Protestant Image Question in Western*

and Eastern Europe, London, 1993, pp. 6–7, citing Martin Luther, *Werke*, ed. Weimar, 1883–1929, I, p. 235.

3 Michalski 1993, op. cit., pp. 6–7 and Luther, *Werke*, ed. 1883–1929, op. cit., I, p. 598.

4 Michalski 1993, op. cit., p. 7, and Martin Luther, *Werke*, ed. 1883–1929, op. cit., VI, pp. 43–5.

5 A recent overview of Luther's biography is M. Gretzschel, *Martin Luther. His Life and Places of Work*, Hamburg 2016.

6 Homily 50, "On the Gospel of Matthew", 3–4. See PG 58, cols. 508–9. English translation taken from

The Divine Office. The Liturgy of the Hours According to the Roman Rite, 3 vols., London, 1974, III, pp. 480–2.

7 Useful for the spirituality of Luther's time is *The Reformation in Medieval Perspective*, edited by Steven E. Ozment, Chicago, 1971 and, in that collection, Ozment's own essay, 'Homo viator: Luther and Late Medieval Theology', pp. 142–54.

8 *De Imitatione Christi*, Paris, 1934, I, 4, pp. 2–3 (author's translation).

9 Michalski 1993, op. cit., p. 7.

10 Ibid., see also Luther, *Werke*, ed. 1883–1929, op. cit., VI, p. 211.

11 Michalski 1993, op. cit., pp. 9–10.

12 See *Martin Bucer, Strasbourg et l'Europe*, exhibition catalogue (Strasbourg, Églises Protestantes d'Aslace et de Lorraine, 1991), Strasbourg, 1991, pp. 116–7.

13 See Michalski 1993, op. cit., pp. 13–14; Martin Luther, *Werke*, ed. 1883–1929, op. cit., X, pp. 26–36.

14 See K. Schuetz, 'L'Évangile selon Füllmaurer', in, *Évangile selon saint Matthieu, saint Marc, saint Luc, saint Jean*, 4 vols., Milan, 2002, IV, pp. 203–11.

15 See my essay about Piero di Cosimo's painting in Part Two of this volume.

16 See Savonarola's sermon on the Friday following the third Sunday of Lent, 1496: in *Prediche e scritti: Girolamo Savonarola*, edited by Mario Ferrara, Milan, 1930, p. 387. See also Marcia B. Hall, 'Savonarola's Preaching and the Patronage of Art', in *Christianity and the Renaissance. Image and Religious Imagination in the Quattrocento*, edited by Timothy Verdon and John Henderson, Syracuse, NY, 1990, pp. 493–522.

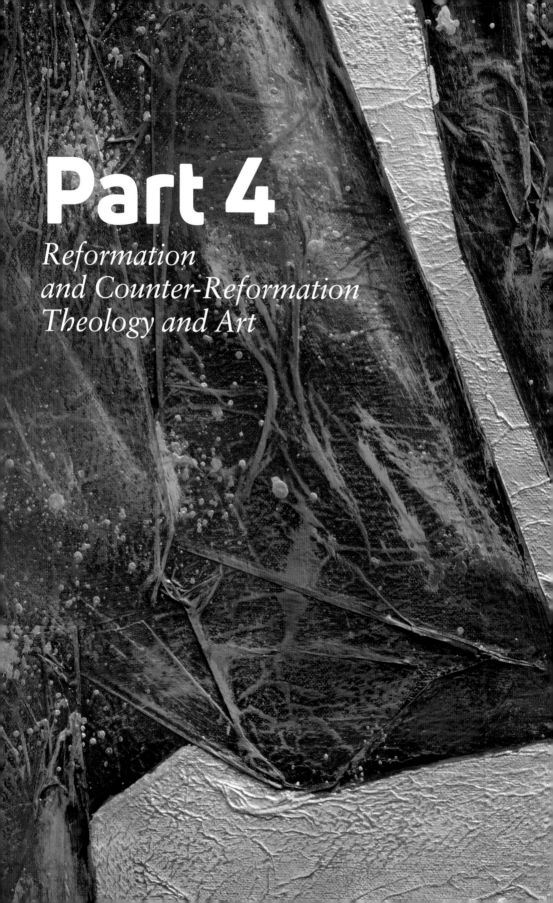

Part 4

*Reformation
and Counter-Reformation
Theology and Art*

The Influence of the Reformation on the Visual Arts from the 16th Century to the Present

JÉRÔME COTTIN

It has long been said that the Reformation produced nothing in the arts – that it was iconoclastic, not iconophilic. But, looking at the numerous works inherited from the Reformation or simply inspired by it, this kind of judgment must be strongly qualified and even corrected. We know that the Reformation accorded a privileged role to music as a church art, and that across the centuries it produced some of the greatest musicians of the western world (Dietrich Buxtehude, Heinrich Schutz, Johann Sebastian Bach).[1] We know as well, thanks to recent scholarship,[2] that while iconoclastic movements accompanied its diffusion, the Reformation did not identify itself with iconoclasm: Luther energetically fought the iconoclasts at Wittenberg, and if Zwingli authorized iconoclast decisions at the institutional level in the city of Zurich it was with the sole objective of neutralizing popular iconoclastic claims.[3] As far as Calvin is concerned, he arrived in Geneva only in July of 1536, after the city's iconoclast decisions.

With regard to the reformers and their theology, it would be better to speak of iconophobia (criticism of images) and aniconism (absence of images) than of iconoclasm. What did the reformers say of art and of images (the 16th century did not yet distinguish these two notions, as Hans Belting has rightly shown[4])? To

tell the truth, they said very little, for these issues were not central to their theology. They were concerned above all to take their distance from Roman Catholic piety, which had made images sacred objects and had confused them with the cult of relics and the veneration of the saints or the sacrifice of the Mass. All these notions and practices were violently rejected by the Reformation in the name of *sola gratia*, *sola scriptura* and the *solus Christus*.

And yet the reformers were not completely silent on these questions. We might sum up their thought in the following way: Luther certainly accepted images, but was indifferent to aesthetics.[5] For him the image was merely an efficacious pedagogical tool serving to illustrate Bible texts in order to help people better remember them. For Calvin the opposite was true. He rejected all images, without exception, in places of worship. But he developed a theological aesthetic, a theology of beauty. In his case we can speak of an aesthetic of *soli deo gloria*.[6] Thus the two principal reformers (Zwingli should be studied separately) had complementary approaches, Luther accepting images but not aesthetics, Calvin aesthetics but not images. Today these two approaches could be considered together, since they are complementary, not opposed to each other as they were long believed to be; in that way one would reach a veritable Protestant theology of images.[7]

But what did the Reformation produce directly – in church spaces – or indirectly, through a culture impregnated with these ideas –, in the visual arts? That is the object of the present essay, to pass from thought on images to their actual making, from the theological level to that of artistic gesture.

The idea is to show that the thought of the two chief reformers also generated an artistic tradition whose developments we can follow right down to the contemporary era. To be sure, to put the art produced in culturally Protestant European countries in direct relation to the reformers' ideas would smack of apologetics. Other historical, aesthetic and philosophical influences must be taken into account. What is more, artists – and it was one of the indications of modernity – increasingly sought to emancipate themselves from traditional models of all kinds (political, religious, aesthetic). But no one can deny that, indirectly at least, Protestant culture – Lutheran, Reformed (and, in England, Anglican) – stimulated and oriented the arts and artists from the 16th to the 20th centuries, in ways that we shall now specify, citing specific examples.

We will limit ourselves to the Lutheran and Reformed/Calvinist traditions, showing several works and speaking of certain artists representative of the two currents of historical protestantism. We will conclude by speaking of two aesthetic characteristics proper to these two currents of the Reformation.

Luther and Lutheranism
At the time of the Reformation:
Cranach and others

Thanks to Lucas Cranach the Elder, official painter of the Prince-Elector of Saxony, friend of Luther and a convinced "Lutheran", the Lutheran Reformation has artworks of the highest level.

I will mention two of Cranach's pictures, which present biblical texts up to that time never (or rarely) represented in Christian art: *Jesus Welcoming and Blessing the Children* (Mk 10:13–16) and *Jesus and the Adulteress*

(Jn 8:1–11; fig. 1). Why create paintings relative to these two texts? Because in a narrative way they perfectly translated the central idea of the Reformation: God's grace and pardon unconditionally offered to all (gratuitous salvation), and especially to those who are weaker (children, women) and who are border-line (the adulteress). *Jesus Welcoming and Blessing the Children* (1539) is in the Stadtkirche of Naumburg, in Saxony. In it we see Cranach's particular style: elegant forms, large areas of color, dark backgrounds against which the handsomely dressed personages stand out, rich fabrics and feminine grace made fully evident. This could also be a genre of painting: the scenes of the child hanging on to his mother's dress, or of the little girl with a doll in her arms, seem to be studied from life. Yet this painstaking aesthetic is at the service of precise theological convictions. In this painting it was a question of taking an equal distance from Roman theology (by emphasizing sexuality and procreation) and from the radical reformers (the *Schwärmer*, or "enthusiasts") who contested the validity of infant baptism (here the blessing given to the children should be understood as an allusion to this sacrament).

Another picture by Cranach, *Jesus with the Woman Taken in Adultery* (Kronach, Fränkiche Galerie), calls attention to itself for the particularly painstaking representation of the sinful woman, presented here as the ideal of feminine beauty. By contrast her accusers are shown with particularly repulsive features. This painting has two peculiarities: it was purchased by the Prince-Elector of Bavaria, Maximilian I (the head of the Catholic league, and thus an enemy of Lutheranism) for his residence in Munich; and the purchaser subjected the painting to important modifications in order to 'erase' its excessively Protestant character. In effect we know the first version of the work thanks to a very exact old workshop copy in the Germanisches Nationalmuseum of Nuremberg, destroyed in the war but of which a (single) photograph survives. In relation to the original, the changes made for Maximilian I were the following:

- the monochrome background became an architectural interior;

1. Lucas Cranach the Elder, *Jesus and the Adulteress*, Kronach, Fränkliche Galerie.

- additions (since removed) increased the dimensions by a good third;

- Jesus's left hand, which seized the adulterous woman, was 'effaced' by the folds of his tunic, covering the woman's right arm: it was a question of eliminating the close union between the Son of God and the sinful woman, and of reinforcing Christ's hieratic aspect.

On the original monochrome background, above Jesus's head, there was an inscription in Latin: QUI SINE PECCATO EST VESTRUM IN EAM | PRIMU[M] LAPIDEM MITTAT | IOHANNIS OCTAVO ("Let the one among you who is guiltless be the first to throw a stone at her / John eighth"; Jn 8:7).

Lutheran art was essentially a biblical art that aimed at translating into images the Gospel accounts and certain particularly important Old Testament texts, like the Ten Commandments, of which Cranach realized an enormous painting in 1516.[8] But the biblical art of Luther's time was not restricted to the production of Cranach and his atelier. The

largest work of visual art of the Reformation, the *Mömpelgarder Altar* (c. 1542; fig. at p. 139),[9] is by another artist, Henrikus Füllmaurer. The altarpiece is made up of a central panel and two sets of lateral panels painted on both sides which move on hinges: to see them one must turn these lateral panels like the pages of a book. The altarpiece has 157 painted panels depicting almost all the scenes of the gospels. These are prettily colored; the biblical personages are represented in a bucolic landscape reminiscent more of south and central Germany than of Palestine; the personages around Jesus are 'actualized': that is, they wear 16th-century clothing (fig. 2).

There are three particularly Lutheran features in these representations:

- The biblical texts (with chapter references) invade the space of the visual representations, in the upper third of the image. The texts thus offer themselves twice to viewers, who at the same time read them and see them depicted.

- Jesus is present in every image, but never represented frontally. It was a question of avoiding the creation of a new devotional relationship between Christ (often represented frontally in the medieval tradition) and the viewer.

- The scenes are not simply illustrations of the biblical texts, but actualized interpretations as well. In what is shown the text is not only written but also proclaimed and preached. For example, in the parable of the mote of dust and the wooden beam, the man with the beam in his eye is shown in rich clothing, while the man with a mote in his eye is dressed as a peasant.

The Lutheran Reformation produced only biblical paintings. For the sake of completeness, we should also mention its dogmatic images, which present in image-form Lutheranism's central dogma: justification by faith. That is how a whole series of paintings and engravings were born, entitled "Law and Gospel" or "Law and Grace", in turn giving birth to a rich iconographical tradition.[10] There are of

2. Henrikus Füllmaurer, *Mömpelgarder Altar*, detail, Vienna, Kunsthistorisches Museum.

course also polemical delineations in black and white, most often woodcut illustrations of tracts denouncing the papacy and the abuses of the Roman Catholic Church.[11] Thus we can say that Lutheranism was at the origin of religious caricature, which is to say of the art of caricature *tout court*.

From Romanticism to the German Expressionists

We now leave the Reformation era and look at Lutheran influence in later centuries. I will omit the Baroque period (of which much could be said, there being high quality Baroque art in north, central and east Germany in the 17th and 18th centuries) in order to discuss the contemporary era. The 19th century and the Romantic period – with such great Lutheran artists as the Romantic Kaspar-David Friedrich (1774–1840), inventor of the "spiritual landscape", or the realist painter Fritz von Uhde (1848–1911) –, should also be studied.

The artists of the late 19th- and early 20th-century Avant-garde are more difficult to situate in the Lutheran orbit, since they are part of a movement determined to free art from the various restrictive institutional frameworks imprisoning it, among which the framework of the Church, particularly conservative in questions of art.

That notwithstanding, several of these artists, born in a deeply Lutheran cultural milieu, do preserve traces of their origins, emphasizing three elements that are direct products of Lutheran piety:

- Bible stories, and particularly those of the four gospels, as a source of artistic inspiration;

- concentration on the figure of Christ; we know that Christ, and even the crucified Christ, is at the heart of Luther's theology of salvation freely offered to all;

- and finally the very Lutheran idea that Christ is first of all Christ for me (*pro me*), whom I receive in an interior impulse of faith open to my own subjectivity. We reach the paradoxical situation that the artists whom we will now name, who left their Church of origin or were in conflict with it because of the Church's inability to understand the deep spirituality of their atypical Christ figures, are those who have left the most moving representations of a Christ at once suffering, contemporary and near to human beings.

Most of these Christs – by Barlach, Nolde, Beckmann, Schmitt-Rottluff, Giess – were denounced by the Nazis, who put them on view in the 1937 exhibition of *Degenerate Art*, without the Lutheran Church making the least protest. Waiving the more exhaustive presentation these works merit, here I will simply cite a few of the atypical Christs of these pre-expressionist and expressionist artists.

Of Lovis Corinth (1858–1925), one thinks of *The Great Martyr* (1907, Regensburg), where Christ on the cross is totally nude, and *The Red Christ* (1922, Munich), where the blood of the Crucified splashes the entire landscape, or again the *Ecce Homo* (1925, Basle), which shows Christ as a prisoner surrounded by a psychiatric doctor and a Wehrmacht officer.

Emil Nolde (1867–1956) is without doubt the expressionist artist who has left the 20th century the greatest number of biblical paintings. We recall his immense poliptych in nine parts, *The Life of Christ* (1911–12, Seebüll), of which the central part (a Christ on the cross) is inspired by the crucified Christ of Grünewald's *Isenheim Altarpiece*. Nolde's masterpiece had a strange fate, for it was refused by the civil authorities, by the church authorities (Catholic and Lutheran) and by the Nazis. Nolde shocked the public because he dared to represent a 'Semitic' Christ; the intensity Nolde's emotions was expressed by the use of lively, at times strident colors, and by a nervous, almost hysterical brushstroke.

Ernst Barlach (1870–1938), a complete artist (sculptor, engraver, writer, dramaturge) realized a small, calm sculpture with the double title, *The Reunion/Jesus and Thomas* (1926, Hamburg and Güstrow; fig. 3). In that period of nostalgia for the heroes of the Great War, of rearmament and of justification of military retaliation, some of his radically pacifist bronze sculptures were melted down, with the blessings of the Lutheran church and of the city of Güstrow, where he resided.

Finally Max Beckmann (1884–1950), more post-expressionist than expressionist, in 1917 realized two paintings of large dimensions

3. Ernst Barlach, *The Reunion/Jesus and Thomas*, Güstrow (Mecklenburg–Western Pomerania, Germany), Gertrudenkapelle (Ernst Barlach Memorial).

forming a diptych: *Christ and the Adulteress* (St Louis, USA) in which he represented himself as Christ, and *Descent from the Cross* (New York). "An artist who wants to succeed must wrestle with his art like Jacob with the angel" (see Gn 32,27) wrote Beckmann, to whom moreover we owe a cycle on the Apocalypse.[12]

In conclusion we must still name that unclassable figure Otto Dix (1891–1969), whose life and œuvre traverse the greater part of the 20th century; he was enrolled as a soldier in the two world wars and survived all the atrocities. Beside the fact that he remained a figurative artist, one must define him as 'unclassable', so much did his work change style in the different eras of this protean century. Originally a supporter of the "new objectivity" (*Die neue Sachligkeit*), he then took to painting "in the manner" of the German primitives (in part to thwart Nazi censure), and ended his career with a simple and naïf style, the opposite of what he had done in the years of his youth. His Lutheran culture evolved toward a Christian agnosticism, but at the end of his life he admitted his attachment to the Bible, which remained his main source of inspiration: "the Bible is, in effect, a marvelous history book. Everything in it is borrowed from a great truth. One may say that it is the book of books, an extraordinary book from every point of view". That is how this stylistically polymorph artist expressed himself in 1963, in his own way re-inventing Luther's *Sola scriptura*.

Calvin and Calvinism
In the Reformation period: aniconic images
Calvinism, differently from Lutheranism, produced no work of art of quality in the Reformation period. With Calvin, at Geneva, there was no great artist of Cranach's stature, and, what is more, the reformer had emptied places of worship of all forms of visual art, including stained-glass windows (which Zwingli, his elder contemporary at Zurich, preserved). The only visual forms authorized in Calvin's time were certain signs (like the trigram IHS, a Latin abbreviation of IHESUS) or aniconic forms such as the circle, which would become a *sun* in the emblem which came to signify Calvinist Geneva. The exceptions are rare.

Théodore de Bèze (1519–1605), a French theologian and humanist, Calvin's successor at Geneva, was also an artist (draughtsman, poet, dramaturge)! To him we owe a collection of forty-four emblems (*Emblemata*) drawn up in 1581 (following the author's *Icones: Les vrais portraits d'hommes illustres*), in which decorative or aniconic forms coexist with short aphorisms. Thus the *Emblem I* represents an empty circle above a landscape, with the saying: "Anyone wanting to seek the beginnings of a circle, finds them in the same place in which the end is attached. So it is with you who love Christ ardently and without dissimulation. At the end of your days your life will begin". In *Emblem III* we find more or less the same drawing, but with a cube in the middle of the circle: "This circle which you see sustaining a square teaches you to pay attention to the true course of your life".[13]

4. Tobias Stimmer, *Astronomical clock*, detail, Strasbourg, Cathedral of Our Lady.

We find the same "aniconic obsession" in a painting on the astronomical clock of Strasbourg Cathedral. The astronomical clock of Strasbourg (1547–71), a work of technical prowess, was realized as a Protestant *manifesto* in favor of astronomical science (and in particular of Copernicus's discoveries) during the Cathedral's protestant period (1529–49 and 1559–1681). It is decorated with paintings by Tobias Stimmer, a Swiss Reformed Christian from Schaffhouse who did not want to represent God the Creator in the scene depicting the creation of Eve from Adam's side (Gn 2:21–2), and so replaced the traditional image of God as creator (often shown with a Christ-like head) with a simple disk of light in which God's name is inscribed in three languages (Hebrew, Greek, Latin; fig. 4).[14] Through the centuries, artists of Calvinist convictions or culture would show similar reticence – or even refuse – to represent God or Christ.

From Rembrandt to Mondrian
In its own time the Calvinist Reformation thus produced neither art nor artists worthy of the name. Yet – and it is a paradox that invites us to reflect – in later centuries Calvinism produced some of the world's greatest artists. I will mention the three most famous:

In the first place, Rembrandt (1606–69). In 2011 an important exhibition at the Louvre was dedicated to Rembrandt and the Figure of Christ. For the first time, the Amsterdam master's many 'portraits' of Christ were brought together in a single place. International experts stressed that Rembrandt had invented "a radically new image of Christ",[15] which does not in any way draw upon the iconographic tradition of Christ images and is even opposed to it. To be sure, that novelty can be explained by the painter's own genius, but also by his Calvinist sensibility and by the cultural climate of Reformed Protestantism, which since 1648 had been the official and majority religion of the Dutch United Provinces.

Our second example is Vincent van Gogh (1853–90). A minister's son, he studied theology and was an apprentice "evangelist" (a sort of deacon) in a poor mining region of French-speaking Belgium. He became a painter only because he was not ultimately accepted by the Reformed Church as either a minister or an evangelist. While he realized few biblical paintings, he still had a "spiritual" conception of landscape (his picture the *Sower with Setting Sun*, of June 1888, for example, is an evident allusion to the parable of the sower). In perfect Calvinist fashion, he refused to represent Christ. In his biblical painting *The Resurrection of Lazarus* (May 1890), inspired by a print of Rembrandt, whom he admired, he replaced Christ with a sun.

For the first half of the 20th century we should mention the Dutch artist Piet Mondrian (1872-1944), whose hereditary Calvinism was very marked. While he rapidly evolved toward theosophy, he nonetheless maintained an asceticism, a rigor, a sense of the fullness of the void, an attraction to whiteness (symbol of the spirit's clarity), which are signs of a Calvinist ontology. In Mondrian, considered the "father" of geometric abstraction, it became clear that Calvin's radical refusal of figurative art, for a long time experienced as a weakness, in reality is a strength. In his own time, Calvin could certainly not have imagined it, but his 'spiritual' aesthetic proclaimed and without doubt prepared the way for the abstract art which plays the main role in contemporary artistic creation.

If we sum up these aesthetic tendencies in the Reformed or Calvinist context, the following characteristics emerge:

- Attribution of value to light, to whiteness, at times for practical reasons (everyone has to read the Bible for himself) and symbolic ones (the clarity of exterior light signifies the role of the Holy Spirit, who makes clear that which is obscure).

- No representation of Christ, not even of Christ as the man Jesus. Man, he is also God, and one may not represent God (unless 'from behind' or with the mediation of signs).

- Signs more than images. The only possible material realities are signs, which refer us to something other than themselves.

- An aniconic art that exalts harmony of proportions, empty spaces, the beauty of simple forms.

Two Reformation Inventions

I will conclude this all too brief incursion into the visual arts indirectly inherited from the Reformation by mentioning two other characteristics, this time common to the two branches, Lutheran and Reformed/Calvinist, and more directly tied to the Reformation.

Black and white as colors

An aspect insufficiently emphasized is the new value which the Reformation gave to the two "non-colors", black and white. In the refusal of polychromy people have seen a weakness, a sign of austerity, but the opposite is true: it

5. Hans Baldung Grien, *Die Speisung der 5000*, woodcut, in 1535 Bible, in Martin Bucer's *Kürtzer Catechismus* (1537), in *Leienbibel* (1540 and 1542), in *Neues Testament* (1542).

6. Sylvie Tschiember, *Blue indigo*, Paris, Faculté de Théologie Protestante.

is a sign of modernity which founds a new aesthetic that we might qualify as minimalist and utilitarian. The exclusive use of black and white is a direct result of the invention of printing (black ink on white pages) but also of the woodcut, powerfully re-evaluated in 16th-century art after the success of Dürer's *Apocalypse*, and then by the Reformation, which produced numerous prints.[16] The reasons were certainly as much economic and practical as aesthetic: images printed in black and white could easily be reproduced and distributed, and what is more were inexpensive. They thus contributed in an effective way to the diffusion of Reformation ideas, both as biblical images in books

and as polemical images in illustrated tracts (*Flugschriften*). Michel Pastoureau, a historian of colors, has written on the "chromoclasm" of the Reformation,[17] which constitutes an important contribution to modernity and which extends into the contemporary period with, for example, the choice of black and white for the art photograph.[18]

Writing which becomes image

The introduction of symbols and writing into the visual space of figurative art is also one of the Reformation's contributions. To be sure, images have been accompanied by writing in all periods. But the writing was in the borders, outside the picture space; or in the form of simple words permitting the identification of the figures. With the Reformation, biblical writing occupies a more important place, often within the representation itself: that is, in an autonomous manner. When this happens, the image becomes writing, or, on the contrary, the written text offers itself as an image to be looked at. We read and look at the same time. One of the most typical examples is the Dinkelsbühl altarpiece, where the sole subject of the picture is the text which we read. Elsewhere, biblical words and verses in church spaces either accompany altarpiece images (Lutheranism) or replace them (Calvinism). Frank Muller has shown moreover that the first visual representations of the *tetragram* are found in a Strasbourg Anabaptist manuscript.[19] Since the Reformation the four letters of the divine name YHWH fill prints, drawings and paintings, church ceilings, pulpits, ambos and communion tables, but also, at times, house facades (for example a bourgeois dwelling at Bautzen in Saxony). In an immense modern painting (500 × 200 cm) by Samuel Buri entitled *Mark 16:1–8* (1997) and exhibited in 1997 in the Reformed church of Saint-Etienne-Réunion at Mulhouse, we find these characteristics: a black and white painting and a visual interpretation of the account of Mark 16:1–8 uniquely in the form of letters and text. Other contemporary creations – above all installations –, like those of the artist Sylvie Tschiember, are essentially plastic and graphic stagings of biblical verses: her painting *Blue indigo* (fig. 6), for example, on a verse of the letter to the Romans (Rm 12:5; 2011, Paris, Institut protestant de théologie),[20] or her installation *The Instant of Eternity* (Mk 1:15), exhibited in 2009 in the Lutheran church des Billettes in Paris.[21]

Unable to illustrate everything, I have mentioned only a few significant examples. Were it possible, I would speak of many more works and artists and artistic currents. And while it remains unsure whether all of these are marked by the ideas and aesthetics born of the Reformation, it is difficult to maintain the opposite. Above all when it is the artists themselves, or their commentators, who say so. ∎

1   See Beat Föllmi's essay in this publication (pp. 193–201).

2   *Iconoclasme. Vie et mort de l'image médiévale*, exhibition catalogue (Bern, Bernisches Historisches Museum, 2000–1), edited by Cécile Dupeux, Peter Jezler, Paris, 2001.

3   Charles Garside, *Zwingli and the Arts*, Yale, 1966.

4   Hans Belting, *Image et culte. Une histoire de l'art avant l'époque de l'art*, Paris, 1998.

5   In itself, aesthetics is a modern intellectual discipline, born precisely not in Luther's era but in the humanist milieu of the Italian Renaissance, far from central and east Germany, where the reformer lived.

6   Jérôme Cottin, 'Calvin and the Visual Arts: the Aesthetics of Soli Deo Gloria', in *The Ecumenism of Beauty*, edited by Timothy Verdon, Brewster, MA, 2017, pp. 1–13

7   Jérôme Cottin, *Le regard et la Parole. Une théologie protestante de l'image*, Geneva, 1997.

8   It was formerly in the court house of the City of Wittenberg; today it is in the Luther Museum of the same city.

9   The entire altarpiece measures 4 × 3 m; formerly at Mömpelgard, it is now in the Kunsthistorisches Museum of Vienna.

10   Jérôme Cottin, 'Loi et Evangile chez Luther et Cranach', *Revue d'Histoire et de Philosophie Reli-*

gieuses, 76/3 (1996), pp. 293–314, Law and Gospel according to Luther and Cranach, in *Luther Digest*, 7 (1999), pp. 2–9.

11 Jérôme Cottin, 'Le *Passional Christi und Antichristi* (1521): une théologie militante et polémique en images', *Revue d'Histoire et de Philosophie Religieuses*, 97/3 (2017), pp. 361–84; Bobby Dykema, 'Reading Visual Rhetoric: Strategies of Piety and Propaganda in Lucas Cranach the Elder's *Passional Christi und Antichristi*', in *ReVisioning. Critical Methods of Seeing Christianity in the History of Art*, edited by James Romaine, Linda Stratford, Cambridge, 2014, pp. 225–42.

12 *Max Beckmann. Apokalypse. Der Wiederaufgefundene handkolorierte Zyklus*, exhibition catalogue (Wiesbaden, Wiesbaden Museum, 2004–5; Frankfurt, Museum für Moderne Kunst, 2005), edited by Miriam Olivia Merz, Wiesbaden, 2004.

13 Ruth Stawarz-Luginbühl, 'Les "Emblemata/ emblèmes chrétiens" (1580-1581) de Théodore de Bèze: un recueil d'emblèmes humanistes et protestants', *Bibliothèque d'Humanisme et Renaissance*, 67/3 (2005), Geneva, pp. 597–624.

14 Jérôme Cottin, 'Tobias Stimmer et l'horloge astronomique de Strasbourg', in *La Cathédrale de Strasbourg*, edited by Christian Grappe, forthcoming.

15 L. Dewitt, 'La tradition à l'épreuve de la nature. Rembrandt et son image radicalement neuve du Christ', in *Rembrandt et la figure du Christ*, exhibition catalogue (Paris, Musée du Louvre, 2011; Philadelphia, Philadelphia Museum of Art, 2011), edited by Lloyd Dewitt, Paris, 2011, pp. 109–46.

16 Frank Muller, *Heinrich Vogtherr l'Ancien. Un artiste entre Renaissance et Réforme*, Wiesbaden, 1997.

17 Michel Pastoureau, *Une histoire symbolique du Moyen Âge occidental*, Paris, 2004, pp. 151–93: 188, "The Protestant Reformation contributed to the massive diffusion of the black and white image. In so doing it took part in the profound cultural revolution that overturned the universe of colors between the 15th and 17th centuries: all medieval images were polychrome; most images in the modern era are black and white. This mutation has had noteworthy repercussions, and has contributed to bringing black and white out of the category of colors".

18 See the works of Swiss photographer Olivier Christinat, an artist of Calvinist culture: Olivier Christinat, *Photographies apocryphes*, Paris, 2000.

19 Frank Muller, 'Les premières apparitions du tétragramme dans l'art allemand et néerlandais des débuts de la Réforme', *Bibliothèque d'Humanisme et Renaissance*, 56 (1994), pp. 327–46.

20 Sylvie Tschiember, *Blue indigo*, 2011, based on Romans 12:5: "In the same way, all of us, although there are so many of us, make up one body in Christ, and as different parts we are all joined to one another".

21 Sylvie Tschiember, *The Instant of Eternity* (Installation), the verse is Mark 1:15: "'The time is fullfiled and the Kingdom of God is close at hand. Repent and believe the Gospel!', written in black and white letters on the ground and in the upper part of the work".

The Reformation and the Multiplication of Printed Images in German-Speaking Areas

FRANK MULLER

The beginnings of the Reformation are generally associated with the appearance of numerous woodcuts illustrating pamphlets and Bibles.[1] In reality, from a strictly quantitative point of view, that multiplication existed from the years 1480–90 onwards, chiefly in German-speaking areas, and naturally is tied to the rise of printing. But it was above all a matter of change both in the support and function of these images. Before 1520, the year in which Reformation propaganda through images effectively began, the image had a mainly illustrative function in works of profane as well as of religious character, whether narrative, scientific (medical texts, for example), or purely ornamental. But there were also loose sheets with devotional images: often pilgrimage 'souvenirs' which, affixed to a wall, could serve as objects of adoration. Well-known are the three different kinds of souvenir woodcuts made for the pilgrimage to Einsiedeln, in Switzerland, much visited at the end of the Middle Ages. Produced by Master E.S., active in the Upper Rhineland in the years 1450–60, they were certainly commissioned by the abbot of Einsiedeln on the occasion of the 500th anniversary of the legendary 'angelic consecration' of the abbey's Lady Chapel. What is interesting is that these prints, of different sizes and levels of complexity, were evidently realized for categories of pilgrims with different budgets, and in that way adapted themselves to a nascent art market.

We cannot therefore speak of a clean break with the past in 1520, but rather of an iconographic revolution which used what had been developed in previous decades in order to subvert it. A good example of this process is Hans Baldung Grien's portrait of Luther, dated 1521 (fig. 1), first published as the title-page of Luther's writings edited by Johann Schott at Strasbourg, then as a loose sheet. After having first realized a woodcut portrait on the basis of an engraving by Cranach (which he reversed), Baldung, using the same pose *en buste*, freed the figure of its niche (which alluded to a saintly effigy in a church), strongly accentuated the Reformer's features and clothing with vigorous cross-hatching, and surrounded him with rays of light from the halo around his head; he then placed the dove of the Holy Spirit above the figure, which, together with the book, indicated Luther's quality as prophet, presenting the Reformer as a "quasi-saint". What is more, contemporaries, accustomed to this way of representing saints, understood perfectly, as we know from a dispatch addressed to the Vatican by the nuncio Aleander, the pope's emissary at the Diet of Worms, stating that people bought the print and embraced it. Baldung Grien's woodcut was thus at once a new kind

1. Hans Baldung Grien, *Portrait of Martin Luther*, woodcut.

posing Jesus's actions with those of the pope, who was compared to the Antichrist, the accent usually being on the temporal dimension of the antithesis, Christ's poverty and humility contrasted with the luxury and money-management of the papal court, all concluding logically with Christ's Ascension and the pope's descent to hell. Thus the opposition Christ/Antichrist visualized the antinomy between the good and the bad Churches. What is interesting is that these powerfully 'speaking' images were reinforced by texts which were themselves antithetical. In effect it seems that the biblical citations which accompany the images relating Christ's actions were chosen by Melanchthon, whereas the extracts from the decretals and canon law which 'comment upon' papal actions were chosen by the jurist Schwertfeger, the whole process probably supervised by Luther himself. It was thus possible to address two different publics: cultured people, able to connect the text and the images, and those who had to be content with the images alone.

The profusion and change of function of these images are evident results of the rapid adherence of the great majority of printers to Luther's cause. It has often been said that the reasons for this phenomenon were first of all economic, printers and their proof-readers understanding that Luther's writings and the anticlerical pamphlets guaranteed a sure profit. At a deeper level, though, printers and proof-readers were often humanists or in any case influenced by humanism and thus open to the new ideas. What is more, even in cities that would more or less rapidly pass over to the Reformation, official censure was not always indulgent, and more than one printer had occasionally to pay a fine or do prison time, in particular if the question involved political attacks or texts of dissident groups. But we may say that all the great printing centers of the German-speaking area – Augsburg, Basel, Nuremberg, Strasbourg, and still others (with the exception of Cologne) –, and with these Wittenberg and Zurich, the places of residence, respectively, of Luther and Zwingli, took part in this large-scale change. And we must add, as far as images are concerned, that the great artists of the period also rapidly joined the Reformers'

of 'saintly' image and the portrait of a real man, a contemporary, the more striking in that the portrait was then a rather new artistic genre.

This first example clearly shows that a title-page illustration could be transformed into a single sheet image with a text of its own, whereas the opposite was decidedly more rare. Always beginning in 1520 we can therefore distinguish three kinds of support in the religious domain, adding to the categories of biblical illustrations and loose sheets that of pamphlets (*Flugschriften*), generally short and small in format, in which the title-page image constituted a sort of résumé of the text, permitting an uncultured public to form some idea of the contents, even if these were often more nuanced than what was communicated by the 'shock image' on the title-page, the intention of which was almost always violently anticlerical. There were also, right from the beginning, various series of antithetical images, usually explained by a short text: the *Passional Christi und Antichristi* produced by the Cranach workshop in 1521 is the most striking example (fig. 2)[2]. The principle was simple: it was a matter of juxta-

camp, with some exceptions, especially Hans Burgkmair. In the artists' case it was clearly the conviction of a just cause that swayed them, for they had rapidly grasped that the golden age of large ecclesiastical commissions was over, as is attested by the petitions addressed by painters and sculptors to certain city councils asking the authorities to help them find work. Some artists even became partisans of the iconoclast movement, the best known case being that of Jörg Breu the Elder at Augsburg.

Returning to the transformation of images, we can immediately note that antipapal propaganda became apparent even in biblical illustrations (and not only those regarding the Apocalypse) which, given their price, were reserved to a limited category of the population; we will cite some examples below. But it was above all in the illustrated single sheets and pamphlets, which in number and diffusion constituted the spear-head of this propaganda, that traditional visual motifs took a new direction, and novel themes were developed (even if in

some cases there were Hussite precedents, as in the above-mentioned *Passional*): the good Church and the bad; Law and Grace; the pope as Antichrist, etc., as we will say presently. But first we should consider, for the brief period 1521–5, the appearance of a new, positive personage, the Peasant, archetype of the *gemeine Mann* (common man), as he is represented under the generic family name of *Karsthans* (*John Hoe*) in the eponymous dialogue printed at Strasbourg in 1521 (fig. 3) and replicated in several later publications. In medieval literature and in rare visual representations depicting him, the peasant is generally considered a vulgar rustic or, at best, a simple-minded fellow. But in this anonymous dialogue, written by a man of culture (perhaps the Strasbourg humanist Nikolaus Gerbel), it is precisely the peasant, with his sturdy good sense, who convinces his son, a student, of the righteousness of Luther's ideas.[3] In that debut appearance, Luther succeeded in preventing *Karsthans* from resorting to violence against the Reformer's

Lucas Cranach the Elder, woodcuts, in Martin Luther, *Passional Christi et Antichristi*, 1521, pls. 11–12.

3. Attributed to Erhart Schlitzohr, woodcut, in *Karsthans*, 1521.

enemies (in this case the Franciscan Thomas Murner, the most talented of the anti-Luther polemicists). The attitude changed in the second round, however, with Karsthans's reappearance in the *Göttliche Mühle*, published in Zurich and written by two friends of Zwingli, but with title-page iconography probably attributable to Zwingli himself. Without trying here to interpret the whole complex allegory, suffice it to say that the peasant overshadows the entire scene, and, even as he threshes the wheat destined to furnish spiritual 'bread', he threatens the clergy, in evident prefiguration of the 1525 Peasants' War.[4]

Biblical images remained in overall continuity with pre-reformation prototypes, with numerous novelties however, particularly the appearance of what are called 'archeological images', which generally show, in addition to a Jewish priest, depictions of the Ark of the Covenant, of the Temple of Jerusalem, of the decorations of Solomon's throne and, later, maps of the Holy Land. But everywhere we note the insertion of polemical images, of which the prototype is beyond doubt Cranach's *Whore of Babylon* in the *Septembertestament* (the *New Testament* in Luther's translation) of 1522 (fig. 4), an interpretation of the text of Revelation 17 as free as it is partisan, since the whore in question wears a papal tiara. In later depictions this personage emerges from the background of a city which is Rome, generally characterized with the silhouette of Castel Sant'Angelo,

this evidently to accentuate the assimilation of Rome to Babylon. More generally, in almost all the illustrated bibles of the first decades of the Reformation, whatever their place of printing, there are anticlerical images attacking the pope, the Catholic hierarchy and monks.[5] There is also a small number of pedagogical images aimed at making the new theological ideas explicit. Let us take as example the visualization of the *Calling of the First Disciples* (Mt 4:18–22) created in the workshop of Heinrich Vogtherr the Elder, one of the principal illustrators of Strasbourg, in the *Leienbibel*, published in Strasbourg by Wendel Rihel in 1540 (fig. 5).

For the Lake of Tiberias, the print shows the Ill, the river whose waters bathe Strasbourg, and the scene unfolds in front of fortified towers connected by bridges, in a place that is still perfectly recognizable today, called *Ponts-couverts*. Beyond the local patriotism inherent in this kind of image, there is a deeper intention in all this: the desire to show that the biblical episode is still symbolically actual, leading those who see the image to identify with the disciples. In the same work, a sort of biblical summary for laypeople, an illustration by an anonymous Strasbourg artist depicting Jesus who teaches in the synagogue at Capernaum (Jn 6:26–59) shows two ministers distributing the Supper under both species, a logical consequence of Jesus's long discourse juxtaposing the spirit and the flesh; the image is entitled "bread of life" and very clearly announces the institution of the Supper.[6] This same metaphor of the Bread of Life was already present in 1527, in the title-page of a New Testament published by Johann Grüninger, where the four evangelists distribute the spiritual bread – that is, the bible –, to ecclesiastical and lay dignitaries who do not seem very interested,[7] recalling, in the *Göttliche Mühle*, both Luther kneading the same bread and Zwingli offering it to the pope and his henchmen, who refuse it. Many of these images clearly generated others which are not actually copies, even if copies too were very numerous.

Let us look now at some examples of the themes mentioned above, knowing that they appear principally in the form of loose sheets in which the text explains the image, or of title-page illustrations expected to synthesize the contents of a pamphlet. Among numerous examples of the directly antipapal theme, let us take three of different degrees of complexity, illustrating the themes of the pope as Antichrist and of the Good and Bad Churches.

An example of very direct attack is the threatening personage, half man, half animal, by Heinrich Vogtherr the Elder, adorning the title-page of a collection of sermons on the Antichrist given by Rudolf Gwalther, published in 1546 at Zurich by Christoph Froschauer.[8] Identified as the pope by his tiara, but bearded, horned and therefore diabolical, this figure has the nether body of an ass and, with a diabolical dance, with his shoes crushes two books which are evidently the Old and New Testaments. Brandishing a sword in one hand (which puts us in mind of warrior popes like Julius II), in the other he holds a flaming Bull – a *Teufelsbrief* –, which is the very antithesis of the Bible.

Our second example depends directly on the Bible and precisely on the famous passage of the Acts of the Apostles relating the conversion of Saul, which it adapts to the needs of the Reform cause. In effect, to illustrate the *Practica der Pfaffen* (vers 1535), a pseudo prophecy in all likelihood of joachimite origin on the end of the papacy, the Strasbourg printer Jacob Cammerlander, who may also be the draughtsman, on the title-page used an engraving that had appeared for the first time at Haguenau in 1528, supposed to represent the *Road to Damascus* (fig. 6), the iconography of which had long been codified. The Christ appearing in the clouds who apostrophizes Saul – "Saule, was verfolgest du mich?" ("Saul, why are you persecuting me?"[9]) is shown in the classic way, but the personage falling from his horse is not the future Paul, founder of the Church, but the pope. The pope is thus designated as the persecutor of Christ who represents the false Church – a message reinforced by the contrast between the cross held by Christ and the pope's crosier. On the other hand we recall that in the Bible story Saul, a Jew, was on his way to persecute the Christians of Damascus, and it is evident

4. Lucas Cranach the Elder, *Whore of Babylon*, woodcut, in *Septembertestament*, 1522.

5. Workshop of Heinrich Vogtherr the Elder, *Calling of the First Disciples*, in *Leienbibel*, 1540.

6. Jacob Cammerlander (?), *Road to Damascus*, woodcut, in *Practica der Pfaffen*, around 1535.

7. Anonymous artist, *Das sibenhabtig Pabstier* (*The seven-headed papal beast*) – *Offenbarung Johannis Tessaloni. 2. Cap.*, woodcut.

that the 'falseness' of Judaism is here being referred to Catholicism, and we are clearly before a misappropriation of the medieval anti-Judaic theme of the Church and the Synagogue.

The third image is certainly the most complex: a loose sheet by an anonymous artist (fig. 7) probably published at Nuremberg around 1530, on a text by Hans Sachs. The title, *Das sibenhabtig Pabstier* (The seven-headed papal beast) – *Offenbarung Johannis Tessaloni. 2. Cap.*, gives the tone, mixing the Beast of Revelations 17 with an allusion to 2 Thessalonians 2,3–4 which treats of the personification of Evil, "the lost One who … enthrones himself in God's sanctuary and flaunts the claim that he is God", all under the influence of Satan. This rather obscure passage, influenced by the Jewish apocalyptic literature, has often been used in anti-Catholic polemics, which interpret it as referring to the Antichrist and thus to the pope. The commentary by Sachs, the cobbler-poet, is an inventory of all the misdeeds of the popish Church, which, it finally concludes, "Doctor

Martin" has mortally wounded, expressing the hope that God pulverize it.

But it is above all the illustration that interests us, in that it appropriates an iconographic theme current at the end of the Middle Ages, the Mass of St Gregory, which visualized transsubstantiation but was also connected with indulgences. And, in effect, on the desolate earth, "Regnum Diaboli", stands a rather curious altar, which is nothing other than a chest meant to collect the money given by the faithful who have bought indulgences, on top of which a cross is placed, bearing the *Arma Christi*, as was actually done during the indulgence sales campaigns. The usual inscription INRI is replaced by a pseudo letter of indulgence with its official seals (again a kind of *Teufelsbrief*), which bears the words "Umb gelt ein sack vol ablas" ("A sack full of indulgences in exchange for money"). And in place of the apparition of Christ on the altar normally seen in representations of the Mass of St Gregory, here there is a monstrous Beast, flanked by papal banners to right and left and provided with seven heads of churchmen, monks, bishops and cardinals, the centermost head being that of a hirsute pope, recalling the medieval Wild Man and, evidently, a creature of the Devil, whom we see writing beneath the chest in vertical prolongation of the pope's cross, suggesting that the pope is an offshoot of Satan (a diabolical birthing taken up in other loose sheets as well). The 'transubstantiation' operated here is that of the money given by the faithful and transformed into diabolical power.

To conclude, let us consider a pedagogical image, an even more widespread genre due to the diffusion of new ideas and to objectives more and more catechetical in character. But the loose sheet in question, a sort of remarkable synthesis of the themes mentioned above, has visibly been conceived rather as a support tool for preaching directed at adults who already know Scripture well. Entitled *The Old and the New Churches*, it is the work of a certain 'Monogramist H' active in Saxony, and completes a dialogue published in Iena in 1524, in which a Christian debates with a Jew 'about Christ as the cornerstone', according to the words of the title (fig. 8). In the image's very elaborate geometric ordering, Christ on the cross constitutes the center in every senses (we read the number 1 on his torso, and understand that everything begins with him), and the superimposed circles are ordered on the vertical axis, the most immediately comprehensible, obviously to be read from the top down, from divinity to human sinfulness and the devil. It is a kind of *abrégé* of Christian cosmology: the three Persons of the Holy Trinity are, as is often the case, superimposed, in a new-milled version of the medieval Throne of Glory. Above and below Christ are John the Baptist and Daniel, supposed to be the last prophets, and Peter and Paul, the 'new prophets' of the Gospel. To one side and the other are Mary and John, traditional witnesses of the Crucifixion in medieval iconography, while in the squares around Christ appear the symbols of the four evangelists all around the Crucified, and in the corners of the large square we see effigies of Moses, David, Job and Isaiah, the square itself being read evidently as the Cor-

nerstone. The upper part of the lowest circle shows the consequences of original sin: Adam using his spade, Eve weaving, and Cain murdering Abel – which means that one can also read the image from below upwards, since it is Christ's sacrifice which ransoms humankind from its sin, all of that corresponding to traditional medieval Christian conceptions.

Finally, in the two lower parts of the lowest circle the antithesis between the Old and New Churches begins, which we can also read from above downwards, again according to a medieval pattern, with the 'good' on the viewer's left (that is, on Christ's right), and the 'bad' to our right (Christ's left). In effect, the door opened by an angel in the upper left, which reveals Christ the Savior, corresponds to the door in the lower part of the same side, which a devil tries in vain to force: the closed door of the Good Church. By contrast, on the right (Catholic) side, an angel with a sword guards the closed door of heaven, an evident allusion to Adam and Eve expelled from Paradise and

8. Monogramist H, *About Christ as the cornerstone, The Old and the New Churches*, woodcut.

therefore to sinful humanity, while below a laughing devil throws open the gate of hell. Farther up, on the same side, the Whore of Babylon, riding the Beast with seven heads, clearly recalls the Cranach print mentioned above, and serves as a pendant for the seven-branched candlestick in the upper left, an allusion to Christ as the light of the world. At the center, two crowds face each other: one, on the bad side, is led by the pope and a king; the other, made up of simple folk, echoes the 'common man' theme, representing ordinary people who understand the Gospel better than the great of this world.

Finally, beneath the two thieves on their crosses, are two preachers: the one on the left characterized as an 'evangelical preacher like Luther and others', protected by a knight on horseback, who is evidently the prince protector of Protestantism, here probably the Elector of Saxony. On the right is a preacher of indulgences such as 'Eck, Emser or Cochleus', Luther's chief Catholic adversaries; the sun and moon present here are also very ancient symbols of 'light' and 'darkness'. So complex is the image that we could doubtless illustrate still other parallelisms, again showing misappropriations of classic Christian iconographical motifs and their reorganization in a new discourse.

In conclusion, we should also remark that these processes of change are contemporary with the iconoclast phenomena meant to desacralize images: as if the numerous cultic 'images' (paintings, statues) were being replaced with a torrent of multiple images serving the needs of propaganda and instruction but by their very nature excluding adoration. More generally, we should not forget that here we have considered only images related to the religious struggles of the time, the number of which would sharply diminish in the second half of the century, when the Empire's politico-religious equilibrium more or less stabilized. Then, in effect, the mass of printed images of all subjects increased practically everywhere in Europe: a phenomenon that was one of the indices of early European 'modernity'. ■

1   I have decided to limit the number of my notes in this field whose bibliography grows ceaselessly since the publication of the reference text of Linda and Peter Parshall, *Art and the Reformation. An Annotated Bibliography*, Boston, 1986.

2   On the *Passional*, see the recent article by Jérôme Cottin, 'Le Passional *Christi und Antichristi (1521)*: une théologie militante et polémique en images', *Revue d'Histoire et de Philosophies Religieuses*, 97 (2017), pp. 361–84.

3   For a rapid synthesis of the Karsthans personage and this appearances, see Frank Muller, *Images polémiques, images dissidentes. Art et Réforme à Strasbourg (1520-vers 1550)*, Baden Baden, 2017, pp. 19–26.

4   On the *Göttliche Mühle*, see especially Christine Göttler, 'Das älteste Zwingli-Bildnis? Zwingli als Bilderfinder. Der Titelholzschnitt zur "Beschribung der

göttlichen Muly"', in *Bilderstreit. Kulturwandel in Zwinglis Reformation*, edited by Hans-Peter Altendorf and Peter Jezler, Zurich, 1984, pp. 19–39.

5   See for example, for Strasbourg, the examples cited in Muller 2017, op. cit., figs. 77–9, 82–3, 95–6. One could multiply the number of examples.

6   Reproduction and comment in ibid., pp. 312–13, fig. 97.

7   Reproduction and comment ibid., pp. 269–71, fig. 71.

8   On this theme see generally Frank Muller, 'Le thème du Pape-Antéchrist dans la polémique visuelle anticatholique dans le Rhin supérieur au XVIᵉ siècle', *Simpliciana*, 22 (2000), pp. 75–90, with a reproduction of the image on p. 88.

9   These words appear, it seems, only in earlier uses of the image.

Icons, Likeness
and Reformation Spirituality

WILLIAM DYRNESS

In this paper I want to challenge the common assumption that, with respect to art and aesthetics, the Reformation represents a sharp break with the medieval period. To make this case I will focus specifically on the practice of praying before Icons in the Orthodox tradition, especially as this came to influence the use of images in medieval Europe, and, eventually, the developing liturgical notions in Protestant worship. I argue that Protestant ideas of sight and seeing were as much a *development* of this western tradition as a departure from it. Moreover, I believe, recalling ideas of prayer and worship involving icons provides a lens with which, *mutatis mutandis*, later Protestant practices can be more fruitfully understood and evaluated.

Prayer and the Icon

St John of Damascus made clear the embeddedness of images in creation: "the mind which is determined to ignore corporeal things will find itself weakened and frustrated. Since the creation of the world the invisible things of God are clearly seen by means of images".[1] In this way physical seeing was not despised but enhanced, as St John of Damascus says, "leading us through matter to the invisible God".[2] Moreover the correspondence of the image to its prototype moreover involved an important

likeness. This was not a physical likeness of course, but a theological one, which Orthodox theologians insist could be traced back to Christ himself (fig. 1). Each of the icons then provided a veridical window into the heavenly reality, indeed into the very reality of salvation as this was accomplished by the Incarnation and embodied in the liturgy.[3] Icons then represented a particular notion of "symbol" that is important to my argument. The images – of Christ Pantokrator, or the Theotokos, represent the "presence" of what is symbolized. The goal of praying with these figures is that worshipers become themselves an "icon" capable by word and deed of creating external icons, embodying this divine life in the world.[4]

The Medieval appropriation of Icons

Byzantine portrait icons were foundational to the development of western panel painting. As Italian painters took over these images in the 1200s, however, they gradually began to emphasize the emotional affective element on the one hand and an increasing realism on the other. To the theological and didactic purposes of art that had been constant from the Early Church, gradually a third "empathic" purpose was added.[5] Here the idea of *presence* is undergoing a subtle shift. Presence here invokes not the divine presence in the painting, which in the West had always aroused suspicion, but the presence of the viewer and the experience the image was meant to solicit. In arguably the most influential theological text of the 14th century, the illustrated *Meditations on the Life of Christ*, by an anonymous Franciscan monk, the reader is encouraged to ponder the images of Christ's life reproduced and described.[6]

As in the *Meditations*, the object of these Saints Plays, as of the Mass, was to call observers to participate in the recurring drama of redemption as this was described in Scripture and presented in the Mass. But as this was impacted by the Franciscan focus on emotional identification and later by the humanist movement, the observer was increasingly asked to participate – to be present – in the dramatic

1. *Christus Pantokrator*, Sinai (Egypt), St Catherine's Monastery.

action performed. While images no longer necessarily carried the same theological content of icons, in their multiple forms they were freed up to encourage a greater variety of affective responses – an increasing subjectification.[7]

Facilitating this was an increasing realistic intent, elaborated in narrative terms in 'Sacra conversazione' paintings such as Fra Angelico's *Madonna delle Ombre* (fig. 2), in which viewers are to share in the conversation portrayed. We earlier noted that with icons the likeness was theological rather than physical – the question of actual resemblance to some person was secondary. But this was changing dramatically in the 15th century. There one finds a markedly different emphasis. As Alasdair MacIntyre notes, "the heavy eye-lids, the coiffed hair, the lines around the mouth, undeniably represent some particular woman, either actual or envisaged" (fig. 3).[8] But what are we to make of this changing focus on what we see? Is it the case, as MacIntyre suggests, that "resemblance has usurped the iconic relationship"[9]– does it represent the triumph of the didactic, as Orthodox critics argue, featuring "more and more the representation of a human model, made solely by the hand of man"?[10] Rather, I suggest this represents a changing conception of the world, underway already in the 13th century, one that makes way for a new way of understanding God's presence and activity, and, as a result new ways of "seeing" and responding to this presence.

The Fate of the senses in the Reformation

John Calvin is often given credit (or blame) for the fundamental change in Reformation spirituality moving the focus from what is seen in the medieval images and sacramentals, to what is heard in the proclamation of the Word.[11] But a growing number of scholars have come to challenge this characterization, arguing that for Calvin the senses were indispensable to knowing God. Randall Zachman's summary of Calvin's views resonates with the history I have traced: "We must use our eyes and our ears in order to behold the living images that God presents to our view in order to be led from the visible to the invisible, from the earthly to the

2. Fra Angelico, *Madonna and Child with Saints* (*Madonna 'delle Ombre'*), Florence, Museo di San Marco.

heavenly, from the present to the future, from the carnal to the spiritual".[12]

Sight carried deep theological significance for Calvin. God has made himself known by means of things that can be seen. As Calvin famously argued, we are to see creation itself as a marvelous theater for the glory of God. This involved a deeply emotional and volitional, even aesthetic response to things seen. The emotional and dramatic response that medieval worshiper found in the elevation of the host, Calvin finds, in the first instance, in humankind's response to the wonders of the theater of creation. Calvin argues in words that recall St John of Damascus, in his comments on Romans 1:19: "By saying, that God has made it [God's power and divine nature] manifest, he means, that man was created to be a spectator of this formed world, and that eyes were given him, that he might by looking on so beautiful a picture, be led up to the Author himself".[13]

The possibility of seeing God in what he has made, Calvin recognizes and problematizes at the same time. The problem is not that this knowledge is unavailable, but that humans are so blinded by ignorance and malice that they cannot "see" this. Humans "do not appre-hend God as he offers himself", Calvin writes, "but imagine him as they have fashioned him in their own presumption".[14] In other words the likeness of things has been distorted by false human imagining, what Calvin calls our blindness. Note, the problem is not that God's glory is invisible or that human eyes are not capable of seeing this – the problem is theological not optical. And the solution itself involves a reorientation of our sight, involving both a vision of God, and a corrected apprehension of the visible world – that is a recognition of its true likeness. But how does Calvin seek to redirect the gaze of believers?

Calvin's humanist training and his understanding of the role of rhetoric in his preaching led him to a figurative view of language that elicits emotional response. In Calvin's preaching, figures are not meant to be interpreted intellectually; they are meant to be felt and experienced in the drama of the preaching – as an instrument of the Holy Spirit to move the heart to *pietas* – reverence and love for God. For example, Calvin stressed that God is our "enemy". Such expressions Calvin notes "have been accommodated to our sense (*ad sensum nostrum*) that we may better understand how

3. Domenico Ghirlandaio, *Portrait of Giovanna Tornabuoni*, Madrid, Museo Thyssen Bornemisza.

miserable and ruinous our condition is apart from Christ".[15] That is God wants us to see not simply that we are lost, but more viscerally, to feel we are an "enemy of God".[16] Matthew Boulton believes Calvin has in mind a "kind of poetic distillation, a vivid rhetorical icon meant to instruct and persuade, and ultimately to form and sanctify". This formation, Boulton thinks, is central to Calvin's understanding of the worship experience and to the formation of his *Institutes*.[17]

A new way of seeing the world was being proposed and celebrated in performance of the Protestant liturgy, but this was not simply a detached cold gaze on what was there. In the performance of preaching a space was opened for one to see and experience the presence of God. But one needed ears to hear this music; eyes to perceive this icon. This space was not an icon in the Orthodox sense, of course, but the encounter believers were meant to have reso-

nates with experiences that Orthodox believers had praying before an icon. After all a proper vision of what God has done for the world in Christ, an insight into this 'likeness', is not merely a lens that makes everything clear, but an apprehension of "the doctrine of salvation of which it is a part" – as Leonid Ouspensky says of the doctrine of the icon[18]– and of the human participation in this.[19]

The corporate experience of hearing the Scripture proclaimed, singing together and participating in the sacraments, in Calvin's Geneva, was meant to be formational so that believers would create external icons.[20] The dramatic movement is not centripetal toward the raising of the host as a symbol of the cross, but centrifugal from the substance of that "astonishing change of things" accomplished by Christ outward, into the believers' lives – who, in Calvin's dramatic language, are called to play their own role in the theater of the church. They were encouraged to see the play outside as a great drama of redemption – a theater of God's glory. And they were able to have eyes for this drama – to create external icons – precisely because they had their vision corrected. But, here is what I want to underline: this performance, with its dramatic impact accompanied and enhanced by the corporate prayers and singing of the Psalms, was meant to bring about a similar spiritual transformation as these earlier practices. The images of Christ and the Saints were forbidden in this space, of course. But these images, which Calvin dismissed as 'dead images', were to be replaced with 'living images' represented in the preaching of the Scriptural promises, and embodied in baptism and the Eucharist.[21] In this way the space of the church became a formational space, what one scholar has called a "sanctifying space" – a space in which a particular saving grace shines forth in multiple ways.[22]

Protestants: seeing the theater of the world

In resisting the necessary mediation of the Icon and the Mass, I argue, Calvin opened the way for experiencing God's work and presence in a wider variety of situations. Regina Schwartz in fact has suggested a con-

4. Jacob von Ruisdael, *Three Great Trees in a Mountainous Landscape with a River*, Pasadena, CA, Norton Simon Museum.

nection between the Reformers' rejection of real presence in the Eucharist and the ability to see the world as a stage of redemptive significance. Her argument is that it was the elimination of the transformative work of the sacrament that opened the way for poets and playwrights to develop what she calls a sacramental poetics. Despite its supposed opposition to ritual, she argues, when the Eucharist became more about remembrance than sacrifice, the Reformers began to emphasize, "less the power of ritual… than the catharsis of spectacle".[23] Contrary to the view that realistic theater represents a secular development, Schwartz argues, Shakespeare's craving for redemption is itself religious. His plays represent not the absence of rituals, but rituals refilled with moral outrage.[24] Recall that Calvin's rhetoric had as its goal the enlistment of the congregation as players in the theater of the world.

Notice that art objects have been removed from the realm as carriers of the sacred and have become "representational signs"– liberated commodities. But here I want to stress that this development, which scholars are quick to celebrate as a secularization of art, at this point was nothing of the kind. Artists of this period were able to use this broader focus on the theater of the world, as a canvas on which can be inscribed deeply spiritual even theological realities. To illustrate this we turn to 17th century Holland.

Holland in the 17th century: the art of describing

As is well known 17th-century Dutch art is primarily known for its landscapes and portraits, the two elements celebrated as typifying the secular turn in art after the Reformation. Scholarly attention to the naturalism of 17th century Dutch painting has struggled to come to terms

5. Rembrandt van Rijn, *Self-Portrait*,
Pasadena, CA, Norton Simon Museum.

with the theological influence on what has been called the "art of describing".[25] While many factors were at work it is clearly a mistake to see the turn toward landscape and portraits in purely secular terms.[26] Calvin, who deeply influenced developments here, says nature holds up for us a mirror in which we can see God, but it also reflects the responsibility to remake that world in the ways God intended.

One could not find a better example of this staged naturalism than the landscapes of Jacob van Ruisdael, a contemporary of Rembrandt. Consider the painting *Three Great Trees in a Landscape* from 1667 (Norton Simon Museum Pasadena; fig. 4). What first appears as a natural beauty, when more closely examined, is shown to reflect a 'selected naturalness'. If we look carefully we can see a spiritual drama being played out: there is a broken down house by the river, and three stricken beech trees in the foreground. As John Walford argues in his study of this painter, the best reading of the *vanitas* theme so common in this period is "brokenness".[27] The dramatic presence of sin and the fragility of life have given the beauty

of Ruisdael a depth that is absent, for example, in his contemporary Claude Lorraine. Creation is both a theater for the glory of God, and also the dramatic site of sin and brokenness. Still there is hope, light breaks through the clouds, and the men are going out to their labor until the evening as in Psalm 104:23 – a familiar text of the time.[28]

Von Ruisdael offers an image that may be enjoyed on many levels. Dutch burghers could bring this picture into their homes and visit these pleasant places via their imagination from the comfort and safety of their home. But in order for it to be seen and properly appropriated, it must be placed into a larger frame; it must be 'textualized' by the Reformed narrative of creation and redemption. So the delights of rural life are typically mixed with signs of darkness, and of struggle. The light in the sky could signal hope, but the darkness reminded them of the fragility of life – a threat that Dutch people viscerally understood living in a land threatened by the sea. These images reflected the new dramatic situation that had been defined by the Reformed narrative of creation and redemption, a narrative that allowed one to see the world as it truly is.

This landscape seems to be far removed from the focused Orthodox image with which we began. And in many respects, it is. But there is this similarity: both open up to a broader presence that defines and gives a spiritual meaning to the image, and both seek a theological likeness. My attempt to understand how these two very different artistic periods reflect a common Christian tradition suggests a further way to understand what the 17th century might contribute to this common Christian heritage, and to ecumenical conversation more generally: on creation as a theater for the glory of God.

Praying before an icon, celebrating a sacred liturgy in which icons are central, encourages a fully embodied response of the worshiper – something that is often thought to have been lost in Reformed worship. But my argument has been the refusal to restrict the special presence of God to particular images (cf. icons), or sacramental practices (cf. medieval Eucharist), may have expanded the possibilities of seeing and responding to that presence more broadly

6. Rembrandt van Rijn, *The Toilet of Bathsheba*, New York, Metropolitan Museum of Art.

in the drama of redemption being played out in the world.

Perhaps there is no better support for this claim than the late portraits of Rembrandt van Rijn (1606–69; fig. 5). While the majority of Rembrandt's portraits date from 1630s, a decade later they began to take on a more deeply psychological and spiritual dimension. In this respect Rembrandt has often been thought unrepresentative of Dutch art in this period, unlike Vermeer's paintings, for example, which offer the viewer a "flood of observed, unmediated details drawn from nature".[29] Rembrandt by contrast, Svetlana Alpers asserts, displays an estrangement from his own context, "offering a rare entry into invisible human depths".

Now it is important that we carefully understand what Rembrandt's achievement – his estrangement from his context – amounts to. It does not mean reading our post-romantic notions of the person back into these portraits. Rembrandt's self-portraits for example (there were probably around 40 of them), should not

be read as exercises in self-examination.[30] It is also important to recognize that the outpouring of portraits in this period often celebrated more broadly the status of the sitter and the skill of the artist. For the latter, artists often sought *voncken* (sparkle), skin that appears to be real flesh, i.e. simply true naturalness in Alpers' sense of the word. Rembrandt's later works rejected these qualities and for that reason were often considered "unfinished". His response to this charge was to say a work was finished if it "achieved [the artist's] intention in it".

But what was his intention? As many commentators have pointed out, from the 1640s this involved, especially for his biblical subjects, capturing a moment of recognition. And this psychological insight displayed a special connection to the artist's purposes. During the 1630s one can trace Rembrandt's work from the commissions and patrons, from 1641 to 1654 there were few commissions and the artist seems to have chosen subjects he was drawn to.[31] This is seen for example in his 1643 *The*

Toilet of Bathsheba (New York Met Museum; fig. 6). Here typically the figure is highlighted, thrust forward as Simon Schama puts it, "a summation of character through body language and the illumination of face and hands".[32] Here, Rembrandt exhibits the *nae t'leven* that glows with "the robust warmth of full blooded life".

These cannot be described as icons in any traditional sense, but neither do they fit with the developing realism, the anti-thesis of iconography as MacIntyre called it, of the 15th century; these works constitute a new kind of icon.[33] As Simon Schama notes, the frame of these pictures is not a window, surely not a window to heaven as in the icon, but more a self-dissolving threshold "through which both beholder and beheld may unnervingly pass".[34]

The drama of Bathsheba is a drama that we too share.

We are drawn closer to the living person, but like Calvin, our guide here clearly mistrusts the evidence of sight – consider how often Rembrandt was drawn to paint the blind. Alpers suggests this is because Rembrandt's images show us that "it is the word (or the Word) rather than the world that conveys the truth".[35] Because in the figure of Bathsheba Rembrandt captures the depths of the human drama that we are meant to live out as external icons. The material world, creation, is not diminished but its dramatic dimension, the tragic content of human entanglement, is laid bare. Rembrandt has given us, in the icon of a human figure, a theological likeness of the redemptive drama – every-day life, awaiting redemption. ∎

1   St John of Damascus, *De imaginibus*, English translation with the title *On the Divine Images*, by David Anderson, New York, 2002 (1st ed. Crestwood, NY, 1980), p. 11.
2   "I salute all remaining matter with reverence, because God has filled it with his grace and power", ibid., p. 20. The following quote is from p. 67.
3   See Leonid Ouspensky, 'The Meaning and language of Icons', in *The Meaning of Icons*, edited by Leonid Ouspensky and Vladimir Lossky, Crestwood, NY, 1982, pp. 23–49: 27–8. See also p. 30: icon painting corresponds "to what the Gospels preach and relate".
4   Ibid., p. 36.
5   Sixten Ringbon notes that after Nicea II it was increasingly common to have a "deeply emotional experience" before religious images. But, he notes, only later in the medieval period does the individual reaction before images begin to attract attention. Ringbom believes even Gregory suggested the need for emotional response in one of his letters, but this only becomes commonly expected in later medieval devotional images. See Sixten Ringbom, *Icon to Narrative: The Rise of the Dramatic Close-up in 15th c. Devotional Painting*, Abo, 1965, pp. 12–15.

6   *Meditations on the Life of Christ: An Illustrated Manuscript of the 14th Century*, edited by Isa Ragusa, Princeton, 1961, p. 2: in such reflection, he says, "through frequent and continued meditation on his life the soul attains so much familiarity, confidence and love that it will disdain and disregard other things and be exercised and trained as to what to do and what to avoid". Later quote is from p. 50.
7   See the complaint of Evdokimov, that the West always limited images to ornamental purposes, which he thinks poisoned art at its source, thus accounting for the dead ends of contemporary art. Pavel Nicolaevic Evdokimov, *L'art de l'icône. Théologie de la beauté*, Bruges, 1972, reference ed. *The Art of the Icon: A Theology of Beauty*, Torrance (CA), 1990, p. 167.
8   Alasdair C. MacIntyre, *After Virtue: A Study in Moral Theory*, Notre Dame, IN, 1981, pp. 176–7.
9   Ibid., p. 176.
10   Evdokimov 1972, ed. 1990, p. 170. His reference to the "hand of man" is meant to contrast with the Holy Face which is made by God's own hand.
11   Hans Urs von Balthasar concludes his discussion of Protestant views by noting they ensured the elimination of aesthetics from the whole of the

Christian life and more broadly "the expulsion of contemplation from the act of faith the exclusion of 'seeing' from 'hearing'": Hans Urs von Balthasar, *Herrlichkeit. Eine theologische Ästhetik*, Einsiedeln, 3 vols., 1961–9, English trans. by Erasmo Leiva Merikakis, 7 vols., San Francisco, 1982–9, I, p. 70.

12 The discussion is summarized in Randall C. Zachman, *Image and Word in the Theology of John Calvin*, Notre Dame, IN, 2007, pp. 3–7. Quote is from p. 7.

13 Romans 1:19, in underlines the importance of this late (1556) insistence on the role of the spectator and the potential of contemplation of so beautiful an image to lead one to God. See Zachman 2007, op. cit., p. 33. In a sense Calvin reverses the medieval journey toward God, by insisting that one must begin with a vision of God; see John Calvin, *Institutionis Christianae Religionis* [1559]; trans. by Ford Battles, edited by John McNeill, Philadelphia, 1960, I, 1, 2: "It is certain that man never achieves a clear knowledge of himself unless he has first looked upon God's face and then descends from contemplating him to scrutinize himself".

14 Calvin, *Institutionis*, ed. 1960, op. cit., I, IV, I.

15 Ibid., II, XVI, 2.

16 Matthew Myer Boulton, "'Even more deeply moved": Calvin on the Rhetorical Formational function of Scripture', in *Calvin and the Book: The Evolution of the Printed Word in Reformed Protestantism*, edited by Karen Spierling, Gottingen, 2015, pp. 137–45: 145. Quote which follows is from p. 144.

17 In fact Boulton (2015, op. cit., p. 143) thinks the best definition of *Institutes* is "deeply formative education".

18 *The Meaning of Icons* 1982, op. cit., p. 28.

19 Which Boulton (2015, op. cit., p. 145) describes as "a sphere in which by the Spirit's rhetorical engagement, disciples are cultivated, dispositionally and spiritually into human beings fully alive and fittingly grateful".

20 Hans-Georg Gadamer, *Die Aktualitat des Schonen : Kunst als Spiel, Symbol und Fest*, Stuttgart, 1979, English trans. by Nicholas Walker, Cambridge, 1986, p. 4, calls attention to the influence of this on the art of music. The Reformation "brought a new kind of art into prominence, a kind of music based on the participation of the congregation, as in the work of Heinrich Schutz and Johann Sebastian Bach".

21 On Calvin's living images, see Zachman 2007, op. cit., pp. 7–9.

22 The notion of "sanctifying space" is argued in the recent dissertation of Edward Yang, *Sanctifying Space: A Reformed Theology of Places for Corporate Worship*, Ph.D. Diss., Fuller Theological Seminary, 2016.

23 Regina Schwartz, *Sacramental Poetics at the Dawn of Secularism: When God left the World*, Stanford, CA, 2008, loc. 1093.

24 Ibid., loc. 820, 864. She disputes Stephen Greenblatt's assertion that these rituals are emptied of religion: she thinks Othello is a play about the longing for justice (loc. 952), Desdemona's death is a redemptive sacrifice (loc. 1024).

25 Svetlana Alpers, *The Art of Describing: Dutch Art in the Seventeenth Century*, Chicago, 1983.

26 A brief survey is found in Reindert L. Falkenberg, 'Calvinism and the emergence of Dutch Seventeenth Century Landscape Art – A Critical Evaluation', in *Seeing Beyond the Word, Visual Arts and the Calvinist Tradition*, edited by Paul Corby Finney, Grand Rapids, 2000, pp. 343–68.

27 Ewan John Walford, *Jacob van Ruisdael and the Perception of Landscape*, New Haven, 1991. On *vanitas* theme see pp. 33–8.

28 Light breaking often conveyed divine providence and redemption in von Ruisdael. See *Jacob von Ruisdael* 1991, op. cit., p. 99.

29 This is supportive of her general thesis that Dutch art of this period displays a frame of the world as seen, what she calls the art of describing. Alpers 1983, op. cit., p. 222. Quote which follows is from 225.

30 See Ernst van de Wetering, 'The Multiple Functions of Rembrandt's Self Portraits', in *Rembrandt by Himself*, exhibition catalogue (London, National Gallery, 1999) edited by Christopher White and Quentin Buvelot, London and New Haven, 1999, pp. 8–38 for this whole paragraph. Rembrandt quote is from p. 35.

31 See Gary Schwartz, *Rembrandt: His Life, His Paintings*, London, 1985, p. 226.

32 Simon Shama, *Rembrandts Eyes*, London, 1999, p. 338.

33 MacIntyre's claim is that Rembrandt achieves a synthesis: "The naturalistic portrait is now rendered as an icon, but an icon of a new and hitherto inconceivable kind". MacIntyre 1981, op. cit., p. 90.

34 Shama 1999, op. cit., p. 473.

35 Alpers 1983, op. cit., p. 227.

The Catholic Reformation and Art

TIMOTHY VERDON

The work which best expresses the artistic theory and practice of the Catholic Church in the age of the Reformation is the new Basilica of St Peter's in Rome, historically and symbolically linked to the papacy and thus to the entire system of thought and usage brought into question by Protestant reformers (fig. 1).[1] The art of what used to be described as the 'Catholic Counter Reformation' in fact had an institutional and traditional character that insisted upon ideal continuity with the past, and the Church of Rome used the monumentality of its buildings and their magnificent decoration as means of defending its historiographic claims. While the preferred Protestant art form, the popular print, was employed to denounce Catholic abuses, the Catholic Church continued imperturbably to erect the enormous Vatican Basilica with resources derived from the scandalous commerce of indulgences.[2]

As distinguished from Protestant images, which from the start were explicitly polemic, Catholic art, at least in the first quarter-century after Luther's publication of his theses, remained insensible of any need to respond, as if convinced that the German trouble was a passing episode. This myopic disregard began to seek remedies only in 1534 with the election of Alexander Farnese as Pope Paul III, who two years later, in 1536, formed a commission to

study the question, and in 1537 made a first effort to organize the church-wide council which finally opened at Trent in 1545. A fresco executed in 1544 by Giorgio Vasari, showing Paul III personally directing the building of St Peter's Basilica, can suggest the new approach of Catholic art at that time (fig. 2).[3] The theme is again the basilica, the symbolic value of which was beyond question, but the pope is now presented in the vestments of an Old Testament high priest, with a golden *ephod* adorned with gems and little bells: as Esdra, the post-exilic leader who had launched the rebuilding of the Jerusalem Temple and acknowledged that the sins committed by the Chosen People had brought divine punishment (Esd 9:6–15). This unusual iconography implies that Paul III acknowledged the sins of the Church of Rome, punished by the brutal 1527 sack of the city, and committed himself to purify the Church, just as Esdras had done for the People of Israel. The Vatican work site remained open, in any case, and construction of the basilica went forward, because the Church, God's new 'chosen people', needed its temple.

Only in the 1540s, that is, did the Roman Church implicitly recognize the Reform then long underway, and tacitly admit its own guilt. Both factors – acknowledgment and admission of guilt – are perhaps present in Paul III's most

1. Basilica of St Peter's, Vatican City, Rome (view from the back).

2. Giorgio Vasari, *Paul III Farnese Directing the Continuance of St Peter's*, Rome, Palazzo della Cancelleria.

important pictorial commission, Michelangelo's *Last Judgment* in the Sistine Chapel, where the threatening Christ figure may allude to the papacy's consciousness of having sinned (fig. 3). In this perspective it is useful to note that the advisory group formed by Paul III to study the questions raised by the Reformers published its report while Michelangelo's *Last Judgment* was being painted, with the title: "On the Church to be reformed", *De emandanda Ecclesia*.[4]

This willingness to admit a measure of culpability was short-lived, however, fading before a new sense (reinforced by the first sessions of the Council of Trent) of the intangibility and therefore also invincibility of the Catholic system: a sort of 'conceptual triumphalism' first expressed in art in the sculptural program of the Florence Cathedral choir enclosure, begun in 1547 at the behest of Duke Cosimo I de' Medici, with a colossal statue of *God the Father* by Baccio Bandinelli on the high altar (fig. 4) – a statue whose menacing gesture seems inspired by the Christ in Michelangelo's *Last Judgment*, then still quite new.[5]

The image of a menacing God the Father, rare in Christian iconography, was probably introduced here in response to the terminology of one of the first decrees issued by the Council of Trent, that on original sin formulated in 1546, which states that, because of the sin of Adam and Eve, humanity merits the *iram et indignationem Dei*, the anger and indignation of God, and in consequence deserves death and captivity in the Devil's power.[6] And, in effect, the program of the Florence choir enclosure situated statues of Adam and Eve to right and left of the tree of their sin (fig. 5), on which the serpent was perfectly visible, as well as a colossal statue of Christ, sacrificed to redeem humankind from its sins, on the same altar, just below the figure of God the Father threatening (fig. 6). The close resemblance between Adam and Christ in Bandinelli's statues probably alludes to the Pauline idea of a structural identity between the first Adam, who "prefigured the One who was to come" (Rm 5:14), and Jesus Christ, who in his paschal mystery entirely refounded human nature (Rm 5:15–21). The Tridentine *Decree on Original Sin* cites the Pauline texts relative to the 'first Adam' and the 'future

Adam', and the Decree on Justification, also drafted in 1546, insists on the sinner's authentic renewal, *unde homo ex iniusto fit justus, et ex inimico amicus, ut sit heres secundum spem vitae aeternae* – "through which a man who is not just becomes just, and from enemy becomes friend, that he may, through hope, inherit eternal life".[7] Against the position then attributed to the Protestant Reformers, of justification as a kind of mantle covering sin, the Council of Trent proclaimed its faith in the radical sanctification of the human being.

In Florence a major program thus translated the Tridentine decrees into images. The patron of the new choir enclosure, Duke Cosimo I, more ambitious than pious, followed the conciliar debates in real time through reports sent by his two agents at Trent, Bernardino Duretti and Pietro Camaini, and through his brother-in-law Don Francisco de Toledo, who represented the Emperor Charles V at the Council.[8] Later, after the return of the Council from Bologna to Trent in 1551, Cosimo received

3. Michelangelo Buonarroti, *Last Judgment*, detail of Christ in Glory, Vatican City, Sistine Chapel.

4. Baccio Bandinelli, *God the Father*, Florence, Basilica of Santa Croce.

5. Baccio Bandinelli, *Adam and Eve*, Florence, Museo Nazionale del Bargello.

6. Baccio Bandinelli, *Dead Christ with the Angel*, Florence, Basilica of Santa Croce.

7. Michelangelo Buonarroti, *Pietà Bandini* (on its altar-like base), Florence, Museo dell'Opera del Duomo.

reports from Monsignor Giovanni da Fonseca, Bishop of Castellamare, who was directly involved in discussing the question of the real presence of Christ in each of the two species, in the bread and in the wine. In the same year, 1551, at Cosimo I's behest Bandinelli carved the enormous Christ figure for the high altar of the Cathedral.

Bandinelli's program thus had a new polemic character, forcefully emphasizing the Catholic interpretation of the most important doctrines brought into question by the Protestants. Above all his enormous *Corpus Christi* positioned on the altar table, in front of the priest who there consecrated the bread and the wine, gave a three-dimensional response to the Protestant idea that the Lord's body and blood were not present in the Eucharist except as a sign: *in Eucharistia non esse revera corpus et sanguinem Domini nostri Jesu Christi, sed tantum in signio*, as we read in the list of ten heretical articles studied by Catholic theolo-

gians.[9] In an earlier formulation of this article, dateable to 1547, the year in which Bandinelli's choir enclosure was commissioned, a still more heinous offense was attributed to the Protestant reformers: after the words *sed tantum in signio*, the text continues: *sicut vinum dicitur in circulo ante tabernam* –"If not as a sign, as we say that wine is 'present' in the sign hanging outside a tavern". The official record of the Council attributes this blasphemous error to Zwingli.[10]

The sculptural program realized in Florence Cathedral was the most monumental instance of this new taste for doctrinal combat, but hardly the only one. In the same years Catholic art offered many similar 'answers' to questions raised by the Protestants: the *Pietà* carved by the aged Michelangelo between 1547–55, for example, intended for placement on or near an altar, in which the eighty-year old artist himself lowers the Savior's body onto the *mensa* (fig. 7);[11] or the altarpiece by Moretto da Brescia,

dateable *c.* 1550, which shows two saints adoring the consecrated host in a monstrance set on
an altar, even as the glorified Christ appears to
them above the host, surrounded by the instruments of his sacrifice (fig. 8).[12]

In Florence Cathedral itself, Cosimo I completed the sculptural program of the choir with
a titanic fresco in the intrados of the dome
where the same message is transmitted (fig. 9):
in the central portion, right above the high altar with Bandinelli's statue of the dead Christ,
there is a figure of Christ in glory surrounded
by angels and saints; Adam and Eve are there,
transformed from not just to just, from enemies
to friends. At Christ's right (the viewer's left) is
the Virgin Mary, whose role Protestants ques-
tioned, and she is shown in prayer, in refutation
of the protestant notion that the saints in heav-
en do not intercede for believers on earth. And
around Christ's resurrected body is a glorious
aureole with rays that recall the shape of a
Eucharistic monstrance, as if to insist upon the
legitimacy of the Catholic custom of adoration

of the host. The circular aureole in the dome
echoes the arch framing Bandinelli's statues
on the altar below, as if to reinforce the idea
that the bread and wine consecrated at Mass
contain the totality of the mystery of faith in
the Christ who died and rose.

The author of the polemical theology of the
dome program, Vincenzo Borghini, a Vallom-
brosan monk, must have been well acquainted
with the earlier program of the choir. In reality
choir and dome constituted a single program
in two parts, developed in a single physical
space, the cathedral crossing, at the behest of
the same patron, Cosimo I, whose portrait appears in the group of Catholic princes in the
dome. And between the program's two parts
there was absolute temporal continuity: the
sculptural decoration of the choir area was
completed on 23 May 1572, and the decoration of the dome began 19 days later, on 11
June. The 3600 square meters of fresco, painted
by Giorgio Vasari and, after his death in 1574,
by Federico Zuccari, were finished in 1579.

8. Moretto da Brescia, *Eucharistic Vision of Saints
Bartholomew and Rocco*, Castenedolo (Brescia),
Church of San Bartolomeo.

9. Giorgio Vasari and Federico Zuccari, *Last Judgment*,
east segment, Florence, Cathedral of Santa Maria
del Fiore, vault.

10. Pierre Legros, *Religion Overthrowing Heresy and Hatred*, Rome, Church of the Gesù.

11. Giovanni d'Enrico and Morazzone, Chapel of the Ecce Homo, Varallo Sesia (Vercelli), Basilica of the Sacro Monte.

This first major program of the Catholic Reform defined an intellectual style of total immersion, with catalogued doctrines and devotions that surrounded believers on the walls and ceilings of churches: a veritable catechism in pigments and marble. It is clear moreover that, challenged by the Protestant refusal of images and by an aesthetic austerity of Calvinist inspiration, this pre-Baroque Catholic choice to populate the place of worship with saints and angels was polemical, a combative answer to transalpine iconoclasm, an ideal 'restitution' of that which the heretics had eliminated. At the end of the 16th century the Roman church would go still further, using iconographical weaponry to allegorize the defeat of heresy, as in Pierre Legros' statuary group for the sumptuous altar of St Ignatius of Loyola in the main Jesuit church in Rome, the Gesù, where, beneath the apotheosis of the founder of the Society of Jesus, 'Catholic Truth' triumphs over 'Protestant falsehood', as the language of the time put it (fig. 10).

Even when not directly fighting heresy, Catholic art of the second half of the 16th century exalts Catholic doctrines contested by the Reformers, as in Moretto's altarpiece, mentioned above, with its emphasis on Eucharistic adoration and on the veneration of the saints and of relics. Traditional priesthood and hierarchical dignity were exalted with images of the age's new spiritual heroes, St Ignatius of Loyola and St Philip Neri, vested for Mass in chasubles, and of St Charles Borromeo robed as a cardinal even as he reads Scripture and does penance.

Under the influence of St Charles, archbishop of Milan, in Lombardy and Piedmont a new form of catechetical art was developed, halfway between sculpture and theater: the 'Sacro Monte', 'Sacred Mountain', where, on a hillside, a series of small chapels was realized, each containing a 'habitable' tableau illustrating an episode of the life of Christ, Mary or a saint (fig. 11). The pilgrim (like Charles Borromeo himself, who visited the Sacromonte at Varallo four times), after reading the devotional 'guidebook' with its meditation themes, visited the chapels, sometimes by night, contemplating the dramatic life of the personage represented.[13] Inspired by earlier Franciscan spirituality, but with a psychological emphasis derived from the Ignatian method, the Sacred Mountains translated the ideas on art formulated by the Council of Trent and finally published in 1582 by

12. Caravaggio, *Conversion of St Paul*,
Rome, Basilica of Santa Maria del Popolo.

13. Gianlorenzo Bernini, *Ecstasy of St Theresa of Avila*,
detail, Rome, Church of Santa Maria della Vittoria.

14. Gianlorenzo Bernini, *Longinus*,
Vatican City, Basilica of St Peter.

cardinal Gabriele Paleotti in his *Discourse on Images*, which stressed the need to stimulate a deep affective response in the faithful.[14] The Sacred Mountains reveal the extraordinary capacity of Catholicism to exploit its own past in a contemporary key, insisting on the validity of 'tradition' and underlining its 'modernity'.

This was the religious and artistic world which gave birth to Caravaggio, who was a child when Paleotti's *Discourse* appeared, and an apprentice in a Milanese workshop when Charles Borromeo died in 1584. Caravaggio's realism, which corresponds to Paleotti's demand for 'authenticity', would become a common element of both Catholic and Protestant art – of Ribera as of Rembrandt. In Caravaggio there is nonetheless a mystical substratum: the Christ in his *Calling of St Matthew*, for example (see p. 19 of the present publication), makes his entry in a broad swath of light and summons Matthew with a gesture of his hand beneath a window whose structure has the shape of a cross.[15]

In Caravaggio's iconography, at once realistic and mystical, there is a double frame of reference: the intense social work of then new

15. Gianlorenzo Bernini, St Peter's Square, Vatican City (aerial view looking toward St Peter's).

religious orders among the poor, the young and prostitutes, and the Catholic search for religious experiences beyond the everyday, able to definitively change people's lives, as in the case of St Matthew and even more in that of St Paul, thrown to the ground by the Lord whom he had previously persecuted (fig. 12). Catholic art of this period in fact insists on the possibility of converting from enemy to friend of Christ: in addition to Caravaggio's dramatic *Conversion of St Paul*, of 1600–1601, we think of Bernini's *Longinus* of 1629 (fig. 14), or Rubens' *Lance Blow* of 1620, all equally theatrical. Another theme is mystical love, the ecstasies of women consecrated to the heavenly Bridegroom, such as St Margaret of Cortona, in the 1620 canvas by Lanfranco, St Theresa of Avila in Bernini's group of 1645 (fig. 13), and still more Bernini's Blessed Lodovica Albertoni of 1674. In Spain Zurbarán treats the same idea from the male perspective, in his *Vision of St Peter Nolasco*, and in France Georges de La Tour interprets it in a key of intimate erotism in his *St Sebastian Cared for by St Irene*.

Where Protestant art, Calvinist and puritan, bore witness to the ethical integrity of ordinary Christians, Catholic images, that is, dramatized the exaltation of the saints: St Theresa's ecstasy serves to edify the work's noble patrons, installed in what look like theater boxes to right and left of the chapel's altar. Even the adoration of the Host became 'spectacle' during the Jubilee of 1650,[16] and in front of St Peter's Basilica, on the site of an ancient Roman circus, the indefatigable Bernini created the 'theater of the papacy', on whose stage the successor of a man martyred by the emperor Nero shows himself in eschatological glory (fig. 15), while inside the titanic church Bernini invited believers to venerate the throne of the Prince of the Apostles, sustained by four Doctors of the Church beneath the Holy Spirit who, entering the Catholic Church, sheds light on the Chair of Christ's Vicar (fig. 16).[17]

It was the triumph of the Institution, a belated and excessive answer to the polemical prints of the early Protestant Reform. A Dutch master of the period parodied this hyperbolic idiom: Vermeer of Delft, in his *Allegory of the Catholic Faith* (fig. 17), which pokes gentle fun at the Catholic style which Vermeer knew well, having a Catholic mother and a Catholic

16. Gianlorenzo Bernini, *Chair of St Peter*, Vatican City, Basilica of St Peter.

17. Jan Vermeer, *Allegory of the Catholic Faith*, New York, Metropolitan Museum of Art.

wife, and living in his Catholic mother-in-law's house. In Vermeer's day, Protestant churches, freed of traditional decoration, invited believers to the silent inwardness found in that painter's customary figures; Catholic churches prepared them for an experience of ecstasy.[18] And ecstasy became the official Catholic style right up to the French Revolution, from Palermo to Turin, from Spain to Bavaria, Austria and Poland. 20th-century Catholic taste, by contrast, often reflects Protestant aesthetics: one thinks of the architecture of Rudolph Schwarz, Hans van der Laan and Alvar Aalto. Le Corbusier, author of the most famous 20th-century Catholic church, that at Ronchamps, was Protestant! ∎

1 See Timothy Verdon, *La Basilica di San Pietro. I papi e gli artisti*, Milan, 2005, pp. 117–35.

2 Woodcut by Hans Schwalb, done in Augsburg in 1521, in *Martin Bucer. Strasbourg et l'Europe*, exhibition catalogue (Strasbourg, church of Saint-Thomas, 1991), edited by Frank Müller and Christian Krieger, Strasbourg, 1991, pp. 72–3.

3 See Timothy Verdon, *L'arte cristiana in Italia. II. Il Rinascimento*, edited by Timothy Verdon, Cinisello Balsamo, 2006, pp. 308–88: 310–11.

4 See Timothy Verdon, *Michelangelo teologo. Fede e creatività tra Rinascimento e Controriforma*, Milan, 2005, pp. 121–6.

5 Timothy Verdon, 'Immagini della Controriforma: l'iconografia dell'area liturgica di Santa Maria del Fiore', in *Atti del VII centenario del Duomo di Firenze. II.2. La cattedrale come spazio sacro*, Florence, 2001, pp. 520–43. See also Timothy Verdon, *L'arte sacra in Italia. L'immaginazione religiosa dal paleocristiano al postmoderno*, Milan, 2001, pp. 256–69.

6   *Enchiridion symbolorum definitionum et declarationum de rebus fidei et morum* (35th edition), edited by Heinrich Denzinger, Adolf Schonmetzer, Barcelona–Fribourg–Rome, 1976, pp. 366–7, nos. 1511–12.

7   Ibid., p. 328, no. 1528.

8   See Arnaldo D'Addario, *Aspetti della Controriforma a Firenze*, Rome, 1972, pp. 335–6.

9   *Enchiridion symbolorum* 1976, op. cit., pp. 407–8, nos. 1739–40. See also *Histoire des Conciles d'après les documents originaux. X. Les décrets du Concile de Trente*, edited by Albert Michel, Paris, 1938, pp. 239–87.

10   *Histoire des Conciles* 1938, op. cit., p. 240.

11   Timothy Verdon, 'Michelangelo and the Body of Christ. Religious Meaning in the Florence Pietà', in *Michelangelo's Florence Pietà*, edited by Jack Wasserman and Franca Trinchieri Camiz, Princeton–Oxford, 2003, pp. 127–48.

12   See Verdon 2006, op. cit., pp. 331–3. See also *Gesù. Il corpo, il volto nell'arte*, exhibition catalogue (Turin, Venaria Reale, 2010), edited by Timothy Verdon, Cinisello Balsamo, 2010, p. 298.

13   William Hood, 'The Sacro Monte of Varallo. Renaissance Art and Popular Religion', in *Monasticism and the Arts*, edited by Timothy Verdon, Syracuse, NY, 1984, pp. 291–311.

14   See Paola Barocchi, *Trattati d'arte del Cinquecento tra manierismo e controriforma. II. Gilio, Paleotti, Aldrovandi*, Bari, 1961, pp. 117–28.

15   See Timothy Verdon, 'Le stagioni del Barocco', in *L'arte cristiana in Italia. III. L'età moderna e contemporanea*, edited by Timothy Verdon, Cinisello Balsamo, 2006, pp. 6–121: 9–16.

16   See Carlo Rinaldi's engraving entitled, *Teatro eretto nella Chiesa del Gesù a Roma nella quinquegesima l'Anno Santo 1650*, reproduced in Verdon 2006, op. cit., p. 77.

17   See Verdon 2005, op. cit., pp. 144–8. See also Timothy Verdon, *Breve storia dell'arte sacra cristiana*, Brescia, 2012, pp. 223–5.

18   See Timothy Verdon, 'Introduction', in *The Ecumenism of Beauty*, edited by Timothy Verdon, Brewster, MA, and Barga (Lucca), 2017, pp. VII–XIX.

Tridentine Theology in the Florence Cathedral Dome

GIANNI CIOLI

The iconographic program of the intrados of the dome of Santa Maria del Fiore, the Cathedral of Florence, was conceived by Vincenzo Borghini, who documented his 'invention of the Cupola', as he called it, in a letter addressed to Giorgio Vasari, who had been commissioned by Duke Cosimo de' Medici (later Grand Duke Cosimo I) to execute frescoes in the dome (fig. 1).[1] The letter, undated, was presumably written around 1571, or in any case after the 1568 decision to undertake the project and before its inception in 1572.

Borghini, a Benedictine monk of the Florentine Badia and director of the city's Foundling Hospital (Ospedale degli Innocenti), was above all a man of culture: a theologian, philologist and historian. Cosimo de' Medici had appointed him his personal representative in the Florence Academy, and regularly involved him in planning sacred and profane decorative programs.[2]

Borghini was born in 1515, two years before the beginning of the Lutheran reform (1517), and died in 1580, a year after Federico Zuccari finally completed the pictorial decoration of the dome in 1579. The years of the Council of Trent (1545–63) thus filled the middle period of his life, and those of the decoration of the Cathedral dome its final phase, and it is natural to suppose that the Council's theology

influenced his iconographic program. It will be interesting to ask how it did so, and, in answering, to follow the logic of his 'invention'.

The exaltation of the saints and their role

Borghini believed, first of all, that – for its vast scale and strategic position – the space of the dome was an opportunity not to be lost: "in short, the best opportunity for painting in the world".[3] The location of the space to be painted, the "heaven of the church", struck him as "most suitable" to the heavenly Last Judgment, and the vastness of the dome led him to imagine depicting, with Christ the Judge, not only the traditional figures – the apostles, Mary and St John the Baptist – but all "the court of Paradise". In short, Borghini imagined "Jesus Christ's tribunal" thronged with Old and New Testament saints, distinguished from each other and distributed according to a certain order, "the which saints should sit on clouds which float all around the dome: an assembly, practically Our Lord's court come to judge the world, as was promised to the apostles and to all who like them would follow him".[4]

Borghini extends to the whole host of saints, in their specific categories, as we shall see, the prerogative of sitting in judgment with Christ in the Last Judgment. This was a prerogative that traditional iconography assigned to the twelve apostles, on the basis of Mt 19,28. The representation of the Judgment that Borghini conceived, that is – while rooted in a centuries-long iconographic tradition –, transcended the tradition, tending toward what we might call an exaltation of the glory of the saints, a jubilant triumph of sanctity as Catholicism understood it. The role of the saints – as Borghini makes clear when he speaks of the Florentine saints and city patrons –, should not really be interpreted as that of 'tribunal' but as prayerful intercession.

   This is the first and most obvious Tridentine theological orientation that we can indicate in Borghini's program and in its pictorial realization by Vasari and then Federico Zuccari. The Council, in fact – in its decree of December 3, 1563 –, had established that the faithful should be diligently instructed "regarding the interces-

sion of the saints, and on how to invoke their help, on the honor due to relics, and on the legitimate use of images", teaching that "the saints, who reign with Christ, offer God their prayers for humankind".[5] We can therefore affirm that Borghini's program was in line with Tridentine doctrine both in its contents and in its method: in its contents because it exalted the function of the saints, just as the Council asked; and in its method because it did so, again following Trent's indications, through visual art, to which it attributes extraordinary importance.[6]

   To be sure, the Last Judgment theme is not foreign to post-Tridentine spirituality, as is clear from Vasari's decorative apparatus for the high altar of the Dominican convent of Bosco Marengo in 1569, commissioned by Paul V, where the Last Judgment is the main subject,[7] as can be evinced from the Catechism

1. Giorgio Vasari and Federico Zuccari, *Last Judgment*, Florence, Cathedral of Santa Maria del Fiore, vault.

2. Mosaics on the vault of the Baptistery of St John, Florence.

published by the Council in 1566, which urges priests to remind the faithful of the doctrine of the Last Judgment, distinguishing it from the Particular Judgment.[8]

Yet, as Cristina Acidini noted,[9] the choice of this subject for the dome of Santa Maria del Fiore was probably dictated, more than by the influence of the Council, by the opportunity to link the nearby Baptistery of St John, and its Last Judgment iconography (fig. 2), to the Cathedral, which like the Baptistery has an octagonal dome, albeit much greater in size. The lesser height of the Baptistery dome had made it possible to conceive the mosaics that cover

it as a compendium of all of salvation history, culminating in the Last Judgment event, which, in effect, occupies only three of the Baptistery dome's eight sections.

For the Cathedral dome an analogous program would probably not have been legible, given the greater distance separating viewers from what would have been small and detailed narrative scenes. Borghini was thus stimulated to imagine an innovative kind of Last Judgment scheme, exalting – as the Tridentine decree urged – the presence and function of the saints. He was, moreover, able to conceive a surprising and emotionally involving articulation of the heavenly court, by combining various categories of saints with symbolic images and allegories inspired by Christian numerology, and – like the Gospel scribe – in bringing "out from his storeroom things both new and old" (Mt 13,52).

Traditional sevenfold systems and the Doctrine of Justification

In writing his "invention", Cosimo I's theologian was challenged by the octagonal shape of the dome, to make, as he puts it, "of necessity a virtue".[10] Stimulated by the great octagon, Borghini intuited the opportunity to create an iconographical program focused on the sevenfold systems dear to Christian tradition and above all to the Middle Ages. He managed to assemble the pieces of a puzzle which, together with the Last Judgment, seeks to exalt the reality and the function of the saints in order to lead believers to conversion, placing them before the alternative of eternal salvation or damnation. And so, beginning in the upper part of the dome, just below the twenty-four "Elders of the Apocalypse" situated in the pictorial extension of the lantern,[11] in the area of the intrados that represents 'heaven' he suggests depicting the Angelic Choirs and the "Mysteries of the Passion";[12] then, in the area just below, he places the various categories of saints, and, below them, allegorical personifications of the Gifts of the Holy Spirit, the Beatitudes and the Virtues. Finally, in the lowest area, corresponding to 'earth' and 'the mouth of hell', he places animal symbols of the Capital Sins. In reality, his only true sevenfold systems are the Gifts of the Spirit and the "seven Deadly Sins", as Borghini calls them.[13] Despite the fact that the Angelic Choirs are nine and the Beatitudes eight, Borghini manages to harmonize these numbers with the sevenfold scansion of the Gifts and "Deadly Sins", assigning the Cherubim and Seraphim,[14] and the last Beatitude – "Blessed are those who are persecuted in the cause of right" (Mt 5,10: identified with the Church 'militant' which becomes 'triumphant') –, to the segment of the dome corresponding to Christ the Judge.[15]

As far as the Virtues go, on the other hand, Christian tradition had long known the sevenfold system constituted by adding the three theological virtues to the four cardinal ones, depicted by Giotto, among others, in the Scrovegni Chapel in relation to the Last Judgment. Borghini however preferred not to follow this list, because the three "Virtù Theologiche", as he calls them, "do not correspond to a single Sin",[16] and so he asks that they be represented together with Christ the Judge, giving preeminence to Charity, centrally placed between Hope and Faith – which was certainly in line with the Scholastic tradition, but also consonant with Trent, which contested the position of those who sustained the exclusive value of Faith for salvation.[17] And so, to reconstitute a sevenfold system, Borghini added to his three cardinal virtues[18] (having excluded Fortitude, as already present among the gifts of the Holy Spirit), four others,[19] suitable to the categories of saints depicted and susceptible of coordination with the Gifts, the Beatitudes, and, conversely, with the relative Deadly Sins.

As he elaborated sevenfold systems in his letter to Vasari, Borghini hypothesized the possibility of further enriching the program with allegories of the Works of Mercy[20] and of the Planets. These last had been depicted in the lozenge-shaped reliefs of Giotto's Bell Tower, together with the Virtues, the Liberal Arts and the Sacraments. Citation of the Works of Mercy would have been especially timely, agreeing with Tridentine teaching on the importance of 'works' in order to obtain salvation, but also because related to the Gospel account of Mt 25:31–46, the chief scriptural source for Last Judgment iconography. The Works of Mercy were not finally depicted, however, probably due to the difficulty of convincingly coordinating them with the other sevenfold systems.

The pictorial cycle realized in the dome – begun by Vasari working with Sabatini and finished by Zuccari – is substantially faithful to Borghini's program, despite sometimes significant adaptations and modifications. The articulation of the sevenfold systems, as it appears in the murals, is the following:

In the north-east sector (fig. 3) are the Apostles and Evangelists with, above them, the Angelic Choir of the Thrones bearing the cross as

3. Giorgio Vasari and Federico Zuccari,
Last Judgment, north-east segment.

4. Giorgio Vasari and Federico Zuccari,
Last Judgment, north segment.

the relevant Mystery of the Passion. Below are personifications of the Gift of Wisdom, of the Virtue of Brotherly Love, and of the Beatitude of Peace-making. Lower down the hydra appears as a symbol of the Sin of Envy.

In the north sector (fig. 4) are popes, bishops and priests, above whom the Choir of Powers bearing the column. The Gift is Understanding, the Virtue Prudence, the Beatitude Meekness, and, lower down, an ass symbolizes Sloth.

In the north-west sector are the religious, and, above them, the Archangels bearing the hammer, nails and pincers (fig. 5). Below are the Gift of Piety, the Virtue of Temperance, the

Beatitude of Purity of Heart, and – in the lowest area – the boar symbolizing Lust.

In the western sector is "the Holy People of God", with, above, the Choir of Angels bearing Christ's tunic and the dice (fig. 6). Below, the Gift is Fear of the Lord, the Virtue Humility, the Beatitude Poverty. And a monstrous figure of Lucifer symbolizes the Sin of Pride.

In the south-west sector are holy monarchs and, above them, the Choir of Principalities bearing the crown of thorns (fig. 7). Below, the Gift is Counsel, the Virtue Justice, and the Beatitude Mercy. Lower down a toad symbolizes the Sin of Avarice.

5. Giorgio Vasari and Federico Zuccari, *Last Judgment*, north-west segment.

6. Giorgio Vasari and Federico Zuccari, *Last Judgment*, west segment.

In the south sector (fig. 8) are the doctors of the Church and, above them, the Choir of Dominations bearing the sponge. Below are the Gift of Science, the Virtue of vigilance (or perhaps of sobriety?),[21] the Beatitude of Hunger and Thirst for Justice, and, still lower down, Cerberus symbolizes the Sin of Gluttony.

In the south-east sector (fig. 9) are the martyrs, and, above them, the Angelic Choir of the Virtues bearing the lance and chalice. Below, the Gift is Fortitude, the Virtue Patience and the Beatitude is Affliction. Finally, in the lowest area, a bear symbolizes Anger. In the eighth and final sector, to the east (fig.

10), at the center is Christ the Judge surrounded by seven angels, flanked by Mary and St John the Baptist in the traditional *deesis* arrangement, and with Adam and Eve and Florentine saints shown interceding. Above are the Choirs of Cherubim and Seraphim and, as Mysteries of the Passion, the *Titulus crucis* and a placard with the words *Ecce Homo*.[22] Below the Judge are personifications of the three theological virtues, and, at the lowest, earthly, level, allegories: of the Church which from 'militant' becomes 'triumphant', and of Nature, Time and Death which have finished their course and exhausted their function.[23]

7. Giorgio Vasari and Federico Zuccari, *Last Judgment*, south-west segment.

8. Giorgio Vasari and Federico Zuccari, *Last Judgment*, south segment.

The program's articulation, which in fact takes its cue from the sevenfold system of the Gifts of the Spirit in relation to the various categories of saints, does not seem to materially depend either on the Council's teaching or on the *Tridentine Catechism*. This last, moreover, develops its moral teaching on the paradigm of the Ten Commandments rather than those of the tradition's sevenfold systems.[24] As Gilberto Aranci has shown, the erudite Borghini seems to have been inspired by Scholastic theology, used in various ways in 16th-century catechesis, which he reworked with freedom and originality.[25]

I believe nonetheless that, from a formal point of view, the key to Borghini's sevenfold systems can be found precisely in Trent's teaching on Justification, developed through the categories of Thomist theology.[26] The seven gifts of the Holy Spirit, subordinated to the three theological virtues depicted below Christ the Judge, seem in effect to allude to the primacy of grace emphasized by the Council of Trent in its decree on Justification. Justification, as the Council recalled, 'is not simple remission of sins, but sanctification and renewal of the inner man through his free acceptance of divine grace and of the gifts which accompany

9. Giorgio Vasari and Federico Zuccari,
Last Judgment, south-east segment.

10. Giorgio Vasari and Federico Zuccari,
Last Judgment, east segment.

it, thanks to which man, from unjust, becomes just, and from enemy, friend, so as to become an heir "looking forward to inheriting eternal life"'(Tt 3:7).[27]

At the same time the combination of beatitudes, virtues and gifts of the Spirit, and their contraposition to the seven deadly sins, call to mind the other pole of Tridentine teaching on Justification, to wit the assertion that that man, justified by grace, is called to grow from virtue to virtue, becoming ever more 'just',[28] in order to attain blessedness, and that the "good works of a man who has been justified" are also his "merits";[29] Trent furthermore warned

that grace and eternal blessedness can be lost due to sin.[30] In this sense one can agree with Timothy Verdon's recognition of a "Tridentine reflection" in Federico Zuccari's depiction of Hell, somewhat different from Borghini's original idea.[31]

Returning to the combination of the theological elements, one must observe that the exact placement of Gifts of the Spirit in relation to Beatitudes and Virtues is a genuine riddle for the iconologist. In practice the seven triads of Gifts, Virtues and Beatitudes depicted in their respective sectors below hosts of saints are constituted by winged and haloed female figures

11. Giorgio Vasari and Federico Zuccari,
Last Judgment, detail of the east segment.

flanked by two other figures without either wings or haloes. The central figures are clearly preeminent, but they do not always represent the same sevenfold category.[32]

Eucharistic references to Baccio Bandinelli's altar?

Timothy Verdon and Francesco Vossilla agree on the hypothesis of continuity between the pictorial program of the dome and the altar of Santa Maria del Fiore, realized for Cosimo I to a design by Baccio Bandinelli between 1547 and 1572. The iconological analogies, although not numerous, are objective and pertinent.[33]

To be sure, a weak point of the hypothesis of a unitary program, as Verdon himself notes, is the fact that Borghini's letter makes no mention of Bandinelli's altar. "A plausible answer to the question of unity or lack of same", the author says, "would be that the two parts of the program *became unified*: that a series of ideas related to the questions" discussed at Trent "gradually created a unified message, coloring

the Judgment to be painted with the meaning of the 'Sacrifice' already realized in sculpture in the underlying sanctuary".[34]

Bandinelli's altar was characterized by a monumental statue of the dead Christ disposed on the table and by a statue of God the Father, seated, on the altar dossal (fig. 12). This statuary group, realized in concomitance with the Tridentine debates, probably alludes both to the doctrine of the Sacrifice of the Mass and to the real presence of Christ in the Eucharist.

It is certainly possible to hypothesize a unitary reading of the program of the altar and that of the dome in light of the Catechism of the Council of Trent, which recalls that the Eucharist also has an eschatological meaning since it preannounces "the fruit of eternal happiness and glory, which we will receive in the heavenly fatherland, as God has promised".[35]

Verdon, though, proposes a deeper and more subtle interpretation of the Eucharistic meaning of the dome murals: like Cristina Acidini, with whom he agrees,[36] Verdon interprets

12. Bernardo Sansone Sgrilli, *Elevation of the Altar and Part of the Choir*, engraving, in *Descrizione e studi dell'insigne fabbrica di S. Maria del Fiore, metropolitana fiorentina, in varie carte intagliati*, Florence, 1733, pl. XV.

the posture of Zuccari's Christ, who – flanked by the Virgin – looks upwards as if to show his wounds to the Father (fig. 11), as developed from the 'Double intercession' iconography of an early 15th-century painting still in the Cathedral when the dome was decorated.[37] In this reading, Zuccari, probably with Borghini's consent, distanced himself from Vasari's idea[38] and used Christ's pose to represent not the act of judgment but that of intercession for humankind, in the exercise of his eternal priesthood (see Heb 7,24), according to the language of the Letter to the Hebrews, the theology of which was the foundation of the Tridentine doctrine of the Mass as 'sacrifice'. According to Verdon, it was precisely the Council of Trent that inspired an image of Christ "who does not

judge the world but saves it", appearing "before God in our favor" as "high priest of our future blessings": One who died on the cross but through God's grace now lives forever to intercede for God's many sons whom he must lead to glory.[39]

This very attractive hypothesis opens an interesting perspective on present-day ecumenical dialogue regarding the Eucharist. Or, to put it differently, perhaps the depiction of Christ in the dome of Florence Cathedral synthesizes theological implications inspired by the Council of Trent's teaching but open to modern ecumenical development, going beyond what Borghini and Zuccari – and before them the Council itself – presumably meant to communicate. ■

1 Vincenzo Borghini, 'Invenzione per la pittura della Cupola, data da Vincenzio Borghini a Giorgio Vasari', in *La Cupola di Santa Maria del Fiore illustrata con i documenti dell'archivio dell'Opera secolare. Saggio di una compiuta illustrazione dell'opera secolare e del tempio di Santa Maria del Fiore*, edited by Cesare Guasti, Florence, 1857, pp. 132–40.

2 See Cristina Acidini Luchinat, *Taddeo e Federico Zuccari fratelli pittori del Cinquecento*, 2 vols., II, Milan, 1999, p. 65.

3 Borghini 1857, op. cit., p. 132.

4 Ibid., pp. 133–4.

5 *Concilium Tridentinum, Sessio 25, Decretum de invocatione, 3 dec. 1563. Enchiridion symbolorum definitionum et declarationum de rebus fidei et morum* (35th edition), edited by Heinrich Denzinger, Adolf Schonmetzer, Barcelona–Fribourg–Rome, 1976, pp. 366–7, no. 1821.

6 See *Il Concilio di Trento e le arti (1563–2013)*, proceedings of the symposium (Bologna, 10 December 2013), edited by Marinella Pigozzi, Bologna, 2015; *Immagini e arte sacra nel Concilio di Trento*, proceedings of the symposium (Rome, 2–3 December 2013), edited by Lydia Salviucci Insolera, Rome, 2016.

7 See Anne-Sophie Molinié, 'Giorgio Vasari, Francisco Pacheco et le Jugement dernier', *Mélanges de la Casa de Velázquez*, 41/2 (2011), pp. 165–84; Gianni Cioli, 'Il Cristo Giudice e la spada nella volta della cupola di Santa Maria del Fiore', *Giornale di bordo*, 3rd series, no. 38 (2015), pp. 9–20: 13.

8 *Catechismo, cioè istruzione secondo il decreto del Concilio di Trento a' parochi, pubblicato per la prima volta per comandamento del Sommo Pontefice Pio Quinto e tradotto poi per ordine del medesimo in lingua volgare dal Rev. Padre fr. Alessio Figliucci dell'Ordine de' Predicatori e ora ristampato per ordine di N.S. Clemente XIII*, Rome, 1761, pp. 68–73.

9 Cristina Acidini Luchinat, 'Il Giudizio universale: dal Battistero alla Cupola', in *La cattedrale di Santa Maria del Fiore*, edited by Timothy Verdon, Florence, 1993, pp. 40–63.

10 Borghini 1857, op. cit., p. 134.

11 Ibid., pp. 139–40.

12 Ibid., p. 136.

13 Ibid., p. 134.

14 Ibid., p. 135.

15 Ibid., p. 140.

16 Ibid., p. 134.

17 *Concilium Tridentinum, Sessio 6, Decretum de iustificatione, 13 ian. 1547*, chapter 7; see *Enchiridion* 1976, op. cit., nos. 1530–1.

18 Prudence, Justice and Temperance.

19 Brotherly Love, Vigilance, Humility and Patience.

20 Borghini 1857, op. cit., p. 138.

21 For the triad of the south sector Borghini had suggested representing "Science as the gift of the Spirit, and – as Beatitudes – Abstinence and Sobriety: *Qui esuriunt et sitiunt iustitiam*: … the Virtue of Vigilance: all things appropriate to learned teachers and scholars and to those who continually exercise their intellect and mind, without ever giving rest to the body" (ibid., op. cit., pp. 137–8). 'Sobriety', as the term is used by Borghini, is identified with the beatitude of Thirst for Justice. But Vasari, in his 'Dichiarazione della invenzione della Cupola presentata … al Principe Francesco de' Medici', perhaps due to a mistaken interpretation of Borghini's indications or in order to intentionally correct these, assigns to this section "the Gift of Science, the Beatitude: *Beati qui esuriunt et sitiunt iustitiam* … and the Virtue of Sobriety" (in *La Cupola di Santa Maria del Fiore* 1857, op. cit., p. 143).

22 The placard with the words ECCE HOMO is an original feature in which Borghini believes firmly: see Borghini 1857, op. cit., p. 136. The placard's text was discussed at length in relation to the evolution of Florentine humanism in the light of Tridentine theology in the 1995 symposium *L'uomo in cielo*: see Timothy Verdon, 'L'uomo in cielo. Teologia, antropologia e arte', in *L'uomo in cielo. Il programma pittorico della Cupola di Santa Maria del Fiore: teologia ed iconografia a confronto*, proceedings of the symposium (Florence, 18 ottobre 1995), edited by Timothy Verdon, Bologna, 1996, pp. 13–24: 23–4; see also Severino Dianich, '*Ecce homo*: il Cristo giudice e il Cristo giudice nel complesso pittorico della Cupola del Duomo', ibid., pp. 57–72.

23 Borghini 1857, op. cit., p. 135.

24 *Catechismo, cioè istruzione* 1761, op. cit., pp. 287–388.

25 Gilberto Aranci, 'La catechesi a Firenze al tempo della programmazione iconografica degli affreschi della Cupola. Rilievi e confronti', in *L'uomo in cielo*, op. cit., pp. 99–118.

26 Thomas Aquinas, *Summa theologiae*, I–II, q. 68 a. 8; q. 69 a. 1.

27 *Concilium Tridentinum, Sessio 6, Decretum de iustificatione, 13 ian. 1547*, chapter 7.

28 Ibid., cap. 10.

29 Ibid., cap. 32.

30 Ibid., cap. 23.

31 Verdon 1996, op. cit., p. 21.

32 Vasari, in the four sectors which he partially realized, puts the Gifts of the Spirit at the center, perhaps to imply the primacy of grace over human merit; by contrast Zuccari, in the sectors which he painted, always puts in the center the Beatitudes, and in this seems more faithful to Borghini's original indications (see Borghini 1857, op. cit., p. 139). Disagreeing with the reading recently proposed by Lucrezia Giordano, Lucio Bigi, Mario Mureddu, *Gli affreschi della Cupola di Santa Maria del Fiore. La Cristianità. I suoi simboli. Il Giudizio universale*, Florence, 2015, pp. 26–30, I believe that, in the parts painted by Vasari,

the identification of the central figure with the Gift of the Holy Spirit is always clear. It is unquestionably so in the north-east sector (fig. 3), where the Gift of Wisdom is flanked by the Virtue of Dilection (characterized by the presence of babies, as in Charity) and by the Beatitude of the Peace-Makers (bearing an olive branch). It is also clear in the north sector (fig. 4), where the Gift of Intelligence is flanked by the Virtue of Prudence (with the usual attributes of the mirror and the serpent) and by the Beatitude of Meekness (arms crossed on bosom), and it is clear above all in the south-east sector, where the Gift of Fortitude is identified, at the center, with the unmistakable attribute of armor. The identification is also plausible for the south sector (fig. 8), where the winged and crowned central figure, scattering jewels with her left hand and holding a book in her right, unquestionably corresponds to one of the Gifts of the Spirit depicted in a Pentecost altarpiece painted by

Vasari for the basilica of Santa Croce in 1568, according to a program suggested, again, by Borghini (see Nadia Bastogi, *La pala di Santi di Tito nel Santuario di Santa Maria del Soccorso*, Prato, 2002, p. 28).

33 Verdon 1996, op. cit., pp. 17–24. See Francesco Vossilla, 'Dal Coro alla Cupola: linee del mecenatismo di Cosimo I a Santa Maria del Fiore nell'epoca del Concilio di Trento', in *L'uomo in cielo* 1996, op. cit., pp. 41–56.

34 Verdon 1996, op. cit., p. 21.

35 *Catechismo, cioè istruzione* 1763, op. cit., pp. 176–7.

36 Cristina Acidini, 'La pittura specchio della teologia', in *L'uomo in cielo* 1996, op. cit., pp. 25–40: 39.

37 Verdon 1996, op. cit., p. 16.

38 Acidini Luchinat 1996, op. cit., pp. 37–40.

39 Verdon 1996, op. cit., pp. 18–19. See Heb 7:25; 9:11–24.

Esthetics and Kerygma

Protestant Sacred Music from the 16th Century to the Baroque Era

BEAT FÖLLMI

Music and theology in the 16th century

Lutheran musical practices are universally recognized thanks to the great compositions of the 17th and 18th centuries: those of Schütz, Dietrich Buxtehude, Georg Phillipp Telemann and above all Johann Sebastian Bach. The importance that music had in Lutheran culture is often attributed to Luther's own high esteem for this art. The 19th century thus created the image of Luther the musician, playing the lute surrounded by family and singing friends. Luther's biography as a musician and his hymnodic production became one, and in the year 2000 Finnish composer Kari Tikka (born in 1946) wrote an opera entitled *Luther*,[1] which, in sketching the reformer's biography, situates Luther's songs at crucial stages his life, with the result that the songs all seem to have a biographical *Sitz im Leben*. And for the 2017 Reformation centenary, French composer Jean-Jacques Werner (1935–2017), for his opera *Luther and the Begger of Grace*,[2] used the chorale *Ein feste Burg ist unser Gott* in a perspective at once biographical and historiographical.

In my view, however, the importance of music for Lutheran devotional practice cannot be explained primarily on the basis of Luther's personal preference. I propose to change pace, therefore, attempting a theological approach to music from the Lutheran point of view. I am well aware of the difficulties of such an approach. Luther did not write a 'Theology of Music' for the simple reason that music is not one of the *loci theologiae*. Music is generally considered to be an object exterior to theology, of which people speak from a liturgical, ecclesiological or anthropological point of view. That is how most 16th-century theologians expressed themselves on music: Erasmus, Melanchthon, Calvin. Calvin attributed great value to music and an important role in worship, specifying that:

> A thing very expedient to the edification of the Church is to sing some psalms in the form of public orisons by which prayers are made to God, or to chant his praises so that the hearts of all are moved and incited to formulate similar prayers and render similar praises and thanks to God, animated by the same sentiment ... The psalms can incite us to raise our hearts to God, both to invoke him and to exalt the glory of his name by our praise.[3]

This quotation – in a January 1537 request addressed to the council of Geneva – well defines the role of music in the framework of humanist Christianity: song is a form of prayer (the sung word); it assumes the role of praise to exalt God's glory; the musicality of the word makes this more moving, more emotional. We should not underestimate the positive role attributed to music in this Calvinist perspective; some Fathers of the Church were considerably more reticent regarding music.

The Roman Church too believed that music in worship is an aid in making the word effective. The Bull *Docta sanctorum* (the first pontifical text to legislate on music), promulgated in 1324–5 by Pope John XXII, already attributed to music an emotional quality that incites devotion:

> When they [the faithful] speak in words, they accede by the words and by music to a devout state. It is therefore prescribed that in God's churches the psalms be sung in order to stimulate the devotion of the faithful.[4]

The Council of Trent, in its 21st session, 17 September 1562, moved in the same direction when it mentioned the need for visible and audible signs to arouse piety:

> Now the nature of man being such that he cannot easily and without some kind of external help lift himself to the meditation of the things of God, the Church, like a good mother, has established certain customs … to excite the spirits of the faithful – through these sensible signs of piety and of religion – to the contemplation of the great things contained in this Sacrifice.[5]

In the first collection of Catholic songs (German Catholics were familiar with vernacular collections as early as the 16th century), published in 1537 by Michael Vehe on the suggestion of Archbishop Albrecht of Mainz, the author justified song explaining that it allowed "the layman to sing to praise and honor God, to awaken his own spirit and to incite himself to devotion, both in church and outside, before and after the sermon".[6] Praise and the awakening of devotion are thus the two functions that the Catholic tradition attributed to song in the context of worship.

Among Lutherans too, with the exception of Luther himself, the same conventional arguments were invoked to justify spiritual song. For Melancthon, in a 1544 anthology of Christmas songs, music is a precious aid in memorizing doctrine:

> Divine doctrine can be better spread, and can become a more permanent component of the memory of posterity, if it is accompanied by harmonies and songs. People avidly listen to sweet and charming melodies and the memory of these remains inscribed for a long time.[7]

And twenty years after Luther's death, in the preface of his anthology of songs published in 1586, Lucas Osiander (1534–1604), a Lutheran preacher at the court of Stuttgart, wrote: "We should not hesitate to praise, with mouth and tongue, the great wonders God has done for us".[8]

Luther's theology

An echo of what Luther's 'theology of music' was can be found in Cyriacus Spangenberg (1528–1604), castle preacher and dean of Mansfeld, who in one of his *Liedpredigten* (Sermons on choral singing) of 1569–70 says:

> Through Luther's spiritual songs and lovely melodies, just as through David's harp, the Holy Spirit has powerfully worked to make God's praises grow and multiply, in order to put the devil to flight, to console souls that are afflicted, to defeat death and to soften many hard hearts and convert them to God.[9]

To put the devil to flight, console afflicted souls, defeat death and convert hearts: no small affair. Luther's theology of music is far from conventional. We will outline it in four points.[10]

Music is a gift of God (ontology)

Luther often defined music as a gift of God.[11] That definition is frequent in his "Table Conversations",[12] but appears only three times in his published writings. It is difficult to identify the origin of the expression. In the 16th century, in any case, a certain number of authors of treatises on music use it, often without particular emphasis: Heinrich Finck (whom, in his "Table Conversations", Luther juxtaposes to Josquin Desprez[13]), Johannes Oridryus, Ambrosius Wilphlingseder, Gallus Dressler and Peter Eichmann.[14] But in the 16th century the opposite concept existed also: the idea, that is, that music had been invented by *man* after the Fall, as we read in Genesis 4:21, "Jubal… was the ancestor of all who play the lyre and the flute".[15]

Following the custom of his contemporaries, Luther at times used the expression in a conventional way, as we read in the preface to his 1538 *Symphoniae iucundae* (an anthology of polyphonic songs): music is, "as all agree, a divine and excellent gift".[16] Luther goes on to specify that music was "from the beginning placed in the world and created at the same time as the creatures of the universe, for individual and collective use. Nothing is without sound or without sonorous number".[17] That affirmation is less the result of his biblical studies than it is an echo of ancient and medieval speculation, as taught, among others, by Boethius, Thomas Aquinas and Jean Gerson. Luther's remark in *David's Last Words*, of 1534, is similar: he writes that music reinforces the positive effects deriving from reading the psalms, for it is a "creature and miraculous gift of God".[18] In the unpublished draft of a 1530 text "On Music", Luther again specifies that music is "a gift of God and not of man".[19]

Luther's locution *donum Dei* depends upon theology: music is a gift in as much as created "by God and not by man". He does not conceal his admiration for the talent of composers who create, and for musicians who interpret, but music is in the first place of divine origin: *concreata*, created at the same time as the creatures of the universe. In this, Luther remains within the framework of speculative ontology: "nothing is without a sonorous number", he says. Music is not a simple object among the other objects created by God; rather, for its numbers, its proportions, its harmonies, it is the ontological foundation of all creation.[20] God is thus a sort of "composer", as Luther suggests in a letter to a musician friend.[21]

The term *donum* also refers to God's love for man, the love which God offers man. Music is thus an expression of divine goodness, and man, on his side, should receive this gift with joyful appreciation. This gift makes man's praise of God concrete, in the joyous song he raises to God.[22]

Music procures joy (anthropology)

The terms *gaudium* or *laetitia*, in English 'joy' or 'gladness', are recurrent when Luther speaks of music. The gladness that music procures has its place in his concept of human feelings, born of Neoplatonism. There the human soul is described as a ship pitching on the sea of passions. Luther uses that image in the *German Bible*:[23]

> For man's heart is like a ship afloat on a raging sea, shaken by strong winds blowing from all directions. At times the heart feels anguish and fear in the face of a future accident, at other times unhappiness and sadness before a present ill. Or again hope and audacity take form at the prospective of future wellbeing, or certitude and joy breathe upon us thanks to some present good.[24]

It is worth noting that Luther enumerates all the benefits of music (the healing of sadness, putting the devil to flight, procuring innocent pleasure…) without taking into account the ambiguity of the effects it can produce – for music can also evidently lead to debauchery or hatred. Calvin, on his side, compares music to a funnel by which words are injected directly into the human heart and concludes that the words sung should be chosen with care.[25] For Luther, by contrast, all music is good since it procures "an innocent pleasure". The innocence of music begins with birdsong[26] and extends to the song of justified human beings.

Singing the Gospel (theology)

Music, as we have seen, is a divine creation. This divine quality, inherent because of music's numerical relationships and proportions ("harmonies"), is sometimes inaudible (mathematical), sometimes audible (musical). Thanks to its divine origin music is perfect. Luther held that it had not been corrupted by the Fall, as would have been the case if it had been a human creation. When it makes itself heard it resounds like the Word that comes from God. Christ, the incarnate Word, thus becomes a singer. Luther defines the difference between the Old and New Testaments in 'musical' terms:

> In the New Testament we find the better form of worship of which the psalm speaks: Sing to the LORD a new song, sing to the LORD all the earth. For God has filled our heart and soul with joy by his well-beloved Son whom he has given us to deliver us from our sins, from death and from the devil. Anyone who seriously believes this cannot help being joyous and cannot stop himself from singing and speaking of it with pleasure, so that others hear him and draw near. If someone wants neither to sing it or say it, this is a sign that he doesn't believe, and that he depends not on the New Testament but on the lazy, sullen Old Testament.[27]

In the German Bible Luther gives a definition of the term "evangelium" which takes account of the musicality of the Good News: "For *Euangelion* is a Greek word which is translated good news, good message, good announcement, good rumor, which we sing and speak about and which makes us joyous".[28]

In the famous Christmas hymn *Vom Himmel hoch, da komm ich her* (From heaven's heights I come to you), the Angel says: "I bring you Good News of which I want to sing and speak". Luther insists that song brings the Gospel not only in a metaphorical sense; he is convinced that the learned music of his time truly *is* an expression of the Gospel:

> And so God preaches the Gospel through music too, as we see in Josquin [Desprez], all of whose compositions flow gayly, spontaneously and with sweetness, not subject to or restrained by rules, like the song-music of Finck.[29]

The expression "the song-music of Finck" – *Finckengesang* – is deliberately ambiguous. In the first place it designates the song of a finch, God's sublime gift being already manifest in birdsong. But *Finckengesang* is also a song written by the composer Heinrich Finck. Bearing in mind Luther's esteem for the great master Josquin Desprez, one can easily under-

stand his juxtaposition of these two musicians. Josquin's music takes its cue from freedom, that is from the Gospel, whereas *Finckengesang* (the song both of the finch and of the musician) is subject to the Law – that of the Old Testament. A remark posthumously attributed to Luther (in 1566) returns to this idea: "Josquin … is the master of his notes, which must bend to his will, while other song-masters must bend to the will of their notes".[30]

Music is the "new song" (kerygma)

The proclamation of the Gospel is thus musical and procures us immense joy; that joy, in turn, makes our heart overflow and, unable to speak, we sing. Luther describes this process in his 1545 *Bapstsches Gesangbuch*: "Anyone who seriously believes cannot help being joyous and cannot stop himself from singing and speaking [of what he believes] with pleasure, so that others hear and draw near". There is a circularity therefore: a man who has received grace cannot do otherwise than sing, for words would be insufficient. The song he produces is the Gospel, which in this way is announced and brings others to the faith. Evangelical song is nothing else than the *canticum novum*, the new song: it is the right expression of the Gospel itself.

This is what Luther wrote in the dedication of a copy of the Bible which he offered his musician-friend Wolff Heintz, referring to Psalm 149:

> To new wonders one must respond with a new song, new thanksgiving and new speech. But these are God's new wonders: in his well-beloved Son he has split open the true Red Sea of death, and rescued us from the true Pharaoh, Satan. That is what "singing a new song" means: the Holy Gospel and giving thanks to God. May God help us.[31]

Luther's first musical creation, a song dated 1523 in memory of two martyrs of the faith burned alive at Brussels, begins with the words: "We intone a new song". The proclamation of the Gospel passes through song, the new song *is* the Gospel, the Gospel procures an exuberant joy that makes us sing, and by our sung proclamation we draw others to the Gospel.

The evolution of Lutheran music
Definition of style
The second part of this paper considers the consequences of Luther's theology for the evolution of Lutheran music. We should note first that Lutheranism does not have a musical style of its own, such as we find in Calvinism and in the Catholic tradition. Calvinism defines ecclesiastical music as having "weight and majesty",[32] Catholic tradition declares that the musical expression proper to the Church is "Gregorian chant and 16th-century polyphonic music". In both cases liturgical musical practices are subordinate to a given framework of style. Such a definition is doubly problematic. First, the definition itself often raises problems, referring to fluid aesthetic categories which do not allow us to circumscribe a concrete musical style. How does a composer realize 'weight and majesty?' With slow, somber music? Or on the contrary with glittering, splendid music? And which 'Gregorian chant' do we mean? That of the Carolingian reform of the 8th and 9th centuries? The plainchant of the Ancien Régime? The 19th-century restoration realized at Solesmes? Or the Gregorian Chant which today fills the shelves of record shops?

On the other hand, a style that is circumscribed does not evolve. The style itself may remain fixed, but people's aesthetic perceptions do not. What for one generation is "majestic", for the next will be merely sentimental (read: laughable). Sublimity can become sentimentality; accords, harmonies, sequences and rhythms all work in their own time period. Calvinist music, which from the 16th century on favored a textually and musically limited repertory, excluding all stylistic development, did not evolve until the 18th century, when the early practices were finally abandoned in favor of others.

Lutheranism, by contrast, has no stylistic definition for its musical practices. When, in his 1526 *German Mass*, Luther reused the Gregorian model adapting it for singing in German, he was only proposing *one* possibility without excluding others. For him, the *canticum novum*, being the expression of the Gospel, should be a 'new song' both theologically and esthetically. The new song should correspond to the newness of the offer of grace, as a song of Johannes Zwick states: "All Morgen ist ganz frisch und neu / des Herren Gnad' und große Treu" (The morning is all fresh and new, full of grace and of the Lord's faithfulness). But the absence of stylistic and aesthetic definitions has consequences for the development of Lutheran music that are still more important. To assume its kerygmatic role, music can take the most varied forms and borrow the most different styles. And this is effectively what happened. Lutheran musicians were open to the styles of their own time. There were no confessional boundaries, they drew inspiration from Protestant and Catholic repertories, from sacred and profane styles.

Let us take the example of the Lutheran musician Michael Praetorius (1571–1621), Kappelmeister successively at Brunswick, Dresden and Sondershausen. Although he had probably never been to Italy, Praetorius easily used the Italian style, especially the *stile concertante*, adapting it to German liturgical practices. At the beginning of the 17th century, Praetorius published – at the behest of his prince, Heinrich Julius of Brunswick-Wolfenbüttel – a monumental anthology of Lutheran chorales (*Musae Sioniae*, 1605–10), in which he codified the *corpus* of hymns of the first century of the Protestant Reform under the form of *a cappella* motets, and at the same time, with his *Polyhymnia caduceatrix et panegyrica* (Wolfenbüttel, 1619), he presented forty chorales transformed into Italian concerts, with several choir-pieces and instrumental ensembles, thus adapting Gabrieli's Baroque polychorality to the German style. Nothing impeded his being at one and the same time Lutheran and Catholic, German and Italian.

The introduction of the church cantata at the beginning of the 18th century, which we know from Johann-Sebastian Bach, aroused lively debate in the Lutheran world. In the previous century, apart from princely courts, Lutheran musical practices had been relatively stripped down. The chorale for four voices now became the general rule, to which were added organ pieces and motets sung by the *Kantorei*. The "cantata quarrel", which developed principally at Hamburg, an important Lutheran city, raised the question of the modernity of sacred music.

Since 1678 Hamburg had an opera house, the Oper am Gaensmarkt (Opera on the Goose Market), where the works of composers like Händel, Keiser and Telemann were performed in German.[33] It was in this city that novelties at the level of compositional techniques and aesthetics were presented and debated.[34]

Between 1702 and 1726 the theologian and poet Erdmann Neumeister (1671–1756) published the first cantata librettos. For Pastor Neumeister, church music had an important role as a prolongation and continuation of the proclamation of the divine Word. To respond to this ministry, he said, sacred music should use the most contemporary and advanced means and techniques. In other words, sacred music has a radically contemporary vocation. At the beginning of the 18th century such a view could only mean that sacred music should model itself on operatic music. Neumeister resumed his viewpoint in the preface to his first anthology of cantatas as follows: "A cantata has, at the end, no other form than that of an opera: it is composed of *recitatifs* and arias".[35] Stylistically, the church cantata was thus a fragment of profane opera and a piece of contemporary music in the service of preaching. In other words: contemporaneity and profane origin are marks of Lutheran music.

Such a concept provoked a strong reaction from pietists, who were shocked by "theatrical Church music".[36] The Kappelmeister of Hamburg cathedral, Johann Mattheson (1681–1784), defended his musician colleague. His own position was close to Neumeister's: since worship without music could not exist, only the best music is worthy of worship, and at that time the best music was opera music. Another musician who helped Neumeister and Mattheson, the Silesian Gottfried Ephraim Scheibel,[37] also declared that music was necessarily an integral part of worship. The vocation of music, both sacred and profane, was to arouse the passions, and – Scheibel asked – why should opera alone have the privilege of touching listeners to the point of tears?

A similar debate would develop in the Catholic Church at the end of the 19th century, following the *Kulturkampf*, but with the opposite result. Modern music was banned and substi-

tuted with a backward-looking style: the Cecilian movement (or 'cecilianism', after St Cecile, patron of sacred music) would find its reference in Gregorian chant and in the vocal music of the 16th century. There was no question of drawing inspiration either from contemporary music or from the profane repertory (operatic music in particular was rejected).

Music and liturgy

Luther's theology also favors the liturgical use of music, both song and instrumental music. At the same time, the important role of music in Lutheran worship shapes liturgical expression. As we saw, for other confessions, especially Calvinism, musical practices were more frequently limited and subject to rules. Thus, for a long time Calvinists sang nothing but the psalms, excluding every other kind of music. In consequence, their liturgical forms did not evolve.

Among 17th- and 18th-century Lutherans the most varied liturgical forms were elaborated, using different musical styles and genres. It is sufficient to follow the musical evolution of Heinrich Schütz, who was active as a church musician between 1613 and his death in 1677. On his return from a first sojourn in Venice, Schütz began his career at the court of the Elector of Saxony promoting the polychoral style he had learned from Giovanni Gabrieli in the Lagoon City, as it had been practiced by his predecessor Michael Praetorius.

His first printed work of sacred music, opus 2 of 1619, *The Psalms of David*,[38] is a monumental composition. Those motets had their place in the liturgy of the Elector's court, celebrating both the glory of God and the magnificence of the prince, Johann Georg I. The eight-voice motets are accompanied by instrumental ensembles at full strength and by 'preferred choirs' (*cori favoriti*). It was an aesthetic of monumentalization very far from the Lutheran practice of Luther's own lifetime.

The restrictions of the Thirty Years War forced Schütz to completely change his style, thus modifying devotional practices and liturgical forms. The *Little Spiritual Concerts*,[39] published in 1636 and 1639, are musical miniatures: one or more soloists (up to five), accompanied only by a *basso continuo*, explore the interiority and intimacy of the word. That introspection invites believers to meditate the biblical text and to experience the affective (emotional) dimension which the Scriptures contain.

Toward the end of the devastating war, Schütz again renewed his music with the Italian style. In the second part of his *Symphoniae Sacrae*[40] of 1647, he brought together Italian vocal ostentation with the expressivity of the madrigal tradition, this time in German. And in the last compositions of his career, Schütz changed style yet again: his *Christmas Story*,[41] published in 1664, is not an oratorio (in the sense of Catholic non-liturgical oratorios) but a setting to music of the Nativity account according to Luke and Matthew: in a simple but expressive tone, the evangelist sings the biblical text, broken up with *intermezzi* of Italian inspiration. That musical form anticipates the sacred cantatas of the 18th century, especially those forms which use a narrative plot taken from the Bible, such (for example) as the six cantatas of Bach normally grouped together under the title *Christmas Oratorio* but which are really liturgical cantatas.

The sacred cantata of the 18th century modified the way in which the word was heard during worship, for the cantata was at the same time a bearer of the word (textually based on the reading of the day) and an announcer of its meaning (amplifying and actualizing the scriptural text), as well as serving to transmit emotion (shaking the listener, touching his feelings).

These mutations in religious experience were made possible by Lutheranism's open attitude to music. The stylistic changes of music, which modified its function, inevitably led to liturgical change. That possibility of adapting to every era, to every society, to every listener and to every culture was in perfect harmony with the "theology of music" found in Martin Luther's thought. Music indeed has a kerygmatic function and for that reason, as the reformer said, occupies "the second place after theology".[42] ▪

1   *Luther*, opera in two acts, *libretto* by Kari Tikka and Jussi Tapola, staged 8 December 2000 at the Temppeliaukio church in Helsinki (DVD, Ondine, 2004).

2   *Luther et le mendiant de la grâce*, opera in eleven scenes, composed by Jean-Jacques Werner, *libretto* by the composer after Gabriel Schoettel, staged 5 November 2017 at Saverne.

3   *Articles baillés par les prescheurs*, Geneva State Archives, Council Registers, vol. 30, fol. 151; also reprinted in: Pierre Pidoux, *Le psautier huguenot du XVIe siècle*, 2 vols., Basel, 1962, II, p. 1 (Documents).

4   "...dum loquuntur verbis, in ipsum quoque cantibus devotionem accendunt. Inde etenim in ecclesiis Dei psalmodia cantanda praecipitur, ut fidelium devotio excitetur". See Michael Klaper, '"Verbindliches kirchenmusikalisches Gesetz" oder belanglose Augenblickseingebung? Zur Constitutio Docta sanctorum patrum Papst Johannes' XXII', *Archiv für Musikwissenschaft*, 60 (2003), pp. 69–95: 72.

5   *Le Saint Concile de Trente oecumenique et general, celebré sous Paul III, Jules III et Pie IV, souverains pontifes*, translated by Abbé Chanut, Lyon, 1696 (3rd edition), p. 243; see Edith Weber, *Le concile de Trente (1545-1563) et la musique: de la reforme à la Contre-reforme*, Paris, 2008, p. 89.

6   "… gesanglyder … welche vom gemeynen Leyen Gott zu lob und ehren / zu auffweckung des geysts / und anreytzung der andacht / möchten in und ausser der kirchen / vor und nach der predigt … gesungen werden…": Michael Vehe, *Ein New Gesangbüchlin Geistlicher Lieder*, Leipzig, 1537, Répertoire international des sources musicales (RISM) 1537/06; Harmonised Database (HDB) 263; reprinted in Christian Möller, *Kirchenlied und Gesangbuch. Quellen zu ihrer Geschichte. Ein hymnologisches Arbeitsbuch*, Tübingen and Basel, 2000, p. 99.

7   Georg Rhau, *Officia de nativitate*, Wittenberg, 1545, edited by Franz Krautwurst; reprinted in Möller 2000, op. cit., p. 122.

8   "Wir sollen uns aber auch nit schemen / die grosse wolthaten Gottes / so er an uns gewandt / mit unserm mund und zungen zu loben unnd zu preisen…". *Fünfftzig / Geistliche Lieder und / Psalmen. / Mit vier Stimmen / auf Contrapunctus weise (für die Schulen vnd Kirchen im löblichen Fürstenthumb Würtenberg) also gesetzt*, Nürnberg, Katharina Gerlach, 1586 (RISM 1586/11; HDB 868); reprinted in Möller 2000, op. cit., p. 125.

9   "Wie denn auch der heilige Geist / nicht weniger / durch Lutheri Geistliche Lieder und schöne Melodeyen / als bey Dauids Harffen / krefftig gewesen / GOTtes Lob uuermehren und außzubreiten / Den Teufel zuuertreiben / Betrübte hertzen zu trösten / Den Tod zu uberwinden / Und viel harter hertzen zuerweichen / und zu Gott zubekeren…". Reproduced in Möller 2000, op. cit., p. 104.

10   For a fuller discussion of the theology of music see Beat Föllmi, 'Luther et la musique: concepts théologiques et anthropologiques', in *Lutero, la Riforma e le arti. L'articolato rapporto con la pittura, l'architettura e la musica*, proceedings of the symposium (Gazzada, 23–5 February 2017), edited by François Boespflug and Emanuela Fogliadini, Milan, 2018, pp. 99–122.

11   The affirmation is actually less frequent than people think. It has become a *tópos* in the literature on Luther and music, as for example Miikka E. Anttila, *Luther's Theology of Music. Spiritual Beauty and Pleasure*, Göttingen, 2013, pp. 70–1.

12   *Musica maximum, immo divinum est donum*, TR 1,968; "Musica est insigne donum Dei et theologiae proxima", Tischreden (TR, that is Luther's *Table Talk*) 3,3815; "Musica optimum Dei donum", TR 5,4441; "Musica est optimum donum et divinum", TR 2,2387.

13   TR 2,1258.

14   See Beat Föllmi, *Das Weiterwirken der Musikanschauung Augustins im 16. Jahrhundert*, edited by Peter Lang, Berne, 1994, p. 122.

15   So says Johann Walter, an eminent musical collaborator of Luther at Wittenberg and first Protestant *cantor* at Torgau, in his *Lob und Preis der löblichen Kunst Musica*, Wittenberg, 1538; the first edition is lost, and we know only that done at Wittenberg in 1544 by Joseph Klug, *Geistliche Lieder Zu Wittemberg/ Anno 1543* (RISM 1544[05]; HDB 334). The poem is reproduced in Martin Luther, *Werke*, ed. Weimar, 1883–1929, XXXV, pp. 483 ff. and in Möller 2000, op. cit., p. 213.

16   "…donum illud divinum et excellentissimum", Luther, *Werke*, ed. 1883–1929, op. cit., L, p. 368.

17   "Musicam esse ab initio mundi inditam seu concreatam creaturis vniuersis, singulis et omnibus. Nihil enim est sine sono, seu numero sonoro…", ibid., L, p. 369.

18   "…ein wunderliche Creatur und gabe Gottes", ibid., LIV, pp. 33–4.

19   "donum Dei non hominum est", ibid., XXX/2, p. 695.

20   On this point Anttila 2013, op. cit., pp. 85–6, seems to have underestimated this speculative aspect of Luther's musical thought.

21   "[The governments of the whole world] let God and all of reason compose and institute very good things, but they sing so badly that they would deserve pork sausages…", letter of Martin Luther to Matthias Weller dated 18 January 1535, (Martin Luther, *Briefwechsel*, ed. Weimar 1930–1985, VII, p. 154); translated by Hubert Guicharrousse, *Les musiques de Luther*, Geneva, 1995, p. 35.

22   For this second point, I gratefully use the results of the excellent study on Luther's theology of music by Anttila 2013, op. cit., pp. 70–84.

23   Four of the feelings listed by Luther are found in Richard of St Victor (1110–73). Missing are only *odium* (hatred), *amor* (love) and *pudor* (shame), see PL 196, col. 6.

24   "Denn ein menschlich hertz ist wie ein schiff auff eim wilden meer, welches die sturmwinde von den vier orten der welt treiben. Hier stoesst her furcht unde sorge fur zukuenfftigem vnfal, Dort feret gremen her vnd traurigkeit von kegenwartigen vbel. Hie webt hoffnung vnd vermessenheit von zukunfftigem glueck. Dort bleset her sicherheit vnd fruede ynn gegenwertigen guetern" (Martin Luther, *Die Deutsche Bibel*, ed. 1906–61, X/1, p. 101).

25   John Calvin, *La forme des prières et chants ecclésiastiques*, Geneva, 1542 (preface); reprinted in *Joannis Calvini opera quae supersunt omnia*, edited by Johann Wilhelm Baum, Eduard Kunitz and Eduard Reuss, Brunswick, 1867, pp. 169–70; see also Pidoux 1962, op. cit., II, pp. 20 ff.

26   "Voran die liebe Nachtigall", Wittenberg collection, 1544 (RISM 1544[05]; HDB 334); reprinted

in Luther, *Werke*, ed. 1883–1929, op. cit., XXXV, pp. 483 ff. and in Möller 2000, op. cit., p. 213.

27 Martin Luther, preface to "Babstsches Gesangbuch", *Geystliche Lieder. Mit einer newen vorrhede / D. Mart. Luth.*, Leipzig, 1545 (RISM 1545/02; HDB 341), Luther, *Werke*, ed. 1883–1929, op. cit., XXXV, pp. 476 ff.

28 "Denn Euangelion ist eyn kriechisch wortt, vnd heyst auff deutsch, gute botschafft, gute meher, gutte newzeytung, gutt geschrey, dauon man singet, saget vnd frolich ist...", Luther, *Die Deutsche Bibel*, ed. 1906–61, op. cit., VI, p. 3.

29 TR 2,1258; translated by Guicharrousse 1995, op. cit., p. 29; see also TR 3,3516.

30 "Josquin, sagt er, ist der noten meister, die haben müssen machen wie er wolt, die andern Sangmeister müssens machen, wie es die noten haben wöllen", Johannes Mathesius, *Historien von des Ehrwirdigen in Gott seligen thewren Manns Gottes, Doctoris Martini Luthers, Anfang, lehr, leben und sterben*, Nuremberg, 1566, sermon 12 'Von Doctor Luthers historien, vom vierzigsten jare', p. 152; translated by Guicharrousse 1995, op. cit., p. 29.

31 Dedication in a Bible offered to Heintz in 1541, Luther, *Werke*, ed. 1883–1929, op. cit., XLVIII, p. 85; translated by Guicharrousse 1995, op. cit., pp. 36–7.

32 For example: in the preface of *La forme des prieres et chantz ecclésiastiques*, Geneva, 1542, and therefater reused in several collections. Reprinted in *Joannis Calvini opera quae supersunt omnia*, edited by Johann Wilhelm Baum, Eduard Kunitz and Eduard Reuss, Brunswick, 1867, pp. 169–70; see also Pidoux 1962, op. cit., II, pp. 20 ff.

33 See Laure Gauthier, *L'Opéra à Hambourg (1648-1728): Naissance d'un genre, essor d'une ville*, Paris, 2010.

34 See Sieghart Döhring, 'Theologische Kontroverse um die Hamburger Oper', in *Festschrift Klaus Hortschansky zum 60. Geburtstag*, edited by Axel Beer and Laurenz Lütteken Tutzing, 1995, pp. 111–23.

35 "Es siehet eine Cantata nicht anders aus, als ein Stück aus einer Opera, von Style Recitativo und Arien zusammen gesetzt". Preface to the *Geistliche Cantaten* (1702).

36 On this debate see Dorothea Beck, *Krise und Verfall der protestantischen Kirchenmusik im 18. Jahrhundert*, Ph.D. Diss., Halle, Martin Luther Universität, 1951.

37 Johannes Elias Schlegel, *Zufällige Gedancken Von der Kirchen-MUSIC*, Frankfurt and Leipzig, 1721; reprint Stuttgart 2002; Scheibel wrote: "Unter allen Jahr-Gängen sind keine besser als diejenigen, welche zeithero der Weltberühmte und vortreffliche Theologus zu Hamburg, Herr Erdmann Neumeister, welchen man mit Recht den Deutschen Assaph oder David mag nennen, verfertiget ... Telemann hat es bewiesen, wie sie noch Geistreicher klingen".

38 *Die Psalmen Davids sampt etliche Motetten und Concerten mit 8 und mehr Stimmen, nebenst andern zweien Capellen / daß dero etliche auff drey und vier Chor nach beliebung gebraucht werden können*, Dresden, 1619, Schütz-Werke-Verzeichnis (SWV) 22–47; modern edition: *Heinrich Schütz, Psalmen Davids. Neue Ausgabe sämtlicher Werke*, vols. 1–3 (1979), vol. 4 (1981), W. Breig, 1994.

39 *Kleine geistliche Concerte*, 1st part: Leipzig, Gregor Ritzsch, 1636, 2nd part: Dresden, 1539.

40 *Symphoniarum sacrarum secunda pars: Deutsche Concerten*, Dresden, 1547; modern edition: *Heinrich Schütz, Symphoniae sacrae II. Neue Ausgabe sämtlicher Werke*, vols. 15–17, 1964 and 1965.

41 *Historia der freuden- und gnadenreichen Geburt Jesu Christi*, Dresden, 1664; modern edition: *Heinrich Schütz, Historia der Geburt Jesu Christi. Neue Ausgabe sämtlicher Werke*, 1, 1955.

42 "Primum locum do Musicae post Theologiam", Luther, *Werke*, ed. 1883–1929, op. cit., XXX/2, p. 696.

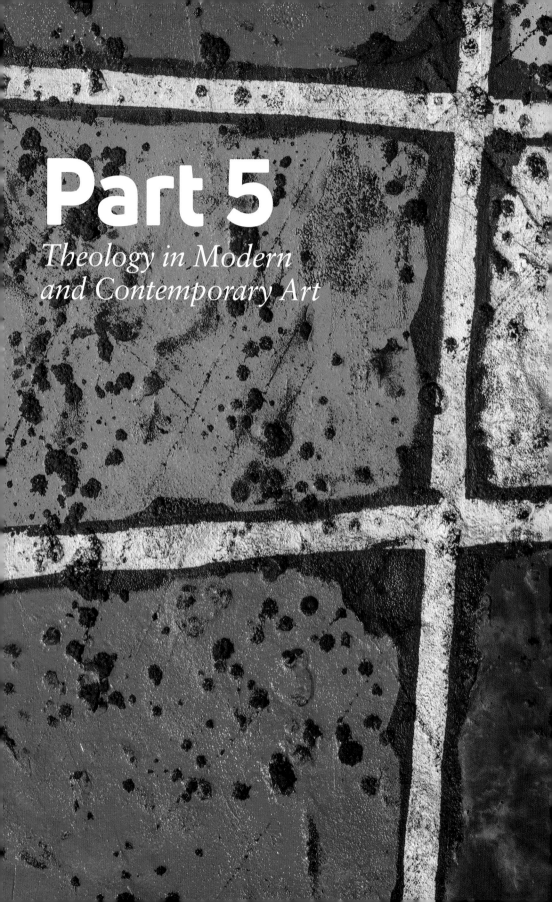

Part 5
*Theology in Modern
and Contemporary Art*

Pedagogical Function and Speculative Dimension of the Image

in the Lutheran Tradition from the 16th Century to the Present

RÉMY VALLÉJO

Rhennish mysticism has a special place in the Lutheran tradition beginning with the 1516 edition of the *Theologia Teutsch* by Martin Luther, whose preface to that 14th-century treatise enthusiastically praised Johannes Tauler. On the one hand, Rhennish mysticism partially nurtured the doctrine of grace, and, on the other, took part in the reform of the inner man. Its quality of "reforming" teaching would moreover, in the 17th century, give rise to the *Pietismus* of Philipp Jakob Spener (1635–1705).

If the speculative reality of Rhennish mysticism did not immediately influence Lutheran tradition in its theological and iconic dimensions, it nonetheless gave rise, against all expectation, to the "dis-imagination" of Caspar David Friedrich (1774–1840), who was not only a landscape painter but also a precursor of Abstraction. Far from reducing itself to the poetic and philosophical ideas of the Iena circle, the work and of this reflective Romantic artist reveals a rootedness in the pietistic milieu and, consequently, in the spiritual teaching of the Rhineland mystics. Thus, in the art of Friedrich, the *Entbildung*, or "dis-imagination", of Meister Eckhart (1260–1328), Johannes Tauler (1300–61), Henry Suso

(1295–1366) and subsequently of Nicholas of Cusa (1401–64) was one of modern Abstraction's sources. In it the essence of the visions of Hildegarde of Bingen (1098–1174), for whom the mystery of the Deity is beyond every word, concept or image, found its most pure expression.

Pedagogical function and speculative dimension of the image in the Lutheran tradition

From the first decades of the 16th century, the Lutheran reform assigned a pedagogical function to images, as various works of the art of drawing and painting in the Germanic world attest. In his *New Testament*, published in Strasbourg in 1527, Hans Grüninger accomplished the *tour de force* of introducing each of the epistles of Paul, Peter, James and John with a frontispiece which, in a skillfully orchestrated composition, sums up the epistle's theme in its different dimensions: literal, moral, allegorical and anagogical. Without precedent in the medieval tradition, these mnemo-technical frontispieces are in no way inferior to the theology lessons of Lucas Cranach the Elder (1472–1553), who, after painting the altarpiece of the Marienkirche at Wittenberg in 1527, worked at a series of drawings, prints and paintings known under the title *Law and Grace*, such as the Prague and Gotha panels, executed in 1529, and the one in Weimar, done in 1553. Lucas Cranach the Elder's *Law and Grace* illustrates Lutheran theological discourse in an iconographic register which, far from breaking with the medieval *Biblia pauperum* and *Speculum humanae salvationis* tradition, perpetuates the literal, allegorical and typological readings of the figures of salvation. The novelty is more in the underlying idea, in its theological, ecclesiological and spiritual dimensions, than in the form of representation in itself.

In the 19th century, in the wake of pietism, this pedagogical function distinctive of Lutheran Reformation images tended to disappear in favor of a speculative dimension. And that is precisely what we see in the paintings of Friedrich, where conscious recourse to the *Entbildung* process of the Rhineland mystics (whom the painter himself never mentioned by name) transforms the statute of images in the Lutheran tradition.

The *Entbildung* process of the Rhineland mystics

Inspired by a dionysiac tradition, which in Hildegarde of Bingen has several dazzling features, the *Entbildung*, or "dis-imagination" of the Rhennish mystics can be seen in various ways.

All through his preaching career, Meister Eckhart advocated 'abandoning all images'. Precisely that is the point of his *German Sermons*, which – marked by neoplatonism (both Augustine's middle neoplatonism and Proclus's more absolute version), remain deeply rooted in the aniconic tradition of Old Testament revelation.

Where the creature ends, God begins to be. Now, God asks no more of you than to come out of yourself according to your way of being and let God be God in you. The least image which takes shape in you is as big as God is big. Why? Because for you it is an obstacle to a total God. Precisely there, where there is an image, God and all his godhead must be put aside. But when the image leaves, God enters.[1]

Less categorical than Mesiter Eckhart, his disciple Johannes Tauler did not systematically underestimate what images – whether figurative, verbal or conceptual – represent, because he gave them a pedagogical statute, like that of a path to take in order to interiorly lift oneself by traversing it from one end to the other. We must therefore "go through images to go beyond images".[2]

Man must use images to lift himself, through them, above them, and pass from exterior and sensible practices to interior ones, to return to himself, to the inmost depths where God's kingdom really is – the inmost depths where living truth shines.[3]

Conscious of the insufficiency and inadequacy of every figure, concept or illustration of the mystery of the divine essence, Henry Suso recommended that we "expell images with images".

How can we give form to that which is without form, and mode to that which is without mode? What we give by way of similitude is a thousand times more dissimilar than that which has no resemblance at all. However, in order to expell images by way of images, I now want to speak to you in images, to show you in a language of images, at least as far as possible, how these imageless thoughts are truly to be taken.[4]

Inspired by Dionysius the Areopagite's *Mystical Theology* and the work of several medieval authors, among whom Hildegarde of Bingen, the very term *Entbildung* belongs, *stricto sensu*, to the language of the Rhennish mystics. It emerged in agreement with the tripartite Augustinian schema *creatio - conversio - formatio* which Meister Eckhart translated into a quadripartite schema. In this process, in a general way, beyond "imagination" (*Bildung*) there must be not only a "dis-imagination" (*Entbildung*) but also a "uniting" (*Einbildung*) when every image fully conformed to the exemplary Image – that which is at the beginning of all things – finally becomes the object of a "higher imagination" (*Überbildung*).[5] That 'higher imagination' manifests the influence of the *Mystic Theology* of the Pseudo-Dionysius, whose process of excess fundamentally transforms the Augustinian schema.

Dionysius the Areopagite's *Aphaeresis*

Dionysius's *Mystical Theology* is a treatise of neoplatonic inspiration that belongs to a body of writings dating to the 5th century. Marked with the seal of apostolic authority,[6] Dionysius's work had an important influence on medieval thought. Commented upon by numerous theologians, among whom Albert the Great, the *Corpus areopagiticum* inspired not only the first chapters of Thomas Aquinas's *Summa Theologiae* but also the work of Meister Eckhart and his disciples.

Dionysius the Areopagite's thought is characterized not only by apophatism, or the "negative way", but by *aphaeresis*, or the abstraction required by every approach to the divine mystery, the essence of which is deeply inaccessible to all sensible or reasonable knowledge.

> The divine Shadow is the inaccessible light where God dwells (1 Tm 6:16). It is invisible due to its transcendent clarity, and it is inaccessible due to the superabundant outpouring of its light. In this Shadow is born every man worthy to know and see God. Aware that it transcends all that is sensible and intelligible, the prophet proclaimed: "Such amazing knowledge is beyond me, a height to which I cannot attain" (Ps 139:6). This is what we say of the divine apostle Paul, that he knew God because he knew him to be beyond all knowledge. Paul also affirmed that God's "ways" are impenetrable (Rm 11:33), his gifts "beyond all telling" (2 Co 9:15) and his peace "beyond our understanding" (Ph 4:7). For he had found Him who is beyond everything, and understood, beyond all knowledge, that He who is the cause of everything is beyond everything.[7]

A pure creation of the School of Cologne,[8] the *Commentary on the Mystical Theology* by Albert the Great (1200–80) infused Dionysius's thought into scholastic reflection, giving rise to the neoplatonic tone of preachers who, emboldened by his authority, did not at all hesitate to propose the way of *aphaereris* to the faithful,

as the German sermons of Meister Eckhart and Johannes Tauler attest.

The visions of Hildegarde of Bingen

If Pseudo-Dionysius was one of the *auctoritates* to whom medieval preachers referred, the true source of inspiration of the Rhennish mystics was Hildegarde of Bingen. Abbess, writer, musician, visionary and prophetess, she was not only one of the great figures of the Rhine valley, but also one of the most astonishing women which the culture of the Middle Ages produced. Beginning in 1141, she consigned her quasi-encyclopedic knowledge, her reflections and her visions to several volumes, among which *Scivias* ('Know the Ways'), the *Liber Vitae Meritorum* ('Book of Life's Merits') and the *Liber Divinorum Operum* ('Book of Divine Works'). Each of her works unfolded in agreement with visions which are described and commented upon in a systematic way. These visions are at the origin of an iconography which is unique in its kind, in which representations of the Trinity and of the Godhead – of the essence of the Trinitarian reality, that is –, have a special place.

In the second vision of the second book of *Scivias*, Hildegarde gives a description of the Trinity, or, more exactly, of the Trinitarian mystery. It is a veritable theology lesson, in which images, in the different sensitive qualities which they suggest, take the place of concepts.

> I saw a dazzling light and, in it, a human form the color of sapphire, all ablaze with a sweet, glowing fire. And that dazzling light invaded all of the glowing fire, and the glowing fire invaded the dazzling light, and that same dazzling light and glowing fire invaded all of that human form, thus forming a single light that had unique power.[9]

The representation of Hildegarde's vision of the Trinity in 12th-century manuscripts is an iconographic hapax apparently without posterity, which gives a clear picture, at one and the same time, of both *epichoresis* and circumcession. The incarnate Son is surrounded by light, before a circle of silver and another of gold. According to Hildegarde's commentary, the "dazzling light" designates the Father, the human form "without any stain of imperfection, of envy, of iniquity" designates the "Son generated by the Father before time began in the manner of divinity", the "glowing fire" designates the Holy Spirit. The commentary itself gives an idea of the movement of the image which manifests the Trinitarian reality of circumcession.

In his preaching, Johannes Tauler in no way refers, *stricto sensu*, to that vision of the Trinity. But thanks to his familiarity with Hildegarde of Bingen's works, the Dominican several times cites the Abbess of Rupertsberg, both to suggest an exemplary life and to mention other visions which, in a purely pedagogical plan, allow him to illustrate his ideas. Johannes Tauler thus alludes to the *Scivias*, one of whose visions is the source of frescoes in the refectory of a convent of Dominican sisters.

> Among other delightful visions, several on this theme were accorded to the noble creature Saint Hildegard. These visions are represented in the saint's book, and also in the refectory of our sisters, in two small paintings … The two personages are barefoot, and the second one is headless. Above him, in effect, is the Godhead (*Gotheit*) on a background of shining gold; that figure does not therefore have a face drawn, but in its place simple rays of gold which symbolize the unknowable Godhead (*Gotheit*); waves of light in effect flow toward the place where his head should be. It is the divinity which is the head, and the image symbolizes true and pure poverty of spirit, of which God himself is the head.[10]

In so describing this figure of Hildegard of Bingen, Johannes Tauler takes the risk of giving an image of the Godhead, or *Gotheit*, the divine essence which, thoroughly unseizable, unknowable and unrepresentable, is nonetheless symbolized by simple rays on a background of glittering gold. This depiction of rays on a gold or glowing background is not entirely new. In effect it belongs to an iconographic vocabulary which since the 5th century had been part of the Byzantine art of illumination, where it was employed to illustrate the manifestation of divine gestures, not only in the gift of the Law

on Sinai, but also in the Resurrection of Christ and in the conversion of St Paul on the road to Damascus.[11] For all the Middle Ages that pictorial modality was a cliché for representing divine actions. We should note, however, that Hildegarde of Bingen's discourse renewed this pictorial modality by attributing to it the task of illustrating the divine essence.

The Godhead in Johannes Tauler

According to Johannes Tauler, although inaccessible to our sensible and rational faculties, Godhead (*Gotheit*) – which is the very essence of the Trinitarian reality from which every being flows forth in its original nobility – can be the object of an experience in which the only possible way is to "suffer God". In the Tauler *corpus*, that experience of the Godhead is thus imagined in the same terms as the prophet Elijah's vision on Mount Horeb.[12]

> However short in duration and however rapid, such a gaze is too far above the capacities of all of nature, which, left to itself, could neither hold it nor conceive it. My children, that momentary vision is truly God. In truth, the Lord is here. My children, that sweetness surpasses all the sweetness of honey and of the honeycomb, which we say is the sweetest thing there is among exterior things. That sentiment surpasses every sense, all intelligence, every faculty, and loses itself in an unfathomable abyss. If a sick eye cannot bear the sun's brightness, nature's infirmity is a hundred times less able to bear this experience of God. My dear children, whatever one may say about it, however great and good one tries to represent to himself this Good, using the senses, words or the intelligence, one remains as far from, and as far below, the reality as if, speaking of a black piece of coal, I were to say: 'Look, that is the bright sun that illuminates the whole world'.[13]

In conformity with the preaching of Meister Eckhart, who, in his German Sermon 71 evoked the conversion of St Paul on the road to Damascus according to the account in the *Acts of the Apostles* (Ac 9),[14] the experience described by Johannes Tauler borders on a blinding of the senses.

It is when Paul sees nothing that he sees God. That is also why Elijah covered his eyes with his cloak when the Lord came. In these situations all the solid rocks are shattered; all that in which the human spirit could find repose must be put aside. And when all these forms have disappeared, then, in a glance, man receives the superior form.[15]

The Godhead according to Henry Suso

Where Johannes Tauler was content to describe Hildegarde of Bingen's figures, in order to make the essence of his preaching intelligible, Henry Suso resorted to drawing to get his ideas across. His *Exemplar*, an autobiographical work which uses his own experience and spiritual doctrine, is thus illustrated with several drawings. Of the twelve known manuscripts, six are illustrated; the oldest of these, dating from the 14th century, today is conserved at the National Library of the University of Strasbourg (MS. 2929).[16] The tenth of eleven drawings of the *Exemplar* is a veritable résumé of the spiritual doctrine of the Rhennish mystics, of which Henry Suso himself provides the explanation.

> The following images show the presence of the nude Godhead in the Trinity of Persons, the ebb and flow of all creatures, the very beginning of a man who goes forward, his advance ordered as a multiplication of effort and the supernatural superabundance of a perfection of being.

Following a process of *exitus-reditus* borrowed from Dionysius the Areopagite, the double movement – of which the Godhead (*Gotheit*) is the beginning and the end – is signified by a line joining the figures which in the area of the heart touches a small ring that represents the 'foundation' or 'spark of the soul', according to the expression of Meister Eckhart and Johannes Tauler. Characterized by a middle-point, this ring, which is in the heart of every being as it is in the heart of each of the Persons of the Trinity, is in the image of the representation of the divine essence. In this process, as Henry Suso allows us to grasp through his image, the first figure is certainly of capital importance, as the brief commentary

which he adds underlines: "This is the eternal Godhead's abyss without mode which has no beginning nor any end".

This Godhead is represented beyond an open tabernacle which shows a veil. The veil is none other than the veil of the Temple, that of the Holy of Holies, behind which the divine mystery is manifest. This – the divine mystery – is represented by three concentric circles which depict the Godhead (*Gotheit*). The three concentric circles allow us to intuit the distinction of Persons, whereas the silver background symbolizes the unity of essence.[17] The middle-point manifests the divine abyss, the bottomless bottom or *Urgrund* of the beginning, the *topos*, the very place from which the Father, in the knowledge which he has of himself, generates the Word who, in the Spirit of Love which binds one to the other in reciprocity, expresses the Father in his fullness while remaining in him. The third strophe of the *Granum Sinapis* or *Mustard Seed*, commonly attributed to Meister Eckhart, explains the meaning of that figure.

> The circle of the Three
> Is deep and awesome,
> That contour
> Cannot be grasped by sense;
> There reigns a bottom without bottom.
> Checkmate,
> Time, form and place!
> The marvelous ring is gushing,
> Its point remains immobile.[18]

Just like the figure of the Trinity in the second vision of the second part of Hildegarde of Bingen's *Scivias*, the figure of the Godhead as it appears in Henry Suso's *Exemplar* is a hapax in the history of the representation of God and of the place between the divine essence and the human soul. Found in only six 14th- and 15th-century manuscripts, *a priori* it has no posterity in the drawing and painting of the Middle Ages, of the Renaissance or of the modern period. Yet we must note that it reappears on the threshold of the 19th century in the context of Lutheran *Pietismus*, in the painter Caspar David Friedrich.

The influence of Lutheran *Pietismus*

Founded by Philipp Jakob Spener (1635–1705), Lutheran *Pietismus* inherited the spiritual tradition of the Rhennish mystics.[19] In view of a renewal of his Lutheran Church, Spener recommended deeper study of the theology inspired by the work of Johannes Tauler and of the *Theologia Teutsch*.[20]

> It would be useful to more often put in students' hands, and recommend their use of, simple little books: the Germanic Theology, Tauler's writings – writings which, together with the Scriptures, made our dear Luther the man he became.[21]

The founder of Lutheran *Pietismus* took advantage not only of the œuvre of Martin Luther, who in 1516 had edited the *Theologia Teutsch*, but also of a work of Jacob Böhme (1575–1624), the *Philosophicus Teutonicus*, which, inspired as much by Johannes Tauler as by Nicholas of Cusa, made Eckhart's language a veritable German philosophical idiom. From that time on it was not only a spiritual doctrine but also a singular mode of expression of the divine mystery which Spener promulgated. That is how the spiritual doctrine of the Rhennish mystics came to flourish again in Germanic and Lutheran territories, not only during all of the 17th century but in the 18th and 19th as well, influencing the arts and letters, music and painting – Johann Sebastian Bach as well as Caspar David Friedrich.

Entbildung in Caspar David Friedrich

Breaking with the pedagogical tradition proper to Lutheran practice, the painted œuvre of Friedrich affirmed a speculative vocation of the image which finds it source of inspiration in Rhennish mysticism. Contrary to all expectations, this landscape painter's imaginary world, in which nothing is ever secondary, became a dis-imagination close to the unseizable *Gelassenheit* of Meister Eckhart and Johannes Tauler. According to Friedrich, the contemplation of nature is an authentic meditation beyond all created things. Long underestimated in favor of merely aesthetic, literary or philosophical interpretations, that source of spiritual inspi-

1. Caspar David Friedrich, *The Cross in the Mountains*, Dresden, Galerie Neue Meister.

ration moreover allows us to grasp how this Romantic painter became a forerunner of Abstraction in Western art.[22]

Born at Greifswald in Pomerania in 1774, and trained in the arts of drawing, engraving and painting at the Copenhagen Fine Arts Academy between 1794 and 1798, Friedrich made his career as a landscape painter at Dresden, where he established himself in 1798 and died in 1840.[23] "This man's works force us to dream, so poetic are they; they admirably communicate the tragedy of landscape", David d'Angers said. But, contrary to that affirmation, the sentiments expressed in the artist's pictures cannot be reduced to tragedy or even melancholy. Although marked by death from early childhood, Friedrich learned to preserve himself from every morbid temptation.

> I must not paint only what I see in front of me, but also what I see in myself. If I see nothing in myself, it is better to stop painting what I see in front of me. For if I dare to paint when I see nothing in myself, my pictures will resemble those pale screens found in hospitals, behind which we expect to find the sick or the dead.

It was therefore the living foundation of things that held the painter's attention. Familiar from youth with the pleasant attractions of

2. Caspar David Friedrich, *Monk by the Sea*, Berlin, Alte Nationalgalerie.

a nature whose charms he was able to enjoy, Friedrich ceaselessly painted plains and mountains adorned with woods and rivers with a candor at times colored with *naïveté*. In reality, his landscapes of the Baltic coasts, of the island of Rügen and of the imposing cliffs of Riesengebirge have an eminently symbolic vocation. His painted work was not a mere evocation of nature for itself, but a total, 'absolute' universe. Influenced in his youth by the preaching of the minister and poet Ludwig Gotthard Kosegarten (1758–1818), who celebrated the Lord's Supper in the open air, on a river bank, Friedrich was heir of the art of the painters of the Low Countries who in the 17th century had breathed religious sentiment into their landscapes, which became contemplations involving sky, earth and sea.

Painted for the altar of the castle chapel of Teschen, *The Cross in the Mountains* (1808; fig. 1) was an effort to replace the traditional symbolism of religious painting with a symbolism inspired by the natural world, which, filled with God, is in itself a book. In this altarpiece, Christ, truly the image of the invisible God, is shown as a crucifix which, turned toward the setting sun and bathed in light, shines on the summit of a rocky peak, where fir trees rich in living sap sink their roots. Abandoning the traditional representation of the Crucified One

in favor of a crucifix planted in nature, Caspar David Friedrich illustrated, as had never been done before, "the icon of the invisible God" according to St Paul's Epistle to the Colossians (Col 1:15). Still more interior, his *Monk by the Sea* (1810: fig. 2) gave landscape the opportunity to unveil the nudity of the human soul. Like a man who, in his solitude, seeks to see beyond the river, the human soul finds its ultimate end on a path stripped of all images. *Monk by the Sea* reveals a process of *Entbildung*, or 'dis-imagination', which we find again in the *Chalk Cliffs on Rügen* (1818; fig. 3) and the *Woman Before the Setting Sun* (1820), where everything concurs, in Johannes Tauler's phrase, "go through the image to go beyond the image".

Friedrich's painted œuvre is not mere illustration of the work of Meister Eckhart or of the sermons of Johannes Tauler. Yet, beyond analysis of his paintings, most of Friedrich's writings, letters, poetry and aphorisms reveal a spiritual sensibility in close complicity with Rhennish mysticism. He painted at the dawn of the 19th century when a young Germany's religious, literary and philosophical world rediscovered medieval mysticism. It was not so much a 'discovery' as a reliving of the sources of the theology of the Lutheran Church and of Pietism.

3. Caspar David Friedrich, *Chalk Cliffs on Rügen*, Winterthur, Museum Oskar Reinhart am Stadtgarten.

That spiritual and deeply biblical rootedness shaped the Romantic painter's thought. Brought up at Greifswald in a pietist milieu, Friedrich did not hesitate to paraphrase the Bible to express his theories on the art of painting. "One could have recourse to the words used by the Holy Scriptures: 'If you had all the wisdom in the world but did not have love, you would be like clanging bronze and a ringing bell'. Or again, if you understand the art of making the brush tremble better than anyone else on the whole face of the earth, but lack life-giving sentiment, all your ability will be no more than dead work".[24] What is more, his sonnets, such as *Der Morgen* and *Der Abend*, are more consonant with the hymns of the pietist *Gebetbuch* than with the poetry of Goethe or Novalis. At Dresden that religious inspiration – revived by Friedrich's participation in a literary cycle whose luminaries were the painter Philipp Otto Runge (1777–1810) and the writer Ludwig Tieck (1773–1853) – rediscovered the spiritual vein of the medieval mystics, whom in 1824 Hegel considered "the patriarchs of German philosophy". Caspar David Friedrich was in perfect accord with the pantheism of the medieval mystics when

he affirmed that the painter who is a "noble man recognizes God in everything, whereas the [painter who is a] common man sees only form and not spirit".[25] His aphorisms, closer in form to a spiritual treatise than to a philosophical discourse, evoke the theme of vision in terms borrowed from the *Theologia Teutsch*.

> Close your bodily eye in order to see your painting first with the eye of the spirit. Then bring into the light of day what you saw in darkness, so that your vision may act upon others, from the outside inwards.[26]

That rootedness in the heritage of the Rhennish mystics thus allows us to comprehend a process of formation strongly marked by an *Entbildung*, or dis-imagination, to which no study of Friedrich has yet called attention, not even in the context of the 2003 exhibition 'Aux origines de l'abstraction (1800–1914)', at the Musée d'Orsay in Paris.[27] A precursor of abstraction, Caspar David Friedrich was also an unexpected heir of the Rhennish spiritual vein.

Caspar David Friedrich's painting is not only a representation of the earth's life, the *Erdlebendbild* theorized by his disciple Carl-Gustav Carus,[28] but also and above all a path of meditation treading which, in conformity with Johannes Tauler's exhortation, man must "go through images to go beyond images". Thus in a small picture today conserved in the Folkwang Museum of Essen (fig. 4), a woman, turned toward the setting sun and bathed in light, ends her journey at the side of a path, in the very place where, in Meister Eckhart's phrase, "the path is pathless". Lost in contemplation, she invites us to become infinitely creative gaze, in order to finally know as we ourselves are known by God, according to the first letter of St Paul to the Corinthians.

> Now we see only reflections in a mirror, mere riddles, but then we shall be seeing face to face. Now I can know only imperfectly, but then I shall know just as fully as I am myself known. (1 Co 13,12)

4. Caspar David Friedrich, *Woman Before the Rising Sun*, Essen, Folkwang Museum.

In fine, in the process of *Entbildung*, that figure unveils the divine essence, or Godhead (*Gotheit*), which leads the soul's eye, the eye of the spirit, beyond every image to Eckhart's divine nothingness.

Conclusion

In its speculative dimension, Caspar David Friedrich's painting approaches the mystery of the divine essence. And precisely that was the object of the Rhennish mystics: to highlight the reality of the Godhead, beyond all images.

Thanks to the diffusion of Johannes Tauler's writings in the Lutheran tradition, Rhennish mysticism had a real influence, which at the very least is surprising and unexpected, on the development of the arts in Reformation culture. This short paper shows once again that to underestimate the spiritual and religious context from which works emerge not only makes it impossible to recognize the source of inspiration which brought them into being, but also and above all to understand the iconic gamble that the works themselves represent.[29] ■

1   Meister Eckhart, *Sermons*, no. 5b (5th edition).
2   Rémy Valléjo, 'Un voyage jusqu'au fond de l'ame', in Johannes Tauler, *Sermons*, Paris, 2013, p. 23.
3   Johannes Tauler, *Sermons*, no. 52.
4   Henry Suso, *Exemplar*, chapter 53.
5   The equivocal use of the word *Bild* in Meister Eckhart et John Tauler should not conceal the sense of the word *form* which, in the writings of the Rhennish mystics, is linked to Augustinian theology, to Aristotelian hylemorphism and to Dionysian noetics. See Wolfgang Wackernagel, *Ymagine denudari. Éthique de l'image et métaphysique de l'abstraction chez Maître Eckhart*, Paris, 1991.
6   Throughout the medieval period, this *corpus* was traditionally attributed to Dionysius the Areopagite, the apostle Paul's only disciple at Athens

(Ac 17:34), whom tradition happily confused with Denis, bishop of Paris.

7   Pseudo-Dionysius, *Letters*, no. 5.

8   The Cologne school was at the origin of a rediscovery of neoplatonic thinkers in the West in the medieval period. Until the 13th century, knowledge of Plato was limited to a few texts: extracts of *Timaeus*, of *Phaedo*, of *Theaetetus* and of the *Republic* which appeared in works of the 3rd to 5th centuries. The *Meno* and the *Phaedo* are translated in the 12th century. Neoplatonism is known in the 13th century thanks to the translation made by Guillaume de Moerbeke (1215–86 of the *Commentary on Parmenides* and *The Elements of Theology* of Proclus [412–85]).

9   Hildegard of Bingen, *Scivias*, Pars 2, Visio Secunda (De Tribus Personis), Paris, 1996, pp. 161–2.

10   Johannes Tauler, *Sermons*, no. 68.

11   That is what the Rubulensis manuscript attests, Siriaque manuscript Pluteo 1.56 of the Biblioteca Laurenziana of Florence (6th century), as does the medieval witness offered by Cosmas Indicopleustes's *Christian Topography*: see Codex vaticanus graecus 699 of the Biblioteca Apostolica Vaticana (9th century), Manuscript 1186 of the Library of the monastery of St Catherine at Mount Sinai (11th century) and the manuscript of the Biblioteca Medicea Laurenziana in Florence (11th century).

12   See Rémy Vallejo, 'L'utilisation de 1 Rois 19 comme paradigme de la naissance de Dieu dans l'âme chez Jean Tauler', in *La naissance de Dieu dans l'âme chez Eckhart et Nicolas de Cues*, edited by Marie-Anne Vannier, Paris, 2006, pp. 73–84.

13   Johannes Tauler, *Sermons*, no. 64.

14   Meister Eckhart, *Sermons*, no. 71 (5th edition).

15   Johannes Tauler, *Sermons*, no. 64.

16   Conserved in the National Library of Strasbourg, the manuscript escaped the fire of 24 August 1870 for the simple reason that it was in Berlin at that time. It returned to the collection of the National Library of the University of Strasbourg in 1907 with the accession number Ms 2929.

17   Oxydized, the silver background has become black in folio 82 of Ms 2929 of the National Library of the University of Strasbourg.

18   Meister Eckhart, *Granum sinapis*.

19   See Remy Vallejo, 'Philipp-Jakob Spener', in *Encyclopédie des mystiques rhénans d'Eckhart à Nicolas de Cues et leur réception. L'apogée de la théologie mystique d'Occident*, edited by Marie-Anne Vannier, Walter Euler, Klaus Reinhard and Harald Schwaetzer, Paris, 2011, pp. 1091–3.

20   Anonymous from Frankfurt, *Theologia Teutsch* [14th century].

21   Philipp-Jacob Spener, *Pia desideria* [1675], ed. Leipzig, 1841, pp. 93–4.

22   Rémy Vallejo, 'Caspar David Friedrich', in *Encyclopédie* 2011, op. cit., pp. 502–4.

23   See Werner Hoffmann, *Caspar David Friedrich. Naturwirklichkeit und Kunstwahrheit*, Munich, 2000.

24   Sigrid Hinz, *Caspar David Friedrich in Briefen und Bekenntnissen*, München, 1974 (1st edition Muchen, 1968), p. 113.

25   Ibid., p. 94.

26   Ibid.

27   *Aux origines de l'abstraction (1800-1914)*, exhibition catalogue (Paris, Musée d'Orsay, 2003–4), edited by Marcel Pochard et. al., Paris, 2003.

28   See Carl Gustav Carus, 'De la peinture de paysage dans l'Allemagne romantique', in *Neuf lettres sur la peinture de paysage*, edited by Marcel Brion, Paris, 1983.

29   See Rémy Vallejo, 'Mystique rhénane, abstraction et culture européenne', in *Culture et transcendance. Chemins de la création culturelle*, proceedings of the symposium (Paris, 6 December 2014), edited by Dominique Ponnau, Michel Morange and Jean Duchesne, Paris, 2015.

The Resurrection of the Image in the English Protestant Imagination

From William Blake to Bill Viola. Part I

BEN QUASH

In an unconscionably brief span, this paper is going to outline the story of the resurrection of visual imagery in English (mainly Anglican) church life, so as to account for its proliferation today. This proliferation would, if it could be disclosed retrospectively to the eyes of a late 16th-century English churchgoer, be utterly astounding.

A harder task is the *qualitative* one of trying to explain not only the fact of such revived visual art within English Anglicanism, but the extraordinary vibrancy it has today. In part II of my essay, I will attempt to offer a few thoughts on this too.

To appreciate its revival, we need first to attend to the circumstances in which visual imagery, by and large, died and was buried in Protestant England. This 'back story' of the suppression and then the neglect of images which precedes their rising again occupies neatly, and almost uncannily, a period of exactly three hundred years: from 1533 until 1833.

It was in January 1533 that Henry VIII married Anne Boleyn, his second wife, in Westminster Abbey. In the same year, the Reformer Thomas Cranmer was appointed Archbishop of Canterbury and annulled Henry's first marriage. In July 1533, the Pope excommunicated both Henry and Cranmer. In the same year, the Act of First Fruits and Tenths transferred taxes on ecclesiastical income from the Pope to the Crown, while the Act Concerning Peter's Pence and Dispensations stated that England had 'no superior under God, but only your Grace [i.e., King Henry]'.

It was in September 1833 that the first of the *Tracts for the Times* were published. Authored by Edward Bouverie Pusey, John Keble and John Henry Newman (all dons at Oriel College, Oxford), they marked the birth in print of what quickly became known as the Oxford Movement (and gained for their authors the title 'Tractarians'). The year marked a watershed in the Church of England's re-engagement with pre-Reformation sources and styles of theology and liturgical practice; a re-engagement that would have its artistic correlates in major programs of church decoration, the Gothic Revival, and sacred painting and statuary.

These bracketing dates of 1533 and 1833 are not of course 'thunderbolt' moments, in which lightning struck from a clear blue sky. They are tipping points, in which numerous factors and forces converged to move things forward. We ought not to neglect the more extended chains of events that give them context.

1. Thornham Parva Retable, Thornham Parva (Suffolk), Church of St Mary.

But as particular dates they are a useful shorthand as they frame a period in which England's once-rich relationship with visual devotional art withered almost to nothing.

The former richness is traceable in a few magnificent (though woefully damaged) survivals. The 13th century Westminster Retable, for example – almost certainly made for the High Altar of the Abbey – is England's oldest known altarpiece. It is made of oak, is around 3 meters long and a meter high, and frames a series of oil paintings on gesso, including one of the Abbey's dedicatee (St Peter). The figure of Christ stands at the center, holding the world, with the Virgin and John the Evangelist on either side of him. Tiny details on the painted earth in Christ's hand include livestock, birds, trees and a boat on water. Four small medallions show a series of miracles that include the raising of Jairus's daughter, the healing of a man born blind, and the feeding of the five thousand. Painted glass set into the border of the retable gives the impression of enameling. It would have been a breathtaking object in its full glory, but it was removed at the time of the Reformation, recorded by an antiquarian in 1725 as being in use at that time as a top for a cupboard housing funeral effigies (having by that stage been covered in gray and white paint), and rediscovered in 1827 by the Abbey Surveyor, Edward Blore, who had it protected by a glass front and put on view again. (Note the date: 1833 was not far off; things were shifting).

Another rare survival is the altarpiece of the parish church of St Mary in the village of Thornham Parva, in Suffolk, made about fifty years after the Westminster Retable in the 1330s (probably originally for a nearby priory at Thetford; fig. 1). Its rediscovery in a hay loft in the village dates to 1927, and indicates that the parishioners of the village had been concerned to protect it from defacement or – worse – destruction at the time of the English Reformation, and so had hidden it; sitting on their secret until eventually they collectively forgot about it altogether.

Like its East Anglian near-neighbor, the Despenser Retable in Norwich Cathedral (made another fifty years later, in the late 14th century), shows an astonishing sophistication. We see glimpses in both works of the sort of confidence in handling space, assurance in applying color, and emotional subtlety, that makes them compositions every bit as beautiful as those to be found on the continent (the frame of the Norwich retable, too, has been judged the equal of the Italian *cassetta* frames of the same period: 'the type and variety of decoration is strikingly rich and well-organized'). In their elegance and complexity, but also in their rarity, they evocatively signal that greater body of work that is now irrevocably lost.

Iconoclasm was on the rise in England as early as the 1520s. The break with Rome, however, did not in itself automatically entail a new policy on the veneration of images; indeed, a change of policy on images does not seem to have been any particular priority of Henry VIII himself at the time that Royal Supremacy was asserted, nor of many of his bishops. In London in October 1533, we hear that religious images were being removed from some churches and thrown away as valueless 'stocks and stones', and that some of the iconoclasts would 'prick them with their bodkins to see whether they will bleed or not'. Eamon Duffy, writing of these events, notes that the ecclesiastical hierarchy profoundly disapproved: "While Stokesley was bishop such 'damnable abusions' were still treated as sure tokens of heresy, and where the culprits could be found they were harshly dealt with …".[1]

Duffy goes on to recount the concern in England about what was happening in Strasbourg at this time:

In September 1535 both the Imperial ambassador and the Lord Chancellor complained to [Thomas] Cromwell about a book lately printed 'touching taking away images'. This was a translation of Bucer's *Das Einigerlei Bild*, a key Reformation iconoclastic tract, which had been produced in 1530 to justify the destruction of all images at Strasbourg. The treatise allowed that in principle images were legitimate as long as they were not worshipped. However, "syth it is so that in churches every were / ymages are honoured / and namley roodes", such is the strength of "old rooted custome" that "though thou prech never so ofte / nor never so ernestly'"there will always be some "whiche wyll hold on styl to put of their cappes unto them orels to lowre and make curtesy to them"and those "snarled" in the Devil's bonds "wyll never refrayne from worshippynge of ymages".[2]

The main concern here on the part of these officials of the English State was that making a doctrinaire fuss about the veneration of images was likely to sow discord and division across the nation, given the popularity of such images and the role they played in the lively day-to-day Christianity of the people.

It is, in retrospect, an irony that what can properly be called the first official doctrinal formulary of the newly-formed Church of England – the Ten Articles approved by Convocation in 1536 – approved the veneration of images (along with the cult of the saints and the practice of intercession for the dead). There were, to be sure, some qualifications:

Images were "representers of virtue and good example", and were meant to be the "kindlers

and firers of men's minds". They might therefore stand in churches, but preachers were to ensure that the people were warned against idolatry. As for "censing of them, and kneeling and offering unto them, with other like worshippings", which had "entered by devotion and fallen to custom", the people were to be instructed that such worship was in reality not offered to the images, but only to God and in his honour.[3]

These qualifications may seem to smack of elements of Bucer's text, referred to above. However, as Duffy goes on to point out, they were "almost precisely those advanced in such impeccably Catholic works as the early 15th-century treatise *Dives et Pauper*, and despite its careful wording this article expressly legitimated 'censing, kneeling and offering 'before images"[4] – hardly things that could be countenanced in Bucerian terms.

As we know, the passage of time, the increase in Cranmer's influence, and the recognition by Henry of the issues on which his surest support base most needed to be appeased, added up to an ever-less covert series of attacks on the use of images in liturgy and devotion. Some even condemned the merely didactic (rather than devotional) use of pictorial imagery, which had for centuries been justified as meeting the needs of the illiterate to be instructed in their faith.

It was Edward VI's accession to the throne in 1547 that sealed the precarious fate of religious images. "All over England [in 1547–8] churchwardens cooperated in the removal and destruction of images and the suppression of traditional services [even though] this cooperation should not be read as approval"[5], observes Duffy.

At the heart of the Edwardine reform was the necessity of destroying, of cutting, hammering, scraping, or melting into a deserved oblivion the monuments of popery, so that the doctrines they embodied might be forgotten. Iconoclasm was the central sacrament of the reform, and, as the programme of the leaders became more radical in the years between 1547 and 1553, they sought with greater urgency the celebration of that sacrament of forgetfulness in every parish of the land … In the end … conformity was almost universal.[6]

What the parishioners of Thornham Parva succeeded in doing in saving their altarpiece was thus not only rare; it was illegal and very dangerous. A less risky path may have given some comfort to those with wall paintings in their churches, who were able to resort to the reversible strategy of whitewashing, knowing that their beloved images were still present, though temporarily veiled from sight.

Reverence for the English Bible, however, seems quickly to have established itself even among those who rebelled against the new Protestant conformity. As Duffy puts it, "[n]ew pieties were forming, and something of the old sense of the sacred was transferring itself from the sacramentals to the scriptures".[7] This leads me to the first speculative point I want to make about the 300 years that – with the shortlived interlude of Mary's reign – starved the English religious imagination of visual imagery from the Henrician Reformation onwards. Images did not go away. Just as some lurked beneath the whitewashed walls of churches and cathedrals, some also migrated – translating themselves into new textual forms more palatable to an audience living under a new dispensation.

Take, for example, this section of John Donne's poetic reworking of the *Lamentations*, which dates from the early years of the 17th century:

CHAP. III.

1. I AM the man which have affliction seen,
   Under the rod of God's wrath having been;
2. He hath led me to darkness, not to light,
3. And against me all day, His hand doth fight. 180
4. He hath broke my bones, worn out my flesh and skin,
5. Built up against me; and hath girt me in
   With hemlock, and with labour; 6. And set me
   In dark, as they who dead for ever be.

7. He hath hedged me lest I 'scape, and added more   185
   To my steel fetters heavier than before.

8. When I cry out He outshuts my prayer; 9. And hath
   Stopp'd with hewn stone my way, and turn'd my path.

10. And like a lion hid in secrecy,
    Or bear which lies in wait, He was to me.   190
11. He stops my way, tears me, made desolate;
12. And He makes me the mark He shooteth at.

13. He made the children of His quiver pass
    Into my reins. 14. I, with my people, was
    All the day long, a song and mockery.   195
15. He hath fill'd me with bitterness, and He

Hath made me drunk with wormwood. 16. He hath burst
My teeth with stones, and cover'd me with dust.

17. And thus my soul far off from peace was set,
And my prosperity I did forget.[8]

It is, I would suggest, hard to believe that some readers of Donne's lines at the time when they were written would not have had in their *mind's* eyes (also, after all, a place of visualization; of visual experience) an image of the *Man of Sorrows* (known in more Latin contexts as the *Imago Pietatis*) of the sort that would have been widely available to English Christians for many decades. An example might be that which peeps out at us in Binham Priory in Norfolk (fig. 2) from behind a textual overlay. The poem's textual rendition of the 'man afflicted', which is christologically-constructed just as its pictorial analogues were, is a means by which the world of religious imagery could be sustained and transmitted in the early stages of the 300-year exile of the painted or sculpted work.

We might note too, with Julianne Sandberg,[9] the abundance of imagery derived from the visual arts that permeates the poetry of George Herbert. In *The Windows*, the speaker explores an extended analogy between himself and stained glass, contrasting his current state – 'brittle crazy glass' – to the pellucidity and luminous color of a window in God's house. He strives for this in his hope that he, like the window, may find God's story 'annealed' in him. Alongside this celebration of glasswork, architectural metaphors

2. *Man of Sorrows*, Norfolk, Binham Priory.

abound as well. In *The Altar*, as Sandberg has pointed out, architectural terms define human identity: 'the altar (which stands for the human person) is "made of a heart" (1:2), "cemented with tears" (1:2), and composed of "stone" (1:6, 14).[10] Thus God constructs the "frame" (1:3, 11) of humanity. In *The Church-Floor*, Herbert depicts God as "the Architect, whose art / Could build so strong in a weak heart" (1:19–20), while the poem *Man* also compares the human heart with a building (one that God has "splendidly … built"; 9:1–2). Finally:

> [a]lthough *Affliction* does not overtly describe humanity as a building project, God again engages in the act of construction, for He takes the 'broken pieces all asunder' (1:1) and 'with care and courage build[s]' (5:5) the speaker into a restored being. In *Zion* [likewise] humanity represents '[God's] Architecture' (2:5), making God an architect who constructs mankind's 'frame and fabric' (2:6).[11]

The 17th century, as Barbara Lewalski has shown authoritatively in her discussion of 'Protestant Poetics' and the English literary imagination,[12] is misread if it is read as a time when the image had vanished. It had simply changed form. In my view, the English literary tradition – even in the hands of Puritan dissenters more Protestant in temper than those of the established church (I am thinking, for example, of John Milton and of John Bunyan) – was a sort of 'Noah's Ark' of visual imagery, in which powerful motifs lived on, ready to reactivate on the soil of a new and more receptive visual culture.

As on the European continent, religious illustration persisted – especially in the context of new editions of the King James Bible, and in devotional and moralizing works published for pious instruction. And the continuance of 'history painting' as a genre (though often eclipsed in popularity by portraiture and landscape painting) allowed for biblical locations and scenes to be drawn, engraved or painted, as a special subset of eminent historical subjects. But these were emphatically not liturgical or devotional works. They were like the grand allegorical designs commissioned as decorations for England's great country houses. This was even true of the series of grisaille paintings that Sir James Thornhill undertook for the dome of Wren's St Paul's Cathedral in London – the first ever post-Reformation English cathedral, and thus the first cathedral to be called upon in its design and decoration to express in a visual language the distinct spirit of the Church of England in its Reformed Catholicism. The dome (fig. 3) is decorated much as a fine country house's ceiling might be (the eight scenes in the dome show episodes from the Life of St Paul). The 1715 committee that awarded Thornhill the commission has been described as "Whig", as "low-church dominated", and as "inspired by a moral Anglican nationalism".[13] Thomas Tenison, the Archbishop of Canterbury at the time, is reported as saying "I am no judge of painting, but on two articles I think I may insist: first that the painter employed be a Protestant; and secondly that he be an Englishman".[14] It is not hard to discern here an abiding suspicion of the "popery" – the tendency to idolatry and superstition – perceived to characterize continental

3. Dome of the Cathedral of St Paul, London.

religious painting, and a determination to stay inoculated against it.

Many private collectors, however, *were* buying works of sacred art from the continent, some with mythical and some with religious themes. So the exposure of certain influential men and women to the art of Catholic Europe continued in this period, albeit more often in a connoisseurial than a devotional context.

Notwithstanding the influence of various forms of low-church prejudice and defensiveness, it is worth noting that some of the artistic achievements of the architects and artists of the new London churches of the 18th century involved visually-sensitive and theologically-informed iconography. The reliefs on the exterior of Wren's St Paul's (which is also, of course, in its overall conception a very self-conscious mirroring of St Peter's in Rome) incorporate motifs of wheat-ears and grapes, suggesting that a eucharistic sensibility was being brought to the interpretation of the building. Wren's most skilled pupil and assistant Nicholas Hawksmoor, meanwhile, incorporated into his fascinating small portfolio of London church-

es a detailing that seems (whether consciously or unconsciously) to use sacred heart motifs, while at a more overarching level his concern to echo what he imagined were the architectural excellences of a primitive, classical world was a deliberate attempt to convey in visual terms the theological bonds that the Reformed English Church felt with pre-Reformation 'primitive Christianity' – the Christianity of a Hellenistic world of classical basilicas. It may not have been medieval Gothic in inspiration, but it was concerned to be *old*.

We now approach, in this compressed and accelerated narrative, the period where the end of this 300-year visual fast begins to prepare itself for a feast.

William Blake was not – indeed, *decidedly* and *vehemently* not! – a member of the Established Church. But his influence on the visual art that would recolonize it was highly significant. Blake, as an autodidact and a man of visionary experience and strong opinion, was free to be influenced by no particular school (fig. 4). He loved the freedom of the Gothic style. He was also a deep admirer of the Classical precision

4. William Blake, *Job and His Family*, engraving from the 1826 edition of the *Book of Job*.

of Michelangelo and Raphael, who were early influences on him. Perhaps most significantly of all, he assimilated these artistic styles not as a collector, a dilettante, or an historian, but as a man of passionate faith, who imaginatively inhabited the world of the Bible every bit as much as he inhabited, as a lifelong Londoner, the streets, the slums and the squares of the nation's capital. His artistic vocabulary, idiosyncratic in its fusion of various debts, was put into the service of awakening religious vision in his readers.

Moreover, in his literary fascination not only with biblical literature but with poetry and drama (John Milton's work preeminently important here) – *and as a poet himself* – he was unusually well-placed to unlock the literary image's visual potential. No other single British artist (until, perhaps the 20th-century painter-poet David Jones) was so accomplished in his skills as a maker of textual art as well as visual. He did not just write poetry, he made of it a visual event. The beauty of his words lay not just in their literary resonance but in their appearance – painted or engraved – on

the page, and this beauty was amplified in the figurative images which shared the page with his words. The images of his mind's eye were externalized – so (more broadly) it can plausibly be argued that he helped the mental images of a nation that had been relying on its mind's eye for devotional nourishment ever since the Reformation to find rewards again in a distinctively English new sort of religious painting.

The merits of Blake's visionary style may not have been fully appreciated in his lifetime, although it was a fairly immediate inspiration to a group of younger painters calling themselves 'The Ancients' (Samuel Palmer notable among them) whose work joins Blake's in having a remarkably lively legacy in subsequent English painting. My view is that to understand the potency of Blake's example, one needs to interpret it as channeling important aspects of past English religious sensibilities, and anticipating future ones.

Blake's work seems to me to breathe the spirit of 'mystical empiricism' which animates the so-called 'metaphysical poetry' of the 17th century; the sense of a divine spirit alive in the

material, corporeal, often very local particularities of time and place: of 'England's green
and pleasant land'. It is everywhere to be found
in the poetry and the poetic prose not only of
Donne and Herbert, whom we have already
acknowledged, but of others like Thomas Tra-
herne and Henry Vaughan. Like Blake, they felt
themselves to be living, moving and breathing
inhabitants of the world of the Bible, whose
characters they found encountering them in the
woods, on the hills, by the streams and in the
church buildings of their daily lives. Giotto in
the Italian *quattrocento* and Stanley Spencer in
20th-century England share the same sensibility. To paint this experience, whether in words
or in pigment, was to offer a powerful artistic
witness to a theology of incarnation that has
always been powerful in English Christianity
(even among its agnostic sons and daughters
– George Eliot, for example).

Blake aimed to make sense of his historical
and geographical environment (however un-
promising it may seem; however far from grace)
as a place of revelation and divine touch. His
similarity with his 17th-century forebears is evi-
denced by an examination of poems like Henry
Vaughan's *The Search*.[15] The poem describes a
journey through a series of biblical locations,
which correspond to episodes in Christ's life,
but – as the episodes themselves do – pick up
Old Testament resonances too (Jacob's well
is a singularly important stopping off point,
even though it sounds less like a well and more
like a Welsh water-source: 'the angry spring in
bubbles swelled', says Vaughan). The journey
begins in Bethlehem, moving through Egypt,
Jerusalem, Sychar, and back to Jerusalem again,
to the hill of Calvary. But the poem is only half
over. Where is there to go now? Perhaps rather
surprisingly, Vaughan's inner promptings take
him off to the wilderness, where while still
alive Christ both faced temptation and found
retreat. Here the ascended Christ still feels near
to Vaughan. And this, Vaughan surmises, is the
place the true Church now finds her destiny
lying. As with his evocation of Jacob's well, it
is hard not to hear his descriptions of this desert space as descriptions of the Welsh valleys:
"What silent paths, what shades, and cells, /
Fair, virgin-flowers, and hallowed *wells*…"

Vaughan's neoplatonic leanings often lead
him to assert the transitoriness of the material
creation, and look for a better vision beyond
the world's 'shell', but he cannot get away
from the fact of the incarnation. Jesus Christ
sat on the ground, drank from springs, and
wandered the earth's paths, as Vaughan does
now. In a powerfully beautiful phrase, used
of the seraphim with whom Jesus shared the
wilderness, Vaughan says that he 'heavened
their *walks*'. The desert is sanctified, and the
'wild shades' are made a paradise. The aptness
of the verses from the Book of Acts is apparent
– 'he be not far off from every one of us, for in
him we live, and move, and have our being'.
Vaughan achieved an extraordinary thing, as
Blake would too, in his relatively unforced im-
position of a scriptural palimpsest upon the
landscape he lived in.

David Jones suggests in an essay in *The
Dying Gaul* that there might be a distinctive
English aesthetic marked by its special interest
in, and attention to, *found detail*. He relates
it to the style of needlework known in medieval times as *Opus Anglicanum*, and his idea
finds a certain resonance with later writers
like Geoffrey Hill: "In tapestries, in dreams,
they gathered, as it was enacted, the return,
the re-entry of transcendence into this sublu-
nary world. *Opus Anglicanum*, their stringent
mystery riddled by needles: the silver veining,
the gold leaf, voluted grape-vine, masterworks
of treacherous thread".[16]

Jones notes that *Opus Anglicanum* is "*the
one art which has taken its name from us*";
that in the poetry of the Middle Ages "again
and again the image evoked, the thing lifted
up, is a flowery, starry, intertwined image";
that the Victorian poet Gerard Manley Hopkins's "dappled things" likewise express "an
intensely native feeling"; and that indeed
England itself is "a most mottled, dappled,
pied, partied and brindled land". Jones, too, is
very obviously characterizing in these phrases
his own painting and writing. His painting
of the crosses of Golgotha transposed into
a history-saturated British landscape (*Vex-
illa Regis*) does visually something of what
Henry Vaughan did poetically three centuries
earlier.[17]

As the late literary scholar Graham Pechey has pointed out,[18] the European counter-enlightenment initiated a revaluation of pre-modern representation, and as a consequence we find in England not only William Blake's attachment to a 'bounding outline' and to the sublimity of 'minute particulars' in his own composite art but also those places in the work of Samuel Taylor Coleridge where a complex metaphysical argument is enacted in a closely observed detail derived from the natural world – as, for example, in the "cinque-spotted" water-insect in the *Biographia Literaria* whose active-passive swimming upstream reflexively figures the imagination. This is where Blake does not only look back to a more immediately post-Reformation world of artistic imagination, but forward to the Romanticism of the later 19th century; the period in which an English visual art will assay representation of the highest religious themes once again, while always retaining a characteristic concern with the local and the particular (believing that all great mystical encounters will tend to have, in Shakespeare's words, "a local habitation and a name").

Hans Urs von Balthasar writes of an English tradition of what I would call "foundness": "[a] mistrust of the value of universal concepts" which is a consciousness, he says, "as old as English intellectual life".[19] He praises what is a hallmark of the concern of John Ruskin, Walter Pater, Matthew Arnold, John Henry Newman, and of course Gerard Manley Hopkins too: the necessity of *paying due attention* to the God-given, glorious 'reality' that is before one in nature – not meddling with it, or allowing one's own shadow to fall distractingly upon it – and *never* abstracting.

Balthasar thus identifies in English aesthetics a particular celebration of "the irreducibility of the individual, be it material or personal" which has its summit in Shakespeare, "the greatest creator of unique, incomparable characters". There is no place in this English perspective for spurious ideas of "perfection in general". There is instead "the absolute, hard reality in which alone the true glory of being shines forth". There is a celebration of the "uniqueness ... of each image met with every day in nature or the world of men"[20]. Blake (as we know from his objections to the work of Sir Joshua Reynolds) would concur.

To the extent that English theology shares this focus on the concrete form – "the unique, the irreducible" – then Balthasar rejoices to celebrate its advantages over his own continental tradition, for "reared in an hereditary empiricism" it has "preserved the native rights of imagery in religious thought ... right up to the present day".[21] And for this reason, it makes perhaps a better sense to an English mind to say that the theologian should talk to the poet.

It also, in hindsight, makes sense of what I said at the outset would have been an astonishing fact if predicted to a late 16th-century English Protestant, namely, that English Anglicanism would in the 19th century find itself patron and seedbed of some of the most prolific manufacture of world-class visual art – in multiple media, including stained glass, wood and stone carving, fabric, metalwork, mosaic, and painting. The belief in revelatory particularity that has been a perennial feature of Anglican thought – in which the concrete and the mystical are not at odds – makes it a tradition congenitally prone to the 'imaging' of its faith. Visual art was bound to reassert itself.

In the wake of the first Tractarian publications in 1833, the doctrinal initiatives of the Oxford Movement soon found themselves with aesthetic outriders like John Mason Neale (1818–66), who, "as a passionate undergraduate at Trinity College, Cambridge", set up the Cambridge Camden Society in 1839 with his friends Edward Boyce and Benjamin Webb. They were tireless and effective promoters of a more visually rich style of church architecture and furnishing. As the prominent evangelical Francis Close, later Dean of Carlisle, memorably put it, what was being "taught *analytically* at Oxford [was] taught *artistically* at Cambridge ... it is inculcated theoretically, in tracts, at one University, and it is sculptured, painted and graven at the other...".[22]

The Church of England has never looked back – to the extent that even its most charismatic and evangelical wings are now busy commissioning painted altarpieces and using visual imagery (both static and moving) in

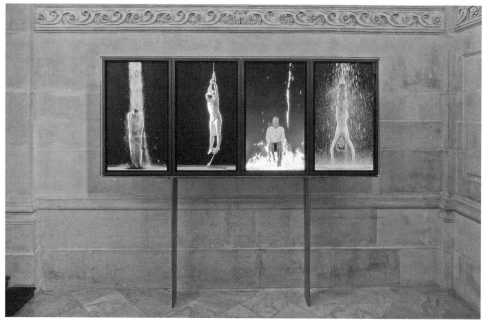

5. Bill Viola, *Martyrs*, London, Cathedral of St Paul.

worship – recognizing that visual imagery is the *lingua franca* of our time.

One final question that could be asked in concluding this paper is whether the influence of a particular doctrine of eucharistic presence is discernible in this tradition – and therefore of the consecrating power of the Holy Spirit: a "presencing" which is real but local; found and not brought or imposed. If so, consciously or unconsciously – and even in the most recent art installations like Tracey Emin's pink neon sign in Liverpool Cathedral (*For You*, which finds its own unexpected resonance with Acts 17:27–28) and the deeply incarnational emphasis of Bill Viola's *Martyrs* in St Paul's Cathedral (fig. 5) – we still see the effects of a commitment to the importance of searching, and of finding, in a historical trajectory which is profoundly embodied, and in its perennial distrust of impersonal, universalist sublimity prefers intimacy over abstraction. This is something I will explore further in Part II of this essay. ■

1   Eamon Duffy, *The Stripping of the Altars: Traditional Religion in England 1400-1580*, New Haven–London, 2005 (1st ed. New Haven–London, 1992), p. 381.

2   Ibid., p. 386.

3   Ibid., p. 392.

4   Ibid., pp. 392–93.

5   Ibid., p. 462.

6   Ibid., p. 481.

7   Ibid., p. 586.

8   John Donne, *Poems*, edited by E. K. Chambers, 2 vols., London, 1896, I, pp. 202–3.

9   Julianne Sandberg, 'The Formation of Spiritual Identity: Visual Art, George Herbert, and The Temple', in *Sigma Tau Delta* (International English Honor Society), Alumni Epsilon Newsletter (Spring 2010). <https://sites.google.com/site/alumniepsilonnewsletter/home/the-formation-of-spiritual-identity-visual-art-george-herbert-and-the-temple>, accessed 12th June 2019.

10   Ibid.

11   Ibid.

12   Barbara Lewalski, *Protestant Poetics and the Seventeenth-Century Lyric*, Princeton (NJ), 1979.

13   See Tabitha Barber, 'Thornhill, Sir James (1675/6-1734)', in *Oxford Dictionary of National Biography*, Oxford, 2004, *ad vocem*.

14   Ibid.

15   Elements of the discussion of Henry Vaughan that follows are reproduced from, variously, Ben Quash, *Abiding: The Archbishop of Canterbury's Lent Book 2013*, London, 2012; 'Community, Imagination and the Bible', in *The Bible: Culture, Community, Society*, edited by Neil Messer and Angus Paddison, London, 2013, pp. 99–122; Ben Quash, *Found Theology: History, Imagination and the Holy Spirit*, London, 2013, pp. 146–62.

16   Geoffrey Hill, *Mercian Hymns*, London, 1971.

17   See my discussion of these themes in Ben Quash, 'Wonder-Voyaging: the Pneumatological Character of David Ford's Theology', in *The Vocation of Theology Today*, edited by Tom Greggs, Rachel Muers and Simeon Zahl, Eugene, OR, 2013.

18   Graham Pechey, 'Pointed Remarks: Scholasticism and the Gothic in the English Counter-Enlightenment', *Christianity and Literature*, 57/1 (2007), pp. 3–33.

19   Hans Urs von Balthasar, *Herrlichkeit. Eine theologische Ästhetik*, Einsiedeln, 3 vols., 1961–9, English trans. by Erasmo Leiva Merikakis, 7 vols., San Francisco, 1982–9, III, pp. 354–5.

20   Ibid., pp. 355–7.

21   Ibid., p. 354.

22   Susanna Avery-Quash, 'Collector Connoisseurs or Spiritual Aesthetes? The Role of Anglican Clergy in The Growth of Interest in Collecting and Displaying Early Italian Art (1830s–1880s)', in *Sacred Text – Sacred Space: Architectural, Spiritual and Literary Convergences in England and Wales*, edited by Joseph Sterrett and Peter Thomas, Leiden, 2011, pp. 269–95: 272.

The Painting as Biblical Metaphor

Interpreting Van Gogh through Paul Ricoeur

JÉRÔME COTTIN

Protestant spirituality has only one source, the Bible. Images and art are part of that spirituality only if they are biblical; that is if they position themselves as interpretations or actualizations of the biblical accounts.

In the contemporary era, however, that conviction no longer works, for, with some rare exceptions, art is no longer a biblical art. To be sure, 20th-century art is still marked by symbols inherited from the Bible and, more broadly, from Christianity (the cross; the image of the Crucified; the *Pietà*; the face of Jesus; Mary, the Child's mother).[1] But the Bible as an ensemble of inter-related accounts, the Bible as the framework of a history of salvation, hardly plays any role in contemporary art. And yet it is possible to find a 'biblical spirit' – and thus a Christian or Protestant spirit – in an art that is no longer such. That conviction was already affirmed in the mid-20th century by the German-American theologian Paul Tillich, who saw in Picasso's *Guernica*, a militant antifascist work, "a great Protestant painting".[2] We cannot, however, avoid feeling that Tillich exploited Picasso's painting improperly, projecting onto it religious convictions found neither in the work nor in its author (Picasso was an atheist and a militant Communist).

One way of responding to this objection is to more deeply examine the notion of metaphor as it was developed by the philosopher Paul Ricoeur, Tillich's successor at Boston University, and to relate it to two paintings by Vincent van Gogh which are also metaphoric in character. That is what the following pages seek to do.

Van Gogh and Ricoeur

The painter Vincent van Gogh (1853–90; fig. 1) and the philosopher Paul Ricoeur (1913–2005; fig. 2), are very far from each other. If I bring them together, it is because they were two Reformed Protestants in *diaspora*, although Van Gogh had abandoned his vocation as a minister to become the immense artist that we know, and Ricoeur – one of the great philosophers of our time – did not want to be called a 'Christian' philosopher, and still less a 'Protestant' one. The writings of both[3] abound with biblical citations, however, and these are omnipresent in Vincent van Gogh's correspondence with his brother Theo.

As far as Paul Ricoeur is concerned, he was also a specialist of textual biblical studies,[4] the comprehension of which field he modernized through his work on story poetics and narrative fiction.

1. Van Gogh, *Self-Portrait*,
Otterlo, Kröller-Müller Museum.

2. The philosopher Paul Ricoeur.

The two are thus world-class figures of art and thought, situated at the heart of Protestantism and yet both careful to distinguish themselves from it, that is to diverge from it.

Van Gogh and the Bible

I will not review Van Gogh's tormented biography, except to recall that he became a painter only because he failed the theology exam necessary to become a minister, and that for several months he exercised the ministry of preacher-evangelist at Petit-Wasmes, in a poor mining region of Belgium. We still possess some of the painter's sermons. Afterwards, spiritual questions continued to haunt our artist, but in a very personal manner, outside of any Church or religious community. We are nonetheless astonished at how little space the Bible and its stories occupy in his painting, where, in effect:

- Jesus is never represented. He is in a single painting, *Pietà* (Saint-Rémy, September 1889), but it is, to be exact, the dead Christ, within a subject that is not *stricto sensu*,

biblical, and it is a 'copy' of a work by Delacroix;
- Van Gogh moreover gave his own face to Christ. It is as if the painter had multiplied the mediating factors, in order to not directly represent Christ.
- He painted only two biblical accounts: the *Good Samaritan* (Saint-Rémy, May 1890) and the *Raising of Lazarus* (Saint-Rémy, May 1890).

Despite the almost complete absence of Bible stories and personages, however, his painting can be considered fundamentally biblical. Why? How? Because it expresses that idea which Paul Ricoeur would explore from the point of view of philosophy: "a work of art can be biblical without its subject being so". Better still. "It can be more biblical if it does not show the Bible, but evokes it metaphorically". In 'showing' a Bible story, art becomes illustration; in not showing the Bible story art becomes symbolization, which is much stronger. Symbolization (or metaphorization)[5] is the capacity of a word, of an image, of an object, to say more than it shows, opening an infinite range of possible meanings, beyond the thing's merely literal sense.

The reader will say: 'Yes, of course, but the symbolic dimension of a work is insufficient to deliver a biblical message'. Symbolization, however, is the very stuff of art, that is why we should specify that in Van Gogh these metaphors and symbols are sustained by a biblical atmosphere. If his paintings are not directly biblical, they are indirectly so. I will give three hints:

- Van Gogh was a great admirer of the Bible painter *par excellence*, his compatriot Rembrandt. About the Amsterdam master, Van Gogh wrote to his brother Theo: "I have rented a little room at Montmartre, which you will enjoy ... I am going to tell you what prints I put on the wall: Rembrandt, *The Reading of the Bible*: evening, a candle on the table where a young mother, seated near her child's cradle, reads the Bible; a seated old woman listens, there is something to think about".[6] In a letter of July 1880, he went so far as to say: "There is something of Rembrandt in the Gospel and of the Gospel in Rembrandt".

- There is an 'eschatology' in Van Gogh's thought, the expectation of a better world, the anticipation of a world that is 'other'; what Christians call the Kingdom. His is not an art with its roots in the past, like Historicism; nor is it an art of the present alone, like Expressionism. He imagines a world that is other, that is different, more beautiful and, for that reason, more true. He begins with a utopian idea so as to reach the present. His is 'messianic' art, prophetic art.

- Behind Van Gogh's sunflowers, his Provençal landscapes, his depiction of a pair of old shoes, other meanings are hidden, often religious, sometimes even biblical. Van Gogh himself said so moreover. In a letter of December 26, 1878, to his brother Theo, he described a snow-covered landscape in which what stood out were "the bramble-covered paths and twisted old oak trees showing their roots"; and added: "with the snow of these last days, all of that has the effect of writing on white paper, like the pages of the Gospel".

Van Gogh's *Sower with Setting Sun*
I would like to propose a double reading of Van Gogh's work: pictorial (or literal) and biblical

3. Vincent van Gogh, *Sower with Setting Sun*, Otterlo, Kröller-Müller Museum.

(or symbolic/metaphoric), beginning with the interpretation of a single painting, *Sower with Setting Sun* (Arles, June 1888; fig. 3). I will limit myself to a few general observations:[7]
- The work is unique but at the same time multiple, since Van Gogh made numerous versions of this theme.
- He did it three times, making two 'twin' versions of the theme (allusions to the first Vincent van Gogh, who died a year before our painter's birth, to the very day?).
- Van Gogh borrowed the sower's position from a painting by an artist he admired, Jean-François Millet (the *Sower*, 1850; fig. 4). Millet is known for having created a 'spiritual climate' in his landscapes, in the spirit of his famous picture the *Angelus*.
- In this painting Van Gogh inverts the color code: the sky is yellow (the color of ripe wheat) whereas the earth is made of blue and white. Thus sky and earth are confused, the earth reflecting the sky, which in turn indicates the earth.

These three motifs, even while uniquely agrarian – tied to the harvest cycle and field-work – are also biblical:
- The sower alludes to Jesus's parables on this subject (Mk 4:1–9, 14–20, 30–2).

4. Vincent van Gogh, *Sower* (after Millet), Otterlo Kröller-Müller Museum.

- The sun occurs in the New Testament in Mt 17:2; Rv 1:16, 10:1, as well as in the Fathers of the Church, in Christian art and even in Calvinism;[8] it often refers to the Risen Christ.
- The path: in the painting, the furrow made by a plough gets deeper and becomes a path which begins in the lower part of the image and moves to the upper part—from earth toward heaven. It symbolizes the path of faith or even Christ himself, in as much as he is the 'way' (Jn 14:6, "I am the way, the truth and the life").

But what justifies a symbolic and biblical reading of this painting or of other non-biblical works produced by modern art? How is such a reading coherent with the works themselves? Is it not simply the over-interpretation of a theologian-viewer? Beyond its first, literal, meaning, why *should* such paintings – how *can* such paintings – be open to a second, religious, sense?

The metaphor in Paul Ricoeur
The notion of metaphor in Paul Ricoeur can help us understand that these second meanings (metaphoric, poetic, and finally religious) are already present in the works themselves, deeply inscribed in the works of our culture whether derived from the Bible or from Rembrandt or from numerous other artists (not all however). Every work is at once interpretive and to be interpreted.[9] Every work helps us understand ourselves as *other* than ourselves, and to understand the other/Other as *ourselves.*[10]

Ricoeur, with his notion of metaphor, helps us to interpret an artwork not in a purely scientific or historical way, or – conversely – in a purely subjective one, but by bringing to light a plurality of meanings, that is to say of "interpretational conflicts".[11] And among these interpretations, religious or Christian ones can have all the space they need, without emptying other interpretations of meaning or substituting themselves for them.

Ricoeur, the inventor of modern hermeneutics, emphasizes the role of the interpretive subject. I interpret (a text, a picture) with all that I am. But to understand what I am, I must make a detour through texts and other works of culture. "When one understands these, one understands one's self in the presence of the text. One must not impose upon the text one's own finite capacity to understand, but rather receive from the text a larger self".[12] And again:

> Contrary to the Cogito tradition, and the subject's pretension to know himself through immediate intuition, it is necessary to say that we do not know ourselves except by the great detour through the signs of humanity deposited in works of culture.[13]

According to Ricoeur, Bible stories and symbols, like all works of culture, help us to understand what we are. They interpret us. But they must themselves be interpreted: Biblical faith cannot be separated from the movement of interpretation which lifts it to language. "The 'ultimate concern' would remain mute if it did not receive the power of speech of a continually re-begun interpretation of the signs and symbols which have educated and formed that concern in the course of centuries".[14] Nothing escapes this needful work of interpretation, neither the Bible, nor works of art.

Although limited to written language, Paul Ricoeur's hermeneutics go well beyond texts alone, being adaptable to every kind of message (verbal, visual, auditory): Jean Caune, a philosopher specialized in communication sciences, underlines that

> the fecundity of this proposition [of Paul Ricoeur] is due to its extension: it is valid for artworks which do not proceed from articulated language, and is equally valid for human action and precisely for cultural objects.[15]

Of all Ricoeur's hermeneutical thought, I will focus on the notion of metaphor, equally applicable to literary texts and to works of art; it permits us to get beyond the first level of literal meaning and gives access to a second level, without considering that movement an over-interpretation or a subjectivizing one.

What is metaphor for Paul Ricoeur?

The philosopher underlines the importance of metaphor in the process of constituting sense. Following Aristotle, he defines it as "the transferral to one thing of a name which designates another ... in the manner of an analogical relationship".[16] He thus puts poetics above rhetoric, overall unity (the image, the *Gestalt*) above singular unity (the word, the letter). His definition of metaphor approaches that of the symbol, which gathers together two disjointed parts: "The metaphor holds together, in a simple meaning, two different missing parts from contexts which differ from that meaning".[17] What is more, the metaphor includes a moment that is non-verbal, sensitive, visual: "If metaphor consists of speaking of one thing in the terminology of another, does it not also consist of perceiving, thinking or feeling one thing in the terms of another?".[18]

Metaphor thus has a double function, signifying but also referential. It has a capacity for *re-description*.[19] It does not limit itself to speech but points toward extra-linguistic realities: "In comprehending the sense, we bring ourselves to the reference".[20] Metaphor does not confine itself to suspending natural reality, but opens meaning on the side of imagination;[21] it is what Ricoeur, together with American phenomenology, calls *picture thinking*, a "pictorial power of language".[22] And the philosopher concludes with the complementarity of the image and meaning: "The non-verbal and the verbal are thus closely united at the heart of language's image-making function".[23] Beginning with written or verbal language, Ricoeur finally arrives, thanks to metaphor, at the artwork: "the artwork can have an effect comparable to that of the metaphor, integrating stacked levels of sense, retained and contained together".[24] Thus the artwork, whether literary, biblical or visual, has the capacity to restructure the world of the reader, the listener, the viewer. It jostles his horizon, challenges his expectations, remodels his moods, reworking them from within. Ricoeur goes on to say:

> Is that work not absolutely parallel in language to what is done outside of language, in the arts that cannot be transcribed in language, such

as music essentially but also, different degrees, in painting and sculpture? The possibility to 'speak on' without doubt belongs to the signifying character attached to both verbal and non-verbal signs, and to their capacity to mutually interpret each other.[25]

Amplifying:
when art and the religious meet

Meditation on a painting by Van Gogh and some powerful ideas of Paul Ricoeur on the double function of metaphor, semantic and aesthetic,[26] allow us to propose some elements of synthesis, in the hope of better understanding the spirituality of contemporary art. Today's art is not biblical or even Christian, but remains, from a metaphorical point of view, profoundly 'religious': it continues to bind the human to God and human beings to each other, following a pattern very close to biblical thought. That art can thus *be* – or once again *become* – biblical, even when its theme is not so. We thus return to Paul Tillich's intuition, but in a way that is more precise, honed, actualized.

Again with Paul Ricoeur's help, I would propose two elements of encounter between art and the religious:

Aesthetics and the religious retrieve each other. "Between the aesthetic and the religious there is an area of trespassing",[27] Ricoeur said in a text on aesthetic experience. We must distinguish these two kinds of language, which are not of the same order and do not have the same aims: liturgy is not art and a pretty picture is not a sermon. But the two – the aesthetic experience and the religious one – have an effect of attraction, invite us to go beyond, aim at silencing our "I" to discover the Other: "The good, like the beautiful, is of the order of a *Nachfolge*", Ricoeur says.[28] The German word *Nachfolge*, popularized by the book of that name by Dietrich Bonhoeffer,[29] is a fundamentally technical biblical term evoking the condition of the disciple, called to leave everything to follow the Master. In defining the work of art according to a 'logic of excess', Ricoeur makes of aesthetic experience something close to religious experience:[30] "In respect to the viewer or reader, the artwork carries out a labor of re-figuration which overturns his

expectations and horizon".[31] When he affirms that "the work is like a fire trail coming of itself, that reaches me and then, beyond me, reaches the universality of men",[32] Ricoeur employs the very words that could define religious, even mystical, experience. Art is not a simple amusement, an imitation, a reproduction. It creates a new world and makes us love that world. Art presents itself as outdistancing language, even if it needs language to transmit meaning. On all these counts, the same is true for faith.

This encounter between the vocation of art and the vocation of faith allows us to avoid a double reef: first, that of considering nothing in 20th- and 21st-century art any longer religious (or Christian, or biblical). In that view, art would have made its definitive exit from Christianity; it would be self-sufficient, "an endless objective" (Kant). And second, the opposite reading, according to which everything in art is religious (or Christian, or biblical), because art by its nature is religious. In that way one evolves from religion *through* art to the religion *of* art, an idea which had been defended by the 19th-century German romantics (Goethe). Art is the religion of modern times, which has taken the place of Christianity. Museums are the temples and churches of these modern times, artists are the priests or prophets, art-lovers the believers.

Paul Ricoeur's thought on the metaphor allows us to break free of this false alternative, since, for him, the metaphor is inseparable from the object itself that is read or looked at, and inseparable too from the human subject who reads or looks. It can be applied to the verbal as to the visual, to the poetic as to the aesthetic, to the semantic and to the symbolic.

Example: *Still Life with Bible* by Van Gogh

Nourished by this 'amplifying hermeneutic', as Paul Ricoeur's thought has been called, I want to look again at a painting by Van Gogh, his *Still Life with Bible*, (Nuenen, October 1885; fig. 5). I want to show that a metaphoric reading of the painting can be just as right as, or even preferable to, a literal reading.

The painting represents a large, open Bible. But is it meant to be a hymn to the Bible? A pictorial expression of Protestant faith in the *Sola scriptura*? Nothing is less sure. At the first level, that of literal reading, it could, on the contrary, express Van Gogh's biblical doubts and his distance from his minister father, whose Bible we see here. His father had died a few months earlier, and all that remains is this old Bible, open but without a reader: next to it there is a candle, but it is extinguished. What is more, in front of the Bible is another book, a work by Émile Zola, *The Joy of Living*. We know that Zola was an atheist, and that Van Gogh had argued with his father precisely because of Zola, whom the elderly minister did not like, but whom Vincent greatly appreciated. In the painting we therefore have a kind of revenge of the son on his father, and of profane, contemporary literature on the Book of Books. In this first (literal, not metaphorical) interpretation of the painting, for Van Gogh it was not a question of vaunting the Bible's merits but,

on the contrary, of detaching himself from a Bible that had belonged to his father.

We could call this first reading a non-believer's interpretation, coherent with Van Gogh's state of mind at the moment when he painted the picture: his faith in the Bible as God's word had become shaky, if, indeed, it had not been snuffed out.

But that first reading can be followed by a second, not literalist but metaphoric, in which we will find a faith-based, even biblical, interpretation. These two opposed views – as they were both in 19th-century social history and in Van Gogh's relationship with his father – are here brought close to each other, here come together again. Zola's novel is in front of the Bible, but it is small in size and closed, whereas the Bible is large and open. Who could fail to see that, behind these two books are two personages who find each other again, and, behind the two personages, two biblical figures?

5. Vincent van Gogh, *Still life with Bible*, Amsterdam, Van Gogh Museum.

It could indeed be a metaphor of the Prodigal Son account (Lk 15:11–32): the novel in front of the Bible would signify the prodigal returned to his father, and the open Bible the open arms of the Father of Mercy. Here is how an interpreter of Van Gogh articulates this second reading:[33]

> We get the idea that Van Gogh has, in a veiled way, painted a *Return of the Prodigal Son*. It is this torn and tattered book that bears the world's image and form. The yellow, modern book is at the feet of the Book of Light, the Eternal Book – at its knees. But it is too late for the son to throw himself into his father's arms: the father is no more, the candle is snuffed out. What remains is the Book, large, open: its clarity remains, so that hearts can speak to each other in God.

In a letter to his sister Wilhelmina, moreover, the Flemish painter wrote:[34]

> The work of the French naturalists, Zola, Flaubert ... is magnificent, and it is very hard to say if we belong to our own time or if we know our own time at all ... Let the Bible be enough for us. For the moment, I believe that Jesus himself would say to those who remain melancholy and passive: 'That is not the way. Get up! Why are you looking for the living among the dead?'

We started with the painter Van Gogh, and to better interpret him we made a detour into an aspect of the thought of the philosopher Paul Ricoeur. Then we came back to Van Gogh. We have established a sort of 'circle' (people speak of the hermeneutical circle). At the circle's center there are, in a way sometimes

6. Logo of the Waldensian Cultural Center in Torre Pellice.

hidden, sometimes evident, biblical texts and above all the One to whom the texts refer: the God of Jesus Christ. This biblical God condemns and pardons, calls and saves, hides and reveals himself. He speaks directly in the Scriptures, and indirectly (or metaphorically) in the works of art produced by culture, including contemporary culture.

I conclude with a brief indication which brings us back to Italian Protestantism, strongly colored by the 800-year long history of the Waldensians, disciples of Peter Waldo who in the 16th century joined the Geneva Reformation.[35] Is it pure chance that the logo of the Waldensian Cultural Center at Torre Pellice (fig. 6) reuses the very elements of Van Gogh's painting? We see the sower, the wheat field and the sun (either setting or rising), and the inscription in French: SON ART EN DIEU (His art in God). This logo is one of the very rare authorized images of a strictly Calvinist Protestantism... and this image is without doubt inspired by the Van Gogh painting we have studied in these pages. ■

1 See Jérôme Cottin, *La mystique de l'art. Art et christianisme, de 1900 à nos jours*, Paris, 2007.

2 Paul Tillich, *Theology of Culture*, New York, 1959, p. 68.

3 Van Gogh did not only paint, he also wrote, essentially letters.

4 Paul Ricoeur, *L'herméneutique biblique*, texts reunited by François-Xavier Amherdt, Paris, 2001.

5 In the present context I will consider these two words as more or less equivalent.

6 Letter of Van Gogh of July 6, 1875.

7 For a more complete study of this painting, see Jérôme Cottin, *Quand l'art dit la résurrection. Huit œuvres du VIe au XXIe siècles*, Geneva, 2017, esp. pp. 95–113 (the chapter 'Van Gogh: Le semeur au soleil couchant').

8 The sun is the emblem of Calvinism and of the city of Geneva.

9 See Paul Ricoeur, *La métaphore vive*, Paris, 1975.

10 Paul Ricoeur, *Soi-même comme un autre*, Paris, 1990.

11 Paul Ricoeur, *Le conflit des interprétations. Essai d'herméneutique*, Paris, 1969.

12 Paul Ricoeur, *Du texte à l'action. Essai d'herméneutique II*, Paris, 1986, pp. 116–17.

13 Ibid.

14 Ibid., p. 131.

15 Jean Caune, *Culture et communication. Convergences théoriques et lieux de médiation*, Grenoble, 1995, p. 58.

16 Ricoeur 1975, op. cit., p. 19.

17 Ibid., p. 105. On Paul Ricoeur's interpretation of the symbol, see 'Herméneutique des symboles et réflexion philosophique', in Ricoeur 1969, op. cit., pp. 283–330; on his explanation of the famous phrase "the symbol gives us something to think about", see Ricoeur 1969, op. cit., p. 284. See also his article: Paul Ricoeur, 'Parole et symbole', *Revue des Sciences Religieuses*, 49/1–2 (1975), pp. 142–61.

18 Ricoeur 1975, op. cit., p. 109.

19 Ibid., p. 114 (the word is underlined by the author). Ricoeur cites and comments thoughts open to aesthetics, like those of Mikel Dufrenne, *Phénoménologie de l'expérience esthétique*, Paris, 1953; Monroe Beardsley, *Aesthetics. Problems in the Philosophy of Criticism*, Cambridge, MA, 1981 (1st Edition New York, 1958); Gilles-Gaston Granger, *Essai d'une philosophie du style*, Paris, 1968; Nelson Goodman, *Language of Art. An Approach to a Theory of Symbols*, London, 1969.

20 Ricoeur 1975, op. cit., p. 119.

21 Ibid., p. 267.

22 Ibid., p. 269.

23 Ibid., p. 270.

24 See also Paul Ricoeur, *La critique et la conviction. Entretien avec François Azouvi et Marc de Launay*, Paris, 1995, p. 259.

25 Jean-Marie Brohm, Magali Uhl, *Arts, langage et herméneutique esthétique. Entretien avec Paul Ricoeur*, second part, in <www.philagora.net/philo-fac/ricoeur1.htm>, accessed 21 June 2019.

26 Jérôme Cottin, 'Métaphore et esthétique dans la pensée de Paul Ricoeur', in *La réception de Paul Ricoeur dans le champs de la théologie*, edited by Daniel Frey, Christian Grappe, Karsten Lehmkühler, Fritz Lienhard, Münster, 2013, pp. 105–14.

27 Ricoeur 1995, op. cit., p. 276.

28 Ibid., p. 275.

29 Dietrich Bonhoeffer, *Nachfolge*, Gütersloh, 2002 (3rd ed.; 1st ed. Munich, 1937).

30 In theology: Pierre Gisel, *L'excès du croire. Expérience du monde et acces à soi*, Paris, 1990.

31 Ricoeur 1995, op. cit., p. 263.

32 Ibid., p. 270.

33 Claude-Henri Rocquet, *Vincent van Gogh jusqu'au dernier soleil*, Mame, 2000, p. 52.

34 Quoted ibid., pp. 51–2.

35 See Giorgio Tourn, *I valdesi. La singolare vicenda di un popolo-chiesa: 1170-2008*, Turin, 2008 (4th ed.; 1st ed. Turin, 1977).

Romano Guardini and Van Gogh

YVONNE DOHNA SCHLOBITTEN

Guardini, the *Weltanschauung*, light

With his gaze turned to Van Gogh's aesthetics, Romano Guardini describes "the meeting between the eye and the light in which everything is united".[1] In the context of the present collection of essays on art and theology in ecumenical perspective I would like to consider Guardini's 'everything' as including the Christian churches and ask whether images possess a 'light' capable of 'uniting'.

Guardini himself did not deal directly or in depth with ecumenism. And yet, his idea of Catholic *Weltanschauung* can make a significant contribution to this theme, in view of a renewed theological anthropology.

According to Guardini, no believer can mature a Catholic vision by withdrawing from the world. Abstract internalizations of the world cannot favor spiritual progress, for "to believe in truth also means to dare making a new beginning. Beginnings however cannot be only attempted, they must be implemented".[2] For Guardini, every Catholic vision which merely internalizes an objective sense of the world produces that separation from the world which risks fundamentalism, reducing Catholics to "types" beside other types, and provoking their sectarian marginalization – a risk that,

as everyone knows, was particularly feared by Joseph Ratzinger.[3]

We must therefore dare to make a new beginning and implement what we dare. That is what artists do when they create images: they use forms to implement a new beginning.

The question of the image was immediately a reason for division within the Church. In the early centuries of Christianity each of the geographical areas in which Christian communities arose – and with them the first figurative expressions of Christian art – adopted specific iconographic models and different styles. The different ways of expressing *kerygma* in art assumed a primary role in the early Christian communities, because these interpretative modalities were tied to debated theological issues and their symbolic mediation. If this had not been so – if, as today, artistic expressions had been unrelated to religious beliefs – the beliefs would have seemed abstract, pure theological formulas. Art historians and theologians should never underestimate the role of artistic images, relegating them to simple exteriority or considering them mere illustrations. In his Apostolic Letter *Duodecimum Saeculum* John Paul II affirmed that "the showing of the painted icon allows those who contemplate it to accede to the mystery of salvation through the sense of sight – to approach the mysteries of salvation through sight"[4], and these words seem a clear invitation to seek, in exploring the theme of the image, a new unity among Christians. Where the iconoclast controversy of the end of the first millennium resulted in a cultural division between Eastern and Western Christians[5] that was expressed in different concepts and styles of sacred art, today we may be able to recover an ecumenical sense of art if we learn to distinguish the scope of artistic creation from that of criticism. And Romano Guardini can help.

1. Vincent van Gogh, *Van Gogh's Chair*, London, National Gallery.

Guardini and Van Gogh

In his famous discourse on Van Gogh's image of a chair (fig. 1),[6] Guardini deepened this concept of unity by stating: "The chair is a totality".[7] For him Van Gogh's encounter with the chair was the result of a process in which the chair became

the center around which everything revolves, and that is how the chair is formed: its component parts are arranged around a center in its own constitution. The image appears as a unit"[8] because "it has to do with unity of form.[9]

Guardini focused his anthropology on the idea of *forma*, which, with the exception of man, can only be implemented by looking directly at the image not as a "thing" but as the expression of a ritual action. For him, art and liturgy are in fact apparently related: "sisters" because both are "daughters" of revelation. The two activities – the gaze turned to artistic creation and ritual action –, are complementary, because what the liturgy *mysteriously* implements in the sacraments, art makes *mystically* perennial in perception.[10]

This process of image-*formation* has different characteristics. As Guardini later specified, "I may never behold everything because I, myself, am also just a fragment of everything".[11] Every object we encounter is thus seen only in a "fragment-to-fragment" relationship. But in the process of artistic formation (*künstlerische Formung*) something special happens: every

aspect that emerges from the object, and from the observer when he perceives the part that emerges, creates a sort of power.[12] Around this power, the unity of existence becomes present (*gegenwärtig*) and the whole of the object – the whole of nature, of man and of history – lives in one: "in the chair vibrates the music (the tone) of the universe".[13] In every work of art the "world" is therefore born,[14] a world which manifests itself to our gaze and our perception.

According to Guardini, the artist does not provide an encyclopedia of existence. The artist shows the way in which individual events are transformed into a process of formation. As exemplified by Guardini:

Beauty is born from within. It is the splendor of truth, according to Medieval philosophy. It is not an intellectual element, but the sign of a fullness of internal maturity, something splendid that manifests itself when a thing becomes that which it truly must be, according to its true essence.[15]

Everything happens through the 'how' of the work of art, not the 'what'.[16] This approach

2. Vincent van Gogh, *View of Saintes-Maries-de-la-Mer*, Winterthur, Sammlung Oskar Reinhart «Am Römerholz».

derives from phenomenological thought and especially from Heidegger, and aims at eliminating all forms of dogmatism. Guardini and Heidegger: the theme common to these two exponents of Central European culture is that of artistic perception and *light*. For both of them 'Light as logos' and 'the metaphysics of light' are original statements in artistic creation.

The ritual and terrifying dimension of light also appears in Guardini's critical exegesis of a drawing by Van Gogh, depicting a city on the top of a hill (fig. 2).[17]

"This was the sun, which is a terrifying secret, 'Glory bringing death'. There is a drawing by Vincent van Gogh with a city on the hill … all filled with a monstrous sun. In this moment I understood, like man, in the terror and joy of his heart, he looks and adores in the sun the supernatural".[18]

In his description of the drawing, Guardini refers to Rudolph Otto and speaks of the "Glory that brings death" (*tötende Herrlichkeit*) and of an experience of attack on the heart of the numinous: "What Aristotle says about drama is valid for every work of art, and this shows the ethical meaning of art".[19]

Paul VI and the cry of light

A third authority on these questions is the thoughtful 20th-century pope, Paul VI. In an interview with the philosopher Jean Guitton, Paul VI states:

The thing that struck me from the beginning in the papal chapel was the play of light. The light was at home there, glowing. However, there was no visible light source, only a sail of glass windows that spans the sky. And the light feels at home, it glows. At the same time there is no visible light source, only a veil of light windows creating a sky.[20]

A little further on, Paul VI offers a description of light in relation to beauty:

Beauty is a phosphorescent aura, full of splendor more than light, it is an inner splendor of something, far from any form, far from content, far from the work of art itself; it is more interior than interiority. Beauty has a relationship with man: it is the interiority of man …, the happiest synthesis. Beauty is more than light.[21]

This theme returns in Paul VI's discourse on a *cappella anonima*: "A chapel is an altar in which all lines and lights come together".[22] Citing Cocteau, the pope continues: "Art is a linear sigh (from breath and sigh), the artist must find this imperceptible line – this '*spiaggiamento*' (beaching) as Leonardo calls it – and must be willing to give up everything that disturbs his dialogue with the invisible".[23]

He goes on to write: "Beauty arises from the artist's effort, as he strives to take away things that distance us from God".[24] And later says:

In an empty space God and things can reveal themselves. Space is so filled with Presence! Nothing is more difficult and more precious than the poverty of emptiness, of pure space. Only pure space is more difficult and more precious than the poverty of emptiness. Nothing is more difficult and more precious than the poverty of emptiness, which is pure space. Resurrection does not mean a return to a mortal adventure, but an explosion of being in its new existential form going beyond the forbidden threshold, freedom. The dogma is different because it is based on the experience of man, and so has a testimony of the evidence of light and intimacy.[25]

Paul VI also speaks of the 'cry of light': "The light pierces and penetrates and must always die in a different agony".[26] In that same interview, he cites the Scriptural phrase *et sabbatum illucebat*: the "Sabath dawned" but the verb means "fills with light". So too the chapel of which the pope spoke with Guitton: "Like the last *sabbatum* of the resurrection, it is illuminated: a temple dedicated to light, or – to put it better – to the intimate being of light – *lux intima* – a light of the spirit, a unity that becomes wisdom. Wisdom means unity – with the whole".[27]

Paul VI speaks of a "mystic-religious pedagogy" and of the new "feeling" of Christian art, learned by sentiment as well as knowledge.[28] For him aesthetic experience has two paradigmatic aspects: it is at once a condition and a preparatory pedagogical stage of the experience of faith. Experience of faith, in fact, makes man capable of "proving" in his "feeling" the sentiments of the Christian message, received and lived in the sacraments and in the liturgy. For Paul VI, art, like the liturgy, plays a mediating role between the world of the spirit and the human world.

These reflections are close to Guardini's conviction of an affinity between art and the liturgy, which are "sisters" because they are both "daughters" of revelation. For Paul VI as for Romano Guardini, what the liturgy *mysteriously* implements in the sacraments is *mystically* made perennial in the perception of artistic creation.

Light as a space of truth

Guardini's *tötende Herrlichkeit* (killing glory) also has nothing to do with an education of thought. Instead, it is a feeling of power, "rather of power to initiate again and of the will to do so in the correct way".[29] For Guardini, truth is a space in which the observer enters and from which he/she engages in tension with reality.[30]

His text on the drawing depicting the city on a hill makes it clear that the miraculous thing is not the world, but the light which forms the world and brings it into the visible and offers it its *Gestalt*.[31] Light itself becomes an inner image (*Inbild*) of creative being: an epiphany of God. Light makes objects more than they are because they receive pure transparency in Him, and because in the last *Verdichtung* (materialization) the transformation of matter into light and the transfiguration of the profane (*Irdisches*) take place.[32]

Conclusion

Guardini, as mentioned at the beginning of this article, speaks of the "meeting between the eye and light".[33] This meeting is deeply personal and historical, and thus reflects the dimension of the *Weltanschauung*.

Art has the ability to unite the individual person and the world. Person and world are two poles that are linked, in such a way that one depends on the other, opens to the other and is in the other, revealing itself in space and time received; an encounter of the eye and light that happens in the Incarnation.[34] At that moment, the Word began to speak, leading us toward revelation (*Erscheinungsmoment*).

Guardini exalts the concept of *organicity*, treating the educational idea of *formation*, understood as "putting into shape". *Formation* in Guardini is not the act of falling back into a neutral, abstractly complex vision, but of placing the question of the limit in its positive aspect:

> The individual can realize in himself the various typical possibilities offered by form and act, always only up to a certain point. If form expands into universality, it loses intimate tension, clarity and strength; the essential structure melts.[35] Precisely in this process of shaping form there is a universality, a unity – a "new knowledge"[36]

which is able to coexist with its own opposites, overcoming sectarian and fundamentalist prejudices.

The religiosity of art does not derive from any particular religious content enclosed in the work, but rather refers to the religious nature inherent in the structure of the work of art itself, and in its "pointing toward the future" by implementing itself. For Guardini, a work of art contains within itself a formation process that must be contemplated! The greatness of Guardini is evident in his focus on the intimate gaze which man turns on his own self and on the world (*Anschauung/Weltanschauung*). This *Anschauung* of the world, the gesture of an intimate gaze, embraces contradictions within itself, overcoming the confessional perspective.

The philosopher's perspective must be understood in this sense. We can thus speak of the ecumene in art when we are in the *Anschauung* of the *forma* by means of the virtue that belongs to the eye, to the power of the spirit, and to the vivacity of the heart.[37]

What has just been described is a task that must be transmitted and taught because it accompanies our existence. Guardini writes: "The work of art is a promise".[38] This means, for Guardini, that it becomes one with the man who experiences it, and in this way, transforms him. Guardini's method of exercise in the space of imagination has become the place of encounter with the work of art in which it is possible for man to make a *discernment* and enter into a relationship with the world, with oneself and with God. ■

This article is dedicated to Hanna Barbara Gerl-Falkovitz. I extend my gratitude to her for having aroused in the writer a great interest in the work of Romano Guardini and for having drawn my attention to the designed of the city on the hill of Van Gogh, on which I refer further on. I therefore owe her one of the central themes of this contribution.

1   Hanna Barbara Gerl-Falkovitz, 'Auge und Licht. Annäherung an Romano Guardinis Wahrnehmung von Welt', *Trigon. Kunst, Wissenschaft und Glaube im Dialog. Taschenbuch*, 9 (2011), pp. 27–36: 34.

2   Enrico Garlaschelli, in a conference in Taiwan on 'Christian Universalism in the Test of History'.

3   Joseph Ratzinger, *Einführung in das Christentum. Vorlesungen über das Apostolische Glaubensbekenntnis*, Munich, 1968.

4   John Paul II, Apostolic Letter *Duodecimum Saeculum* of the Supreme Pontiff John Paul II to the Episcopate of the Catholic Church on the occasion of the 120th Anniversary of the Second Council of Nicaea, December 4, 1987, IV, 10.

5   See Georg Ostrogorsky, *Geschichte des byzantinischen Staates*, Munich, 1963 (1st ed. Munich, 1940), pp. 142–3.

6   *Vincent van Gogh. Der gelbe Stuhl mit Pfeife*, Göttingen, 1975. See also Bernd Wengler, *Vincent van Gogh in Arles: Eine psychoanalytische Künstler- und Werkinterpretation*, Kassel, 2013 and Marion Lauschke, Johanna Schiffler, Franz Engel, *Ikonische Formprozesse: Zur Philosophie des Unbestimmten in Bildern*, Berlin–Boston, 2018.

7   Romano Guardini, *Über das Wesen des Kunstwerkes*, Tübingen, 1948, new ed. Mainz, 2005, p. 67: "ein Ganzes".

8   Ibid., p. 23.

9   Ibid., p. 17.

10   Paul VI, *Allocuzione Armonia tra l'arte Sacra e l'attività liturgica*, 4 January 1967, P. Cappelletti, 'La sensibilité artistique de Paul VI', in *Paul VI et l'art*, proceedings of the colloquium (Paris, 27 January 1988), Brescia, 1989, 8–16: 13.

11   Guardini 1948, ed. 2005, op. cit., p. 18.

12 Ibid., p. 19.

13 Ibid., p. 20.

14 Ibid., p. 18.

15 Romano Guardini, 'L'essenzialità dell'opera d'arte sacra', in *Orientamenti dell'arte sacra dopo il Vaticano II*, edited by Giovanni Fallani, Bergamo, 1969, pp. 111–17: 115.

16 Guardini 1948, ed. 2005, op. cit., p. 17.

17 Vincent Willem van Gogh, *View of Saintes-Maries-de-la-Mer*, 1888, 43,5 × 60 cm, Winterthur, Museum Stiftung Oskar Reinhart.

18 "Killing glory: world in the light." Guardini describes and reflects on a light experience in the Fex Valley in the Engadine: the morning was immeasurable, the power of glory was high in the world. How did I realize that beauty burst forth like army columns! Out of the dark shining figures of the mountains, out of every thing that stood in the wonder of that light, it struck my heart, and called up that laughter, and from that depth in which soul and blood are connected. The sun was high, and – but there is no word for it in the German language, because this sun does not exist in Germany – sfolgorava, with this word the Italian says: the sun went down in lightning; it was a burst of long, searing bursts of lightning. That was the sun, which is a frightening secret, killing glory. There is a drawing by Vincent van Gogh, on a hill there is a city, from there to the observer's eye plowed up fields, and the sky above it full of a gigantic glittering sun. Then I understood how man, in the terror and jubilation of his heart, looks and adores unearthly things in this sun". (Romano Guardini, *In Spiegel und Gleichnis: Bilder und Gedanken*, Mainz, 1932, p. 159).

19 Guardini 1948, ed. 2005, op. cit., p. 22.

20 Jean Guitton, *Dialog mit Paul VI*, Munich, 1978, p. 199.

21 Paul VI: "Who does not know the Sublime, the Secret of God, the unexplainable, can not be a true artist" (Ibid., p. 34).

22 Ibid., p. 199.

23 Ibid., p. 89.

24 Ibid., p. 78.

25 Ibid., p. 67.

26 Ibid., p. 66.

27 John XXIII already speaks of the suffering of light: the doctrine of the Popes of the 20th century has turned a very particular attention to artistic perception. The artist and his experience become the place in which the encounter with the divine takes place autonomously. In this direction, John XXIII carried out with his "artist" Manzù a theology of suffering in art. The language of suffering, which the artist lives in his existential path and which translates into the work of art, becomes, as in the case of the Crucifixion, 1947 locus theologicus; in the surface that reveals the face of Christ, His body dissolves in the material of the artifact and appears completely different from the physicality of the other figures of the low-relief. The fragility of the body, which alludes to the fragility of life that reveals itself between matter and light and "manages to render in just a few millimeters of thickness a vibrant representation of an earthly scene or of an allegorical mystique". The artist can thus afford to approach his mystery to the Resurrection with his art. The drama of suffering, expressed by the face and body of Christ, makes clear the idea that, on the one hand, man is part of the reality created by God and, on the other, he is also the culmination of the work of creation. Moreover, and this seems to us a fundamental aspect, the same gesture of artistic creation imposes itself as the privileged place, in which the drama of the human vocation and of the human being is expressed, called as creature to self-realization and to discover one's own freedom. The creative act does not imprison the world in its natural reality. Likewise the molded matter (the "imprisoned image") by the artist is not abandoned to chance, but is marked by the grace of God and is entrusted to the freedom of the creature. The artist's work brings to the fore the traces of the divine plan.

28 See Paul VI, *Allocuzione Armonia tra l'Arte Sacra e l'attività liturgica*, 4 January 1967.

i 29 Guardini 1948, ed. 2005, op. cit., p. 23.

30 Ibid., op. cit., p. 22.

31 Gerl-Falkovitz 2011, op. cit., p. 33.

32 Ibid.

33 Guardini 1948, ed. 2005, op. cit., p. 23.

34 Ibid., p. 34.

35 Ibid.

36 Ibid., p. 35.

37 Ibid., p. 27.

38 Ibid., p. 35.

Contemporary Architecture in the Service of Monastic Prayer

Several European Examples

JÉRÔME COTTIN

I am often invited to speak at conferences in monasteries and religious communities throughout Europe, and on these occasions have discovered that some of them, while remaining faithful to the forms and traditions of the past (liturgy, monastic rule) are nonetheless very innovative when it comes to contemporary art and architecture.

One significant feature of this surprising mixture of tradition and modernity (or even post-modernity) is without doubt the intention to show that monasticism is not opposed to the modern world. On the contrary, it allows us to better understand the world, even as it emphasizes its limits. Another significant feature is the desire to go beyond a solely patrimonial vision of Christianity; monks are not necessarily linked to the magnificent convents and monasteries dating to the Middle Ages, the Renaissance or the Baroque period that are scattered all over Europe, which, though they be artistic gems, are often remote from present-day life. Monks can also live in modern buildings. Our problem in Europe is quite the opposite of the one encountered in the US, for we have too many historic buildings, too many old churches, too much of… the Middle Ages!

A third intention in embracing contemporary art is to show that modern aesthetic forms, being clean, sober and aniconic, convey in themselves an authentically Christian spiri-

tuality. Just as the God of the Bible is allusive and cannot be fixed in a shape or an object, likewise contemporary architecture sometimes conveys better than more classical forms the mystery, the living presence of God, the breath of the Holy Spirit.

I will demonstrate this through several examples that I have discovered and photographed myself. I have had to limit the choice to a representative selection and to three countries (France, Germany, Portugal), out of the many other examples that could be shown.[1] I have further limited the scope to monasteries and convents that are still inhabited by groups of consecrated religious, but one could obviously make the same demonstration by using churches and cathedrals in which another type of Christian community gathers, namely the assembly of ordinary baptized believers.

Finally, I would like to distinguish two different concepts in the connection between past and contemporary architectural forms. The first is *traditional*, in which modernism adds, often discretely, to existing forms to better showcase them. The second is more *radical*, in which modernism substitutes itself for the existing forms, replacing them. In the first case the artistic creation places high value on past history, whereas in the second case it takes its place. I will discuss four examples of each of these two approaches.

1. ARKOSE architectes, The Rule of St Benedict on panels of metal and frosted glass, abbey of St Mary of Maumont.

First approach:
adding contemporary forms to historical ones ('Continuity in creation')

The Abbey of St Mary of Maumont

This is a community of Benedictine sisters whose convent in Southwest France is historic but not very practical. The community subsists mainly through its bookbinding activity.

After Vatican II, and then at the beginning of the 21st century, the sisters decided to modernize their chapel, and also to renovate the convent's entrance. In place of the iron grid work that had made its front look like a prison, there is now a superb gateway, made of letters and phrases cut out of flat iron plate (fig. 1). What do those letters say? They recall the most important elements of the Rule of St Benedict. The visitor, even before entering the convent, can thus read its spiritual precepts, meditate on them and perhaps choose to enter into the community to meet and to pray with it. Because the letters have been cut out of iron plate, they let light penetrate, and when the sun is shining they can be read twice: in the empty space cut out of the gate, and projected as a shadow on the walls to each side.

The stained-glass windows by Pierre Soulages in the Abbey of Conques

At times a building's architecture is so famous that there can be no question of transforming it. On the contrary, it must be showcased. The famous Abbey church of Sainte-Foy in Conques (Southwest France) is known throughout the world as one of the gems of 11th-century Romanesque art and is classified as a UNESCO world heritage site. Equally famous is its tympanum, sculpted in the 12th century, depicting the *Last Judgment*.

Hundreds of thousands of tourists come each year to visit it, but that does not prevent its small Augustinian community from living and praying there each day. In 1986 the French government asked the artist Pierre Soulages (born in 1919), the best-known French artist living at that time, to make new stained-glass windows for the abbey. Rather than proposing figurative windows, which would probably have disrupted the visitor's perception of the abbey's medieval architecture, Soulages spent several years crafting translucent white glass for the abbey's 95 windows, whose stained glass was composed only of this particular white color, cut by parallel black lines that echo the arches spanning the abbey's nave (fig. 2).[2] The particularity of these windows is that they reflect the light, and thus can be viewed from the outside as well as the inside. They thus highlight the strength of the Romanesque architecture on the inside, while they also reflect the sky on the outside. These non-figurative windows create an atmosphere of peace and contemplation which helps nurture reverence and prayer. Soulages himself said:

> From the beginning I was inspired by the desire to serve this architecture such as it has come down to us, by respecting the purity of its lines and proportions, the shifting shades of its stone, the way its light is organized, the life that takes place in such a unique space. Far from attempting to reconstitute, imitate or rethink the Middle Ages, I tried to make use of the technologies of our day to produce glasswork that corresponds to the identity of this sacred building of the 11th century with its emotional and artistic powers.[3]

In the new Soulages museum (opened in 2014) located in the nearby city of Rodez[4] – the artist's birthplace – are displayed the 200 preliminary sketches of the 95 stained-glass windows of Conques.

2. Pierre Soulages, Windows, Conques, Abbey of Sainte-Foy.

3. Memory chapel, abbey of Ettal (Germany).

The new chapel next to the Benedictine abbey of Ettal

This is another instance of modern architecture built alongside a prestigious example of historic architecture, this time Baroque: the Benedictine abbey of Ettal, in Upper Bavaria, Germany (fig. 3). Those who know the Lutheran theologian Dietrich Bonhoeffer know that he spent several months in this abbey (from November 1940 to February 1941), before entering into the service of the Confessional Church, which opposed Hitler, and this led to his death as a martyr.[5] The interior of this church is superb, but the monks must have wanted to remind us that we are

no longer living in the Baroque age (the 17th and 18th centuries), for they recently built, on the eastern flank of the church, a small, modern chapel, constructed in concrete. The roof reminds us of a tent, in order to represent the fragility of the church in today's times. A skylight reveals a rainbow, symbol of the Covenant between God and his people. The altar is made of sheets of translucent earthenware, in which the word 'light' is engraved in numerous languages, to represent the universality of Christianity, which is present on all 6 continents. Once again, as in Conques and at Maumont, we find a cohabitation of historic and modern art forms.

4 Chapel of the church of the Minor Seminary, Braga (Portugal).

The church of the Minor Seminary in Braga[6]

A further step was taken with the church of the Minor Seminary in Braga, Portugal, realized in 2015. The outside of the church, called *Capela Imaculada*, rather ordinary in its architectural style, was conserved. Inside, however, everything is new (fig. 4).[7] We find an alliance of three elements, concrete, wood and light, which are disposed to facilitate prayer and in view of the vocation and training of future priests. The visitor is surprised by the simplicity of the whole, in a country such as Portugal, where, on the contrary, church interiors generally feature a profusion of shapes, of gold, of sumptuous elements and rich decoration. In this renovated church, everything has been considered, everything is symbolic: not only the architecture, but also the interior layout, light sources (both natural and artificial), and liturgical furnishings (under the altar flows a fountain of running water). Natural gems take the place of stained-glass windows, letting in diffused light. On one of the benches is a hu-

man figure: a sculpture of Mary, the mother of Jesus, seated there as if she had come into the church to pray. This very human Mary, in all ways similar to us and thus strangely Protestant – the artist who sculpted her, the Norwegian Asbjorn Andresen, is in fact a Lutheran –, is the only work of sculpture found in this Catholic church built to serve future priests. The church gallery is a more intimate space, built in wood and conceived for individual meditation. It draws meaning from the church's two liturgical actions, namely the proclamation of the Word and the celebration of the Eucharist.

Is this not a genuine case of ecumenism through art?

For the moment we have looked at modernizations of historic churches or modern additions to historic churches, in settings in which the churches serve for the prayer of monastic communities or, at Braga, for future priests. In each of these cases, as in the four that we are about to discover, it was important to create an atmosphere of community, a place in which the worshiper feels at peace, or desires to remain in order to meditate, to pray, to listen to Scripture together, or to celebrate holy communion.

Second approach: the construction of new monastic buildings (*ex nihilo* creation)

Other communities have made more radical choices, by building new churches or convents *ex nihilo*, from scratch. We will look at four examples.

The new monastery of the Poor Clares near Le Corbusier's chapel at Ronchamp

Le Corbusier (1887–1965) was one of the best-known architects of the 20th century. In 1955 he built the Catholic chapel of Notre-Dame du Haut at Ronchamp, near Belfort, in the east of France, not far from both Switzerland and Germany. This chapel is without a doubt the most famous example of religious architecture from the 20th century.[8] Today more than 100,000 tourists come to visit it each year. What is less known is that Le Corbusier was raised in a strict Swiss Calvinist family, which undoubtedly explains his attraction for simple forms, empty spaces and harmonious proportions.

5. Renzo Piano, Convent for the Poor Clares, Ronchamp.

The success of this contemporary church has recently drawn a community of Poor Clares, who decided to establish themselves at the foot of the hill, to better accompany the tourists and pilgrims that Ronchamp attracts. It began as a discrete but innovative architectural project, carried out between 2008 and 2011 by the famous Swiss-Italian architect, Renzo Piano:[9] a horizontal, ecological monastery, which, planted as it is on the flank of the hill, is respectful of the landscape around it (fig. 5). Here is what the architect said on the subject: "We opened the hill, we put the sisters inside, and now nature, silence and prayer have reclaimed their rights".[10]

This religious community has established itself at the foot of the church of Ronchamp, thereby testifying to the fact that Le Corbusier's church is not only a remarkable feat of architectural prowess, but a place of prayer, of silence and meditation. It attracts numerous tourists, but its vocation is to attract pilgrims, men and women in search of faith. This new, half-buried convent is sufficiently discrete so as not to throw a shadow on the prestigious architecture; its role is to assist the chapel of Ronchamp to once again become a place of prayer, and to induce tourists to become pilgrims.

The Friary in La Tourette by Le Corbusier
Just after completing the chapel at Ronchamp, Le Corbusier built a modern monastery: St Mary's Friary in La Tourette, near Lyon (fig. 6).[11] He undertook the project at the request of the Dominican brothers, and in particular Father of Alain-Marie Couturier, director of the periodical *Art Sacré*, which was in conversation with the greatest artists of the time (Picasso, Chagall, Léger, Braque, Matisse).[12] The Dominicans were convinced that Le Corbusier's contemporary architecture corresponded to their spirituality. The friary, which was built between 1956 and 1960, is made of raw concrete, built on stilts, and consists of 5 floors. The areas reserved for meditation, such as the chapel, are closed spaces with skylights. Other areas, intended as meeting spaces, such as the refectory, are very well lit and open towards the outside. Since 2016 this friary, like all the rest of Le

6. Le Corbusier, convent of St Mary in La Tourette, Lyon.

Corbusier's constructions, has been classified as a UNESCO world heritage site. This building – or rather group of buildings – is shaped like an inverted pyramid and is perfectly well integrated into its surroundings. It favors introspective meditation as well as community life. On the inside it is as if we were in an ocean liner, sailing the seas. We feel protected and safe. Le Corbusier said the following about his construction: "This friary built of rough concrete is a work of love. It doesn't speak. It is experienced from the inside of our being. The essential takes place on the inside".[13]

Convent of the Dominican sisters of St Matthew of Treviers

This convent (fig. 7), modern and of modest proportions, is located in the south of France, near Montpellier (St Mathieu de Treviers). It is the Convent of the Transfiguration, which is home to Dominican nuns, and was built between 1971 and 1976. The convent and the chapel were designed by a famous artist, Thomas Gleb (1912–91), a Jew who fled Poland during the war and who, while he did not

convert to Christianity, became closely connected to it.[14] In 1932, in Paris, he changed his name, Yehouda Chaim Kalman, to Thomas Gleb: "Thomas, because I had not believed".[15]

In 1979 Gleb completed *The Sign*: a monumental work (3.70 meters in height) cut into the wall, in the shape of a "Y" (fig. 8). It was created for the former Carmel of Niort, and should have disappeared as a result of a renovation project that transformed the Carmel chapel into a loft. The director of the Hiéron Museum in Paray-le-Monial, Dominique Dendraël, succeeded in saving this sign by having it removed from the wall in which it was embedded and displaying it in her museum. The sign has a threefold meaning: the 'Y', is at once the first letter of YHWH (the divine Name that cannot be pronounced), and of Yeshoua (which is Jesus in Hebrew), and also of Yehouda, the artist's Jewish first name. This 'Y' is blood red in color, like a wound, and it is criss-crossed by thin cords that resemble stitches closing a wound. It therefore represents a scar, which evokes a deep wound. Three other symbolic references are present in connection

7. Convent of the Transfiguration, St Matthew of Treviers.

8. Thomas Gleb, *The Sign*, St Matthew of Treviers, Convent of the Transfiguration.

9. Chapel of the Convent of the Transfiguration, St Matthew of Treviers.

with this wound: an allusion to the life story of the artist (who escaped from the Shoa) and more generally to the dramatic history of the Jewish people in the 20th century, but also – since the wound has been closed – to the possibility of reconciliation between Judaism and Christianity.

We find this same sign, this 'Y', in the architecture of the chapel of St Matthew's Convent in Treviers (fig. 9). This chapel is round in shape, sober in its style, and its light source, which penetrates windows that are partly obscured, helps to foster the community's meditation and worship.

The chapel of the Protestant Deaconesses of Versailles

The last example is of a radically new architectural form within a Protestant religious community, which is a very rare case. It is the Community of Deaconesses in Reuilly (Paris), whose motherhouse is located in Versailles.

10. Marc Rolinet, Chapel of the Protestant Deaconesses, Versailles.

11. Marc Rolinet, Chapel of the Protestant Deaconesses, Versailles.

Rather than enlarging their former chapel, which was of modest proportions and lacking particular artistic qualities, the sisters decided to undertake a modern construction that would be at once economical, ecological and esthetically pleasing. The new chapel, designed and built by the Lutheran architect Marc Rolinet and inaugurated in 2008 (fig. 10), is based on two antithetical principles:[16] a glass *patio*, in the shape of an ascending triangle, similar to the prow of a boat – a space that allows the visitor to communicate with the outside, to contemplate the magnificent grounds in which the chapel is situated.[17] This glass structure encloses or protects the space designated for worship, and thus inverts the logic: it encloses itself. Like the hull of a boat that has been turned upside down (or half of an eggshell), it focuses our gaze on the interior (fig. 11), since there is no opening. This protective

shell is made of strips of pinewood that were strapped into place, one by one.

Sister Evangeline, mother superior of the Protestant Deaconesses of Versailles, visited the Community of Jesus circa 15 years ago and was impressed with the Community's aesthetic and liturgical sensibility, as she told me in a personal letter.[18]

One might add to the description of this almost futuristic construction, that of the pavilion of the novices, which was designed by the same architect several years earlier. He set the building on stilts, which gives it the advantage of taking up less ground space. In addition, it emphasizes the building's shape, which is that of an open book (the Bible). The technical constraints of such a construction have thus been made subservient to the building's symbolic shape!

Conclusion

I hope I have demonstrated three things through the variety of these examples:

- Architectural shapes, be they traditional, modern or postmodern, play a role in the worship life of the community. That is why these communities pay particular attention to the architectural and artistic choices that they make.

- The old and the new are not opposed to one another, and indeed can be useful complements one to another. When modernity makes a *tabula rasa* of all that has come before, following the radical formula of *ex nihilo*, it is often because there is too much of the old: in such cases the objective is to show that Christianity is not a religion of the past, but of the present and even the future.

- Finally, architecture – be it traditional or modern – represents a complete artistic language. Not only because it comprises other forms of artistic creation (stained-glass windows, liturgical furniture, paintings, sculpture), but also because architecture can be approached both from the outside and the inside. It is an art form in which we can live, both literally and figuratively. ■

1   For example see Dossier 'Bénédictins et cisterciens. Une esthétique monastique', *Arts sacrés*, no. 32 (2016), pp. 47–63.

2   See Christian Heck, *Conques. Les vitraux de Soulages*, with a preface by Georges Duby, Paris, 1994.

3   Quoted ibid., p. 39.

4   <http://musee-soulages.rodezagglo.fr/>, accessed 21 June 2019.

5   A commemorative plaque at the church entry records this fact and pays homage to the him.

6   For more pictures and text about this chapel see <www.protestantismeetimages.com/Architecture-interieure.html>, accessed 21 June 2019.

7   Capela Imaculada. Seminário de Nossa Senhora da Conceição, Braga, Portugal. The architectural firm was Imago – Cerejeira Fontes Arquitectos; the architects were António Jorge Fontes, André Fontes; the artist was Asbjorn Andresen.

8   See Yves Bouvier, Christophe Cousin, *Ronchamp. Une chapelle de lumière*, Paris, 2005; Marie-Alain Couturier, *Art et liberté spirituelle*, Paris, 1958.

9   Piano is the author of numerous prestigious international structures, among which the Centre Pompidou in Paris, the New York Times Building in New York City, the renovation and enlargement of the California Academy of Sciences in San Francisco.

10   <http://www.clarisses-a-ronchamp.fr/313_p_37435/histoire-de-notre-communaute.html>, accessed 21 June 2019.

11   <http://www.fondationlecorbusier.fr/; http://www.couventdelatourette.fr/>, accessed 21 June 2019.

12   Antoine Lion, 'Art sacré et modernité en France: le rôle du P. Marie-Alain Couturier', *Revue de l'histoire des religions*, no. 1 (2010), pp. 109–26; available for consultation on line at <http://rhr.revues.org/7567>, accessed 21 June 2019.

13   <https://fr.wikipedia.org/wiki/Couvent_Sainte-Marie_de_La_Tourette>, accessed 21 June 2019.

14   <http://dom.tourelles.free.fr/thomas_gleb.php>; <http://thomasgleb2012.blogspot.fr/p/saint-matthieu-de-treviers.html>, accessed 21 June 2019.

15   <http://www.thomas-gleb.fr/, https://fr.wikipedia.org/wiki/Thomas_Gleb>, accessed 21 June 2019.

16   Elisabeth Flory, *Guide des architectures religieuses contemporaines à Paris et en Île-de-France*, Paris, 2009, pp. 110–11.

17   <www.diaconesses-reuilly.fr>, accessed 21 June 2019.

18   Letter from Sister Evangeline to Jérôme Cottin, 25 September 2017.

Fotis Kontoglou

and the Struggle for an 'Authentic' Ecclesiastical Art in Greece

VASILEIOS MARINIS

Fotis Kontoglou (1895–1965) remains one of the most influential and controversial Greek artists of the 20th century.[1] He was born in Ayvalık, in what was, at the time, the Ottoman Empire, and was educated at the School of the Arts in Athens. He also lived in Paris and traveled extensively, including in Spain, Belgium, and elsewhere. In 1922 Kontoglou moved permanently to Athens, where he worked as a painter, illustrator, and art restorer. He was also a voluminous writer, authoring several articles and books of fiction and nonfiction.

Kontoglou is particularly famous for his unremitting crusade to revitalize Byzantine-style painting in Greece – the only style that he considered appropriate for Orthodox worship. He not only vehemently attacked Westernizing religious art that was conspicuous in Greece at the time, but also doubted whether Renaissance and Baroque painting could be categorized as religious painting at all. Kontoglou's uncompromising attitude and his almost fanatical zeal about this subject led to many and frequent misunderstandings. For many, he remains an extreme conservative and chauvinist who managed to stifle all innovation in the realm of religious painting in Greece and who turned art into a process of slavishly copying supposedly venerated prototypes. For others, surely the majority, Kontoglou is the standard-bearer of Orthodox tradition, the grand master who freed Greek religious painting from the grasp of Western (that is, heretical) influences. It is my contention in this paper that Kontoglou was neither. I argue, rather, that Kontoglou's main assertion – namely that the way a Western painting looks and operates is incompatible with traditional Orthodox spirituality – is essentially valid, at least in the context of 20th-century Greek Orthodoxy. Furthermore, I maintain that the copying of earlier works of art is but one step in Kontoglou's complex and sophisticated process of learning and practicing religious painting.

To understand Kontoglou we must first discuss art production and education in Greece in the 19th and early 20th centuries.[2] Greece became an independent state in 1830. During the following year, the Bavarian prince Otto von Wittelsbach (1815–67) was installed as the monarch of the newfound kingdom. In an effort to reorganize and modernize the nascent state, as well as in an effort to create a national identity, Otto's German consultants and the native *intelligentsia* espoused a narrative that emphasized the state's connections with the glorious age of classical antiquity and downplayed those to the Byzantine and post-Byzantine periods. Art, especially of the post-Byzantine era, was considered to be 'decadent' (or, even worse, 'barbaric'), and in need of drastic amelioration. In general, the shortcomings of Byzantine art, such as its lack of perspective and anatomical inaccuracies, were to be corrected through the application of Western principles of painting.[3] The result was an ecclesiastical visual language that combined a variety of influences, including Neoclassicism, late Academicism, and, primarily, the Nazarene movement. Byzantine idioms, however, were not completely abandoned.

The Bavarian painter Ludwig Thiersch (1825–1909) is perhaps the most outstanding representative of this style. Thiersch was educated in the Akademie der Bildenden Künste, in Munich, and was well versed in Academic art. During his residency in Greece between 1852 and 1855, when he taught at the School of the Arts, he also familiarized himself with Byzantine art, especially the 11th-century mosaic ensembles of Daphni Monastery in Attica and Hosios Loukas in Boeotia.[4] Thiersch was commissioned to decorate several churches, the most important of which was the Russian Church (also known as Soteira Lykodemou) in Athens (fig. 1).[5] These paintings are firmly Academic and Nazarene in style, but they contain reminiscences, however distant, of Byzantine mosaics, especially those in Daphni. Interestingly, Thiersch's selection of many of the saints (depicted either standing or in medallions) was evidently based on their connection to the Athenian Church (fig. 2). Despite his rather brief stay in Greece, Thiersch was very influential, both through his work and through his teaching. Nikephoros Lytras and Spyridon Chatzigiannopoulos, two of the most distinguished 19th–century Greek painters, were his students. They also assisted him with Soteira Lykodemou.

Although in his later texts he is largely dismissive of Western religious art, Kontoglou was, to be sure, an astute student of Renaissance and later Western painters.[6] Early in his career he was a great admirer of painters such as Domenikos Theotokópoulos (known as El Greco; *c.* 1541–1614), Paul Gauguin, Vincent van Gogh (1853–90). Furthermore, he could be critical of Byzantine art, whose compositions he sometimes found unbalanced.[7] But these opinions evolved. The reasons for this evolution were certainly manifold,[8] but one of the most consequential seems to have been his numerous visits to Mount Athos, the most important center of Byzantine monasticism, in the 1920s. There he came into extensive contact with Byzantine and post-Byzantine fresco ensembles and icons, which dramatically altered his philosophy of painting.[9] By 1930, Kontoglou had developed his trademark style and used it in both his secular and religious works (figs. 3, 4). Concomitantly, he began a decades-long campaign to rid the ecclesiastical painting of Greece of Western influences.

For Kontoglou the struggle to re-educate the public took almost mythical dimensions. In one of his letters to the fellow artist Euaggelos Maurikakis he writes: "Here we fight day and night against the powers of darkness".[10] Neither was the church hierarchy safe from his ire. In another letter to Maurikakis, he claims that

We will take care of all those unhappy lovers of the West who think that, if they put inside churches Genevièves and Italian Madonnas, they will be considered modern. But perhaps it is not their fault, because they just know that much. If the bishop feels that way, what can the rest do?[11]

And he continues in the same letter:

The people are good, but the deceivers of the people, the spiritual swindlers, blind them. From the thousand who read my articles, how many were enemies of the tradition and now beg me to write to them?[12]

Nowadays, when the Byzantinizing style is dominant, it is difficult to understand this kind of acrimonious discourse. And yet, in the first decades of the 20th century, the situation was very different. The style introduced by the Bavarians and propagated by their Greek followers had been the norm for more than a century. Virtually all newly-built churches, as well as many existing ones, were decorated with

1. Ludwig Thiersch, *Christ Pantokrator*, Athens, Soteira Lykodemou (Russian Church).

2. Ludwig Thiersch, *Female Martyr*, Athens, Byzantine and Christian Museum.

Western-looking paintings. Both laypeople and clergy were accustomed to worshiping in such contexts. Moreover, the rhetoric of the superiority of Western art, especially in comparison to the 'technically inept' Byzantine technique, had been embedded in people's minds. No wonder Kontoglou met with fierce resistance.

What was it that Kontoglou disapproved of in Western religious art? And why did he believe Byzantine art to be more appropriate for the church? These questions are not always easy to answer. Kontoglou addressed them in many of his writings but not always in a systematic way; furthermore, he was not entirely consistent. For the sake of brevity, I examine here only one of his essays, *The Byzantine painting and its true value*,[13] but I also consider several of his other writings.

The first claim that Kontoglou makes in this essay is that Byzantine art cannot be understood by scholars who approach it only as a field of inquiry or by those who judge it aesthetically. It is only the practicing Orthodox, those who live with this art, who can truly understand it.[14] Byzantine art is incomprehensible when approached through the lens of classical or Italian Renaissance art. Byzantine art does not move people in the way of these other styles. It lacks naturalism and perspective, correct anatomy, and the usual standards of beauty. Yet all these traits, to Kontoglou, are unnecessary. Simplicity is beneficial to both the body and the soul. Byzantine art transforms people from material into spiritual beings. With its mystical forms and colors, it wants to express the divine love that engulfs the saints it paints.[15] Because Byzantine art is spiritual, it cannot be measured with physical means.[16] Byzantine art, argues Kontoglou, reflects the mystical riches of God's Kingdom.[17]

3. Fotis Kontoglou, *Hadji Oustas Iordanoglou of Cappadocia and His Son Homer*, Collection of D. Kontoglou-Martinou.

4. Fotis Kontoglou, *Christ Pantokrator*, Patras, church of St Lucia.

For Kontoglou the fundamental distinction of Byzantine art lies herein: Byzantine icons are spiritual, while the paintings of artists like Raphael are "physical" (i.e., worldly).[18] Even religious Renaissance art is, in reality, secular art, because it expresses the secular spirit of the Catholic Church (which has acquired secular power), especially when it is mixed with the rationalism of ancient philosophy. Thus, Italian Renaissance art is the rebirth of ancient, pagan, and worldly art.[19] The Italian painters did not paint liturgical art; religion, writes Kontoglou, was just an excuse for them to paint "their conceited sentimentalities". Their work consists not of icons to be venerated, but of worldly paintings.[20]

Kontoglou argues that with the revitalization of classical art, Church art lost its spiritual, mystical character and from liturgical became naturalistic. The individual replaced tradition and artistic liberty was exalted. Kontoglou argues, however, that this liberty is an illusion. The master who works with his imagination and seeks, because of his vanity, to show off his mastery, is a slave to his baser passions. By contrast, the iconographer, with his adherence to tradition, is truly free. Iconographers working in the Byzantine tradition follow a given form, but each interprets this form according to his piety. The religious art of the Renaissance lost its catholicity, by contrast, on the altar of individualism.[21] Furthermore, with the involvement of science,[22] art became complex, experimental, fake, and crowded with unnecessary additions.[23]

In Byzantine art, Kontoglou continues, rationalism is eradicated in favor of the wonderful and the apocalyptic. Its lack of perspective suspends time and allows the faithful to see everything.[24] It employs nothing of the abstract symbolism and theatricality of Western paintings. The figures in the icons could not be mistaken for actors in a play, nor icons for paintings of operas.[25]

It is easy to point to Kontoglou's biases. Yet, if we peel back the over-generalizations and contention in *The Byzantine painting and its true value*, many of his observations are quite correct. There are essential – one might say ontological – differences between a Renaissance religious painting and a Byzantine icon. Their divergent styles indicate contrasting systems of viewing, interpretation, and symbolism, and the way that each functions in a worship space is radically different. Kontoglou essentially ar-

5. Fotis Kontoglou, *Deposition from the Cross*, copy of a fresco in Kapsokalývia, Mount Athos.

6. Fotis Kontoglou, *Ajax and Odysseus*, Private collection.

gues that the way a Western painting looks and operates is incompatible with Orthodox spirituality, especially in the 20th century.[26]

Kontoglou was eventually victorious, as the style of Thiersch and his followers has been all but abandoned today in Greece. But his unyielding promotion of the tradition has had some long-lasting consequences. Even a cursory look at the ecclesiastical art in Greece in the 80's and 90's shows an utter disinterest in creativity and personal style. At best, we find insipid copies of earlier prototypes (interestingly, mostly post-Byzantine); at worst – especially in the case of mass-produced icons for the tourist market, both indigenous and foreign – we encounter utter lack of artistic competence and ignorance of the basics of iconography. The usual excuse is that proper and true Orthodox art remains adherent to 'tradition'; any kind of originality or innovation is suspicious, bordering on heresy. Isn't that, after all, what Kontoglou taught us?

Quite frankly, it is not. For Kontoglou, the process of icon painting is a complex and multi-stage affair, one that involves continuous study and learning, and one that presupposes an active spiritual life.[27] Kontoglou firmly believes that the best way to learn is to copy earlier, Byzantine works (fig. 5). Yet, copying is but the first step in developing one's personal style

in the confines of the tradition (fig. 6). Again, in a letter to Maurikakis, he writes:

> This is the most important thing, to absorb the old but give it our own voice, without novelties and easy innovations. We need to respect the existing works of art…

Offering words of encouragement to his younger colleague, Kontoglou continues:

> In general, your progress is notable… because you are not narrowly attached to copying, but you felt the spirit that animates the works in Mystra [Maurikakis had been copying parts of the famous late Byzantine frescoes in the city of Mystra, in southern Greece]… and slowly you create something new. That is, you learn the language and you make your own sentences, without imitating the sentences you learned at school. That is the true way of our art.[28]

In his next letter to Maurikakis, Kontoglou asserts that

> Copying is just training. Only afterwards comes the true work, during which the craftsman absorbs the elements that exist in the prototypes he copied, and gives [them], through his personal sensitivity, a new pulse. In that

7. Fotis Kontoglou, *Christ the Merciful*, Boston, Monastery of the Metamorphosis.

way, he creates his own work, without straying from the tradition.[29]

And in one of his essays, he explains further:

The form of each saint was delivered to us centuries ago, and the iconographers preserved it until today. Those who only know Byzantine art superficially and say that an icon is just a copy of another are wrong. A Byzantine icon is always a living work, autonomous, original, based on a given prototype, but interpreted by each painter according to his piety. It is like the Liturgy, performed by each priest differently, according to his devoutness.[30]

As George Kordis has argued Kontoglou thinks of an icon as comprising two elements: form, or iconographic type; and style. The former is essentially given and cannot be altered. The style, however, ought to be personal, based on the painter's sensitivities. "That way [an icon] can always be a modern creation, without losing its traditional character".[31]

In this context, the obsession with tradition that has plagued religious painting in Greece in the second half of the 20th century and continues in some circles today seems unwarranted. It is clear in Kontoglou's writings that, although

copying earlier works is part of the process of learning, what the serious iconographer should aim for is a personal, individual style. To reiterate one of Kontoglou's favorite metaphors, the tradition offers the iconographer the vocabulary, but he or she is responsible for putting together sentences.

The most correct way to elucidate Kontoglou's relationship with tradition is to study his own paintings (fig. 7). It is impossible to mistake one of Kontoglou's icons for somebody else's. Although the late Byzantine elements that he admired – such as elongated figures, distorted perspective, and exaggerated poses – are present, he has infused them with an original demotic sensibility, an innovative color palette, and several whimsical details. In this sense, Kontoglou's efforts to revive Byzantinizing painting are no different than artistic movements such as Neoclassicism and the Nazarenes. Kontoglou's approach was in line with such movements in that he looked to the past for a cultural framework from which to draw inspiration, which he then adapted to his own sensibilities. What made him different, however, was Kontoglou's conviction that the Greeks had a religious painting of their own, one that made the importation of Western styles unnecessary. ■

1   Due to space limitations, in this essay I only offer essential bibliography. For Kontoglou see *Οἱ Ἕλληνες ζωγράφοι. ΙΙ. Ὁ εἰκοστὸς αἰῶνας*, Athens, 1976, pp. 212–51; Nikos Zias, *Φώτης Κόντογλου, Ζωγράφος*, Athens, 1991; Georgios Kordis, 'Ὁ Φώτης Κόντογλου καὶ ἡ δυναμικὴ τῆς ζωγραφικῆς μας παραδόσεως', in *Φώτης Κόντογλους, ἐν εἰκόνι διαπορευόμενος*, Athens, 1995, pp. 295–306; Stauros Zoumpoulakis, 'Γιὰ τήν ἁγιογραφία τοῦ Φώτη Κόντογλου', *Νέα Ἑστία*, no. 159 (2006), pp. 680–93.

2   See Antonia Mertyri, Η καλλιτεχνική εκπαίδευση των νέων στην Ελλάδα (1836-1945), Athens, 2000; Nikolaos Graikos, Ακαδημαϊκές τάσεις της εκκλησιαστικής ζωγραφικής στην Ελλάδα κατά τον 19ο αιώνα. Πολιτισμικά και εικονογραφικά ζητήματα, Thessalonike, 2011. For historical background see Thomas W. Gallant, *The Edinburgh History of the Greeks, 1768 to 1913*, Edinburgh, 2015.

3   Antonis Danos, 'The Culmination of Aesthetic and Artistic Discourse in Nineteenth-century Greece: Periklis Yannopoulos and Nikolaos Gyzis', *Journal of Modern Greek Studies*, 20/1 (2002), pp. 75–112: 75–86. See also Miltiadis Papanikolaou, *Γερμανοὶ ζωγράφοι στὴν Ἑλλάδα κατὰ τὸν 19ο αἰώνα (1826-1843)*, Thessalonike, 1981.

4   Hanna Kaiser, *Ludwig Thiersch in Athen um 1850: Neobyzantinismus im Kontext des Philhellenismus*, Ph.D. Diss., Munich, University of Munich, 2017.

5   Soteira Lykodemou was originally built in the first half of the 11th century but has undergone considerable alterations and renovations. For the 19th-century iconographic program of this church, see Nikolaos Graikos, *Η «βελτιωμένη» βυζαντινή ζωγραφική στον 19ο αιώνα. Η περίπτωση του Σπυρίδωνα Χατζηγιαννοπούλου*, MA Thesis, Thessalonike, University of Thessalonike, 2003, pp. 193–221.

6   See, for example, Fotis Kontoglou, *Γιὰ νὰ πάρουμε μιὰ ἰδέα περὶ ζωγραφικῆς*, Athens, 2002.

7   *Οἱ Ἕλληνες ζωγράφοι* 1976, op. cit., II, p. 216.

8   See the extensive analysis in Ryan P. Preston, *The 'Eternal Return' of the Byzantine Icon: Sacred and Secular in the Art of Photis Kontoglou*, Ph.D. Diss., Cambridge, Harvard University, 2010, pp. 54–180.

9   This was, in a sense, a paradox. At that time, the dominant style of icon painting in the Holy Mountain was largely inspired by Russian ecclesiastical painting, in a style very close to Academicism.

10   Fotis Kontoglou, *Πρὸς ἁγιογράφον Εὐάγγελον Μαυρικάκην*, Athens, 1997, p. 59.

11   Ibid., p. 63.

12   Ibid.

13   Fotis Kontoglou, 'Η βυζαντινὴ ζωγραφικὴ καὶ ἡ ἀληθινὴ της ἀξία', in *Ἡ πονεμένη ρωμιοσύνη*, Athens, 1963, pp. 96–119. Some of Kontoglou's essays on art have been translated in *Byzantine Sacred Art: Selected Writings of the Contemporary Greek Icon Painter Fotis Kontoglous on the Sacred Arts According to the Tradition of Eastern Orthodox Christianity*, translated by Constantine Cavarnos (2nd ed., 1st ed. New York, 1957), Belmont, MA, 1985.

14   Kontoglou 1963, op. cit., pp. 96–7.

15   Ibid., pp. 101–2.

16   Ibid., pp. 102–3.

17   Ibid., p. 104.

18   Ibid.

19   Ibid., p. 105.

20   Ibid., p. 106.

21   Ibid., pp. 110–12.

22   For the calculation, e.g., of perspective.

23   Ibid., p. 111.

24   Ibid., p. 116.

25   Ibid., pp. 118–19.

26   For the consequences of Kontoglou's campaign see Georgios Kordis, 'The Return to Byzantine Painting Tradition: Fotis Kontoglou and the Aesthetical Problem of Twentieth-Century Orthodox Iconography', in *Devotional Cultures of European Christianity, 1790-1960*, edited by Henning Laugerud, Dublin, 2012, pp. 122–30.

27   On this, see Georgios Kordis, 'Ὁ Φώτης Κόντογλου καὶ ἡ σπουδὴ τῆς ἁγιογραφίας', in Kontoglou 1997, op. cit., pp. 107–45.

28   Kontoglou 1997, op. cit., p. 81.

29   Ibid., p. 83.

30   Kontoglou 1963, op. cit., p. 112.

31   Kordis 1997, op. cit., pp. 122–3.

The Resurrection of the Image in the English Protestant Imagination

From William Blake to Bill Viola. Part II

BEN QUASH

In Britain, traditional Protestant churches are awash with proposals attempting to energize the aesthetic possibilities of sacred buildings or anxious to rephrase the language of religious principles in modern artistic terms. "[A]rt is entering ecclesiastical spaces at such a rate these days that the doorway can barely admit all those clamoring for admittance".[1] In this paper I will offer a British comparator to a US context, and attempt to explain the phenomenal resurgence of visual art in the UK's Protestant churches. Might these in part be the product of a mission-driven agenda which recognizes that the deep-seated imperative to translate the Gospel into all languages must now extend to include a new *lingua franca* of visual images? Might the visionary edge of radical nonconformity have an innate tendency to fuel new artistic experiments, like those of William Blake and his successors? Or might there be in the peculiarities of England's Elizabethan settlement, with its ongoing attachment to a sacramental imagination and a doctrine of the incarnation as sanctifying the particularities of local habitations and of natural as well as human forms, the ground of a "mystical empiricism" that presses for visual realization? Might the "modest Modernism" that is characteristic of a 20th-century British context, and contrasts with some of the more strident and revolution-ary Modernisms of continental Europe and the USA, be in part a consequence of a certain theological temper?

In Part I of this essay, I looked at how the visual arts fared under the sway of British (and, I think, especially *English*) Protestant Christianity in the period between Henry VIII's break with Rome in the 1530s and the Anglo-Catholic revival in the 1830s. Rather remarkably, it is a period exactly three hundred years long, almost to the year.

In this second installment I propose to continue that British (and especially English) story into the 20th and 21st centuries, in the hope that a transatlantic comparator will also be a useful resource for those looking at religious traditions of art in a North American context.

I want to begin by taking you to Chichester, on the south coast of England (its cathedral is the only English cathedral that can be seen from the sea, and the spire was for centuries used by sailors as a navigation point). The cathedral is a medieval building, 900 years old, and to walk around its interior is to be given a glimpse of the history of the English Church's relationship with the visual arts in its successive stages. It is a little like looking at a series of geological strata in cross section; each layer of sedimented deposit distinct and eloquent of its time.

So, for instance, we have the 12th- or 13th-century Lazarus Reliefs, hidden for a long time behind the choir stalls of the cathedral until they were discovered in 1829, and relocated to the south aisle (figs. 1–2). They are remarkable for their emotional intensity; we see a Romanesque imagination interpreting that spare but powerful verse "Jesus wept" to magnificent effect. Who knows what larger scheme these reliefs might once have been part of? But even on their own they have the power to conduct their viewers on a sort of mental pilgrimage to the Holy Land, and they testify to a time when the cathedral's works of visual art would have been an essential part of its teaching of biblical stories, its awakening of emotional responses that were at the same time devotional ones, and its testimony to the fact that God incarnate walked among us, occupying physical space as these carved figures do. (These are, of course, exactly the three purposes of art enshrined in St John of Damascus' classic defense of icons from the 8th century).

Not far away we find the Charter Panels, by the Tudor artist Lambert Barnard. Begun in 1533, their creation anticipated the Act of Supremacy only a year later, and is a visual statement of the long history of the interdependence of church and monarchy in Chichester, as in England more generally. A depiction in the panels themselves of the situation that occasioned them, in which the Diocese was seeking renewed patronage and continued rights to land ownership from Henry VIII, is paralleled elsewhere in the panels with the 7th-century events in which the Diocese was first founded by St Wilfred with the material support of the newly-converted King Caedwalla of the South Saxons, who donated the lands on which Wilfred would found his new cathedral. Though there are points of theological interest and sophistication in them, these are a form of history painting which served also as a piece of political propaganda.

Then we have a bonanza of Victorian stained glass, signaling the revival of an appreciation of Britain's medieval roots and a desire to mirror

1. *Martha and Mary beseech Jesus,*
Chichester, Cathedral Church of the Holy Trinity.

2. *Raising of Lazarus,*
Chichester, Cathedral Church of the Holy Trinity.

their glories in that period. The South Transept window is a big, story-telling visual scheme, exploring in traditional typology the patterns of promise and fulfillment in the Old and New Testaments respectively. Glass like this was in the vanguard of the triumphant return of the figurative visual arts to Anglican churches in the 19th century, with carving, mosaic, fresco and in some cases painted altarpieces close behind.

Then we see the full flowering of this resurrection of the devotional visual image in a host of works, most of them (in Chichester's case) commissioned in the middle decades of the 20th century, and – in this particular cathedral as also in Coventry – of consistently fine quality. In both the quantity and the quality of these works it needs to be acknowledged that Chichester is not typical of all English cathedrals. Its successes have much to do with the assured eye, the passionate drive and the personal connections of the then Dean, Walter Hussey, who had the important support of his Bishop, George Bell. The fruits of their vision are to be seen in Marc Chagall's magnificent stained glass window, based on Psalm 150; in Graham Sutherland's *Noli me tangere* altarpiece; in John Piper's great tapestry panels which hang behind the High Altar; and in a number of other significant commissions.

Commissions of permanent works continue to the present. A recent, permanent installation of quiet emotional intensity is the work of the contemporary artist Michael Clark, whose *Five Wounds* (fig. 3) are located at different points in the cathedral, and (when noticed, for they do not 'shout', as some have found the Piper tapestry to do) transform one's relation to the building, turning its fabric into a body, and incorporating the viewer within that body.

In bringing this story up to the present, we should also mention more transient works, for you will find in Chichester (as in nearly any English cathedral nowadays) a variety of temporary installations, or works that are not made for particular spaces and that are moved around as occasion demands. Some seem to me to be of questionable value (Galia Amsel's *Connection*, and Diana Brandenburger's *The Refugee* are cases in point, to my mind), and some

3. Michael Clark, *Five Wounds*, Chichester, Cathedral Church of the Holy Trinity.

work very powerfully (two recent installations in the North Transept, which is currently set aside for this purpose: Carrie Fertig's *Homing*; Anna Freeman Bentley's *Descent*; fig 4).

So there we have it: an artistic palimpsest. What does it tell us, though, about the changing ways in which art has been used and related to in each of these periods in British church

4. Anna Freeman Bentley, *Descent*, Chichester, Cathedral Church of the Holy Trinity.

history, and (perhaps most importantly for our purposes here) the way in which art in churches is being used and related to today?

We cannot easily be certain of what was the perceived importance – the visceral, affective importance – of images in people's lives in the 13th, in the 16th or even in the 19th centuries, and thus where the continuities and discontinuities between these eras might lie. My colleague at King's College London, Robin Griffith-Jones, suggests that in considering the medieval period we might reach for words like "presence, protection, assurance", and imagine works of sacred art giving their viewers a sense of being "at the intersection of earth and heaven where Christ and the saints – and the salvific effects of Christ's sacrifice on Calvary and in the Mass – were most palpably present".

In the unusual Charter Panels of Tudor Chichester, we see a different sort of power being exercised; the power of visual works of art to consolidate a particular interpretation of contemporary events and political arrangements; to allow past stories with both regional and national dimensions to frame a sense of future prospects. These are not images held up for pious veneration; Lambert Barnard did not paint these panels so that candles might be lit in front of them. They are more like an ecclesiastical mission statement in visual form.

By the 19th century, we seem to see a self-conscious revival of medieval and pan-European religiosity in the face of an industrialized and urban and already secularizing Britain, and in deliberate contrast to lower churchmanship.

And in the 20th and 21st centuries? Well, as Griffith-Jones says, "tricky: but a more consciously aesthetic, artistic enjoyment of a long and now beleaguered culture?"

He puts a question mark at the end of this suggestion, and the question he makes is one that has been very sensitively explored, and at helpful length, by Jonathan Koestlé-Cate, whose recent intelligent and lively book *Art and the Church: A Fractious Embrace* I quoted at the beginning of this paper. I thoroughly recommend it for its nuanced critical analysis of many of the recent adventures that the institutional church has embarked on in the company of contemporary artists. Some of these

adventures have been ill-advised – perhaps even reckless (the jury is still out on David Wynne's millennium piece *Blessed Virgin Mary* (2000) in the Lady Chapel of Ely Cathedral, and I remain unimpressed by Jonathan Clarke's *Way of Life* (2000), also in Ely, for its heavily-obvious symbolism). Others have returned great treasures. Koestlé-Cate is generous in his readiness to celebrate occasions when commissions in churches (whether permanent or temporary) have had an illuminating, inspiring, or appropriately challenging effect, usually when they have worked with a significant degree of sympathy towards the history, purposes and practices of the buildings they are made for and the communities which use those buildings. At the same time, he is rightly skeptical about the difficulties of letting 'arts policies' govern decisions about commissioning, and advocates the benefits of a 'less-is-more' approach on the part of churches and cathedrals; a concern to maintain the appropriate intensity of the 'event' character of a piece of art in a church or cathedral.

What I propose to do in the short space available to me here is to try to complement Griffith-Jones's pointed question and Koestlé-Cate's extended analysis with a more explicitly theological set of categories. Griffith-Jones may be right that many people (Christian and non-Christian) look at artworks in churches and cathedrals these days with a more conscious awareness of themselves as aesthetic consumers than their forebears had, enjoying the effects of innovative interventions in some of the nation's prime heritage sites. But there are other forces in play that deserve consideration, including a creative concern on the part of clergy and congregations with the dynamics of their worshiping life and their public ministry, and what part visual art might play in these things. Koestlé-Cate, meanwhile, combines sociological, philosophical and art-critical approaches to great effect in analyzing recent ecclesiastical commissions, but also keeps theology somewhat at arms' length in his book.

The theological categories I propose to deploy may help us to distinguish and to track three influences that – so it seems to me – animate the very lively new relationship that now obtains between visual art and British churches whose Reformation inheritance didn't use to make them hospitable to images at all. My three categories are prophecy, mission and sacramentality.

Prophecy

The first theological category – prophecy – helps us to isolate an influence whose significance I began to trace in Part I. My contention there was that after the Reformation's suppression of images – indeed its wholesale destruction of them in most parts of the country – *the mind's eye took over*. A visualization of the biblical stories and their actors was sustained in a predominantly literary medium. George Herbert and Henry Vaughan, in an Anglican tradition, and John Milton and John Bunyan, in a Puritan vein, are preeminent examples of the 'visuality' of this literary imagination. My case was that, although a tradition of artistic brilliance in its own right, this textual legacy allowed also for something akin to a 'cryogenic preservation' of a native tradition of religious visual imagery in Britain, which in the right conditions was ready to spring to life again.

The first really suitable conditions for this resurrection, interestingly, were fostered where the innate conservatism of the Established Church did not extend its dead hand. William Blake's influence on the visual art that would recolonize that Church was highly significant, even though he was avowedly nonconformist. The fact that this first strand of influence on modern Christian art is Britain has nonconformist roots is not surprising; 'prophecy' is generally practiced at an angle to the mainstream consensus of its time. But calling it 'prophetic' also helps us to make sense of its inclination to visualization. Prophecy has typically deployed words in the service of the communication of intense visualizations of divine life and truth, and this is why biblical prophets are called 'seers' even though their legacy to us is words. Like them, Blake turns his religious vision into words *and* pictures, knowing from his own experience how both words and pictures can awaken religious vision.

Frances Spalding, in her excellent survey of 20th-century British Art, observes that in Britain:

Innovation has [often] been made through a return to personal convictions or native traditions, to a revival of narrative, for example, or a realist approach. The individualism inherent in British art has liberated artists from unthinking adoption of fashionable styles.[2]

I think she is right, and I think that all these qualities are presaged in Blake's religious work. Its personal conviction is everywhere evident. It undoubtedly has roots in native traditions of imagining God incarnate and present "in England's green and pleasant land" (Cicestrians, incidentally, like to suppose that this notion came to Blake while living for three years just outside Chichester, in the coastal village of Felpham). A fascination with narrative, especially biblical narrative, is also powerful in Blake's work, and so is a concern to explore the human body. 20th-century art in Britain has tended to sustain rather than reject these priorities, and often with just the eccentricity of 'personal conviction' that in Blake I am calling prophetic. This sets it apart somewhat from the avant-garde modernisms of Europe and North America. In Spalding's words, a certain *sort* of concern with modernism (governed largely by "an obsession with the move towards abstraction") has

blinkered critical evaluation of twentieth-century art, encouraging historians ... to look for a linear evolutionary development, a tendency which has helped banish into temporary obscurity much that did not uphold the dominant avant-garde ideology.[3]

When evaluating the British context this needs to be balanced, so she argues, by attention to more realist and figurative traditions, many of which are religiously inspired or informed (Paul Nash, Stanley Spencer, Eric Gill, David Jones, Henry Moore, Barbara Hepworth, Graham Sutherland, John Piper), and no less imaginatively inventive for that. Might this resistance to the 'unthinking adoption of fashionable styles' itself precisely be a form of prophetic witness?

A prophetic legacy, I would argue, is alive and well in contemporary churches and cathe-

5. Mark Wallinger, *Ecce Homo*, installation in the St Paul Cathedral (London), 1999.

drals (less cautious and less conservative than they used to be), and is now often an explicit reason why they welcome specific works of art into their spaces.

Gerry Judah's twin white crosses in St Paul's Cathedral, London (2014), echo in their pale forms the countless war graves which are a special focus of remembrance, especially in the centenary years of the First World War, but when viewed in detail reveal on their surfaces the shattered cityscapes of war-torn cities of the contemporary world. Such a work in such a context is powerfully affecting. One question we might ask of it, I admit (and one we might also put to Bill Viola's two moving-image artworks in the Cathedral), is whether they represent a new sort of internationalism in contemporary taste (there is something very Californian about Viola's work), and whether by the same token their prophetic mode of address is not quite that natively British one which is still traceable in the mid-20th century. But does this matter? Perhaps not, and in any case the British style is arguably still traceable in other artists' work. Mark Wallinger's *Ecce Homo* (1999; fig. 5) seems to me a case in point. Either way, their presence confirms my thesis that prophetic impulses of various kinds remain a significant motivation for the making of new works for ecclesiastical spaces in the United Kingdom.

Mission

In a large West London Charismatic-Evangelical church, Victorian Gothic in its architectural style, you can see this vast triptych by the Northumbrian-born artist Charlie Mackesy. Like many churches of its kind, St Paul's in Hammersmith has taken out its pews, carpeted the floor, and made it as comfortable and flexible a space as possible. The altar is frequently out of sight behind a worship band. What is rarely out of sight, however, is the vast, faux-tenebrist crucifixion in the central arched space in the east wall, and the spaces to left and right of it. The space on the right shows one of Mackesy's favorite scenes, the return of the Prodigal, which he revisits many times in different media (sometimes making the son into a daughter). The left-hand space is, to the best of my knowledge, still unfinished, but the intention of both the artist and his patrons (the parish community and above all its Vicar, the Revd Simon Downham) is that it will depict Jesus emerging with joyous laughter from the waters of his baptism.

Citing the erstwhile Evangelical John Ruskin as one of the inspirations behind his initiative, Downham has stated his belief that art can play more than a simply decorative role in worship, even within a church of a traditionally aniconic stripe like his own. He has insisted on art's ability to "mediate God's grace" in its demonstration of inspired and inspiring creativity.[4] The creative capacity of art is central to Downham's belief that it can act as a way to God; on these grounds he challenges the principle that art serves only its own ends (he is, in other words, suspicious of the idea of 'art for art's sake'). Meanwhile, in an argument that has a long Orthodox and Catholic pedigree, Downham also cites the materiality of Christ as a justification for the making of Christian images, and sees them as a valuable bulwark against various contemporary manifestations of Gnosticism (Theosophy in the early-20th century; various forms of New Age spirituality in more recent times).

The most interesting aspect of the St Paul's commission for me, however, is its careful consideration of how the works might speak effectively to those not closely familiar with the biblical narratives or with Christian doctrine. The church wanted not only to focus and deepen the devotion of the regular faithful, but to captivate and draw in those beyond that circle. Mackesy especially planned the flanking panels with this in mind. Those coming to church only for the occasional offices, like weddings, funerals and baptisms, would still, he hoped, be able to relate to the attractive symbol of a hug and the unexpected sight of Jesus laughing. The crucifixion, meanwhile, though more conventional for the center of an altarpiece, causes the lone figure of Christ to loom startlingly into our space, somewhat confrontationally seeking an intimacy with us, and certainly taking the unsuspecting visitor by surprise.

Part of the surprise may simply be that a church whose informal style is proclaimed in its publicity, its furnishings, its music, and so on, and whose tradition is a Reformed one, should so consciously announce that it wants a piece of the action where visual art is concerned. The fact that the style of the central panel is so heavily and comfortably reminiscent of Counter-Reformation European art is especially revealing. This is a post-denominational move, made by mission-minded church leaders who correctly see that early 21st-century Britain is a place where art is a common currency for everyone. Old Masters and street art alike are

widely viewed – not least by smart Londoners – as a shared cultural inheritance. They do not respond to these images with wary caution that the subliminal semiotics of Catholicism might corrupt them. St Paul's Hammersmith has here chosen to present "an intimate, joyful, relational and ultimately sacrificial God",[5] in a hybridization of artistic forms, styles and subjects that oddly continues to proclaim its status as 'art' even while bringing it into a sanctuary space again.

The primary influence at work in this case study, as I see it, gives me my second theological category for evaluating the relationship between Protestant churches and visual art in modern Britain: mission. Not only are the visual arts a cultural arena in which some of the deepest possible questions of life and death, meaning and purpose, continue to be raised; they are also the medium through which the 21st century is increasingly communicating. In the digital domain, where millions now interrelate, the visual arts have become a preferred form of communication across internet platforms, and particularly through social media. We are witnessing what in retrospect may look like a revolution in the use of visual imagery, as images become a new *lingua franca*. Inevitably, missionary-minded Christians are asking how this new *lingua franca* can be 'spoken' in the service of proclaiming the Gospel to all people and in every language, and are experimenting with visual ways of doing so. That, I think, may help to explain what we are seeing here, and in churches like it – even if the works of art make only brief appearances as part of the powerpoint slideshows designed to accompany worship.

Sacramentality

In *The Glory of the Lord*, Hans Urs von Balthasar celebrated British theology's characteristic focus on the concrete form – 'the unique, the irreducible' – indicating its advantages over his own continental tradition, for "reared in an hereditary empiricism" it has "preserved the native rights of imagery in religious thought … right up to the present day".[6] In hindsight, this concern with the "native rights of imagery" in Britain may help us to make sense of what would have been an astonishing fact if predicted to a late 16th-century British Protestant, namely, that Anglicanism in the British Isles would in the 19th century find itself patron and seedbed of some of the most prolific manufacture of world-class visual art – in multiple media, including stained glass, wood and stone carving, fabric, metalwork, mosaic, and painting. As I argued back in Part I of this essay, the belief in revelatory particularity has been a perennial feature of Anglican thought. It is an outlook in which the concrete and the mystical are not at odds, and this makes Anglicanism, at its best, a tradition congenitally prone to the "imaging" of its faith.

Frances Spalding – while pointing out that there are "sufficient contradictions [in modern British art] to keep talk of national characteristics at bay" – talks nevertheless of "[a] leaning towards the romantic and particular".[7] This combination of "romantic" and "particular" is what I would call the 'mystical empiricism' of a certain British tradition. It has religious roots, and continues to manifest itself in new works for Christian contexts. As Spalding points out, Graham Sutherland and Paul Nash were aligned with this tendency when they took aspects of Surrealism from the European continent and absorbed it into the British landscape tradition. Stanley Spencer is also one of mystical empiricism's best exemplars. Spalding writes:

> Spencer's originality lay in his merging of the descriptively literal with the visionary and imaginative. Behind his entire career lies a consistent purpose: to see the wholeness of things, to unite body with spirit, the sacred with the profane.[8]

And although the insularity of his resolutely local village life in Cookham was shattered by World War I, Spencer "continued … to search for the supernatural in the local and particular [and] to hallow the ordinary".[9] This mystical empiricism cannot wholly be separated from the prophetic strand which was the first line of influence I traced in this account of modern and contemporary religious art in Britain. I discussed this interweaving in Part I;

to encounter God's action in your midst and in your time is to find yourself and your context unsettled, as the prophets knew! I think, though, that the effects of a certain *sacramental* theology are also at work here, and must be acknowledged alongside Blake's nonconformist visionary passions. That is why I propose this as a third distinct line of influence, which I believe generates for us a third theological category for the evaluation of modern and contemporary church art in British contexts. In a British context, the sacramental presence of God tends to be articulated as a distributed, non-homogeneous presence, discernible (in principle) in each place and person and in each figure and form that surround us. This attitude is christologically-grounded, and is informed by the hereditary empiricism that von Balthasar highlights. Such sacramentality celebrates historical and geographical differences and looks at the variant forms emergent out of these differences in the expectant hope that the divine life can be discerned in them. It is an attitude advocated by Samuel Taylor Coleridge (see, for example, his poem *Frost at Midnight*), and it thrives on the soil of late-19th- and 20th-century British Catholicism, in Newman's acute sense of the revelatory value of historical modulations, in Hopkins's love of "pied beauty", in G.K. Chesterton's rejoicing in the quirky and the eccentric, and (to echo Shakespeare) in Tolkien's delight in small-scale and local "habitations" and "names".

In recent cathedral commissions, I see this sensibility in, for example, Christopher Le Brun's attention to the delight of the small domestic dog in his *Return of the Prodigal Son* (made for Liverpool Anglican Cathedral). If I am right, the identification of a "mystical empiricist" tradition helps us to understand how his landscapes can seem so mystically charged – humans and non-humans bound by a shared spiritual energy – as well as being so closely observed, making room as they do for the antics of the Prodigal Son's family pet. And in the same cathedral, I would propose we see some important continuities (though in a radically different medium and style) in Tracey Emin's *For You* (2008; fig. 6). What it has in common with Stanley Spencer, David Jones and others is a quirky but profoundly human concern with the way that the touch of the immediate may mediate the infinity of God; the God who is only and always Love. "In him we live and move and have our being", as Acts 17 has it, and we are invited to "feel after him, and find him". Emin's "I Felt You And I Knew You Loved me" seems to have done just this.

Artists like Le Brun and Emin in Liverpool make sacramental "nests" within the grand architectural spaces of the buildings that host them, just as they suggest moments of heightened and particular presence in the great sweeps of historical process and geographical expanse that threaten to render our individual experiences inconsequential. This can in itself be a form of powerful witness to the humility of the incarnation of God as Christianity witnesses to it – and the still, small voice of a Craigie Aitchison *Crucifixion* can be a source of powerful resistance to the great totalitarianisms of the noisy and violent times in which we live. For the greatest and most enduring truths will not be found in earthquakes, wind, and firestorms.

This may be reason enough to celebrate what Spalding calls 'the essentially provincial nature of [British art's] achievement' in its re-colonizing of church spaces like Manchester Cathedral (for which Mark Cazalet has made work) and St Mary the Virgin, Iffley in Oxfordshire (where Roger Wagner has). In Spalding's words: "Twentieth-century [and we may add 21st-century] British art represents, like many English gardens, an enclosed world which

6. Tracey Emin, *For You*, installation in the Cathedral Church of Christ (Liverpool), 2008.

holds our attention, not so much through its immediate impact, but through the slow revelation of the subtlety and complexity of species contained within it. It is this multiplicity, together with the sustained imaginative effort that gives to [such work] a quiet intensity, which links British art of this century with the greatness of its past".[10] ■

1   Jonathan Koestlé-Cate, *Art and the Church: A Fractious Embrace. Ecclesiastical Encounters ithw Contemporary Art*, London–New York, 2016, p. 20.

2   Frances Spalding, *British Art Since 1900*, London, 1986, p. 7.

3   Ibid.

4   All quotations of Simon Downham's words are from an interview with him on the 01 March 2011; I am indebted to my former student Sophie Young for conducting this interview.

5   I am grateful to my former MA student Sophie Young for this summary, and for her illuminating

work on Mackesy's triptych on which I have drawn in this section.

6   Hans Urs von Balthasar, *Herrlichkeit. Eine theologische Ästhetik*, Einsiedeln, 3 vols., 1961–9, English trans. by Erasmo Leiva Merikakis, 7 vols., San Francisco, 1982–9, III, p. 354.

7   Spalding 1986, op. cit., p. 8.

8   Ibid., p. 81.

9   Ibid., p. 84.

10   Ibid., p. 9.

Enchanting Secularity:
In praise of...

JEFFREY L. KOSKY

A late addition to the list of participants in this yearlong symposium on 'sacred arts' I was of course pleased to be welcomed, and I remain thankful for the invitation. But I need to point out that the book that led to my being invited, *Arts of Wonder*,[1] does not say "sacred" or "holy", "religion" or "religious," in its title, and in fact, it bears the subtitle *Enchanting Secularity*. This might make it surprising that I am included. Firstly because of the book's subject matter: the art it treats comes from the avant-garde or, more specifically, earthworks movement. This work is not often associated with religion or religious traditions, and the artworld for which it is canonic is commonly taken as emblematic of a godless and irreligious secular modernity. Secondly because of its subtitle: for an audience accustomed to thinking of 'secular' and 'religious' as opposites, the idea that a book about secularity would hold anything of significance to the sacred approaches the unthinkable. Which means: the phrase designating my project, *Enchanting Secularity*, is an oxymoron. Most scholars, including myself, are accustomed to equating modernization, secularization, and *dis*enchantment; 'enchanting secularity' is an untenable paradox.

In *Arts of Wonder*, I tried to hold to this untenable paradox. Responding to a sensation that there are many seculars today who are disenchanted with modern disenchantment, I approached 'enchanting secularity' by staging intimate encounters with significant artworks of 20th- and 21st century modernity. I chose big names and big works. These included Walter De Maria's *Lightning Field*, James Turrell's *Twilight Epiphany Skyspace*, and the works of Andy Goldsworthy, along with a few others. Here I found an art that does not invite suspicion or disenchantment, but is received in wonder. De Maria's *Lightning Field* in the New Mexico desert (fig. 1) and Turrell's *Twilight Epiphany Skyspace* (fig. 2), for instance, do nothing if they do not put you on earth under an open sky, wondering where you are and what you are doing here, in the widest sense. They invite the asking of big questions, searching questions, ones that wonder and seek.

They also encourage attention to mundane things. The paradox is worth highlighting: these earthworks invite the asking of big questions at the same time as they encourage attention to small things, as if the mundane itself was an invitation to wonder. They invited me to slow down and wait, wait for the light

1. Walter De Maria, *Lightning Field*, installation in Quemado (New Mexico), 1977.

to set or dawn at the *Lightning Field* so that I could see it materialize in those glorious poles. And they asked me to attend events I could not stop from happening – like the slow drift to the sea of an Andy Goldsworthy stick dome. In this sense works like this ask me to be patient, not agent, of my world. Such patience is quite the opposite of the everyday desperation that despairs of waiting and quits attending to these events it cannot control or make happen, running on instead to the next available thing and more productive business. I wasted a lot of time waiting in these places, to be sure, but I learned that it can be glorious to be given time to waste, especially when it affords a glance at such majestic sights.

My encounter with earthworks taught me to value the patience that waits on what is given and then to celebrate the moment in which I was attendant on something whose coming to be does not originate with me. Moments like this are hard to affirm within the framework of modern disenchantment. Not so for religion. More sensitive to a life in which we are not in control of the conditions of our everyday seeing and doing, religion has language and practices that celebrate what happens there, key terms in Christianity being *grace* and per-

haps *liturgy*. The theologian Josef Pieper says that the Christian life is organized around the word 'grace', a term signifying that "everything gained and everything claimed follows upon something given, and comes after something gratuitous and unearned; that in the beginning there is always a gift".[2] Its fundamental mood, he continues, the mood in which such graces are received, is appreciative, thankful. This appreciation takes shape in the leisurely celebration of praise – that is, in liturgy, a life lived leisurely precisely because, as thanking, it is not calculated to produce any desired outcome, having already received. Call it festival or liturgy, celebration or praise, it is a response that acknowledges with thanks what we cannot account for on the basis of what we know or make for ourselves and our world. This is markedly different from the response of a disenchantment that appreciates little it sees or writes about so suspiciously and critically – perhaps in an effort to defend its autonomy and independent originality.

When I wrote about the earthworks I visited, therefore, I found my response to them invoking a vocabulary that was anything but that of the disenchanted modern I was in the habit of being. That response had its origin in words

2. James Turrell, *Twilight Epiphany Skyspace*, Houston, Moody Center for The Arts - Rice University.

like "wonderful" or "magnificent," rather than interrogations like 'what is it, what is it saying'. I did not begin suspiciously with 'what's *really* going on', but 'Look' or 'I see', exclamations the works elicit by pointing majestically to a glorious landscape I could not grasp. The writing that articulated my response tried to remain faithful to this sense of awe and wonder. It is, I would like to think, akin to praise, a free response in which glimpses of glory seen in wonder take form.[3] By inviting such a response, works like this were the beginning of my essay at an alternative to the disenchantment of the world. They perhaps contribute to something like a liturgy of enchanting secularity.[4]

To colleagues in the secular academy, this may sound naïve, simple-minded, and unenlightened. Wonder is insufficiently critical, and the praise that issues from it frequently deluded or willfully unknowing. If asked where the art came from, we critical thinkers would hardly ever answer 'wonder'. We are far more likely to claim, as Rita Felski documents in *The*

Limits of Critique, the art emerged from power relations prevailing in surrounding historical context, a context composed of economic, political, social, and technological realities. And because the work encodes the operations of power, we believe we are deluded when we stand before it contemplatively and appreciate its appearance with words that say something like 'magnificent' or 'beautiful'. We in the secular academy are instead motivated suspiciously – to 'lift the veil', to 'demystify', and to otherwise expose and explain what is really going on, in truth, an explanation that can be offered only when the wonder has been overcome and the mystification banished.[5] To the degree that it speaks praise on the basis of wonder, enchanting secularity seems alienated from the norm of secular reception of the work of art.

But, the fact that I approach 'enchanting secularity' through a canon composed of avant garde 20th century art makes it seem equally alienated from religion. This is not the case, however. For, if an enchanting secularity takes form in works of praise originating in wonder, it surely has a thing or two to learn from religious tradition and traditional religion – which is after all learned and practiced, rich and resourceful, in techniques and examples of praise.

The target of my 'enchanting secularity', then, is not the secular or the religious as such but the disenchantment that pervades certain secularist and also religious understandings of self and being in the world. The disenchantment of the world risks making it unappealing and charmless, which rightly echoes in our disenchantment with it and frequently leads to an understandable desire to deny or negate it, indeed to flee it, sometimes in frightening movements and gestures. This disenchantment, of the world and with the world, found in both secularism and religion, is what enchanting secularity hopes, against hope, to counter. Art and religion can be allies in this, an effort to praise or appreciate what disenchantment sees only to dismiss or demystify without appreciating.

＊

It might now be time to address the notion of disenchantment. Those of us accustomed to using it as a diagnosis of modernization and secularization look to Max Weber for its canonic definition. In his famous essay, *Science as a Vocation*, Weber concludes dramatically: "The fate of our times is characterized by rationalization and intellectualization and above all by 'the disenchantment of the world'". This means, he specifies, "there are no mysterious incalculable forces that come into play, but rather that one can, in principle, master all things by calculation".[6] Before describing us, then, disenchantment is a thesis about the world: mysteries banished, the world that remains is one we can count on, reliably and predictably, precisely because it is one we can count up, measure and compute in a calculative science.

Disenchantment could also be considered a mood, if we keep in mind that moods are not located simply in me: they are how the world is in me and I in it. They are how the world appears.[7] But, disenchantment is a strange sort of mood, one that denies it is moody at all. The barest minimum of mood, it is buffered, shel-

tered, from the disturbances that come from the world that is received in our moods. It is not incorrect, then, to say 'no world appears in it' – except the one whose constitution I manage and direct by my own self-directed, self-controlled activity, an agency enabled by the buffering its moodless mood provides. In short, the world is not given to appear in disenchantment; it is constructed by it and constructed according to the interests of the disenchanted agent. What Hans Blumenberg, decades ago, called "the self-assertion of reason through the mastery and alteration of reality" is thereby founded on this mood and its thesis of the world.[8]

It would be a mistake, then, to take disenchantment to mean, at least at first, that we are too sunk in malaise to act or to make. Quite the contrary. The disenchantment of the world authorizes a frenzy of self-assertive activity to make and order reality, precisely because the disenchanted world can be counted on, reliably, to be accessible to calculations and technical means of counting it up. This lets the world be managed into being, as it were, by the efforts and administrations of disenchanted self-assertion, *rationalization* in Weber's term. This truth pertains equally to the reality of a life well-lived: we can make our life's happiness as readily as our cars. Done imploring unreliable spirits with prayers of unpredictable effect, disenchantment asserts itself and turns happily to the reliable rule of the calculable, where success is assured to one whose activity adheres to methodical plans. The sense of 'well' in a life 'well-lived' thereby comes to mean 'self-assertively', and the 'life' of the life well-lived is composed of activity realized in and empowered by a rational pursuit of calculated interests integrated into a systematic whole. I see it, for example, in the CV of my undergraduate students who take great pains when selecting courses to see that everything they do is accounted for on the transcript, is counted for credit, and counts toward a credential. Everything has a reason that accounts for it, and if it does not count and is not counted, it is not accounted worthy. Little to no time or energy is wasted in devotion to what cannot be accounted for in this way.

*

When discussing modernization and disenchantment with my students, I also try to show it to them, using an image, the frontispiece to Christian Wolff's classic of European enlightenment, *Reasonable Thoughts on God, the World and the Human Soul, and All Things in General*. The banner unfurling above the smiling sun says *Lucem post nubila reddit* [He/It brings back the light after the clouds]. This is a depiction of the climactic event that ends the dark times of the past: light returns triumphant, clouds dissipate, shadows vanish, and all there is (God, the world, the human soul, and all things in general) appears distinctly in the illuminated clearing made by the one light. It is an image of unveiling and demystification – thanks to which a day dawns in which everything fits into a unified picture of the world, embraced in the one cone of light shined by the 'reasonable thoughts' that are rendered for all things.

When I ask students what the sun symbolizes, who or what shines the light that lets us see the world in a truth that is clear and distinct, unified and whole, responses are generally divided: some say 'God'; others, 'Reason' or 'Science'. All are right. In both cases, there is a single point of view, an undisturbed perspective above it all, from which mastery of order is possible. You have only to stand there to be certain that what you see is seen truly.

The students' response tells me it is not only the secularist who buys into the disenchantment of the world. Indeed, there is a lot of religion, not all of it but much, that is about providing access to that position of uncontested vision and explaining the totality from there. Even though I do not stand there now, it says, I can know what is seen from that place, if I adhere to the divinity who occupies that position. This adherence is one way to understand what is meant by 'belief'. Belief affords access to the one who occupies the position from which mysteries are banished, questions answered, and explanations provided. Such belief risks becoming a form of disenchantment of its own. It is the opposite of faith – faith whose true opposite is no doubt but objective certainty and whose true 'object' is not explanation but mystery and glory, desire of the searching question.

This position and the belief that accesses it also operate in the suspicion and unmasking that dominate the critical enterprise of academic explanations of art. In this, the suspicious critic Felski describes resembles the allegorizing of believers who are out to find confirmation of creeds: her critiques find another figure of, for instance, the power relations that underlie everything that appears. In both cases, truths already possessed are confirmed in cases unveiled by the light brought to bear by such truths. Much knowledge has been produced thereby, and such demystification has brought important social and political change, but there is little of the searching question, little wonder, and little praise. We are very good at saying what we know about works of art and cultural objects, but less good at saying what is appealing to us about them.

Looking back to our image of modern disenchantment, we could see it through the subtle eyes of Friedrich Nietzsche. Readers of Nietzsche will see this as an image of the will to truth, whose contemporary realization he often figured in terms of high-noon. We have come to a noontime, it says, when the power to illuminate and explain (render reasons) means that truth is laid bare in a knowledge that unveils and uncovers all that hides in shadows or remains veiled in darkness. As things become clear, all can be seen distinctly. But, worried Nietzsche, what is seen clearly and distinctly grows shallow and brittle when the shadows that lend depth and weight to the surface of reality are forgotten. "One will hardly find us again on the paths of those Egyptian youths who endanger temples by night", he writes, "and want by all means to unveil, uncover, and put into a bright light whatever is kept concealed for good reasons. No, this bad taste, this will to truth, to 'truth at any price', this youthful madness in the love of truth, have lost their charm for us".[9] No longer charmed by the disenchanted gestures of a demystification that responds to beautiful appearances by lifting the veils and shining a light on everything, Nietzsche sees that too much brightness flattens things; without shadows, their surfaces become only superficial, and they lose body – seem less there, less radiant with a glory that makes it bearable for us to, in Nietzsche's words, "carry existence across the river of becoming".[10]

*

An enchanting secularity knows this, too. It sees that all too often secularity lets disenchantment triumph in a secularism that calculates very well, unmasks truth very successfully, but leaves a thin, insensible, mostly unappealing reality with very little to delight in seeing. Left with a calculable world, one might well wonder whether all the counting counts on things that count, whether what we are counting and counting on counts at all anymore.

It seems obvious that for what we are counting to count it has to be appreciated and appreciation is in a significant sense a matter of praise. What is less obvious but no less significant is the connection of this to art. The poet Susan Stewart helps. Writing about the relation of praise, the work of art, and making things count, she says,

> We could say that the most fundamental act of artistic making is the act of creating value by praising, for in praising creation we also set out a field of discrete choices [a realm of possible calculated decisions] that are necessary to human thought ... To thank is to specify and recognize, to make something count.[11]

In other words, praise or appreciation is also a matter of acknowledging with thanks given received. This acknowledgment, in praising, holds to the ground or origin of worth and value; it lets something count; and this (letting it count by praising and thanksgiving) is the work done in the work of art.

My own effort at holding to the ground of worth was organized by earthworks art. Lingering with such works, I learned the praise that celebrates being on earth under the sky.

At the *Lightning Field*, for instance, the poles opened a celebration of praise (fig. 1). Somewhat like a lyric poem as Robert von Hallberg describes it, the poles don't explain anything or say very much at all.

Lyric poems can seem intellectually modest, and not only because they are cut short. Poets behold and approve the value of the women, men, and landscapes that move them, but they don't *explain* that value. The identification of value is itself intellectually ambitious in a context dominated by skepticism and irony.

The poles are lyrical. Not signs that say something, they are pointers, indicators, designating or marking worth, value, meaningfulness, by their work of witnessing. Gathering earth and sky, shadow and light, into this desert, the art says "Behold...",[12] pointing with approval and appreciation to all there is. In the gesture of this work, praise and the opening of a world become one and the same.

Quite a few visitors describe the poles as "singing", lyrically, in the light of the dying sun, "a chorus of soft hues".[13] Akin to the experience of music, we feel the presence of the poles without them needing to explain themselves. As when language becomes song, the poles benefit from an authority beyond the signification of words. In that sense, again, the *Lightning Field* does something more original than explain, account for, or even communicate something about the world: it presents it immediately, as if musically, by beholding and approving it. A celebration of being on earth under the sky. While the song of the poles might not offer a reliable account of itself, putting it at a disadvantage with regard to the explanatory power of disenchanted discourses, the affirmation it conveys gives something, some things, pointed to with approval – and that is what is needed to make all the explaining and the accounting count for something.

If the art seeks to arrange a relation by pointing with approval, scholarship falls short, without being wrong, when it treats the poles as communicating some content – for instance, when it examines the statement they make about the commodification of art in the gallery system of presenting it. One could instead treat the poles as doing something, having an effect on us – more specifically, presenting the world to me and inviting me to receive it in wonder. Religion can help the scholar here, for when it thinks about a relation to the divine majesty, glory, or mystery of creation, it knows a higher way to be than theoretic knowledge and it knows truths other than those contained in propositions. This relation is praise, where the important thing is not so much what is known or said but the address to, the fact of maintaining a relation with the divine mystery. Religion knows that the use of names and naming in praise is not first of all a matter of explaining the other but, more pragmatically, acknowledging him and calling to him, in short arranging a relation in which a whole field of meaningful acts and statements opens. In fact, praise risks becoming idolatry when one believes its words and concepts adequate to its target, the mystery of God. The language of praise in this sense does not issue from comprehension but, as Susan Stewart said about art, from wonder and thankfulness, and thanksgiving, it is important to remember, is not so much an act of knowledge as it is an acknowledgment of others, even if unknown, and the gift whose presence preceded me. John Calvin, before Stewart, also noted as much when, commenting on the phrase with which the Christian praises God in the Lord's Prayer, "Hallowed be thy name", he says "[the glory of God] should captivate us with wonderment for him and impel us to celebrate his praise".[14] Cultivating wonderment in the face of the divine mystery, Calvin tells us, means recovering the ground of praise, an act of acknowledgment of this mysterious presence.

This is something enchanting secularity can learn from religion. Thanks to Calvin's lesson, I could linger with earthworks art, rather than restlessly try to clarify what they meant or were saying. They appealed to me in wonder; they did not invite suspicion that sought greater certainty, a form of quasi-ungratefulness to them that risks closing the appearing of the mystery of being on earth under the sky. My response hoped to be articulated as praise letting things appear majestically.

We might also find a world open in the praise that issues from wonder in a James Turrell skyspace. If ever there was a work of art that gave us to experience "Behold…", this would be it. Sitting and looking at what it points out to me, I become intimate with things appearing in its depth: clouds shapechanging; a leaf adrift; birds passing from and to elsewhere. They all draw near, yet none are grasped by the work that indicates them in the distance, passing.

Turrell's art thereby separates what disenchantment connects: seeing from mastering and perhaps therefore knowing from manipulating. It gives us over to experiences of sight that are perhaps best understood as something like contemplative wonder: a vision that does not grasp what it sees but rather wonders before and about it. Looking into the profound blue, I can only admire what appears so gloriously. The birds on their way through the skyspace are 'magnificent', whereas ordinarily I overlook them or they are a nuisance, eating my blueberries. The clouds that pass through the frame of the oculus are 'beautiful', not something to banish so that I might see the eclipse or enjoy the picnic this afternoon. Such language ('magnificent', 'beautiful') is the language of one who, in Von Hallberg's words, "wants only to name, not to explain"; it is, he observes, the language of worship or adoration, where names are used pragmatically to enter approvingly into relation with that other invoked – and praised.[15]

Bringing the birds, the leaves, and the clouds into focus, Turrell's work enlarges reality, makes it more capacious. This, too, is the work of praise, as Susan Stewart again writes:

> Traditions of praising a Creator intensify and multiply the gifts of creation … the specifying act of praise enriches the manifold of the world. 'I will praise; I will magnify', claims the speaker in Psalm 69 [69:30] – to praise is to enlarge.[16]

Turrell's works do the work of magnification that is praise. I cannot help but think of a skyspace as a magnifying lens. Far from eliminative, the aperture or frame in it magnifies – both enlarges and praises, at the same time, making our world more grand, in contrast to the critics' too frequent reductionism that often leaves a pale and shrunken world seen in explanations that are clear and powerfully effective but dull and charmless.

*

'Enchanting secularity' can learn from works of art like these, for such art presents a world that is worth counting: a world that is pointed to with praise, appreciation, or approval is one where we might hope our calculations count on things that count. I do not intend by this to say that art fills a place left vacant by religion. That is triumphant secularism talking; it supposes a subtraction of religion from contemporary life and culture. What I prefer to say is that the work of art can provide places that incite and sustain longings and desires, attitudes and dispositions, that religion is *also* expert at cultivating. In fact, venturing one step further, I would say that my 'enchanting secularity' learned from religion how to encounter works of art in ways that might break the spell of modern disenchantment – in this case by accepting the invitation to linger in the wonder and let it take shape in praise. ■

1 Jeffrey L. Kosky, *Arts of Wonder: Enchanting Secularity, Walter De Maria, Diller + Scofidio, James Turrell, Andy Goldsworthy*, Chicago, 2013.

2 Josef Pieper, *Leisure: the Basis of Culture*, San Francisco, 2009 (1st ed. New York, 1952), p. 36.

3 Praise is the articulation of wonder. The poet Susan Stewart writes: "Human beings begin in response, and the most fundamental, preliminary act of response is the expression of wonder. What follows such awe is praise's articulating and articulated forms … Humans can praise with things they have made". See Susan Stewart, *The Poet's Freedom. A Notebook on Making*, Chicago, 2011, pp. 30, 32.

4 This liturgy of enchanting secularity differs from the secular liturgies described by James K.A. Smith in his book, *Desiring the Kingdom. Worship, Worldview, and Cultural Formation*, Grand Rapids, MI, 2009. Smith restricts his account of secular liturgies to the shopping mall. This seems shortsighted – untrue to secularity and its potentialities. He may be right that the shopping mall is "a material ritual of ultimate concern", one that expresses and more importantly shapes dispositions and desires, and he is right that seeing it this way opens a much desired critical space for escaping it. But there are, I venture, other liturgies of secularity.

5 Rita Felski, *The Limits of Critique*, Chicago–London, 2015. Almost predictably, therefore, the works preferred by the secular critic, observes Felski, are those engaged in the very process of disenchanted critique that we imagine for our own enterprise.

6 Max Weber, *Science as a Vocation* [1917], in *From Max Weber: Essays in Sociology*, edited by Hans H. Gerth, Charles Wright Mills, New York, 1946, pp. 139, 155.

7 This is not the place to develop a theory of moods. Let it suffice it to say they are how the world appears, both in the adjectival/adverbial sense of 'how' and, more importantly, also in the active, verbal sense of 'how'.

8 Hans Blumenberg, *Die Legitimat der Neuzeit*, Frankfurt, 1966, English translation wit the title *The Legitimacy of the Modern Age*, by Roger M. Wallace, Cambridge MA, 1983, p. 137.

9 Friedrich W. Nietzsche, *Nietzsche Contra Wagner* [1889], in *The Portable Nietzsche*, translated by Walter Kaufmann, New York, 1954, p. 682.

10 Friedrich W. Nietzsche, *The Gay Science* [1882], ed. by Bernard Williams, Cambridge, 2001, p. 104. In context, the citation runs: "Honesty would lead to nausea and suicide. But now our honesty has a counterforce against our honesty that helps us to avoid such consequences: art as the *good* will to appearance … then it is no longer eternal imperfection that we carry across the river of becoming – we then feel that we are carrying a *goddess*, and are proud and childish in performing this service … an aesthetic phenomenon existence is still *bearable* for us". In an editor's note, Walter Kaufmann rightly notes that this passage echoes an earlier one from *The Birth of Tragedy*, with a significant difference: in the earlier work Nietzsche wrote that existence is *justified* as an aesthetic phenomenon; now he says it is *bearable*. Justification or explanation, the rendering of reasons or an accounting, is precisely what existence does not need; it needs to be praised, turned into a goddess so that we can carry it proudly.

11 Stewart 2011, op. cit., p. 32.

12 Robert von Hallberg, *Lyric Powers*, Chicago–London, 2009, pp. 17, 35.

13 Erin Hogan, *Spiral Jetta: A Road Trip through the Land Art of the American West*, Chicago–London, 2008, p. 125.

14 John Calvin, *Institutionis Christianae Religionis* [1559]; trans. by Ford Battles, edited by John McNeill, Philadelphia, 1960, p. 904.

15 Hallberg 2009, op. cit., p. 34.

16 Stewart 2011, op. cit., p. 40.

The Arts and the Need of the World

DEBORAH SOKOLOVE

In *The Community of the Beautiful*, the late theologian Alejandro Garcia-Rivera describes the call of beauty – which he spells with a capital B – that he first heard as a young man.

> It was Beauty at her most beautiful. Subversive, yet gracious, ever hoping and fresh, Beauty crossed barriers and created community. Beauty's call made possible the impossible and made visible the invisible. Beauty could cross differences made long ago. Indeed, Beauty loved difference.[1]

While the gender that Garcia-Rivera assigns to beauty raises a lot of issues that I don't have time to address here, I love the thrill of discovery and excitement with which he describes an experience in which he sees the difference between false, deceptive beauties and what is truly beautiful. In looking for a way to discern this true beauty, he suggests that there is a third type of knowing that is neither perception nor cognition, but takes a middle place between them. Relating perception to what he calls the Community of the True, and cognition to the Community of the Good, this third type of knowing moves the heart through the senses not in some ethereal other world, but precisely in what he calls "the garden of good and evil". Here, for Garcia-Rivera, the aesthetic norm is revealed as that which lifts up the lowly in the ongoing creation of the Community of the Beautiful.[2]

In many discussions with theologians, pastors, artists, and ordinary Christians, not to mention people who don't fit any of these categories (or fit more than one) it has become clear to me that this is not what most people mean when they talk about beauty. In contemporary, Western culture, the word *beautiful* is slippery, applied with equal ease to spectacular sunsets, sleek cars, stylish clothes, Renaissance paintings, and certain women, usually those who are young, slender, and possessing regular features. For this reason, as well as because of its connection with the cosmetics/fashion/entertainment industrial complex and the inevitable slippage from that realm to the quite different discursive realms of the church and the art world, I find beauty a troubling notion.

Too often, especially in religious communities, arguments for the arts hinge on an expectation that what will be produced or acquired will be beautiful. What people usually mean by this is that it will please their eyes or ears,

1. Massachusetts militiamen with fixed bayonets surround a group of peaceful strikers in the 1912 Textile Workers Strike at Lawrence, MA.

or at least uplift their spirits. The ensuing arguments over whether this or that piece of art is beautiful or ugly reveals more about their personal taste than about the intrinsic worth of the artwork.

Rather than engage that argument, I would like to share with you some artworks that are not necessarily intended to be beautiful in any conventional sense of the word, but rather exhibit elements that Garcia-Rivera identified with the Community of the Beautiful. Some of them were made by professional artists, working in anguished response to brokenness of the world around them. Others were made in and for specific communities, often in collaboration with other artists as well as social workers, chaplains, and ordinary folk from those communities. Some were not intended to be art at all, but rather were made by grieving, hurting people on their road towards healing.

Let me begin with a poem called *Bread and Roses* written by John Oppenheim in 1911. Later set to music, it was sung by the women who marched on the picket lines at the American Woolen Company in Lawrence, Massachusetts (fig. 1), in 1912 as they struck for fair pay and safe working conditions. It goes like this:

As we go marching, marching, in the beauty of the day / A million darkened kitchens, a thousand mill lofts gray / Are touched with all the radiance that a sudden sun discloses / For the people hear us singing, bread and roses, bread and roses. / As we go marching, marching, we battle too, for men, / For they are women's children and we mother them again. / Our days shall not be sweated from birth until life closes, / Hearts starve as well as bodies, give us bread, but give us roses. / As we go marching, marching, un-numbered women dead / Go crying through our singing their ancient call for bread, / Small art and love and beauty their trudging spirits knew / Yes, it is bread we fight for, but we fight for roses, too. / As we go marching, marching, we bring the greater day. / The rising of the women means the rising of the race. / No more the drudge and idler, ten that toil where one reposes, / But a sharing of life's glories, bread and roses, bread and roses.

I have so many memories of this poem that I no longer know if it is beautiful, or even very good. What I do know is that everyone needs to live in a world where they not only have enough bread to sustain their bodies but also enough roses to sustain their spirits. Both physical sustenance and spiritual food, found in the expressiveness of the human-created arts as well as in the beauty of God's created world, are necessary for a fully human life.

Often, spiritual food grows in places of pain. While officially thought of as a form of urban blight and prosecuted as vandalism, graffiti might more usefully be understood as a creative response to feeling unseen and unheard. As Italian photographer Gusmano Cesaretti observes,

> A Chicano kid grows up with walls of many kinds around him. When somebody is born into that situation, there are several things he can do. He can ignore the walls and sink into apathy. Or he can become violent and try to blow up the walls. But there is a third way, a way that people have used for centuries. And that is to perform a kind of ritual magic to neutralize the force of the walls by decorating them with signs, symbols, and art.[3]

While I cringe at some of the words I find myself reading on the sides of buildings when I ride the Metro in Washington, D.C., I admire the courage and resourcefulness of the young people who climb over fences and all kinds of other obstacles with their pockets filled with cans of spray paint, merely to play with form and color. With little or no training, but lots of heart, many of them make artworks that are bold, well-designed, and free just for the looking.

In the barrios of East Los Angeles, the walls are covered with what some call 'graffiti', and others give the more dignified label of 'mural'. Some, like this one at the entrance to a low-income housing project called Estrada Courts, are made by friends and neighbors to commemorate the all-too-frequent deaths of young people who fall prey to violence or drugs (fig. 2).

Others are made by professionally trained artists, like this one called *The Wall that Cracked Open*, by Willie Herrón. It was painted in 1972 near the site where Herrón's

2. Mural at entrance to Estrada Courts, 1987.

younger brother was beaten up and stabbed in the neck by local gang members. While not quite convincingly illusionistic, and certainly not beautiful in any conventional sense of the word, the mural depicts the young man and his attackers breaking through the wall on which they are painted. Intentionally incorporating the existing graffiti, it questions the separation between art and everyday life, as well as the alienation from the larger society felt by both the gang members and their victims.

The connections between art, spirituality, and healing are unquestioned in most non-Western societies. From Navajo sand paintings to Buddhist *mandalas* and *tankhas* to masks and songs and dances and effigies, the arts are intrinsic to healing rituals in many parts of the world. In the 20th century, various psychosocial therapeutic models began to be augmented with visual art, music, dance, and other modes of creative expression, to gain access to the thoughts and feelings of clients for whom talking therapies were insufficient. As the interconnection between the mind, body, and spirit becomes increasingly well understood in the scientific community, the potential of the arts to affect physical, as well as psychological, healing is being realized in more and more places. Hospitals turn their hallways into art galleries; senior centers recommend storytelling to help clients with dementia recover memories and reconnect with loved ones; and countless workshops, seminars, retreats, and conferences are offered for people to learn to use the arts in their own quest for healing.

This therapeutic aspect of the arts is not reserved solely for those with time and money to seek it out. In 2001, David Harris found both a voice and a home when he joined a creative writing group at Miriam's Kitchen, a breakfast program for people who are homeless in Washington, D.C. Writing poetry became a means for him to combat the fear, loneliness, and physical privation of life on the streets. Privately published as *Street Corner Majesty* by the members of a church group that calls itself The Pilgrimage. Harris now lives in a subsidized apartment, and shares his story and poetry through the National Coalition for the Homeless Faces of Poverty Panel and through

teaching his own Creative Writing Workshops. In "Small Blue Poem #2", he writes of a perfect moment in the midst of life on the street:

> The Sun peeks through layers of thick gray clouds and / bathes me in a warm spotlight. Says the Sun: / Here is a small blue thing / lying forgotten in grass and clover. / Here's a weed / to be plucked from a lush green lawn. / Now I've been purged – you can gaze upon perfection.[4]

At N Street Village, another shelter in Washington, D.C., homeless women learn to find their voices through sustained, disciplined participation in drama. Life Stories is a program of the Theater Lab School of the Dramatic Arts, a non-profit institution whose mission is to transform lives through the theater, with summer camps, weekend workshops, and classes in acting, playwriting, and public speaking for children and adults at all levels of experience. At N Street, Theater Lab faculty members give the clients enough instruction in writing and acting to present their stories as polished monologues, allowing themselves and others to see their stories as something larger than their own, private tales of woe.

A few years ago, some of these stories were gathered into a scripted performance called *My Soul Look Back in Wonder*, which was presented at the Kennedy Center Terrace Theater in early 2012. At a gathering a few months later, the women told new stories of lives redeemed – one had gotten her GED, another had gone to cosmetology school and was working as a hairdresser, another was writing a book, and yet another had reconciled with family from whom she had been estranged for many years. All of them attributed their success to the skills and self-discipline that they had learned as members of the Life Stories workshop.

A documentary film called *How I Got Over* was made about this process by Nicole Boxer. The trailer at <https://www.youtube.com/watch?v=ieFavfyYBKo> will give you a taste of what I am talking about.

Even when life is cut short, the arts can help people find a meaning in their suffering.

When I first came to Wesley Theological Seminary as an Artist-in-Residence in January 1994, I met a student named Wesley Maxwell Lawton. Max was an artist before he came to seminary, and he had been given a corner of the studio to paint in. When I arrived, he was working on a painting that he called *Man of Sorrows*. During Advent, he had been alone in his apartment, overcome with grief over the deaths of friends, loved ones, and mentors because of AIDS. In a vision or waking dream, he saw himself sitting on a hospital examination table, naked, and hooked-up to oxygen and IV drips. Suddenly, he wrote,

> the image changed. It was no longer me sitting there, but Christ, covered in AIDS cancer lesions with his head bowed, nude wearing only a crown of thorns. I knew I had to paint it. I quickly gathered my supplies and, in a transcendent experience, I made the first version of *Man of Sorrows: Christ with AIDS*.[5]

While the painting was on display at the seminary, a visiting priest from Cape Town who had been sent by Archbishop Desmond Tutu to Washington, D.C., to research AIDS ministries saw it. Several months later, Archbishop Tutu and his new ministry, Wola Nani-Embrace, invited him to Cape Town to make a similar version of the painting in St George's Cathedral.

While the painting that Max made in Cape Town stirred up a lot of controversy, eventually it went on to tour universities and townships all over South Africa. It now remains at the Wola Nani-Embrace center, reminding all who see it of Christ's healing presence with those living with HIV/AIDS.

Max died in June, 2006. His partner, Ed Grieff, brought the original *Man of Sorrows: Christ with AIDS* to a memorial service at the Seminary and offered it to us as an indefinite loan. Today, it hangs outside our studio, where I first saw Max working on it.

Of course, not everyone living with HIV/AIDS is a trained artist like Max, but art can and does help people from a variety of backgrounds find healing and wholeness, if not a cure. In South Africa, artist Jane Solomon has

been developing a process called body mapping to help people living with HIV/AIDS to reframe their personal narratives as a way towards new self-understanding. Working with clinical psychologist Jonathan Morgan under the auspices of the Regional Psychosocial Support Initiative (REPSSI), an international capacity-building organization, and the Canadian AIDS Treatment Information Exchange (CATIE), Solomon developed a facilitator's guide called "Living with X: A Body Mapping Journey in the time of HIV and AIDS".

Solomon writes,

> Instead of talking about someone who is 'Living with AIDS', we talk about 'Living with X'. We have done this because we do not believe that having HIV or AIDS is the most important thing about a person. There are many other personal qualities that are more important, and we have called those things X. Different people will have different ideas about what X means.[6]

People who have participated in Living with X Body Mapping Workshops learn not to just describe themselves as persons living with HIV/AIDS. Instead, they now describe themselves as persons living with "strong feelings and a smart attitude ... principles and courageous love ... initiative and a love for development ... initiative, bravery and hope ... courage and a leader ... [or] endurance and a good head for business".[7]

Unlike Max, none of these people would describe themselves as artists. Rather, like the women at the N Street Village Life Stories workshop, who learned enough about writing and acting to tell their own stories with artful conviction, the people who participate in Living with X workshops have been through an extended process in which they acquired enough tools and skills to discover their own self-worth, and to define themselves in ways that do not deny their HIV status, but include it as only one of many facets of their being.

There is often a very thin line between art and ritual. In many societies, such as Japan or Mexico, it is customary to create shrines in the home which incorporate elements of both ritual and art. In the 19th-century United States such shrines were common, and might include a daguerreotype of the deceased person, mourning lockets containing the person's hair woven into a wreath, embroidered or painted memorial pictures, and mourning scrapbooks or quilts.

A few years ago, Chaplain Rhonda Cooper and social worker Louise Knight at the Sidney Kimmel Comprehensive Cancer Center at Johns Hopkins Hospital thought it would be a good idea to hold a Service of Remembrance for all the patients who had died in the previous year. They recognized that not only the families, but the doctors, nurses, and other hospital staff who had become attached to patients in the course of long and intense treatment, needed the opportunity to remember and to mourn. Realizing that an artist might offer some skills and perspective that they might not otherwise be able to access, they invited community artist Cinder Hypki to collaborate with them in the design of the service.

Over 300 people attended the event, which included an invitation for family members to call out the names of the deceased. Some held photographs, some merely stood, as those who had died were remembered as loved and valued individuals. As the service ended, everyone was given the opportunity to write a message – a wish, a prayer, a remembrance – on a strip of cloth, and weave that cloth into a sculpture that had been prepared to hold them. More than 250 people contributed to the sculpture by the end of the evening.

This was not some empty ritual. Nor was it meant to be high art in the strictest sense of the word. Rather, it was a means by which people could get in touch with their grief and share their memory with others, contributing to a common project with visual and tactile elements. Hypki reports that many people took out their cell phones and photographed the messages they had written and placed into the sculpture. She concludes,

> In effect, to take a photo and text it, e-mail it, post it on social networking sites, or save it, was to affirm: 'I was here, I did this thing that was important to me and it was a part of

something much larger that validates me and our collective coming together'.[8]

Following the service, staff members expressed their gratitude at the opportunity to reconnect with the families of those whom they had served, and a Service of Remembrance, complete with the opportunity to contribute to a sculpture, has now become an expected annual event.

On reading the article describing this artful service, I found myself awash in tears, deep in my own memories of grief and loss. I contacted Hypki soon thereafter, and in a conversation with her and Cooper as they were planning the third iteration of the service, I asked what would become of the sculptures. On the one hand, the works were meant to be ephemeral, and were too large and fragile to store or exhibit. On the other hand, the strips of cloth with their heartfelt messages seemed somehow sacred, and could not simply be disposed of unceremoniously.

Several weeks later, Hypki reported on what she calls 'the second life' of the messages. Nurses and other staff began braiding the rope this spring, in anticipation of archiving them and freeing up the sculpture itself for this third Service. As I did the first year, they documented each strip by logging it in to a document for that purpose, and they braided three sets of braids which then became the strands for a larger braid about an inch thick and 9 feet long.

Hypki, Cooper, and staff members have decided that the braids from each years' sculptures will be joined together in a continuous rope which will remain at the Kimmel Cancer Center as a witness to the ongoing life of this community of caring.

In this paper, I have offered just a few examples from the countless artworks that have been made intentionally as food for starving souls. I could have chosen other stories, equally moving, equally important, that feed the imagination, soothe heartbreak, and free the mind from the images of war, poverty, disaster, and political nastiness that relentlessly fill the news. As William Carlos Williams once wrote in *Ásphodel, That Greeny Flower*, it is difficult to get the news from poems, but every day people die because they do not have what may be found in them.[9]

Genuine transformation can happen when people in situations of extreme difficulty, as well as those in more privileged situations, are given the chance to participate in artistic experiences. Whether the resulting artworks are beautiful or not, I would suggest that they help to build the Community of the Beautiful, one artwork, one person, one community at a time. Through offering opportunities for people of all ages and all stations in life to participate in the arts, religious communities can address the need of a world that is crying out for far more than bread. ■

1   Alejandro Garcia-Rivera, *The Community of the Beautiful. A Theological Aesthetics*, Collegeville, MN, 1999, p. 3.

2   Ibid., pp. 170–1.

3   Gusmano Cesaretti, *Street Writers. A Guide Tour of Chicano Graffiti*, Los Angeles, 1975, p. 61.

4   David Harris, *Street Corner Majesty*, Bloomington, 2009, p. 20.

5   Wesley Maxwell Lawton, private communication.

6   Jane Solomon, *Living with X. A Body Mapping Journey in the Time of HIV and AIDS: Facilitator's Guide*, Johannesburg, 2008, p. 2.

7   Ibid., pp. 55–7 passim.

8   Cinder Hypki, Rhonda S. Cooper, Louise Knight, 'Memorial Ritual and Art: A Case Study and Exploration of the Potential for Healing', *Community Arts Journal (Maryland Institute College of Art)*, no. 3 (2011). <https://www.mica.edu/About_MICA/Departments_and_Services/The_Center_for_Art_Education/Community_Arts_Journal/Memorial_Ritual_and_Art.html>, accessed 25 June 2019.

9   William Carlos Williams, *Asphodel, That Greeny Flower*, collected in *Journey to Love*, New York, 1955.

Part 6

The artists speak

Art as Prayer

The Spirit Comes to Help Us in Our Weakness

TIMOTHY VERDON

St Paul affirms that "the Spirit ... comes to help us in our weakness. For when we cannot choose words in order to pray properly, the Spirit himself expresses our plea in a way that could never be put into words, and God who knows everything in our hearts knows perfectly well what he means, and that the pleas of the saints expressed by the Spirit are according to the mind of God" (Rm 8:26–7).

Precisely this was the case of the exhibition organized in the context of the international symposium which the present volume documents, *The Arts and Ecumenism*. The exhibition (Florence, Museo dell'Opera del Duomo, 2017; Orleans, Massachusetts, Community of Jesus, 2017–18) was born, that is, in a situation in which all taking part felt the difficulty of choosing 'words in order to pray properly', given that neither side any longer seeks to convince or convert, as once was the case.

What, we all asked, should we ask? For what should we pray? Above all how could we pray together when, for half a millennium each of the main Christian traditions – the Orthodox, the Roman Catholic, the Protestant and the Anglican – has developed its own language, with a distinct syntax and vocabulary. What we needed was something completely new.

We needed an intervention of the Holy Spirit – the same Spirit who hovered over the waters

at the creation of the world, who covered Mary with his divine shadow at the Annunciation, who descended on Jesus at the Baptism and who enlightened the apostles at Pentecost. We needed the 'Creator Spirit' evoked in the exhibition's title, whose presence has often been associated with art and with the power of images to touch the heart. Speaking of art, Christians in fact use terms like 'inspired' and 'prophetic' to emphasize its supernatural force.

The relationship between human creativity and God's original creative act should not be taken for granted, however, and the subtitle of our symposium, *What Theology risks in artistic creativity*, suggested the caution with which Christianity has interpreted art's role in the life of believers: the distrust, at times open, at times veiled, that stripped Protestant churches of images and has often reduced the art made for Catholic churches to mere decoration.

For art to communicate the Divine it must be nourished by prayer, as in the Orthodox tradition, translating the sense of the Scriptures in visible forms and becoming a material sign of spiritual realities. These indeed were the objectives which guided our artists: Susan Kanaga, an American Protestant woman, and Filippo Rossi, an Italian Catholic man. Together they sought to let the Spirit speak in their works – the Spirit who comes to help us in our weakness, praying in us in ways that could never be put into words. Their exhibition in fact evoked Pentecost, the outpouring of the Spirit on Mary and the apostles after the Savior's ascension to heaven – the same Spirit which all Christians receive as a gift in Baptism. And, since Christians are baptized in the death of Christ crucified in the hope of sharing also in his resurrection (Rm 6:3–5), the sign which Kanaga and Rossi proposed was Jesus's cross transfigured by glory. In the exhibition, moreover, the cross had the shape of the Greek letter 'Tau' because, in the Book of Ezechiel, the Tau marks the forehead of those who "sigh and weep for all the abominations" committed in this world; on judgment day God will command his angels to do no harm to those whose foreheads are marked with a Tau (Ez 9:4–6). The Tau-cross is a sign, that is, of the Spirit's greatest gift: salvation.

Kanaga and Rossi communicate the glory of the saving Tau, which invested the apostles at Pentecost, with gold, which transforms the material substance of the cross into light. The idea of a transformation of matter occurs in the New Testament in the same text in which Paul speaks of the Holy Spirit coming to "help us in our weakness": a few lines before that phrase, when the saint states that all of material creation is "eagerly awaiting for God to reveal his sons", since it too is destined for freedom and for glory (Rm 8:19–21). He speaks, that is, of a cosmic transformation at the end of time.

St Paul's text also speaks of a bond between creation's yearning for this future glory and the similar aspiration of the human heart. He says: "From the beginning till now, the entire creation, as we know, has been groaning in one great act of giving birth; and not only creation, but all of us who possess the first fruits of the Spirit, we too groan inwardly as we wait for our bodies to be set free" (Rm 8:22–3). Then, as if to insist on the mystical character of the bond between human beings and material creation, Paul adds:

For we must be content to hope that we shall be saved – our salvation is not in sight, we should not have to be hoping for it if it were – but as I say we must hope to be saved since we are not saved yet – it is something we must wait for in patience (Rm 8:24–5).

Our salvation is not in sight, we should not have to be hoping for it if it were… it is something we must wait for in patience. It was for this reason that Kanaga and Rossi chose the language of abstraction: they wanted to communicate a Salvation that is more than the memory of past events – more than the narrative of the first Pentecost, with Mary and the apostles in the upper room and tongues of fire above their heads. Kanaga and Rossi wanted to arouse the viewer's hope of something that is not "in sight", for which human beings wait with patient intensity. They wanted to inspire in those who saw their works the courage needed to continue waiting for God.

In St Paul's text, right after the phrase "Our salvation is not in sight, we should not have to be hoping for it if it were … it is something we must wait for in patience", the apostle says:

The Spirit too comes to help us in our weakness. For when we cannot choose words in order to pray properly, the Spirit himself expresses our plea in a way that could never be put into words, and God who knows everything in our hearts knows perfectly well what he means, and that the pleas of the saints expressed by the Spirit are according to the mind of God.

Our 'plea' cannot be put into words because no verbal formulation could adequately express its depth, nor are there terms high enough to communicate its meaning. Insufficient too are figurative images, which reduce to iconographic formulae "things that no eye has seen and no ear has heard, things beyond the mind of man, all that God has prepared for those who love him" (1 Co 2:9; see Is 64:3).

For these things that "no eye has seen", Kanaga and Rossi used the language of abstraction, which they paired with fragmentary Scripture texts distributed throughout the exhibit. In fact Christ himself, the incarnate Word, did not hesitate to present himself in terms far from any possible figurative representation, as 'the way', 'the truth', 'the life' and 'the light' of humankind. Above all in the liturgical context, where art is called to accompany rites that urge us to go beyond the external aspect of things, abstraction is often the style best suited to the living mystery which is celebrated.

Kanaga's and Rossi's intention was not to question the value of the figurative tradition, which in church art past, present and future has been, is and will continue to be a fundamental point of reference. But they wanted to recall the principle enunciated by Émile-Auguste Chartier, the philosopher of art known as 'Alain' (1868–1951), according to whom "the work of a true sculptor, like that of a true painter, should conform to the rule that to recognize something does not mean to know it" (Reconnaître n'est pas connaître).[1] Taken from his *System of the Fine Arts*, published in 1920, Alain's assertion was born in the context of a revaluation of traditional aesthetics made necessary by the artistic innovations of the early 20th century, whose central idea had been the refusal of naturalistic mimesis. In sculptural and pictorial images of that time – by masters such as Braque, Picasso, Leger, Duchamp, Mondrian, Klee, Arp, Kandinsky and later Miró – a common denominator in fact was the non-recognizable subject, which nonetheless promised a heightened level of 'knowledge'. Thus the phrase, "to recognize something does not mean to know it", was emblematic of the refusal of an outdated system in which the legibility of the subject might falsify its meaning.

Those who even today claim that only the figurative style is suitable for Christian art should bear in mind St Augustine's words on the art of song: specifically on the 'new song' which Psalm 32 invites believers to sing: "Give thanks to the Lord upon the lyre, play to him on the ten-stringed harp; sing a new song in his honor, play with all your skill as you acclaim him!" (Ps 32 [33]:2–3). Augustine exhorts his reader:

Free yourself of all that is old – you now know a new song. A new man, a New Testament, a new song: the new song is unsuitable for old men. Only new men may learn it: men renewed, through grace, and freed of what was old; men of the New Testament, which is the kingdom of heaven. For that kingdom we yearn with all our hearts and sing a new song; raise a new song not with your tongue but with your life.[2]

According to Augustine, this song raised to God with the believer's life is *abstract*, not figurative: it uses only sounds, that is, not words. After stating that it is God himself who gives the tone, the Bishop of Hippo says to all who want to sing in this way:

Do not seek words, as if you could translate into articulated sounds a song in which God will take pleasure. Sing rather with jubilation; to sing to God with art consists precisely in this: to sing with jubilation. And what does it mean to sing with jubilation? It means to understand and yet not be able to explain what we sing in our heart. In fact, those who sing during the grain or grape harvest, or during any form of intense work, first experience pleasure in the words of their songs, but then, as the excitement grows, sense that words can no longer express what they feel and so vent their emotion with a simple modulation of notes. This is the song we call 'jubilation'.[3]

In ecumenical dialogue this song without words makes it possible to express things that words would inhibit, gathering into unity voices that would otherwise seem divided, harmonizing different tones. It is not man who brings this about, but the Spirit creator of unity, who prays in us in ways that could never be put into words – the Spirit of Pentecost, who lets us understand unknown languages.

One of the languages of the Spirit is art. ■

1   See Leonardo Sciascia, 'I ritratti', in *Mario Pecoraino*, exhibition catalogue (Palermo, Galleria Civica d'Arte Moderna Empedocle Restivo, 1987), edited by Giuseppe Bellafiore, Palermo, 1987, pp. 21–2.

2   St Augustine, *Exposition of the Book of Psalms*, 32.2, 8.
3   Ibid.

My Artistic Journey

SUSAN KANAGA

My artistic journey began early in life. I would describe myself as a creative, someone who didn't quite see things artistically as others did. Color, shape, form, texture, smell and sound were there to be explored. This curiosity has led me in many directions. I'm at heart a painter, but am also a costume designer, mosaicist, professional florist and a professional make-up artist.

I was born and raised in Kansas City and as a child, I was brought up in the Reformed tradition. I have many fond memories of worshiping in St Andrew's Episcopal Church, where I was baptized, confirmed and married.

I was fascinated throughout my childhood with the liturgy and the word, although at the time I didn't have the vocabulary nor experience to fully understand our worship services. Instead, I let my imagination create pictures in my mind to further grasp such phrases as "so great a cloud of witnesses", "I am the light of the world" and "I am the door", to name just a few. In this way, my understanding of abstract ideas took shape in color and form. Worship became more personal but I still felt a void, a disconnectedness.

In High School, I had the opportunity to visit five European capitals. It was at St Peter's in Rome that I finally understood what had been missing from my childhood religious tradition: images. Yes, I was familiar with prayer, the sacraments, the liturgy and the word, but not with the power of sacred art. Here, scripture took two and three-dimensional form. In my mind the image and the word became one and my eyes were opened to an entirely new way of seeing.

In 1983, my husband and I answered a call from God and moved with our two children from Denver, Colorado to live as members of the Community of Jesus. We have been vowed members there for 34 years.

The heart of all activity within the Community is the Church of the Transfiguration. It is filled with images created by artists from all over the world. In 1999, collaborating with Master Sculptor Regis Demange, I received the design commission for sculpture of the eight-ton exterior lintel for the church. In 2004, I again collaborated with Regis, to design a creation cycle for the ten column capitals of the Church of the Transfiguration's atrium. All of the design work was created from my personal interpretation of the Genesis scriptures. From this point on, sacred art became my vocation.

SECTION II

When and how I first met Filippo Rossi pivoted off my decision to go back to school. I had taken many art workshops and continuing art education classes during the time I raised our children but wanted and needed formal training. And so, in 2009 I began four years of study at the Maine College of Art.

It was interesting to me that while I immersed myself in the technical and historical aspects of creativity, I shied away from speaking my truth. I felt it was not an open environment to fabricate and exhibit Christian art; every other "ism" was acceptable just not Christ-centered sacred art. And then, two things happened which changed my life.

In my Junior year after declaring painting as my chosen major, I hit a wall. I was not inspired, and my work fell flat. In an attempt to jump-start my creative spark, I asked for and received a studio visit with Sam Messer, an Associate Dean and Professor of the Yale University School of Art. Sam looked at my studio work and was less than complimentary. In an attempt to engage him in further conversation, I showed him photographs of the atrium column capitals from the Church of the Transfiguration. These images stopped Sam dead in his tracks. He basically asked me, why are you making such awful insipid studio art, when this is where your heart is? I've never forgotten Sam's words and the courage he gave me to just "speak it how I saw it", never mind the repercussions.

The second life changing event occurred during the 2011 Symposium *Life Sources and Creative Faith; Approaching the Sacred in Art Today* held in Florence, Italy. During that time, I had the opportunity to see the work exhibited by Filippo Rossi, and I was intrigued. More than intrigued, I felt a connection with someone I had never met. I knew Filippo was Catholic, but I felt and saw we both spoke the same language. I wanted to learn more.

After graduating in 2013, I moved to Lucca, Italy, where I've been living nine months out of the year working with Filippo, immersing myself in the language of abstract sacred art. I would say the most important thing we do when we work together is communicate. We talk about everything until we fully understand each other; where Filippo as a Catholic and I as a Protestant are coming from. We prayerfully look for those places where we agree. I truly believe the Holy Spirit is fully present when we hammer out our ideas.

We also both try to get our "selves", our egos, out of the way. We must do this to keep the work in balance and we both feel this is important. Some days this can be difficult, especially when I think I'm right. But, it's never about being right, it's about listening to God through prayer and to Filippo to hear what the artwork needs.

SECTION III

Creating abstract sacred art, or any art with spiritual underpinnings, can only truly be realized if one is in essence vulnerable, open. I must be willing to let the Holy Spirit in, in order to be able to listen and see, and to trust in this process while putting my opinions aside. As Filippo and I both work in this manner, I consider us contemplatives. We are each alone with God even while working and creating art together.

Frammenti was first exhibited in Barga, Italy in June of 2015 in the exhibition space for the Villa Via Sacra, home to the Mount Tabor Ecumenical Centre for Art and Spirituality.

In this second show together, Filippo and I approached the idea of how to fabricate an installation reflecting the beauty found within scripture.

1 Corinthians 13:12 became the starting point from which the artwork evolved: "Now I know in part; then I shall know fully, even as I am fully known."

Through Light, our third artistic collaboration, was exhibited in May of 2017, at Villa Via Sacra, opening on the occasion of the Florence portion of this Symposium. The importance of light as a symbol has fueled most of the work Filippo and I have done together. For the Christian, light speaks of truth and salvation as Jesus Christ is the light of the world.

Fabricating art is my life's work. It's answering to the best of my ability a call God has given me. A call to express beauty and truth and the sacrificial life takes on a new meaning when

I enter the studio. All of my artwork springs from personal life experiences.

Tree of Mercy, Tree of Life was inspired by a deep experience with the mercy of God. This tryptic considers how God redeemed a broken relationship with a dear friend, through the gift of forgiveness.

As a Christian artist, I look for what is "unseen", which only occurs when I'm in conversation with God. Angels have been a recurring theme in my work for years. The idea of a protective guardian angel comes from my childhood faith experience. I have passed my belief of God's presence in the form of a guardian angel onto my children and five grandchildren.

Filippo and I both live a faith-centered life and approach the unseen in a similar fashion. It's our willingness to be open with each other, to try to fully understand each other, that makes our collaboration work.

Many times, such as with *Luce del Mondo* and *Frammenti*, we hadn't seen all of the artwork together before it went to the photographer. We weren't sure it would work as a complete exhibit. For me, as a somewhat controlling person, I was surprised I was so calm about those situations. But even from the very beginning, I knew we understood and trusted each other enough artistically, that these exhibitions would speak.

By the time we created *Through Light* and *Spirito Creatore*, we were in synch. Still very different people, with different styles and faith backgrounds, but definitely what I would call an established ecumenical collaboration in action. ■

Art as a Christian Calling

FILIPPO ROSSI

God calls each of us in different ways and at different moments, allowing everyone to give an answer that completely realizes him or her. We in turn have the duty of bearing witness to Him with the tools he puts at our disposal. I, for example, am an artist in search of light, of His light. The beauty I seek to create is born of light – transmitted above all with gold leaf and through a clearly perceived use of signs, which become eloquent.

In my early works I concentrated on signs almost to the exclusion of color. I sought, and still seek, beauty in the service of truth, as I believe every artist does. I seek to create beauty despite my own wretchedness and poverty, answering a call that Christ's Gospel directs to all human beings, artists included. I do this mainly through a non-figurative style, for I believe that spiritual experiences and events cannot be merely narrated but must be lived intensely and transmitted as personal dialogue with God. I received a sort of confirmation of this dialogue at the meeting with artists in the Sistine chapel convened by Pope Benedict XVI in 2009, at which I was the youngest of those invited.

For artists, who transform the material with which they work, to speak of the Salvation Mystery in works of art means speaking of their own relationship with the material itself.

But it also – and above all – means speaking of the relationship between the artist, who is a creature, and the Creator who gave him or her talent: the Creator to whom artists bear witness in their relationships with others. Artists do not, in fact, really 'make' the works they realize, but become responsible, according to their intelligence and will, for that which they represent. My art makes this clear through the theme which I have often treated, of marriage between a man and a woman and the children that God gives them.

The more an artist is aware of the gift he has received, the more he is moved to look at himself and at all creation with eyes able to contemplate and give thanks, lifting a hymn of praise to God. Only in that way can he fully understand himself, his vocation, his mission. In silence he listens to the Spirit and, if he is really 'real' as artist and faithful to what he feels, will be able to create real beauty, which is a reflection of God's uncreated Beauty. That beauty becomes a place of revelation of the Absolute, providing meaningful space for human experience.

Making a work of art is an act of faith, and often the creative process is more fascinating than the work itself. My own aesthetic journey has slowly charted a path at once viable and fragile. During this journey I have had the good luck to meet the protestant artist Susan Kanaga, who came to me for help in developing her painting style. I met her in the context of my first encounter with the ecumenical Community of Jesus, of which Susan is a member – the community which has sponsored parts of the symposium narrated in this volume, which concluded with three days at their monastery on Cape Cod.

In my work with Susan Kanaga I have proposed my own art and its message, through incisive works which try to describe the memory of the event they recount without overemphasis, through allusive passages and hidden cuts, or with grooves, lacerations of humble building material, unimportant and even vulgar bits of wood. Elements which all express lives worn down and worn away, and yet still capable of an unhoped-for power of recovery to which the constant presence of gold-bearing veins bears witness, giving these materials a possible and unexpected redemption. The expressive and evocative force of single passages is thus offered to the viewer's judgment, so that he or she can grasp on this threshold, in this wound between nowhere and redemption, both the wretchedness of the human condition and the presence of yet another providential chance for salvation. Poor, malleable materials and the immutable treasure of the gold leaf! It is the gold of death vanquished, of Love which burns and is consumed with love – which knows only how to give.

Every work encloses in itself the wonder of new and unrepeatable life, in which every sign or scratch, every wrinkle or change of tone, every groove or clot recalls the complexities that all human experience conceals. For, as I said, I believe that spiritual experiences and events must be lived in the first person rather than narrated: they must be communicated in the form of a personal dialogue with God.

My work with Susan Kanaga has deepened my faith, obliging me to both explain myself and to respect her freedom as an artist and as a spiritual person. Our relationship took concrete form for the first time in the joint-exhibit *Light of the World*. The goal was for each of us to maintain personal freedom of expression while also achieving aesthetic harmony and a harmony of message with the other.

My use of signs, and, above all, of the sacred sign of the cross, expresses my deep search for an unimaginable fusion of the expressive force of art – of art with its own voice, not mere repetition – and of the grandeur of the thought developed by Church tradition. When we overcome the inadequate and superficial, we set out on a perilous journey leading to higher mystery. As I think a work through, I ask myself: 'Is my art a direct expression of my inner life?'. My work becomes personal witness, that is: not an aesthetic exercise but an honest 'profession of faith'.

That faith obliges an artist to expose himself – to himself furnish the key to the meaning of his work, which may not be immediately apparent to those who see it. What is important is that – even when the subject of a work is the artist's personal drama or suffering – the viewer's gaze be fixed on Mystery, which always gives a breath of hope. In his work an artist can achieve a synthesis capable of deeply touching others, consoling but also agitating their spirit; he must have the courage to reject what in aesthetic terms is 'evil' – banal, that is, kitsch, closed to the Spirit – and to choose instead the 'good' of a use of his own creativity open to God. And he must do this even if his choice leaves some unsatisfied.

Creator Spirit is an exhibit Susan Kanaga and I did together, last May in Florence, on the occasion of the Italian session of the symposium presented in this volume. When, as in this case, artists work with spiritual content which is also personally meaningful, their art becomes contemplative. When, as they paint or carve, artists also pray, they contemplate God – a *modus operandi* which helps them grow in their creative gift and which helps them in their mission as artists. In this way all that they do is filled with the Spirit of God, who gives life and the possibility to manifest flashes of his divine transcendence. ∎

SPIRITUS VEHEMENTIS ET REPLEVIT TOTAM DOMU

ET CUM COMPLERENTUR DIES PENTECOSTES, ERANT OMNES PARITER IN EODEM LOCO. ET FACTUS EST REPENTE

...UND, THEY HAD ALL MET TOGETHER, WHEN SUDDENLY THERE CAME FROM HEAVEN

...IRE HOUSE IN WHICH THEY WERE SITTING; AND THERE APPEARED TO THEM TONGUES AS OF FIRE; THESE SEP...

...ET SEDENTES, ET APPARUE... ...QUERITUM LINGU... TAMQUAM IGNIS...

REPLETI SUNT OMNES SPIRITU SANCTO

...D OF EACH OF THEM. THEY WERE ALL FILLED WITH THE HOLY SPIRIT AND BEGAN TO SPEAK

SPIRITO

...QUI ALIIS LINGUIS, PROUT SPIRITUS DABAT ELOQUI ILLIS.

...ANGUAGES AS THE SPIRIT GAVE THEM POWER TO EXPRESS THEMSELVES.

...ALS DER PFINGSTTAG GEKOMMEN WAR, BEFANDEN SICH ALLE AM GLEICHEN ORT. DA KAM... ...PLÖTZLICH VOM...

...ZUNGEN WIE VO...

...WIE ES DER GEIS...

...E WENN EIN HEFTIGER STURM DAHERFÄHRT, UND ERFÜLLTE DAS GANZE HAUS, IN DEM SIE WAREN; UND ES ERSCHIENEN IHNEN...

...ALLE WURDEN MIT DEM HEILIGEN GEIST ERFÜLLT UND BEGANNEN, IN FREMDEN SPRACHEN ZU REDEN...

**Ecumenical exhibition "Spirito Creatore",
by Filippo Rossi and Susan Kanaga,
10 May–11 June 2017
Florence, Museo dell'Opera del Duomo**

View of the first section of the exhibition

Exhibition opening at the Museo dell'Opera del Duomo (10 May),
the curator Timothy Verdon's introductive speech

Susan Kanaga and Filippo Rossi.

A moment of the exhibition opening.

IL MIO SPIRITO SOPRA OGNI

Susan Kanaga and Filippo Rossi with Mother Betty Pugsley.

Susan Kanaga and Filippo Rossi with Community of Jesus members
(Mother Betty, Fr. Martin Shannon, Karen Moore).

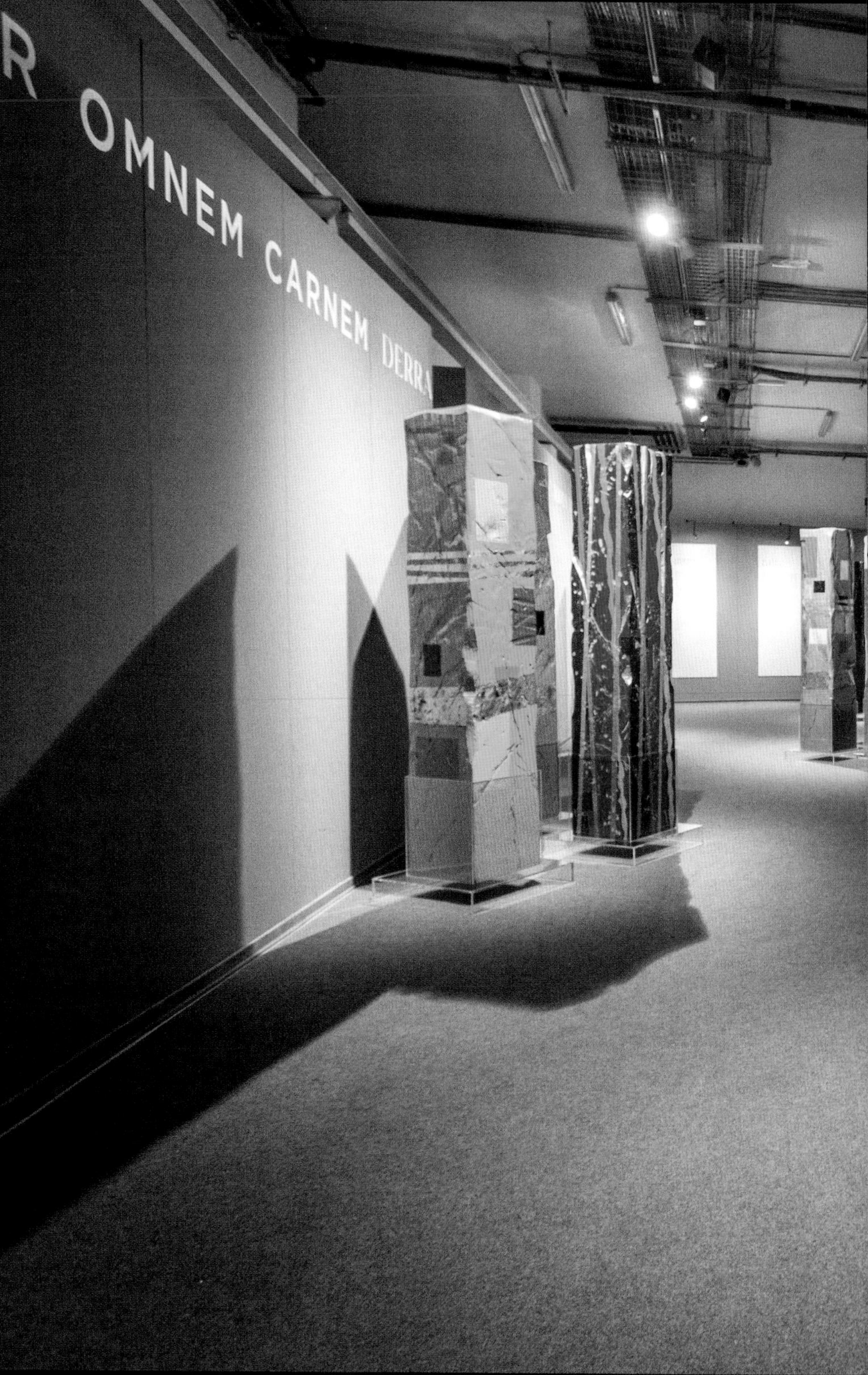
R OMNEM CARNEM DERRA

IO SPIRIT

Susan Kanaga and Filippo Rossi.

Filippo Rossi with his family.

Susan Kanaga.

Event Coordinator Giovanni Serafini.

Ecumenical exhibition "Creator Spirit",
by Filippo Rossi and Susan Kanaga,
28 October–30 November 2017
Community of Jesus,
Monastery and Church of the Transfiguration

Views from outside the pavilion.

Views from outside the pavilion.

Interior of the pavilion.

...ESI REPENTE DE CAELO SONUS...

SUDDENLY THERE CAME FROM HE...

...INCLUE TANQUAM IGNIS, SEDITQUE... ...PRA SENCTOS L...

...PEARED TO THEM TONGUES AS OF FIRE, THES... ...OADATER...

...LLI ET SU... ...TU SANCTO...

...N LANGUAGES AS THE S... ...B...VES.

...DA RAMPU... ...HER EIN BRAUSEN...

...N VON FEUER... ...ON IHNEN LIESS SICH EIN...

...ER GEIST IHNEN E...

...N SPRACHE...

...E L'ESPRIT LEUR DONNAIT DE S'...

...PRIT, ET SE MIRENT À...

The Pilgrim's Progress

Ralph Vaughan Williams's (1872–1958) opera *The Pilgrim's Progress* premiered in 1951, more than forty years after the composer first began to work on the idea. Vaughan Williams's interest in the theme of spiritual pilgrimage appears in a number of his works, but nowhere more thoroughly than in his rendition of the classic allegory by John Bunyan (1628–88).

John Bunyan lived in the midst of the religious and political upheaval that defined Great Britain through the decades of the 16th and 17th centuries. As a 'non-conformist' preacher – essentially what today we might consider a Baptist – Bunyan was imprisoned for his preaching activity in 1660 when the monarchy was restored and gatherings outside the auspices of the Church of England were prohibited. For the next twelve years, Bedfordshire county prison became the studio in which Bunyan wrote the story that would become a distinguished classic in English religious literature, and arguably the most significant work of the Puritan tradition. First published in 1678, *The Pilgrim's Progress* has never been out of print; it has been translated into more than two hundred languages and printed in hundreds of editions. Its thoroughly Protestant character (at times disparaging of the Roman Catholic and Anglican churches) makes it a faithful representative of the Reformed theology that inspired it at the time, even as the overarching idea of Christian pilgrimage can be understood across all theological divides.

Vaughan Williams's fascination with spiritual pilgrimage is what inspired him to write his opera (he constructed the libretto himself) and it is what made the work a fitting part of our observance of the 500th anniversary of the Protestant Reformation. It was performed by the world-renowned Gloriæ Dei Cantores together with a cast of critically acclaimed soloists and the director and members of the Elements Theater Company, in the Church of the Transfiguration, a liturgical space that itself emphasizes the Christian life as a journey from baptism to the New Jerusalem. ■

The Pilgrim's Progress
(Ralph Vaughan Williams's opera),
performed by Gloriæ Dei Cantores
and Elements Theater Company,
Community of Jesus, Church of the Transfiguration
27–8 November 2017

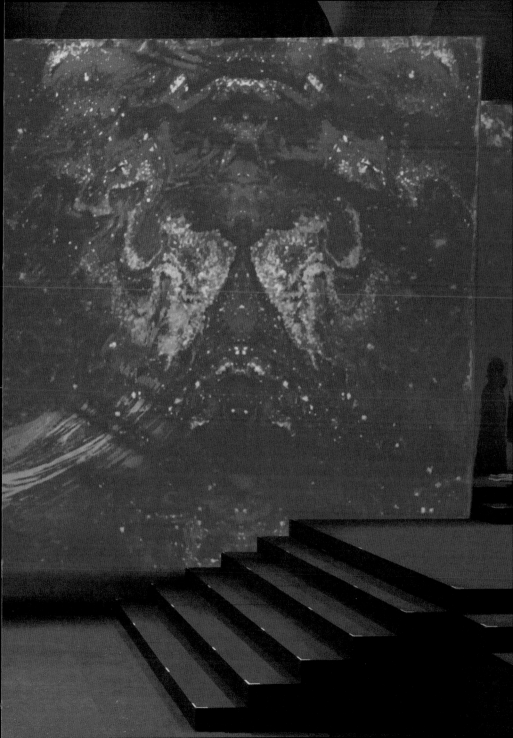

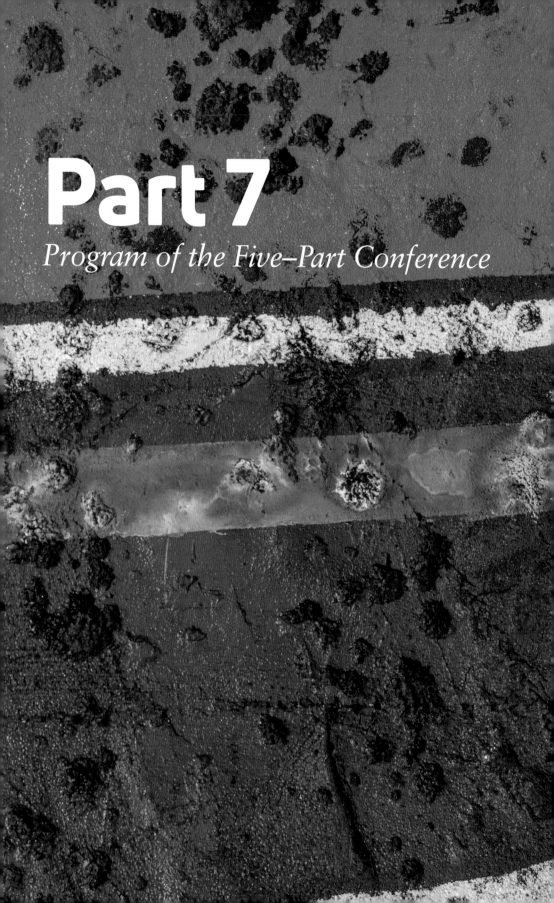

Part 7
Program of the Five–Part Conference

Les arts et l'œcuménisme
La théologie au risque de la création artistique

Le arti e l'ecumenismo
La teologia al rischio della creatività artistica

The Arts and Ecumenism
What Theology Risks in Artistic Creation

Institut Catholique, Paris
Faculté de Théologie Protestante, Université
de Strasbourg
Facoltà Teologica dell'Italia Centrale e Opera
di Santa Maria del Fiore, Florence
Institute of Sacred Music, Yale Divinity School,
New Haven, Connecticut
Community of Jesus, Orleans, Massachusetts

Paris:
12–13 May 2017
Strasbourg:
19–20 May 2017
Florence:
25–7 May 2017
New Haven, Connecticut:
20–1 October 2017
Orleans, Massachusetts:
27–9 October 2017

Avant-propos

Les arts en général revendiquent leur autonomie au nom même de leur exigence de liberté et de vérité. L'acte de création artistique est, en son geste libre, une quête de vérité. Dans une lettre à son ami Stassov, le musicien Modest Moussorgski évoque « la vérité à bout portant ». Les artistes cherchent la vérité en chair et en os, une vérité mise à nu, dépouillée de toute rhétorique ou ornement. Les arts sont en prise avec le réel, tel qu'il est; ils expriment des questions anthropologiques fondamentales. Mais cette vérité « nous enclot dans l'immanence ». Elle nous voue au monde et seulement au monde. Pourtant quand les arts donnent chair à la présence forte de la vulnérabilité humaine et de sa finitude, ils résonnent fortement avec la figure du crucifié. Le corps à corps créateur avec la matière qui fabrique des compositions musicales, des tableaux de peintures, des édifices architecturaux, des vidéogrammes ou des jeux de théâtre peut aussi « envoyer vers Dieu ». Entre la quête de vérité qui prend chair dans l'acte de création artistique et l'accomplissement de la vérité en et par Jésus Christ, retentit plus d'une résonnance. L'art et la théologie s'interpellent.

Pourtant, l'union de ces deux mots peut poser problème. En effet, que peut-il y avoir de commun entre une pratique artistique et créatrice et une pratique discursive et analytique ?

L'écueil principal à éviter est certainement l'instrumentalisation de l'art par rapport à la théologie. L'idée, c'est-à-dire, que l'art est au service de la théologie, étant subordonné à la visée théologique que nul ne remet en cause en tant que telle, et que la théologie évolue certes mais en son ordre propre et en toute autonomie. Selon cette conception, la foi chrétienne reste une réalité permanente parce que transcendante dont la théologie préserve l'intégrité en éclairant le contenu, et les arts ne feraient que prolonger la main du théologien, et seraient réduits à n'être que des outils pédagogiques comme l'affirmait déjà le pape Grégoire 1er. Mais une telle perspective est insuffisante. En effet, les arts, au sein même de l'expérience esthétique qu'ils proposent, ont leur champ spécifique de compréhension et leur fécondité théorique, et ils sont capables d'élaborer leur propre représentation religieuse du monde. En cela, ils sont véritablement capables d'interroger le théologien. Il peut ainsi s'établir entre les arts et la théologie une authentique relation dialogique.

Si nous gardons aux arts et à la théologie leur caractère propre, il nous semble que leur dialogue est de facture herméneutique en deux sens : la création artistique peut être considérée comme une herméneutique en acte de la foi chrétienne et la théologie comme une herméneutique des expressions artistiques parce qu'elles parlent de la foi chrétienne et sont possiblement des chemins vers Dieu.

Ce colloque, se déroulant l'année du 5e centenaire de la Réforme et réunissant des facultés catholiques et protestantes, inscrit sa recherche dans une dimension œcuménique.

Prefazione

Le arti in generale rivendicano la loro autonomia, nel nome stesso della loro esigenza di libertà e di verità. L'atto di creazione artistica è, nel suo libero gesto, una ricerca di verità. In una lettera al suo amico Stassov, il musicista Modest Musorgskij evoca "la verità vista da vicino". Gli artisti cercano la verità in carne ed ossa, una verità nuda, spogliata di ogni retorica e ornamento. Le arti afferrano il reale così come esso è, esprimendo fondamentali questioni antropologiche. Ma questa verità "ci rinchiude nell'immanenza": ci vota al mondo e solamente al mondo. Pertanto quando le arti danno carne alla forte presenza della vulnerabilità umana e alla sua finitezza, esse risuonano fortemente con la figura del Crocifisso. Il creativo corpo a corpo con la materia che realizza le composizioni musicali, i quadri dipinti, gli edifici architettonici, le video-installations o i pezzi teatrali può anche "condurre a Dio".

Fra la ricerca di verità che s'incarna nell'atto di creazione artistica e il compimento della verità in e per Gesù Cristo molteplici sono le somiglianze, e l'arte e la teologia s'interpellano. Eppure l'unione di questi due termini può sollevare un problema, perché, in effetti, che cosa possono avere in comune una pratica artistica e creativa con una discorsiva e analitica?

Lo scoglio principale da evitare è certamente la strumentalizzazione dell'arte in rapporto alla teologia – l'idea che l'arte sia al servizio della teologia, subordinata al comando della teologia, che in sé non rischia nulla di suo proprio. Secondo questa concezione la teologia si evolve, certo, ma nel proprio ordine e in totale autonomia, e la fede cristiana rimane una realtà permanente perché trascendente; la teologia ne preserva l'integrità chiarendone i contenuti, e le arti altro non fanno che estendere la

mano del teologo, riducendosi a non essere altro che strumenti pedagogici, come già papa Gregorio I affermava. Ma tale prospettiva è insufficiente: le arti, al cuore stesso dell'esperienza estetica che propongono, in effetti hanno un loro campo specifico di comprensione e una loro fecondità teorica, e sono capaci di elaborare una loro propria rappresentazione religiosa del mondo. In quel senso, esse sono veramente in grado d'interrogare il teologo. Tra le arti e la teologia è anche possibile stabilire un autentico rapporto dialettico.

Se conserviamo il carattere proprio sia delle arti che della teologia, il loro dialogo sembra essere un prodotto ermeneutico a due sensi: la creazione artistica può essere considerata un'ermeneutica in atto della fede cristiana, e la teologia come un'ermeneutica delle espressioni artistiche, dal momento che queste parlano della fede cristiana e sono potenzialmente sentieri verso Dio.

Questo convegno, i cui lavori vengono svolti nell'anno del V centenario della Riforma, riunendo facoltà accademiche sia cattoliche che protestanti iscrive la sua ricerca in una dimensione ecumenica.

Foreword

The arts in general claim the right of autonomy, in the name of their need for freedom and truth. The act of artistic creation is, in its free gesture, a quest for truth. The musician Modest Mussorgsky, writing to his friend Stassov, evoked this "truth at point-blank range". Artists look for flesh and blood truth, naked truth, stripped of all rhetoric or ornament. The arts come to grips with the real just as it is, and express fundamental anthropological questions. That "truth" "encloses us in immanence", however, vowing us to the world and only to the world. Thus, when the arts give flesh to a strong presence of human vulnerability and its finitude, they resound powerfully with the figure of the Crucified One. Even the creative struggle with matter which produces musical compositions, paintings, architectural structures, videos or theater productions can "direct people toward God".

Between the quest for truth that takes flesh in the act of artistic creation and truth's fulfillment in and through Jesus Christ there is more than one significant echo, in fact, and art and theology beckon to each other. Yet the union of these two words can pose a problem, for, in fact, what can a creative artistic practice have in common with a discursive and analytic one?

The principal danger to avoid is obviously that of reducing art to a tool of theology: the idea that art is at the service of theology, remaining subordinate to the summons of theology, which itself risks nothing. That way of thinking holds that theology certainly evolves, but in its own order and in complete autonomy, and that Christian faith remains a permanent reality because it is transcendent, with theology preserving its integrity and enlightening its content. In that view, the arts do no more than extend the theologian's hand, and are reduced to mere pedagogical tools, as Pope Gregory I affirmed long ago.

Such a view is insufficient. In reality, the arts, at the very heart of the aesthetic experience which they propose, have their own specific field of comprehension and their own theoretical fecundity, being able to elaborate their own religious representation of the world. In that sense, they are truly able to put questions to theologians, and it is possible to establish an authentic dialogical relationship between the arts and theology.

If we preserve the distinctive original character of both the arts and of theology, it seems to us that their dialogue is a two-way hermeneutical product: artistic creation can be considered a hermeneutic "in action" of the Christian faith, and theology as a hermeneutic of artistic expressions, for these speak of the Christian faith and are potential paths leading to God.

Our symposium, which takes place in the year of the fifth centenary of the Reformation and brings together Catholic and Protestant university departments, situates its research within the dimension of ecumenism.

· ·

Paris
12–13 mai/maggio/May 2017
Institut Supérieur de Théologie des Arts (ISTA)
Theologicum-Faculté de Théologie et de Sciences
Religieuses
Institut Catholique de Paris (ICP)
21 Rue d'Assas, 75270 Paris Cedex 06

Création artistique et théologie
de l'Esprit Saint
« *De l'apparaître à l'envol* »

Creazione artistica e teologia
dello Spirito Santo
"Dall'apparire al volo"

Artistic Creation and Theology
of the Holy Spirit
"From Appearance to Flight"

A research project on the artist's creative gesture has made clear the importance of the figures of breath and of the bird. In effect, in poetry or in painting, in sculpture, music, or the other arts, these figures evoke the very act of artistic creation, its necessity, its appeal, its movement, its openness.

A bird's lively presence is conveyed by the suddenness with which it "appears," is it not? And by its song, and its "flight"? The bird thus becomes an expression both of "first beginnings" and of "fulfillment."

The discovery of these figures in art invites us to again examine their biblical meaning as figures of the Holy Spirit, and by that fact bring them back into theological and pneumatological discourse.

The Paris portion of the symposium thus desires to propose a theology of the Holy Spirit open to the risk of artistic creation.

The symposium provides an occasion to present, explore, and question the theological gesture that the Institut Supérieur de Théologie des Arts (ISTA) represents within the theology school of the Institut Catholique of Paris.

Vendredi 12 mai 2017
Amphithéâtre Paul Ricœur

Matin : Problématique et questionnement

Présidence Thierry-Marie Courau, o.p., doyen du Theologicum

9h-10h   Accueil: Salle B01

10h-10h45   Conférence d'ouverture, Thierry-Marie Courau, o.p., Denis Hétier, directeur de l'ISTA

10h45-11h30   Art et théologie : Prof. Christoph Theobald, s.j., théologien, Centre Sèvres-Facultés des Jésuites de Paris

11h30-12h   Pause/café/librairie

12h-12h45   Poétique de la théologie : Prof. François Cassingena-Trévedy, o.s.b., artiste et poète, théologien, Institut Supérieur de Liturgie/Theologicum-ICP

12h45-14h   Pause/repas

Après-midi : La création artistique et la figure de l'oiseau

Présidence Cécile Coulangeon, directrice du département Histoire de l'Art - Faculté des Lettres - ICP

14h-14h15   Introduction

14h15-14h45   De la palette à l'oiseau, Martine Sautory, historienne d'art, diplômée de l'ISTA

14h45-15h15   L'appel de l'oiseau dans la création poétique, Florent Dumontier, poète, étudiant à l'ISTA

15h15-15h45   Pause

15h45-16h15   La musique de l'oiseau, Mgr. André Dupleix, musicien, théologien, ISTA

16h15-16h45   L'envol dans l'art de Brâncuşi, Martine Grenier, historienne d'art, théologienne protestante, Institut Protestant de Paris et ISTA, et Marielle Besançon, peintre, étudiante à l'ISTA

16h45-17h15   Débat avec la salle

17h15-18h   Temps de reprise et de synthèse de la journée, Prof. Denis Villepelet, théologien, ISTA, et Denis Hétier, directeur de l'ISTA

19h   Buffet. Soirée artistique présentée par Mgr. André Dupleix

Samedi 13 mai 2017
Amphithéâtre Paul Ricœur

Matin : Pour une théologie de l'Esprit Saint

Présidence Corinne Lanoir, doyenne de l'Institut Protestante de Théologie de Paris

9h-9h30   Problématique et thématique de la journée

9h30-10h   La vie et L'Esprit dans l'Eglise ancienne, Isaïa Gazzola, o.c., théologien, ISTA et Institut Supérieur de Liturgie/Theologicum-ICP

10h-10h30   L'Esprit Saint dans l'art florentin, Mgr. Timothy Verdon, historien d'art, Stanford University (Florence), et directeur du Musée de l'Œuvre de la cathédrale de Florence

10h30-11h   Pause

11h-11h30   Théologie biblique de l'Esprit Saint et art contemporain, Prof. Jérôme Cottin, pasteur, historien d'art, théologien, ISTA et Université de Strasbourg

11h30-12h15   Pour une théologie de l'Esprit Saint, Prof. Jean-Louis Souletie, théologien, directeur de l'Institut Supérieur de Liturgie/Theologicum-ICP

12h15-14h   Pause/repas

Après-midi : Création artistique et théologie de l'Esprit Saint

14h-14h15   Reprise et proposition des ateliers

14h15-15h15   Ateliers : De l'expérience artistique à la théologie

15h15-15h30   Pause

15h30-16h30   Grande table ronde : L'art : une question à la théologie ?

16h30-17h   Conclusions et perspectives : Denis Hétier, directeur de l'ISTA

· ·

Strasbourg
19–20 mai/maggio /May 2017
Faculté de Théologie Protestante
EA - Équipe de recherche 4378
Université de Strasbourg
9 Place de l'Université, 67000 Strasbourg
Palais universitaire, Salle Tauler

L'apport de la Réforme
à une théologie des arts

L'apporto della Riforma
a una teologia delle arti

The Contribution of the Reformation
to a Theology of the Arts

The risk implied in artistic creation will be explored in the Strasbourg symposium from the point of view of three key moments in the history of theology: first in the biblical writings, where it will be seen that as early as the Old Testament the "image" (or, more simply, the "idol") is presented as a locus of sense and is situated at the heart of the structure of the alliance. The second moment is Rhenish mysticism of the 13th through the 15th centuries, which prepares and announces the Reformation. And the third moment is the 16th-century Reformation itself, which saw the expression of contradictory and even conflicting positions regarding images – positions that today are interpreted as expressions of broad hermeneutic approaches aimed at deploying the Word in the world of the imagination, of the emotions, and of cultural mediation.

It will be asked if such narrative images constitute key moments in the reception and actualization of a Word so original as to escape every possibility of representation, or if narrative images prepare and introduce "images" which, like Words, open a breach in the horizon of the world.

In this exploration, we will not limit ourselves simply to texts but will let images of different periods – and, if possible, the motivations of their authors – speak.

Vendredi 19 mai 2017
Palais universitaire, Salle Tauler

Matin : Vision et expérience visuelle dans la culture de la Réforme

8h45-9h   Accueil – ouverture de la journée d'études

9h-9h30   De Paris à Strasbourg : reprise, Denis Hétier, théologien, directeur de l'Institut Supérieur de Théologie des Arts - Institut Catholique de Paris

9h30-10h15   L'expérience visuelle de Dieu dans l'Ancien Testament, Prof. Jan Joosten, théologien, Oxford University et Université de Strasbourg

10h15-11h   Les visions de quelques mystiques rhénans (Tauler, Hildegarde de Bingen, Nicolas de Cues) : formes, fonctions, sens, Rémi Valléjo, Père dominicain, Directeur du Centre de recherche « Le Rhin mystique », Strasbourg

11h-11h30   pause

11h30-12h15   La Réforme et la multiplication des images imprimées, Prof. Frank Muller, historien, Université de Strasbourg

12h15-13h30   pause repas

Après-midi : Les images et le protestantisme

13h30-14h15   La dimension kérygmatique et esthétique de l'hymnologie protestante, Prof. Beat Föllmi, théologien et musicologue, Université de Strasbourg

14h15-14h45   De la pensée à la pratique des images dans le protestantisme : divergences théologiques et artistiques, Prof. Jérôme Cottin, théologien et historien d'art, Université de Strasbourg et Institut Catholique de Paris

14h45-15h30   God, Language, and Time: The Emergence of a Protestant Aesthetic in the Reformation period, Prof. William Dyrness, théologien, Fuller Theological Seminary (Pasadena, CA)

15h30-16h15   Réaction et Réponse: L'art de la Réforme catholique, Prof. Mgr. Timothy Verdon, historien d'art, Stanford University (Programme

de Florence) et directeur, Museo dell'Opera del Duomo, Florence

16h15-16h45   pause

16h45-17h30   The Resurrection of the Image in the English Protestant Imagination: From William Blake to Bill Viola, Prof. Ben Quash, théologien, King's College (London)

17h30-18h   Synthèse et envoi, Prof. Denis Villepelet, théologien, Institut Catholique de Paris

18h   fin de la journée d'études

Samedi 20 mai 2017

Art et spiritualité chrétienne (protestante)
in situ

Matin   visite du Retable d'Issenheim (1512–15) de Matthias Grünewald, dans le nouveau musée Unterlinden, Colmar

Après-midi   visite commentée de l'exposition « Le vent de la Réforme : Luther 1517 » à l'occasion du Jubilé de la Réforme (1517–2017), à la Bibliothèque Nationale Universitaire (BNU) de Strasbourg.

Samedi 20 mai 2017

Art et spiritualité chrétienne (protestante)
in situ

Matin   visite du Retable d'Issenheim (1512–15) de Matthias Grünewald, dans le nouveau musée Unterlinden, Colmar

Après-midi   visite commentée de l'exposition « Le vent de la Réforme : Luther 1517 » à l'occasion du Jubilé de la Réforme (1517–2017), à la Bibliothèque Nationale Universitaire (BNU) de Strasbourg.

Firenze
25–26–27 mai/maggio/May 2017
Centro Arte e Cultura
dell'Opera di Santa Maria del Fiore
Piazza San Giovanni 7, 50122 Firenze

La vocazione teologica degli artisti

La vocation théologique des artistes

The Theological Vocation of Artists

The arts, which in historical civilizations are born as expressions of the sacred, remain occasions for reflection and tools of communication both inside the faith systems in whose service they are placed, and outside these systems, ever offering themselves as stimuli to spiritual experience and hermeneutic keys to the transcendent. One may in fact speak of the "theological vocation" of artists, particularly apparent in masters of the late Medieval period and Renaissance, still tied to the popular religiosity of the ecclesiastical institution.
Thus, in the context of a multi-session conference focused on the role of art in various Christian traditions from the Reformation to our time, the Florentine meeting recuperates the testimony of the past: of Eastern icons and of the "new" art created in Florence in the era of Arnolfo di Cambio and Giotto, which dissociated itself from the earlier Byzantine style articulating a visual language open to the Western Christian theology of the 13th, 14th, and 15th centuries.
Key themes of the Florentine session are: the sense of the art of the Eastern Church; the sense of the new Florentine naturalism of the later Middle Ages; the Renaissance redefinition of art and of the role of the artist; the art of the Reformation and Counter-Reformation; the impact of architecture upon ecclesial identity. In Florence – in the exposition space of Cathedral Museum – there will be a collaborative exhibit by the artists Susan Kanaga, cj, American and Protestant, and Filippo Rossi, Italian and Catholic.

Giovedì 25 maggio 2017

Pomeriggio: Ospedale degli Innocenti, Sala Poccetti
(Piazza Santissima Annunziata), poi Museo
dell'Opera del Duomo, Spazio espositivo temporaneo
(Piazza del Duomo 9)

Pomeriggio: Gli artisti interpreti della fede

16,30   Ospedale degli Innocenti, Piazza Santissima
Annunziata, *Un frate tedesco nella Firenze degli
artisti: Martin Lutero agli Innocenti*, visita in situ
condotta da Mons. Timothy Verdon

18,30   Museo dell'Opera del Duomo, Spazio
espositivo temporaneo, Piazza del Duomo 9, *Spirito
Creatore* (mostra ecumenica di Filippo Rossi e Susan
Kanaga, CJ)

19,30   cena

Venerdì 26 maggio 2017

Centro Arte e Cultura dell'Opera di Santa Maria del
Fiore, Piazza San Giovanni 7, Sala Brunelleschi

Mattina: La storia antica

Presiede Dr. Antonio Natali, Opera di Santa Maria
del Fiore, già Direttore della Galleria degli Uffizi

9,00   Accoglienza

9,30   Resoconto delle sessioni di Parigi e
Strasburgo: Prof. Jérôme Cottin, Prof. Denis
Villepelet, Prof. Denis Hétier

10,00   Firenze e la vocazione teologica dell'arte
da Giotto e Arnolfo a Michelangelo, Mons.
Prof. Timothy Verdon, storico dell'arte, Stanford
University (Firenze)
e direttore, Museo dell'Opera del Duomo, Firenze

10,30   Spirito e materia, mano d'uomo e fede della
Chiesa: il carattere sacramentale dell'icona nella
teologia orientale, Prof. Basilio Petrà, teologo, FTIC

11,00   Fotis Kontoglou and the Struggle for an
"Authentic" Ecclesiastical Art in Greece, Prof.
Vasileios Marinis, storico dell'arte, Yale University

11,30   discussione, pausa

12,00   Architettura e arti visive nella divisione delle
chiese e nel cammino verso l'unità, Prof. Severino

Dianich, teologo, FTIC

discussione, pranzo

Pomeriggio: Dal Rinascimento a oggi

Presiede Prof. Riccardo Burgiana, Direttore, Centro
Studi Ecumenici

15,00   Le porte del Regno: un'esegesi dei progetti
iconografici realizzati da Lorenzo Ghiberti per il
battistero di Firenze, Prof. Agnese Maria Fortuna,
teologa, Istituto Studi Superiori Religione "Ippolito
Galantini", Firenze

15,30   Piste teologiche tridentine nel programma
di Don Vincenzio Borghini per l'intradosso della
cupola di Santa Maria del Fiore, Prof. Gianni Cioli,
teologo—FTIC

16,00   Orthodox Icons, Likeness and Reformation
Spirituality, Prof. William Dyrness, teologo, Fuller
Theological Seminary (Pasadena, California)

16,30   discussione, pausa

17,30   Romano Guardini e Van Gogh: Per una
ricezione spirituale ecumenica dell'immagine, Prof.
Yvonne zu Dohna Schlobitten, filosofa dell'arte,
Pontificia Università Gregoriana, Roma

18,00   Ricœur e Van Gogh: dall'ermeneutica
biblica alla spiritualità nell'arte, Prof. Jérôme
Cottin, teologo, Université de Strasbourg et Institut
Catholique de Paris

18,30-19,00   dibattito

19,30   cena

Sabato 27 maggio 2017

Visite in situ (facoltative)

09,30   partenza in pullman per Barga

11,30   Visita al Duomo

12,30   Pranzo alla Villa "Via Sacra" seguita dall'ora
media

15,00   Chiesa di Sant'Elisabetta, La Comunità
di Gesù e l'arte, Mons. Timothy Verdon, Direttore
scientifico, Centro Ecumenico di Arte e Spiritualità
Mount Tabor, Barga, e Fr. Martin Shannon

17,00   Rientro a Firenze e serata libera

● ●

New Haven
20–21 October/octobre /ottobre 2017
Yale University
Sterling Divinity Quadrangle
409 Prospect Street, New Haven, Connecticut 06511
Institute of Sacred Music Great Hall

Sacred Arts in North American
Contexts

Les arts sacrés en Amérique du Nord

Le arti sacre nell'America del Nord

The myriad array of religious traditions in North America has given rise to an equally diverse range of artistic expressions. These are informed by practices shaped by individuals and communities past and present, often calling notions of normativity, canon, and authority into question. This Yale session of our symposium lays out a series of case studies that demonstrate a range of these practices, both within and without specific liturgical contexts. We set these in close conversation with the work done by our colleagues in Paris, Strasbourg, and Florence, and look forward to a lively exchange of ideas.

Friday, October 20, 2017

Institute of Sacred Music Great Hall (N100)

Afternoon: Aesthetics and Risk

1:30 pm   Welcome

1:45   Report on the Paris, Strasbourg and Florence Sessions, Mons. Timothy Verdon (Stanford in Florence, Museo dell'Opera del Duomo), Prof. Jérôme Cottin (University of Strasbourg), Prof. Denis Villepelet (Institut Catholique, Paris)

2:15   Modern Poetry and the Language of Faith, Prof. Christian Wiman, theologian, Yale

2:45   break

3:15   The Contribution of Aesthetics to Interfaith Understanding, Prof. William Dyrness, theologian, Fuller Theological Seminary

3:45   The Tutiorism of Risk and the Aesthetics of Worship: Theological Risk-Taking in Ecumenical Worship, Prof. Maggi Dawn, theologian, Yale

4:15   discussion

5:00   end

Saturday, October 21, 2017

Morning: Twentieth- and twenty-first-century situations

9:00 am   Convene and The English Protestant Imagination – Part Two (20th–21st centuries), Prof. Ben Quash, theologian, King's College, London

9:30   The Advent of Urban Praise and Worship, Prof. Josef Sorett, Columbia University

10:00   How a Quaker Metropolis Became an Orthodox Village: Material Christianity in Philadelphia's Greektown, 1900–1930, Prof. Kostis Kourelis, theologian, Franklin and Marshall College

10:30   break

11:00   Material Establishment and the Politics of Sacred Space in Hawaii, Prof. Sally Promey, Yale

11:30   Ecumenical Collaboration and Making Art Today, Susan Kanaga, cj, artist, Community of Jesus, and Filippo Rossi, artist, Archdiocese of Florence, Stanford University (Florence), and Mount Tabor Ecumenical Centre for Art and Spirituality, Barga

12:00   closing discussion

12:45   end

General interlocutors/respondents from the Yale Faculty: John Hare, Peter Hawkins, Vasileios Marinis

●●●●●●●●●●●●●●●●●●●●●●●●●●●●●●●

Orleans
27–28–29 October/octobre/ottobre 2017
Community of Jesus
5 Bay View Drive
Orleans, Massachusetts 02653
Monastery and Church of the Transfiguration

The Word in Color, Action,
Music, and Form

La Parole en couleurs, en scène,
en musique et en sculptée

La Parola in colori, in scena,
musicata e scolpita

Among the contexts of Christian experience
open to the arts and music, today as in the
past, monastic life has particular importance,
its contemplative dimension predisposing the
free creative act in which the Holy Spirit is
present.
The final session of our symposium thus
unfolds in an ecumenical monastery in
the Benedictine tradition, the Community
of Jesus, known for its commitment
to sacred music and art. The session
combines academic papers with examples
of contemporary artistic production and
musical performance, within the typically
monastic framework of solemn liturgical
celebration.
At the Community of Jesus's monastery
there is a second edition of the collaborative
ecumenical exhibition inaugurated in the
month of May in Florence, with works by
Susan Kanaga, cj, American and Protestant (a
member of the Community of Jesus), and by
Filippo Rossi, Italian and Roman Catholic.

Friday, October 27, 2017

Paraclete House

Evening: Prayer and the Symposium

5:00 pm   Introduction and Report on the European and Yale Sessions of the Symposium: Mons. Timothy Verdon, Prof. Jérôme Cottin, Prof. Denis Villepelet

6:00   Dinner, Paraclete House

7:30   Performance of Vaughn Williams's opera The Pilgrim's Progress (Church of the Transfiguration)

Saturday, October 28, 2017

Paraclete House

Morning: Monastic Life and the Arts

8:30 am   Breakfast, with discussion on the theme The Arts in a Community Setting, Mother Betty Pugsley, CJ, Sister Danielle Dwyer, CJ, Christopher Kanaga, CJ.

9:45   Monastic Life and Artistic Creativity, Timothy Verdon, historian of art, Stanford University (Florence), Museo dell'Opera del Duomo, Firenze, and Mount Tabor Ecumenical Centre for Art and Spirituality, Barga, Italy

10:15   The Monastery as Laboratory of the Arts: The Case of the Community of Jesus, William Dyrness, theologian, Fuller Theological Seminary (Pasadena, CA)

10:45   Art contemporain et prière : nouvelles formes architecturales et liturgiques au service de la vie monastique en Europe, Prof. Jérôme Cottin, Université de Strasbourg

11:15   Discussion followed by coffee break

11:45   Ecumenical Collaboration Among Artists, Susan Kanaga, CJ, and Filippo Rossi

12:30 pm   Lunch

Afternoon: Creative and Performing Art

(activities at choice: 2:30 pm-5:30 pm):

• Workshops with demonstration of frescoes, mosaics

• Community of Jesus live visual art demonstrations, Patmos Art Center

• Creator Spirit, ecumenical exhibition, works by Susan Kanaga, CJ, and Filippo Rossi, TBD

• Chant Display in the Chapter Hall

• Paraclete Press Display, Bethlehem House

6:30 pm   Dinner

7:30   The Pilgrimw's Progress (Church of the Transfiguration).

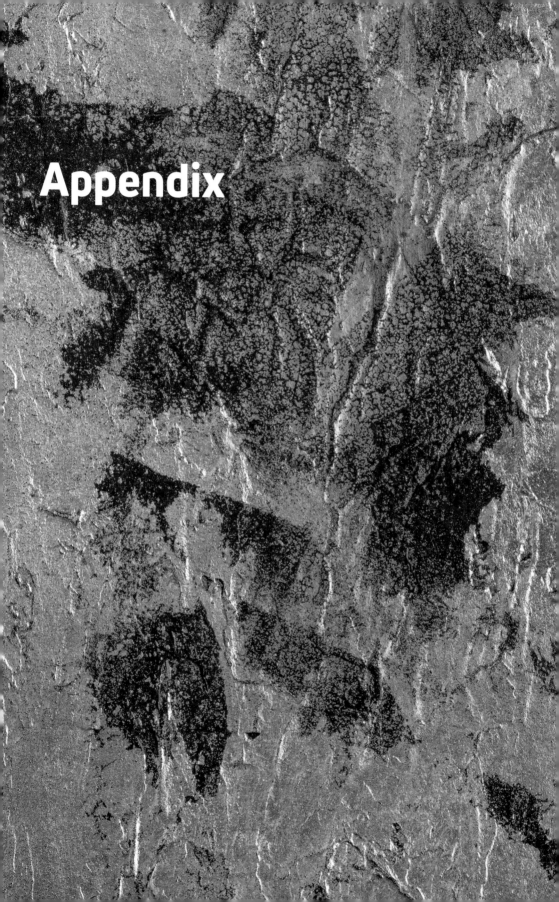

Appendix

Marielle Besançon
Painter, Institut Supérieur de Théologie des Arts - Institut Catholique de Paris

François Cassingena-Trévedy, o.s.b.
Artist and poet, theologian, Institut Supérieur de Liturgie – Theologicum – Institut Catholique de Paris, Faculté de Théologie et de Sciences Religieuses

Gianni Cioli
Theologian, Facoltà Teologica dell'Italia Centrale

Jérôme Cottin
Protestant minister, art historian, theologian, Institut Supérieur de Théologie des Arts - Institut Catholique de Paris and Université de Strasbourg

Severino Dianich
Theologian, Facoltà Teologica dell'Italia Centrale

William Dyrness
Theologian, Fuller Theological Seminary (Pasadena, CA)

Beat Föllmi
Theologian and musicologist, Université de Strasbourg

Agnese Maria Fortuna
Theologian, Istituto Superiore di Scienze Religiose "Beato Ippolito Galantini", Florence

Martine Grenier
Art historian, Protestant theologian, Institut Protestant de Paris and Institut Supérieur de Théologie des Arts - Institut Catholique de Paris

Denis Hétier
Theologian, Director of the Institut Supérieur de Théologie des Arts - Institut Catholique de Paris

Jan Joosten
Theologian, Oxford University and Université de Strasbourg

Susan Kanaga
Artist, Community of Jesus, Orleans (MA)

Jeffrey L. Kosky
Religious scholar, Washington and Lee University, Lexington (VI)

Vasileios Marinis
Art historian, Yale University

Basilio Petrà
Theologian, Facoltà Teologica dell'Italia Centrale

Ben Quash
Theologian, King's College (London)

Filippo Rossi
Artist, Archdiocese of Florence, Stanford University (Florence) and Mount Tabor Ecumenical Centre for Art and Spirituality, Barga (Lucca)

Martine Sautory
Art historian, gratuated from Institut
Supérieur de Théologie des Arts - Institut
Catholique de Paris

Yvonne Dohna Schlobitten
Art historian, Pontificia Università
Gregoriana, Rome

Martin Shannon, Fr.
Theologian and member
of the Community of Jesus

Deborah Sokolove
Director of the Henry Luce III Center for
the Arts and Religion at Wesley Theological
Seminary, Washington, D.C.

Jean-Louis Souletie
Theologian, Director of the Institut
Supérieur de Liturgie – Theologicum –
Institut Catholique de Paris, Faculté de
Théologie et de Sciences Religieuses

Christoph Theobald, s.j.
Theologian, Centre Sèvres - Facultés Jésuites
de Paris

Rémi Valléjo, o.p.
Director of "Le Rhin mystique" Research
Centre, Strasbourg

Msgr. Timothy Verdon
Art historian, Stanford University (Florence),
and Director of the Museo dell'Opera del
Duomo of Florence

Denis Villepelet
Theologian, Institut Supérieur de Théologie
des Arts - Institut Catholique de Paris

DIGITAL CONTENTS

The video "Creator Spirit"
with Susan Kanaga and Filippo Rossi

In English
<https://vimeo.com/gianmarcodagostino/spirito-creatore-eng>

In Italian
<https://vimeo.com/gianmarcodagostino/spirito-creatore>

In French
<https://vimeo.com/gianmarcodagostino/spirito-creatore-french>

© 2019 Mandragora s.r.l. All rights reserved.
via Capo di Mondo 61
50136 Florence, Italy
www.mandragora.it
ISBN 978-88-7461-473-8

© 2019 Paraclete Press. All rights reserved.
Brewster, MA (U.S.A.)
www.paracletepress.com
ISBN 978-1-64060-455-1

Translation
Timothy Verdon

Editor
Marco Salucci
with Francesca Mazzotta

Art director
Paola Vannucchi

Printed by
Grafiche Martinelli, Bagno a Ripoli (Florence)

Bound by
Legatoria Giagnoni, Calenzano (Florence)

Printed in Italy in August 2019.